FREEDOM OF EXPRESSION

Two legal systems founded upon similar Enlightenment philosophical and political values use state coercion differently to regulate a liberty at the core of the Enlightenment: the freedom of expression. This comparative study of France and the United States proposes a novel theory of how the limits of freedom of expression are informed by different revolutionary experiences and constitutional and political arrangements. Ioanna Tourkochoriti argues that the different ways freedom of expression is balanced against other values in France and the United States can be understood in reference to the role of the government and the understanding of republicanism and liberty. This understanding affects how jurists define the content and the limits of a liberty and strike a balance between liberties in conflict. Exploring both the legal traditions of the two countries, this study sheds new light on the broader historical, social, and philosophical contexts in which jurists operate.

Ioanna Tourkochoriti teaches at the National University of Ireland, Galway. She has previously held a lectureship at the Committee on Degrees in Social Studies at Harvard University, a Wertheim Fellowship at Harvard Law School, and fellowships with other universities in North America and the London School of Economics.

ASCL STUDIES IN COMPARATIVE LAW

ASCL Studies in Comparative Law publishes monographs and collections that broaden theoretical and practical knowledge of the world's many legal systems. Published under the direction of the American Society of Comparative Law, the *ASCL Studies* examine legal problems in a comparative light to advance legal science, develop technical insights, and promote greater cooperation across jurisdictional and cultural boundaries. This book series serves legal practitioners and those seeking to improve law and justice by publishing in-depth comparative studies of specific legal problems in every area of law..

The series has two general editors. David Gerber is Distinguished Professor of Law and Co-Director of the Program in International and Comparative Law at Chicago-Kent College of Law, Illinois Institute of Technology. He is past President of the American Society of Comparative Law. Mortimer Sellers is Regents Professor of the University System of Maryland and Director of the Baltimore Center for International and Comparative Law. He is past President of the Internationale Vereinigung für Rechts- und Sozialphilosophie.

Freedom of Expression

THE REVOLUTIONARY ROOTS OF AMERICAN AND FRENCH LEGAL THOUGHT

IOANNA TOURKOCHORITI
National University of Ireland, Galway

CAMBRIDGE
UNIVERSITY PRESS

CAMBRIDGE
UNIVERSITY PRESS

University Printing House, Cambridge CB2 8BS, United Kingdom

One Liberty Plaza, 20th Floor, New York, NY 10006, USA

477 Williamstown Road, Port Melbourne, VIC 3207, Australia

314–321, 3rd Floor, Plot 3, Splendor Forum, Jasola District Centre,
New Delhi – 110025, India

103 Penang Road, #05–06/07, Visioncrest Commercial, Singapore 238467

Cambridge University Press is part of the University of Cambridge.

It furthers the University's mission by disseminating knowledge in the pursuit of education, learning, and research at the highest international levels of excellence.

www.cambridge.org
Information on this title: www.cambridge.org/9781316517635
DOI: 10.1017/9781009042789

First published 2022

A catalogue record for this publication is available from the British Library.

ISBN 978-1-316-51763-5 Hardback

Contents

Acknowledgments

This book began as a dissertation at the *École des hautes études en sciences sociales* (EHESS), completed partly in France and partly at Harvard Law School in the United States. I benefited enormously from the intellectual atmosphere at EHESS, which helped me form my thought on many of the ideas discussed in the book. I am particularly grateful to Olivier Cayla for his supervision and his intellectual support.

I thank Frederick Schauer and Mark Tushnet for their extremely precious comments on the dissertation, and their mentorship during the period I spent as a visiting researcher at Harvard Law School. Richard Tuck provided invaluable comments on early versions of the text and was the most inspiring and supportive chair at the Committee on Degrees in Social Studies at Harvard. His willingness to discuss in length ideas in this book and many other of my papers proved crucial to the formation of my thought on these issues.

I also thank my colleagues and students at Harvard's Committee on Degrees in Social Studies for endless discussions on the ideas in the text and in particular Melanie Adrian, Stephan Bird-Pollan, Kevin Caffrey, Rodrigo Chacon, Healan Gaston, Alex Gourevitch, Matt Landauer, Christopher Meckstroth, Nicolas Prevelakis, Thomas Ponniah, Lisa Stampnitzky, Scott Staring, and Carla Yumatle. Special thanks to Bo-Mi Choi and Bonnie Talbert for reading through the dissertation and giving advice on ideas that could convert it into a book. Our interaction at the Committee contributed decisively to making us all teachers of ideas. It helped us build a community of scholars who share the same social studies approach to reading classical thinkers and using them to make sense of the needs of contemporary societies. Michael Frazer and Andy Jewett contributed significantly to our conversations in Social Studies. I am also grateful to Glyn Morgan for helping me acclimate myself in the Committee and for his support during his tenure as Course Head of Social Studies 10. His teaching style and remarkable sense of humor helped us learn how to teach.

I had discussions with colleagues and received comments at various stages of the project in workshops all around the world. James Q. Whitman, Peter Lindseth, Kim Scheppele, and the participants in the American Society of Comparative Law Works-in-Progress workshop held at Princeton in 2018 provided valuable comments toward the final form of the book. I am enormously grateful to Martin Loughlin for reading and commenting on chapters included in this edition. I owe a particular debt to Eric Heinze for his detailed comments on various chapters of the book and for lengthy conversations on many ideas discussed in this and various other projects we are collaborating on. Mark Graber and Fara Dabhoiwala offered very helpful suggestions for the direction of the analysis in the final version of the book. My colleagues at the National University of Ireland Galway School of Law were very supportive of my efforts to complete the book. The anonymous reviewers for Cambridge University Press offered very valuable insights for the final version of the book.

Finally, I would like to dedicate this study to my parents and my sister: everything begins thanks to them and everything ends thanks to them.

1

Introduction

Speech, Privacy, and Dignity in France and the United States

1.1 ENLIGHTENMENT VALUES IN THE BALANCE

What are the just limits of freedom of expression in relation to the protection of other values like privacy and human dignity? To what extent should offensive speech be protected? What is the proper equilibrium between speech and other rights when in conflict? Is it legitimate for the state to define the content and limits of freedom of expression to protect other values or should civil society accomplish this task by itself? Is it legitimate for the state to intervene to protect its citizens from the danger of forming the wrong opinions? Is it legitimate for the state to intervene to protect citizens from modes of self-expression that could be considered by a part of society as violating the dignity of the person expressing themselves? The answer to these questions would be different in France compared to the United States, despite the fact that both countries share the same philosophical background of the Enlightenment.

Freedom of expression is a liberty at the core of the preoccupations of the Enlightenment. Two legal systems founded upon this similar philosophical and political background use state coercion differently to regulate a liberty at the core of the Enlightenment. This book studies this variety in the protection of freedom of expression to offer a philosophical reflection on the just limits of freedom of speech. France is more willing to accept limitations while the United States has opted for a regime that is very protective of free speech.[1] In the United States, the legal protection of freedom of expression trumps the protection of other values, like privacy or human dignity, a sign of American exceptionalism.[2] Social restrictions from civil society and political correctness limit expression. By contrast, limitations

[1] Robert Post and Peter Molnar, "Interview with Robert Post," in Michael Herz and Peter Molnar, eds., *The Content and Context of Hate Speech: Rethinking Regulation and Responses* (Cambridge University Press, 2012), 11. Frederick Schauer notes the importance of freedom of the press as a check on the government in Frederick Schauer, *Free Speech: A Philosophical Inquiry* (Cambridge University Press, 1982), 43–44.

[2] Frederick Schauer, "The Exceptional First Amendment," in Michael Ignatieff ed., *American Exceptionalism and Human Rights* (Princeton University Press, 2005), 29–56.

to freedom of expression are legitimate in France, in order to protect other competing values. The role undertaken by civil society in the United States is undertaken by the state in France. Civility norms are enforced by the state in France, which is not the case in the United States, where limitations to self-expression, which could be seen as violating the "dignity" of the person expressing themselves, would not be accepted. Examples of this divergence abound, concerning all cases of possible conflict between freedom of expression and other values, such as hate speech, freedom of religion, and invasion of privacy, as well as various modes of expression.

Hate speech is not protected in France.[3] Defamation on the basis of a person's "race" is punished more heavily than "ordinary" defamation and constitutes a "special crime."[4] By contrast, in American law, freedom of speech is a "preferred" liberty even when it is in conflict with other values. The US Supreme Court does not accept content restrictions on speech. Only time, place, and manner restrictions are accepted. In the United States, campus speech codes have been struck down as unconstitutional.[5] According to the Supreme Court, when the government restricts speech because of its communicative impact, even when the speech falls within one of the exceptions to the protection of free speech, limiting hate speech is impermissible viewpoint discrimination.[6] Although the Supreme Court upheld a group libel law in 1952,[7] the decision is no longer treated as good law.[8] Since *Brandenburg* v. *Ohio*,[9] the Court accepts that speech can be limited only if there is an "imminent danger" of causing harm. This criterion requires incitement to an illegal act, which is very likely to be committed, according to John Stuart Mill's conception. This protective regime applies against any state attempt to limit hate speech. In private settings where there is no state action, hate speech can be regulated in the United States too.

The denial of "the existence of one or more crimes against humanity" and "apology for crimes against humanity" (defined in the case law as the publication or public evaluation inciting its recipients to make a favorable value judgment on one or more crimes against humanity and tending to justify these crimes)[10] is a criminal offense in France.[11] The French Constitutional Council held that the

3 See generally Ioanna Tourkochoriti, "Should Hate Speech be Protected? Group Defamation, Party Bans, Holocaust Denial and the Divide between Europe and the US," *Columbia Human Rights Law Review* 45 (2014), 552–622.

4 Code pénal [C. pén] [Penal Code], art. R625-7, modifying arts. 32 and 33 of Loi sur la liberté de la presse du 29 juillet 1881 [Law of July 19, 1881 on the Freedom of the Press].

5 *Doe* v. *Univ. of Mich.*, 721 F. Supp. 852 (E.D. Mich. 1989); *Corry* v. *Stanford*, No. 74039 (Cal. Super. Ct. Santa Clara Co. Feb. 27, 1995).

6 *R.A.V.* v. *City of St. Paul, Minnesota*, 112 US 2538 (1992).

7 *Beauharnais* v. *Illinois*, 343 US 250, 266 (1952).

8 *Nuxoll* v. *Indian Prairie School Dist.*, 523 F.3d 668, 672 (7th Cir. 1985).

9 395 US 444 (1969).

10 Tribunal de grande instance [TGI] [ordinary court of original jurisdiction] Nanterre, Sept. 23, 1987, Gaz. Palais 1987, 2, 672.

11 On the basis of the "Gayssot Law" – Loi 90-615 du 13 juillet 1990, tendant à réprimer tout acte raciste, antisémite ou xenophobe [Law 90-615 of July 13, 1990 against any racist, antisemitic or xenophobic acts], *Journal Officiel de la République française* [JO] [Official Gazette of France], July 4, 1990, 8333.

Gayssot Law, which outlaws denial of the Holocaust, is in conformity with the Constitution as it aims to limit an "abuse" of the exercise of freedom of expression.[12] French legislation criminalizing the denial of crimes against humanity, similar to that which exists in other European countries, has inspired Framework Decision 208/913/JHA[13] of the Council of the European Union, which encourages other member states to enact similar legislation. By contrast, Holocaust denial is protected in the United States.[14] As the US Supreme Court clarified, even demonstrably false statements are protected.[15]

The US Supreme Court has invalidated federal legislation imposing limits on independent expenditures – political campaign communications usually made by corporations independently from the candidate – as a violation of their speech rights.[16] The Supreme Court invalidated legislation prohibiting independent spending by corporations "for speech defined as an 'electioneering communication' or for speech expressly advocating the election or defeat of a candidate."[17] France regulates the funding of political campaigns strictly and imposes upper ceilings to campaign expenditure.[18] In the United States, the newspaper industry was granted an exception from antitrust laws, which has led them to pursue a business model of maximizing monopoly profits.[19] This model has led to a significant crisis with the evolution of new communication platforms on the internet. French legislation gives judges the option of suppressing allegations of facts during electoral campaigns that are "inexact or deceiving" and of a nature to alter the sincerity of the voting process via an urgent requests process.[20] The French Audiovisual Superior Council can unilaterally terminate a contract with a broadcasting corporation when it transmits

12 Conseil Constitutionnel [CC] [Constitutional Council], decision no. 2015–512 QPC, Jan. 8, 2016, JO, Jan. 10, 2016, 20.

13 2008 OJ (L 328), 55.

14 Robert Kahn, *Holocaust Denial and the Law: A Comparative Study* (New York, Palgrave, 2004).

15 *United States* v. *Alvarez*, 132 S. Ct. 2537 at 2547 (2012).

16 *Citizens United* v. *FEC*. 558 US 310 (2010).

17 Bipartisan Campaign Reform Act of 2002, § 441b.

18 Loi 88–226 du 11 mars 1988 relative à la transparence financière de la vie politique [Law 88–226 of March 11, 1988, relating to financial transparency in political life], JO, Mar. 12, 1988, 3288; Loi 88–227 du 11 mars 1988 relative à la transparence financière de la vie politique [Law 88–227 of March 11, 1988, relating to financial transparency in political life], JO, Mar., 12, 1988, 3290; Loi 90–55 du 15 janvier 1990 relative à la limitation des dépenses électorales et à la clarification du financement des activités politiques [Law 90–55 of January 15, 1990, relating to limits on election expenditures and the reporting of political funding activities], JO, Jan. 16, 1990, 639. On the ceilings to campaign expenditures, see the decision of the Commission nationale des comptes de campagne et des financements politiques [National Commission on Campaign Accounts and Political Financing] of November 26, 2007, regarding Nicolas Sarkozy, presidential candidate, JO, Jan. 10, 2008, 574. See the site maintained by the Library of Congress in the United States www.loc.gov/law/help/campaign-finance/france.php

19 Adam Lebovic, *Free Speech* and *Unfree News: The Paradox of Press Freedom in America* (Cambridge, MA: Harvard University Press, 2016), 213.

20 Loi 2018-1202 du 22 Décembre 2018 relative à la lutte contre la manipulation de l'information [Law 2018-1202 of December 22, 2018 on the fight against fake news], OJ, Dec. 23, 2018, art. 1, modifying Code électoral [Electoral Code], art. L. 163–2(1).

"false information."[21] The law applies to corporations broadcasting in France controlled by foreign states. Legislation also obliges online platforms to take measures against the transmission of "false information" that can disturb public order.[22]

The divergence is also obvious in the area of self-expression. Wearing conspicuous religious symbols has been forbidden in "public schools and high schools" in France since 2005.[23] In 2010, the French parliament banned the wearing of the burka.[24] Covering one's face in public places is forbidden in reference to a conception of human dignity that dictates showing one's face to others. The European Court of Human Rights did not find that, by banning the burka, France had violated the right to freedom of religion under Article 9 of the European Convention of Human Rights, considering that the state has the authority to define "the circumstances of living together."[25] Limitations on the wearing of headscarves by students in schools were not accepted in the United States.[26] The hybrid rights doctrine offers strong protection for these claims, as they are founded both on the freedom of expression and freedom of religion clauses of the First Amendment. Prohibitions on facial coverings in public places would be accepted only in narrowly defined circumstances and for limited purposes related to public security.[27]

French courts are more willing to adopt a philosophical conception of human dignity as transcending the individual and imposing obligations toward the self, which must be enforced by the state. The French Council of State upheld the decision of a mayor, taken within his police authority, banning the practice of "dwarf-throwing."[28] For the Court, the respect of human dignity is one of the components of public order. According to the conclusions of Patrick Frydman, solicitor general at the Council of

21 Loi No 2018–1202 du 22 Décembre 2018 relative à la lutte contre la manipulation de l'information, OJ, Dec. 23, 2018, art. 8, modifying Loi 86-1067 du 30 septembre 1986 relative à la liberté de communication [Law 86-1067 of September 30, 1986 on freedom of communication], OJ, Oct. 1, 1986, art. 42–46.

22 Loi 2018–1202 du 22 Décembre 2018 relative à la lutte contre la manipulation de l'information, OJ, Dec. 23, 2018, art. 11.

23 Loi 2004-228 du 15 mars 2004 encadrant, en application du principe de laïcité, le port de signes ou de tenues manifestant une appartenance religieuse dans les écoles, collèges et lycées public [Law 2004-228 of March 15, 2004 concerning, in application of the principle of separation of church and state, the wearing of symbols or clothing demonstrating religious affiliation in public primary and secondary schools], JO, Mar. 17, 2994, 5190. For a presentation, see Jonathan Laurence and Justin Vaisse, *Integrating Islam: Political and Religious Challenges in Contemporary France* (Washington, DC: Brookings Institution Press, 2006), John R. Bowen, *Why the French Don't Like Headscarves* (Princeton University Press, 2006).

24 Loi 2010-1192 du 11 octobre 2010 interdisant la dissimulation du visage dans l'espace public [Law 2010-1192 of October 11, 2010, prohibiting the concealment of the face in public spaces], JO, Oct. 11, 2010, 18344.

25 ECtHR, S.A.S. v. *France*, App. no. 43835/11, Judgment of July 1, 2014.

26 See for instance Consent Order, *Hearn* v. *Muskogee Pub. Sch. Dist.* 020, No: CIV 03–598-S (E.D. Okla. 2004), available at www.justice.gov/crt/spec_topics/religiousdiscrimination/hearn_consent_decree_final.pdf.

27 See Ioanna Tourkochoriti, "The Burka Ban: Divergent Approaches to Freedom of Religion in France and in the U.S.A.," *William andMary Bill of Rights Journal* 20 (2012), 791–852, esp. 824–25.

28 Conseil d'Etat [CE] [Council of State], Assemblé [Ass.] [Assembly], Oct. 27, 1995, 136727, www.legifrance.gouv.fr/affichJuriAdmin.do?idTexte=CETATEXT000007877723.

State, the activity violated not only the dignity of the person being thrown but also the dignity of the spectators and the dwarfism community.[29]

The divergence also concerns cases where expressive interests conflict with privacy rights. The privacy of public figures is strictly protected in France.[30] In French law, the public's right to knowledge about public officials covers only private facts relating to public office.[31] Legislation prohibits the publication of elements of identification of victims of sexual aggression and suspects of crimes.[32] The US Supreme Court has on occasion held that similar legislation is unconstitutional.[33] The European Court of Human Rights has held that the privacy protection standards imposed on the press in France apply to all the member states of the Council of Europe.[34] The US Supreme Court, on the contrary, is predisposed to finding any conceivable justification to refuse media responsibility.[35] The Court has held that the notion of "newsworthiness" has constitutional value.[36] The recent history of the protection of free speech under the First Amendment in the United States shows that it has served as a "powerful engine of constitutional deregulation" in many areas where government regulation is accepted in Europe, such as data privacy.[37] Overall, informational privacy is not considered to be a value significant enough to mobilize state coercion for its protection. The Supreme Court has for example invalidated legislation that barred pharmacies from disclosing information to data miners.[38]

29 Patrick Frydman, Concl., CE Ass., Oct. 27, 1995 (two cases), *Commune de Morsang-sur-Orge* and *Ville d'Aix en Provence*, *RFDA* (1995), 1204–15.

30 Richard Malka, "Le droit à l'information n'est pas le droit à l'humiliation," *Le Monde*, May 16, 2011; Richard Malka, "Affaire DSK: la presse anglo-saxonne s'attaque à la culture française du secret," *Le Monde*, May 17, 2011. See the Opinion of the Conseil supérieur de l'audiovisuel [French Superior Audiovisual Council], May 17, 2011, www.csa.fr/Espace-Presse/Communiques-de-presse/Le-Conseil-appelle-les-chaines-a-la-plus-grande-retenue-dans-la-diffusion-d-images-de-personnes-mises-en-cause-dans-une-procedure-penale; Richard Malka, "Affaire DSK: le CSA appelle les chaînes de télévision à 'la retenue,'" *Le Monde*, May 17, 2011.

31 See Ioanna Tourkochoriti, "Speech, Privacy and Dignity in France and the USA," *Loyola Los Angeles International and Comparative Law Review* 40 (2016), 101–82.

32 Loi 2000–516 du 15 juin 2000 renforçant la protection de la présomption d'innocence et les droits des victimes [Law 2000–516 of June 15, 2000 strengthening the protection of the presumption of innocence and victims' rights], JO, June 16, 2000, 9038.

33 *Cox Broad. Corp.* v. *Cohn*, 420 US 469 (1975); *Florida Star* v. *B.F.J.*, 491 US 524 (1989); *Globe Newspaper* v. *Superior Court*, 457 US 596, 607–8 (1982); *Smith* v. *Daily Mail Publ'g Co.*, 443 US 97, 108–9 (1979).

34 ECtHR, *Von Hannover* v. *Allemagne*, App. no. 59320/00, Judgment of June 24, 2004. This case concerned the publication of pictures of a member of a royal family in public places during activities, which according to the opinion of the court are "private." For the European Court of Human Rights the privacy of a member of the family of one of the European monarchies is protected if the person is in a public place shown in an activity not related to public life.

35 Paul Gewirtz, "Privacy and Speech," *Supreme Court Review* 139 (2001), 140.

36 See *Cox Broad. Corp.* v. *Cohn*, 420 US 469 (1975).

37 Robert Post and Amanda Shanor, "Adam Smith's First Amendment," *Harvard Law Review Forum* 128 (2015), 165.

38 *Sorrell* v. *IMS Health Inc.*, 131 S. Ct. 2653, 2672 (2011). For a comparison with EU legislation in the area, see Ioanna Tourkochoriti, "The Snowden Revelations, The Transatlantic Trade and Investment Partnership and the Divide Between US–EU in Data Privacy Protection," *University of Arkansas Law*

Some overdetermination of the content of freedom of expression by the state is legitimate in France while it is not in the United States. American law tolerates violations of other liberties by freedom of expression, which other legal systems do not tolerate. This book analyzes two different approaches, the American and the French, on the proper limits to freedom of expression. It focuses on the study of the social and political context in which these norms were elaborated. It argues that the difference in the balancing of the two rights can be understood by reference to the philosophical presuppositions underlying the two legal orders. These presuppositions are expressed in legal arguments. They reflect philosophical ideas formed due to different historical, and political contexts. They reflect a difference in the conception of the role of the government regarding the degree of its intervention in civil society. They also reflect a different role for the government in determining the content and limits of freedom of expression. This understanding of the role of the government was formed at the foundation of the two democracies in response to concrete political problems. Legislation limiting speech is frequently invalidated by the US Supreme Court. In France, similar legislation in many cases was not even referred to the Constitutional Council (under the previous system of deferral to the Council based on the initiative of members of the parliament or the president). This indicates that the difference relates to the interplay between law and liberty in the two legal systems. The debates around the French Revolution, the Declaration of Independence in the United States, and the construction of the federal government there are instructive in relation to this interplay between law and liberty. These debates to a great extent formed the understanding on the proper relation between law and liberty.

In comparing the French and American approaches to free speech in this book, I identify, relatively, more and less legitimate exercises of government power in regulating speech. It is possible to distinguish between these more and less legitimate cases and to reflect critically upon both traditions to propose a theory of free speech. In France, the dominant tradition of trust toward the state leads to an overdetermination of the content and limits of liberty, including free speech. In the United States, the tradition of distrust leads to an underdetermination of the same liberty. Understanding how the two traditions emerged can help us to engage in a critical reflection in order to retain the best elements of both traditions. Understanding the origins of legal rules does not mean accepting historical determinism.[39] Limits on free speech are justified in order to protect other values such as human dignity and privacy, and in order to ensure that everybody has access to public debate. When speech violates privacy, it is the dignity of the person whose

Review 36 (2014) 161, 167; Paul M. Schwartz and Daniel J. Solove, "Reconciling Personal Information in the United States and European Union," *California Law Review* 102 (2014), 877; Paul M. Schwartz, "The EU-US Privacy Collision: A Turn to Institutions and Procedures," *Harvard Law Review* 126 (2013), 1966.

39 Cf. Eric Heinze, *Hate Speech and Democratic Citizenship* (Oxford University Press, 2016).

privacy is violated that should be protected over the dignity of the speaker. A presumption in favor of privacy, dominant in France, is preferable in this case, though this area involves difficult ad hoc considerations of public interest.

Limitations to hate speech are justified when it has an individualized target. In this case, the harm caused due to the performative effects of speech is very important. Speech has the potential to accentuate marginalization and oppression. Speech has this performative effect when it targets a person individually. It is less easy to specify its harmful effect when speech has the form of broad statements, even concerning social groups. This means that legal sanctions as understood in France for "group defamation" are not justified. The very existence of an offense of group defamation is a case where the government overdetermines speech. Similarly, there should be no legal responsibility for speech challenging historical facts, even denying the existence of crimes against humanity. In this case, the causal link between a statement that describes a fact and the offense/harm caused is very weak. As I argue, legislation criminalizing the denial of crimes against humanity is justified only in reference to the emotion of guilt.[40] If societies feel guilty for terrible atrocities that took place in their midst, this is a very weak basis to justify limitations to freedom of speech. Therefore, the American solution, which trusts the reason of the individual to decide in these cases, is preferable. In some others, such as the dwarf-throwing case or the wearing of headscarves, government intervention is not legitimate and the individual should decide for themselves how to treat themselves. In both those cases, the reason of the individual should be trusted. The limits on self-expression imposed by French law are not justified. Regarding the regulation of political campaigns, it is imperative to protect the public debate from distortions and corruption. Therefore, in this case, the French solution is preferable to the American one.

The difference in the regulation of freedom of expression can be understood, I argue, in reference to the difference in the understanding of republicanism in France and in the United States. American republicanism associates the need to protect the common good with respecting the "natural liberties" of the individual. Government exists in the United States to protect the natural negative liberties of the citizens. The common good itself is associated with the protection of the liberties of the citizens. This can help us understand why the neo-Roman understanding of republicanism that insists on a mixed system of government has been dominant in America since the Founding Era. A conception of balanced government corresponds to the distrust toward the government. French republicanism protects the rights of the individual only to the extent that they promote the common good. It is closer to the conception dominant in antiquity. Republicanism in France is permeated with trust toward the state, which has its origins in the political theories that

40 See Ioanna Tourkochoriti, "Challenging Historical Facts and National Truths: An Analysis of Cases from France and Greece," in Uladzislau Belavusau and Aleksandra Glyszczynska Grabias, eds., *Law And Memory: Towards Legal Governance of History* (Cambridge University Press, 2017), 151.

were dominant before the French Revolution. According to the French conception, rights are rules that regulate social interaction. They exist only because they are recognized by the state. They do not make sense outside of society and the state. The quality of citizen is primary and serves as the foundation of the rights of man. These ideas, related to the two different conceptions of republicanism, can assist our understanding of the difference in the protection of freedom of expression in France and in the United States.

Freedom of expression is very important both for individuals and societies. Numerous thinkers have emphasized the importance of freedom of speech for the intellectual development of humanity. Locke and Spinoza note the link between freedom of expression and freedom of thought and conscience. Spinoza notes that attempts by the state to limit how a human being thinks, and by extension to limit the expression of their opinions, are pointless.[41] For Spinoza, the very purpose of the state is to allow persons to "use their reason freely."[42] An understanding of the importance of mental autonomy underlies his analysis. Were this freedom suppressed, human beings, while not expressing their opinions, would still retain them, which would lead to generalized corruption in the state and the "good arts." Limitations would bring about stubborn resistance endangering peace in the state. Locke expands on this idea noting that questions of faith and thus expression of this faith belong to the individual.[43] It is impossible for a person to ensure that their faith conforms to the dictates of another. The nature of human understanding is such that it cannot be compelled to the belief of anything by outward force. Penalties, he thinks, are not capable to change one's beliefs. "It is only Light and Evidence that can work a change in Mens Opinions" [sic].[44] Voltaire also notes the importance of protecting expression, which helps human beings elaborate their reason and reach maturity of thought.[45] Criticizing religious fanaticism, he makes a compelling argument in favor of the freedom of speech of minority religious groups.[46] This argument would mean for us today that human beings have an interest in expressing themselves through dress and other choices in ways that are considered eccentric and unusual, an argument relevant to the debate on the permissibility of wearing conspicuous signs of religious affiliation in France.

Milton articulates a powerful critique against prohibition of books and prior restraint for speech.[47] For Milton, freedom of speech is important for civil liberty

41 Benedict Spinoza, *Tractatus Theologicophilosophicus*, trans. Jonathan Israel and Michael Silverthorne (Cambridge University Press, 2007 [1670]), chap. 20, 250–59.

42 Ibid., chap. 20, 240.

43 John Locke, *Letter concerning Toleration* (Indianapolis, IN: Liberty Fund, 2010 [1689]), 35–67.

44 Ibid., 40.

45 Voltaire, *Toleration and Other Essays*, trans. Joseph McCabe (New York and London: G.P. Putnam's Sons, 1912), 27.

46 Ibid., 32, discussing that the Greeks allowed the Epicureans to deny providence and the existence of the soul.

47 John Milton, *Areopagitica* (Cambridge University Press, 1918 [1875]).

but also for the development of the individual themselves; men attain "the utmost bound of civil liberty when complaints are freely heard, deeply considered and speedily reformed."[48] Limiting the circulation of books hinders and crops the discovery that might be made in religious and civil wisdom, he notes.[49] "He who destroys a good book, kills reason itself."[50] According to Milton, revolutions of ages do not recover the loss of a rejected truth, for the want of which whole nations fare the worse. Milton discusses cases where ancient Athens ordered the burning of books. The judges of Areopagus commanded the books of Protagoras to be burned and the man himself banished from the territory because he expressed doubts as to the existence of the divinity.[51] Milton notes that all opinions and even errors are of service and assistance toward attaining the truth.[52] Good and evil are interwoven, he notes: they grow up together almost inseparably.[53] The knowledge of the one presupposes the other. It is the knowledge of what is evil that defines wisdom. Milton's argument stresses the need to protect individual freedom of choice of opinions that are right or wrong.[54] Optimistic as to the possibility to discover truth, Milton notes that it will always prevail.[55] He also brings an interesting nuance in his conception of truth. For him truth is like Proteus: "she may have more shapes than one."[56] Expressing an insight later expressed by Hegel, he notes that truth may be on both sides of an issue "without being unlike herself."[57]

Deontological justifications focus on principled a priori reasons to protect freedom of speech. According to a deontological argument for freedom of speech, human beings have the right to express themselves and to receive information in order to develop their personality. This is a right that should be recognized for everyone out of unconditional respect for their dignity. Freedom of expression is important for intellectual freedom. Freedom of speech allows the public use of reason, which, for Kant, can bring enlightenment in men on its own.[58] As humanity is entitled to unconditional respect, this means that human beings must have the liberty to invent themselves. For Kant, this is a duty that human beings have toward themselves. Other scholars have expanded this insight, noting that human beings have an interest in forming their personality.[59] Freedom of expression allows human

48 Ibid., 2.
49 Ibid., 6.
50 Ibid., 7.
51 Ibid., 8.
52 Ibid., 19.
53 Ibid., 20.
54 Ibid., 20.
55 Ibid., 59.
56 Ibid., 59.
57 Ibid.
58 Immanuel Kant, "An Answer to the Question: 'What is Enlightenment?'" in H. Reiss, ed., *Political Writings*, trans. H. B. Nisbet (Cambridge University Press, 1970 [1784]), 54–60, esp. 55.
59 Seana Shiffrin, *Speech Matters, On Lying, Morality, and the Law* (Princeton University Press, 2014), David A. J. Richards, "Free Speech as Toleration," in W. J. Waluchow, ed., *Free Expression: Essays in*

beings to find meaning in their lives. According to Dworkin, when the government limits a person's speech it is an affront to their dignity as it treats that person as not worthy of equal respect by the government.[60]

In the same spirit, according to an argument inspired by Rawls, freedom of speech is a basic liberty necessary for the development of the moral faculties of every person. It facilitates the formation of moral agency. For Rawls, "freedom of thought and liberty of conscience and so on" are "the background institutional conditions" necessary for the development of the moral powers of a person.[61] Those moral faculties are the capacity to develop a conception of the good and a sense of justice. Freedom of expression allows a person to develop their autonomy.[62] Respect for the humanity of each person dictates that they are allowed to receive information that will help them form their opinions and express them. Freedom of expression can enhance the quality of human life through the experience of various intellectual stimuli including art and social satire.[63]

According to John Stuart Mill's classic consequentialist defense, freedom of expression benefits individuals and societies alike.[64] A society has a better chance of discovering truth in scientific, political, and moral questions if it tolerates the free expression of ideas.[65] Mill emphasizes that when the state suppresses an opinion it assumes infallibility. He is in favor of the intellectual challenge of ideas, to prevent them from becoming dead dogmas. He notes the paradox that truth is very often the result of conciliation and combination of extremes. Optimistic about the rational capacities of humanity, Mill considers that truth prevails against error. He is criticized in this respect by Isaiah Berlin, who stresses that the domain of the irrational is much more complex than Mill imagines.[66] Demagogues and liars are not always stopped in time.[67] In France, bans on hate speech reflect this criticism by Berlin. They are justified by reference to the belief that state rationality can guide the reason of the individual and protect vulnerable individuals from offense.

In philosophy of science the current of phenomenology has made the conception of "objective" scientific truth relative. Husserl and Heidegger have noted that we can

Law and Philosophy (Oxford: Clarendon Press, 1994), 21; Joshua Cohen, "Freedom of Expression," *Philosophy & Public Affairs* 22 (1993), 207.

60 Ronald Dworkin, *Taking Rights Seriously* (Cambridge, MA: Harvard University Press, 1977) 198–99.

61 John Rawls, *Political Liberalism* (New York: Columbia University Press, 1993), 308.

62 For an association of freedom of expression with autonomy see Thomas Scanlon, "A Theory of Freedom of Expression," *Philosophy & Public Affairs* 1, no. 2 (1972), 204.

63 On the importance of freedom of expression for pursuing one's goals and aspirations see also Joshua Cohen, "Freedom of Expression," 207.

64 John Stuart Mill, "On Liberty," in *On Liberty and Other Essays*, ed. John Gray (Oxford University Press, 1998).

65 Ibid., 21.

66 Isaiah Berlin, "John Stuart Mill and the Ends of Life," in *Four Essays on Liberty* (Oxford University Press, 2002), 233; Paul Ricoeur, "The Erosion of Tolerance and the Resistance of the Intolerable," in Paul Ricoeur, ed., *Tolerance between Intolerance and the Intolerable* (New York: Bergahn Books, 1996), 197.

67 Ibid.

only have access to "phenomena" and not objective truths. Thomas Kuhn and others have noted that scientific truth is based on the acceptance of the validity of a - paradigm.[68] The acceptance of this validity varies in time. History of science is a history of succession of paradigms that are accepted as valid by the academic community. Even if one does not accept Mill's postulates on the possibility of discovering "truth," his theory remains a classic as it can be read in parallel with Kuhn's. It suggests a process of discovering intersubjective consensus on a paradigm that is accepted by the academic community and society as a whole in relation to various areas of human activity. Mill's argument in favor of freedom of expression is not inconsistent with skeptical theories. As Frederick Schauer has noted, it maintains its value whichever might be the theory accepted to determine truth, that is, whether it is correspondence, coherence, pragmatism or any other theory.[69]

Mill's conception of the free circulation of ideas as having the potential to allow truth to emerge resonates with Adam Smith's conception of limited government intervention in the economic market. Smith criticized the regulation of the economy by the European monarchs of the eighteenth century.[70] In his opinion excessive government intervention in the economy can distort its processes. Activities that individuals pursue out of self-interest can, in the long term, have positive unintended consequences. They can lead to a good distribution of goods so that everyone has what they need. Government intervention can only distort the free functioning of the market.

Transposed to the "marketplace of ideas" this conception means that the best results can come out of the free competition of ideas. Justice Holmes, in his famous dissent in *Abrams* v. *United States*, made explicit this link between Mill's conception and the "marketplace of ideas."[71] Defending Abrams's right to criticize capitalism and militarism in 1919, Holmes issues a reminder that "time has upset many fighting faiths."[72] He notes that "the ultimate good desired is better reached by free trade in ideas – that the best test of truth is the power of the thought to get itself accepted in the competition of the market."[73] Holmes notes that the US Constitution is an experiment, as all life is an experiment. He advises in favor of "eternal vigilance" against attempts to limit the expression of opinions that "we loathe." Although Holmes's attempt to delegitimize the crime of seditious libel is persuasive, his elaboration of the marketplace of ideas is open to criticism. Appealing as it is, it

68 For Kuhn, science is based on a succession of "paradigms" thought to explain the reality. Factors phenomenally "arbitrary" play a role in making a scientific community accept a scientific paradigm. See T. S. Kuhn, *The Structure of Scientific Revolutions* (University of Chicago Press, 1970). However, for Kuhn freedom of expression can have a promoting role concerning the realization of the insufficiency and the possibility of succession of these paradigms.

69 Schauer, *Free Speech*, 18.

70 See Adam Smith, *The Wealth of Nations*, vol. 1, bk. 4, chap. 5 (Indianapolis, IN: Liberty Fund, 1981 [1776]), 437.

71 *Abrams* v. *United States*, 250 US 616 (1919) at 624, Holmes J. dissenting, joined by Brandeis J.

72 Ibid., at 630.

73 Ibid., at 630.

overlooks social and economic imbalances. All ideas cannot compete equally on the market. Minority opinions have few chances of becoming known to the public.[74] Mill was not in position to foresee the dangers for free speech originating from conglomerates of economic interests. It is possible to argue in favor of some government intervention to create an equal starting point for everyone. Regulation of electoral campaign funding can be a step in this direction.

Mill's conception points toward weighing the utility of the consequences of protecting freedom of expression for individuals and societies alike. Mill admits that the only legitimate reason that a community could have for using force against one of its members is to prevent harm to others. Therefore, opinions lose their immunity, when they are expressed in the frame of such circumstances that make this expression "instigation to a mischievous act."[75] The offense that speech itself causes is not significant enough for Mill to justify limitations.

Freedom of speech is important for democracy. It is a *conditio sine qua non* of a system of government that recognizes that the ultimate power resides in the people. Some democratic arguments in favor of protecting free speech combine deontological and consequentialist elements.[76] The deontological elements exist in the idea that democracy is the regime that unconditionally respects the autonomy of every citizen a priori as a good in itself.[77]

A modern liberal democracy respects everyone's rights and provides the best possible conditions for the search for political justice. Many individual interests are valuable because they are instrumental to social values.[78] Democratic theories contain consequentialist elements too as they point out that free speech as an element of democracy has beneficial consequences for individuals and societies. They emphasize that free speech is a public good, associated with the notion of "popular sovereignty." The formation of voting decisions presupposes access to information, the knowledge of "truths," which are significant to political life. Freedom of expression enables public debate and helps to expose corruption. In short, it contributes to the renewal of the social contract. A state legitimates itself as a democracy through public discourse. Consequentialist elements are mixed in this theory with deontological elements that stress the equal dignity of every person, best guaranteed in a democratic regime. If universal suffrage guarantees self-government, then it must guarantee to the citizens the right to form their opinions, their plans and life decisions as well as allow them to make mistakes.[79]

74 C. Edwin Baker, "Scope of the First Amendment Freedom of Speech," *University of California Law Review* 25 (1978), 964–1040, esp. 980, Stanley Ingber, "The Marketplace of Ideas: A Legitimizing Myth," *Duke Law Journal* (1984), 1–91; David A. Strauss, "Persuasion, Autonomy, and Freedom of Expression," *Columbia Law Review* 91 (1991), 334–371, esp. 349.

75 Mill, "On Liberty," 62.

76 Kent Greenawalt, "Free Speech Justifications," *Columbia Law Review* 89 (1989), 119, 125–29.

77 Ibid.

78 Schauer, *Free Speech*, 47.

79 Ibid, 37.

The thinkers of the Enlightenment noted the importance of freedom of speech in the political sphere. Freedom of the press keeps the spirit of the people alert, as Hume has noted.[80] It allows them to employ their wit and genius to defend their freedom against the government.[81] For Kant, the "freedom of the pen" is "the safeguard of the rights of the people."[82] It can serve as a check toward the government to ensure that legislation respects the principle of the general will. The general will is, for Kant, an "idea of reason." It means the government should limit freedom in a way that it can coexist with the freedom of others in terms of a general law. For Kant, human beings should emerge from their self-incurred immaturity and use their reason in the public sphere.[83] Kant distinguishes between the private use of one's reason that guides a person to consider their own interest and the public use of one's reason, which dictates that a person should see themselves as a citizen. In this quality, a person should think about the common good in ways that may contradict their private good. Kant implies that freedom of speech is essential to designing good legislation that respects the universal right and not the partial interests of any one citizen as a private being.

Democratic arguments in favor of free speech combine deontological and consequentialist elements. According to deontological arguments, freedom of expression should be guaranteed for all opinions out of respect for the dignity of the person who expresses themselves as well as for the dignity of the receiver. Democracy is associated with the notion of equality and equal participation as a matter of principle. Freedom of expression provides access to the necessary information for the formation of voting decisions. This prerequisite to equal participation in the political process can be seen as a component of individual dignity and of equal respect. In this way, the core of the argument moves from the pragmatic or utilitarian calculus of the effective functioning of government toward the moral right to equal participation in the political process.[84] And as self-government is possible when electors obtain intelligence, integrity, sensibility, and generous devotion to the general well-being, freedom of education, the sciences, and the arts are also necessary. And these qualities are obtained by the citizens in a system that allows wide liberty in relation to education, the sciences, and the arts. This is an approach that has a collectivist as well as an individualist echo. It emphasizes the consequences of speech not only as an individual need, derived from autonomy, but also as the needs of the political body.

80 David Hume, "Of the Liberty of the Press," in *Political Essays*, ed. Knud Haakonssen (Cambridge University Press, 2012), 1–3.

81 Ibid.

82 Immanuel Kant, "On the Common Saying: 'This May be True in Theory, but It Does Not Apply in Practice," in *Political Writings*, 85.

83 Immanuel Kant, "An Answer to the Question: 'What is Enlightenment?,'" in *Political Writings*, 54–60.

84 Schauer, *Free Speech*, 42.

According to Rawls' version of the social contract, under a veil of ignorance citizens would agree that freedom of expression is a fundamental liberty that contributes to the protection of the fundamental liberties of all.[85] As Rawls notes, free speech is a "primary good," a basic liberty that must have a special status and absolute weight with respect to reasons of public good and of perfectionist values.[86] It is legitimate to regulate speech as a basic liberty in order to make sure that everyone has the possibility to speak.[87] It is not legitimate though to restrict the content of speech by limiting religious, philosophical, or political doctrines, or discussions assessing the structure of society. Equal political liberty cannot be denied to a social group on the basis that having this liberty can block policies needed for economic efficiency and growth.[88] Theories that associate free speech with democracy insist on the difficulties inherent in viewpoint restrictions. Alexander Meiklejohn notes that no idea can be excluded from public debate on the basis only that someone among those in power thinks that this idea is imprudent or unjust, for this would mean mutilating the deliberative process of the community.[89] He insists that artistic expression should also be protected as it concurs to the formation of citizenship.

Heinze's democratic/deontological approach to free speech notes that citizenship should be protected categorically.[90] For Heinze, it is implausible that democratic citizenship manifests itself only once every few months or years in a fleeting moment within the polling station. There must be some attribute of citizenship even more primordial than voting, which citizens carry always and everywhere within the borders of a democracy. That attribute must be such that it cannot be regulated for the sake of democracy because it constitutes democracy. For Heinze, proposing a deontological foundation for freedom of speech in association with citizenship aims to protect freedom of expression from utilitarian trade-offs as part of legislative, judicial, or administrative balancing. There is no such thing as limiting one's citizenship to ensure some other individual's citizenship. Limits to freedom must not be placed on freedoms attached to any essential element of citizenship. If it is inconceivable to abuse one's citizenship; freedom of speech cannot be abused either. In contemporary, longstanding, and prosperous democracies, viewpoint restrictions should not be accepted. According to this view, protecting security alone could justify limiting speech.

85 John Rawls, *A Theory of Justice* (Cambridge, MA: Harvard University Press, 1971) and Rawls, *Political Liberalism*.

86 Rawls, *Political Liberalism*, 296.

87 Ibid.

88 Ibid., 295.

89 Alexander Meiklejohn, "Free Speech and Its Relation to Self-Government," in *Political Freedom: The Constitutional Powers of the People* (Westport, CT: Greenwood Press Publishers, 1979 [1948]). See also Alexander Meiklejohn, "The First Amendment Is an Absolute," *The Supreme Court Review* (1961), 245–266.

90 Heinze, *Hate Speech and Democratic Citizenship*.

Jürgen Habermas's theory of democracy, premised upon his conception of communicative rationality, contains insightful reflections in relation to the public sphere.[91] According to this "discourse theory of democracy," citizens are engaged in intersubjective processes of reaching understanding in order to coordinate political action. Habermas defines the public sphere as network of spheres all in communication with one another, where citizens discuss issues of public interest in need of regulation. This spans inside and outside parliaments and other deliberative bodies where citizens engage in a rational opinion and will formation. He suggests the image of a decentered society, where the formal procedures of the political system are combined with the peripheral networks of the political public sphere. Protecting freedom of expression in the various fora available to the citizens makes sure that they are able to form their opinion on political praxis. Habermas proposes a version of discursive politics that underlines the need to make legitimate the operation of all government institutions. Within a normative conception of democracy, argumentation is part of legislative politics. A normative understanding of political processes is opposed to a descriptive, which sees it as the arena of power processes motivated by strategic considerations. Habermas builds off the criticisms of Marx and Weber, that economic power and administrative bureaucracies threaten the real and effective legitimacy of current democratic systems. He notes that engaging in communicative action in the various communicative networks can again breathe life into the system. Communicative action has its own rationality, which allows for the hope to reach intersubjective agreement on principles of justice. Participating in the various networks of the public sphere can lead to implementing them through state policies. A normative conception of democracy is possible thanks to communicative rationality and it can be motivated by the need to eliminate social power imbalances. This implies that citizens have the possibility to influence political decision-making through participating in the numerous fora that make up the public sphere. These fora bring together participants from diverse backgrounds who are all motivated by the need to reach understanding.

Habermas notes that deliberative politics is based on the interplay between formal and informal processes, thereby making freedom of expression very important in all these contexts. Participation in the communicative network of public spheres, together with institutionalized procedures of democratic opinion formation, sustain and are sustained by the socially integrating force of solidarity. Preventing democracy from being associated with the domination of majority interests upon minorities presupposes that every citizen can be convinced about the rectitude of policies. For

[91] Jürgen Habermas, *Between Facts and Norms*, trans. William Rehg (Cambridge, MA: The MIT Press, 1996), 299; Jürgen Habermas, *Morale et communication* (Paris: Flammarion, 1999); and Jürgen Habermas, *De l'éthique de la discussion*, trans. Mark Hunyadi (Paris: Flammarion, 1991), in which he elaborates a theory of moral philosophy based in his major social theory book, *Theory of Communicative Action*, trans. Thomas McCarthy (Boston: Beacon Press, 1995). For the significance of this theory for the law, see Habermas, *Between Facts and Norms*.

Habermas, the democratic process must be governed by universal principles of justice, which are constitutive of the body of citizens.[92] In this framework, freedom of expression would allow for the interpretation of needs and wants and the change of prepolitical attitudes and preferences. Any topic considered by anyone as relevant must be open to debate. This openness ensures social integration through reflexivity. For Habermas, communicative action ensures government legitimacy and the reproduction and perpetuation of the "lifeworld" itself. His reflections are enlightening as to the importance of freedom of expression as a matter of principle.

Despite agreement on the need to protect a core for a right to freedom of expression as a matter of principle, there is disagreement among scholars and across legal systems as to its proper limits. The French and the American legal systems are exemplary of this difference. Freedom of expression is protected in the United States by the First Amendment of the Federal Constitution, according to which "Congress shall make no law ... limiting freedom of speech or of the press." Although this negative formulation already indicates distrust toward the government, the clause applied, until the Fourteenth Amendment to the Federal Constitution, only to the federal government. James Madison is famous for having written that

> some degree of abuse is inseparable from the proper use of everything, and in no instance is this more true than in that of the press. It has accordingly been decided ... that it is better to leave a few of its noxious branches to their luxuriant growth, than by pruning them away, to injure the vigor of those yielding the proper fruits.[93]

Alexis de Tocqueville underlined the difference in the approach toward freedom of the press in the United States in relation to France during the nineteenth century. According to the American conception, "in the case of the press, there is really no intermediate solution between freedom and slavery. In order to collect the inestimable goods that freedom of the press assures, we need to know to submit ourselves to the inevitable wrongs that it causes."[94] Does "no law" in the wording of the First Amendment mean in reality that the protection of this liberty is absolute? Although there have been individual justices that have suggested such an approach,[95] the US Supreme Court has never adopted such an extreme position. Obscenity, child pornography, fighting words, and threats are not protected in the United States. Commercial advertising is less protected than other categories of speech.

This protective legal regime for freedom of expression is a result of the work of time. Although elements of a theory for a wide protection of freedom of expression

92 Ibid., 306.

93 Elliott's Debates on the Federal Constitution (1876 ed.), 571. Legal cases today rejecting claims for privacy invasion by the press still contain this quotation from Madison. See for instance *Fellows* v. *National Enquirer, Inc.* (1986) 42 Cal.3d 234, 228 Cal.Rptr. 215; 721 P.2d 97.

94 Alexis de Tocqueville, "De la liberté de la presse aux Etats-Unis," in *De la démocratie en Amérique*, vol. 2, 12th ed. (Paris: Pagnerre, 1848), chap. 3.

95 *Time, Inc.* v. *Hill*, 385 US 374, 400 (1967) (Black, J., concurring).

existed at the moment of the drafting of the First Amendment, First Amendment exceptionalism emerged during the twentieth century. This is when freedom of expression became a "preferred liberty" for the US Supreme Court.[96] The First Amendment initially applied only to the federal government and not to the states. Madison's proposal to include an amendment protecting freedom of the press against state governments passed the House of Representatives and was rejected by the Senate.[97] Making the First Amendment directly applicable to the state legislatures by virtue of the Fourteenth Amendment essentially contributed to the doctrine of strict protection.[98] During the nineteenth century, speech was not protected by state governments as strictly as it came to be protected during the second half of the twentieth century.[99] And even during the twentieth century and the Cold War Eera, Congress enacted significant restrictions to political expression.[100]

Various interpretations of this evolution have been proposed. Some scholars discuss the emergence of a public consciousness for protecting free speech as having occurred after the end of the First World War.[101] Others associate the emergence of the free speech doctrine with the civil rights movement.[102] Some others have most recently associated it with the class war and the compromise between various social and political actors that emerged in the twentieth century around the New Deal.[103] In this book, I complement these theories by arguing that the developments in the

[96] "Free Speech in Twentieth-Century America," *Michigan Law Review* 95 (1996), 299–392. For the American Founders' objections to laws against political dissent see also Stephen D. Solomon, *Revolutionary Dissent: How the Founding Generation Created the Freedom of Speech* (New York, St. Martin's Press, 2016).

[97] Akhil Reed Amar, *The Bill of Rights: Creation and Reconstruction* (Yale University Press, 1998), 22; David Anderson, "The Origins of the Press Clause," *University of California Los Angeles Law Review* 30 (1983), 483.

[98] For an analysis, see Amar, *Bill of Rights*, 280.

[99] David M. Rabban, *Free Speech in Its Forgotten Years* (Cambridge University Press, 1997); Leonard Levy, Emergence of a Free Press (New York: Oxford University Press, 1985); Zechariah Chafee, Jr., "Freedom of Speech in Wartime," *Harvard Law Review* 32 (1919), 932–973, 947; Laura Weinrib, *The Taming of Free Speech* (Harvard University Press, 2016), 3–4.

[100] See Geoffrey R. Stone, *Perilous Times: Free Speech in Wartime from the Sedition Act of 1798 to the War on Terrorism* (New York: Norton, 2005); Mark Tushnet, "United States of America," in Markus Thiel, ed., *The Militant Democracy Principle in Modern Democracies* (London: Routledge, 2009), 357.

[101] These theories are discussed in Rabban, *Free Speech in Its Forgotten Years*, 1; and critically in Weinrib, *Taming of Free Speech*, 5.

[102] Harry Kalven, *The Negro and the First Amendment* (University of Chicago Press, 1966). Mark Graber is offering a nuanced approach on the basis of which a conservative libertarian tradition dominated the approach to freedom of expression from the Civil War until the First World War and a civil libertarian tradition has dominated twentieth-century argument. See Mark Graber, *Transforming Free Speech: The Ambiguous Legacy of Civil Libertarianism* (Oakland, CA: University of California Press, 1991).

[103] Laura Weinrib's book *The Taming of Free Speech* presents a neglected perspective: the contribution of twentieth-century class war and of the labor movement toward forming a conception of civil liberties. The emergence of free speech in America was a calculated bargain between liberals and conservatives during the nineteenth century.

United States in the middle of the twentieth century became possible due to a conception of the role of the government dominant during the Founding Era. By themselves, these theories do not assist our understanding of why, from a comparative perspective, the United States has arrived at protecting speech more rigidly than other democracies that had to handle similar conflicts between political and social interests. The US Supreme Court expressed a profound tradition related to the role of the government and a narrative about the meaning of liberty when it issued its important decisions protecting speech in the 1960s. When government intervention in the economy became acceptable in the United States, the spirit of distrust toward the government dominant during the Founding Era found expression in the protection of freedom of expression. The Progressive Era scholars' ideas who discussed freedom of speech won over only to the extent that they resonated with the distrust towards the government dominant during the Founding Era.[104]

The Supreme Court arrived at a doctrine of rigid protection gradually. *New York Times Co.* v. *Sullivan*,[105] decided at the heart of the Civil Rights Era, was a landmark case for free speech. It concerned a defamation ruling of an Alabama court against a publication by the *New York Times*, which defended the cause of Martin Luther King and the struggle for liberty in the states of the South.[106] The article contained allegations of misbehavior by local police authorities in response to student protests, and contained many inaccuracies. For Harry Kalven, since the judgment of the Alabama court was a response by the South to the civil rights movement, the court was prepared to pay the price of destroying a part of the common law defamation tort.[107] To find a strong premise for freedom of discussion of public questions, Justice Brennan uses a historic-systemic argument, according to which one must consider the case

> against the background of a profound national commitment to the principle that debate on public issues should be uninhibited, robust, and wide-open, and that it may well include vehement, caustic, and sometimes unpleasantly sharp attacks on government and public officials.[108]

The case imposed the rule that publication of inaccurate information concerning public officials does not justify the attribution of compensatory or punitive

104 Lebovic, *Free Speech and Unfree News*. In Jeremy Kessler, "The Early Years of First Amendment Lochnerism," *Columbia Law Review* 116 (2016), 1915, Kessler focuses on the economic aspects of the protection of freedom of expression that became important during the New Deal period. A First Amendment libertarianism emerges in the form of opposition to taxation of Press Corporations.

105 *New York Times Co.* v. *Sullivan*, 376 US 254 (1964); See Antony Lewis, *Make No Law: The Sullivan Case and the First Amendment* (New York: Vintage, 1991).

106 *New York Times Co.* v. *Sullivan*, 376 US 254 (1964), at 256.

107 Harry Kalven, Jr., "The New York Times Case: A Note on the Central Meaning of the First Amendment," *Supreme Court Review* (1964), 191, 200.

108 Ibid., 271.

damages.[109] Only actual malice or reckless disregard for the truth can lead to compensatory damages, a standard difficult to meet.[110] The civil rights movement gave the Supreme Court the opportunity to affirm principles that already existed during the Founding Era, in favor of freedom of expression. Justice Brennan, who wrote the opinion of the Court, cites James Madison, for whom, "If we advert to the nature of Republican Government, we shall find that the censorial power is in the people over the Government, and not in the Government over the people."[111] The right of free public discussion of the stewardship of public officials was, in Madison's view, a fundamental principle of the American form of government. The high value attributed to freedom of speech and the precedent of *New York Times* v. *Sullivan*[112] prevent recovery of compensatory damages by public officials for publication of erroneous factual assertions.[113] The case, by imposing stringent, almost-impossible-to-meet requirements of fault marked the "denigration" of the defamation tort for public officials in the United States.[114]

In France, according to Article 11 of the French Declaration of the Rights of Man and of the Citizen, "the free communication of thoughts and opinions is one of the most precious rights of man: any citizen may therefore speak, write, and publish freely, but shall be responsible for such abuses of this freedom as shall be defined by law."[115] According to Article 4 of the same Declaration, "liberty consists in the freedom to do everything which injures no one else; hence the exercise of the natural rights of each man has no limits except those which assure to the other members of the society the enjoyment of the same rights. These limits can only be determined by law."[116] The positive wording of the article indicates trust toward the legislator to realize this right and impose limitations considered necessary. The ideological foundation of the French Declaration, "moderately liberal,"[117] accepts the possibility to limit this liberty. The French approach, being positive, shows trust in the legislator to realize this liberty and its limitations. It also indicates that the regulation of the forum of ideas, as of civil society in general, is legitimate. As Stéphane Rials has noted,[118] the French clause indicates the general spirit of "*légicentrisme*" (the central role for the law) in the French Declaration. This spirit ensures an important role for the legislature to define the content and limits of this liberty. Freedom of speech is regulated in France by the Law of July 19, 1881 (modified multiple times since), which provides for a number of

109 *New York Times Co.* v. *Sullivan*, 376 US 254 (1964), at 270.

110 Schauer, "The Exceptional First Amendment," 29–56.

111 *New York Times Co.* v. *Sullivan*, 376 US 254 (1964), at 276, citing Madison, 4 Annals of Congress, 934 (1794).

112 See *New York Times Co.* v. *Sullivan*, 376 US 254 (1964), at 254.

113 Ibid., at 279.

114 Harry Kalven, Jr., "The New York Times Case," 205.

115 English translation from the Avalon Project, Yale Law School, http://avalon.law.yale.edu/18th_century/rightsof.asp.

116 Ibid.

117 Stéphane Rials, *La déclaration des droits de l'homme et du citoyen* (Hachette, 1988), 248–49.

118 Rials, *Déclaration*, 248.

criminal offenses committed by speech. They include offending the President of the Republic (Art. 26), the "defamation of a minister for his function" (Art. 31), as well as "members of the parliament, public officials, agents of public authority" (Art. 31). Most of these offenses would be unconstitutional in the United States following *New York Times* v. *Sullivan*.

In the United States, social limitations to speech are acceptable in the form of "political correctness."[119] However, it is not legitimate for the state to enforce these limitations. Violations of the right to privacy by civil society actors like the press are considered less worthy of protection than those committed by the state.[120] Distrust toward the government means that it has no legitimacy to enforce civility rules. Enforcing civility rules would mean the government engaging in positive action beyond the protection of negative liberties.

Structural differences between the United States and France are important.[121] In France and other European countries the requirement to protect constitutional rights applies to both public and private actors. This means that the constitutional protection of privacy can be invoked against private actors like the press. In the United States, the protection of constitutional rights applies only to the state. The concern to protect liberty against limitations imposed by the state, and the distrust toward state intervention in civil society, is expressed by the doctrine of state action.[122] The case law of the US Supreme Court focuses on the protection of the negative aspect of liberty. It does not accept what is considered in Europe as the horizontal effect of the protection of rights (*effet tiers* in French; *Drittenwirkung* in German). According to the doctrine of state action, it is not legitimate for the state to intervene in private relations to enforce respect of the constitutional rights by civil society actors. Such intervention would be unacceptable state action under the Fourteenth Amendment to the Federal Constitution. This structural difference helps us to understand the Supreme Court's reticence to consider the protection of privacy, when the press, being an agent of civil society, violates it. The Court is very diligent to protect this same liberty when state agents violate it.[123] It also helps us

119 James Q. Whitman, "Enforcing Civility and Respect: Three Societies," *Yale Law Journal* 109 (2000), 1397.

120 Peter L. Felcher and Edward L. Rubin, "Privacy, Publicity, and the Portrayal of Real People by the Media," *Yale Law Journal* 88 (1979), 1584.

121 See Ron Krotoszynski, *Privacy Revisited: A Global Perspective on the Right to Be Left Alone* (New York: Oxford University Press 2016), 8.

122 Mark Tushnet, "The Issue of State Action/Horizontal Effect in Comparative Constitutional Law," in *International Journal of Constitutional Law* 1 (2003), 79–98; Charles L. Black, Jr., "Foreword: State Action, Equal Protection, and California's Proposition," *Harvard Law Review* 69 (1967), 69–262; Louis Michael Seidman and Mark Tushnet, "The State Action Paradox," in *Remnants of Belief: Contemporary Constitutional Issues* (Oxford University Press, 1996), 49–71; Robert Glennon and John E. Novak, "A Functional Analysis of the Fourteenth Amendment 'State Action' Requirement," *Supreme Court Review* (1976), 221–61.

123 See James Q. Whitman, "The Two Western Cultures of Privacy: Liberty versus Dignity," *Yale Law Journal* 113 (2004), 1151–221.

to understand its reticence to protect data privacy as well, to the extent that data collectors are agents from within civil society. Thus, when the Supreme Court is called on to decide the conflict between two individual rights, it acts as having an ex ante understanding against any intervention that could be considered as "state action." These structural reasons are indicative of the philosophy of distrust dominant in the United States against state intervention within civil society.

1.2 THE ROLE OF THE GOVERNMENT AND HUMAN DIGNITY

Two legal systems, founded upon the similar philosophical background of the Enlightenment, use state coercion differently to regulate a liberty at the core of the considerations of the Enlightenment. On one side of the Atlantic, human dignity justifies a libertarian conception of freedom of expression. On the other, it justifies limitations of that same freedom. This book proposes a new, in-depth interpretation, from the point of view of political philosophy, on the understanding of the difference in the protection of freedom of speech. This approach is missing in the existing literature on the topic.[124] It proposes that the equilibrium between freedom of speech and privacy in France and the United States relates to the understanding of the concept of positive and negative liberties. By implication it relates to the role of the state in the formation of the human subject.

In cases where freedom of speech is in conflict with other rights, it is the active right that has the potential to violate dignity or privacy. Dignity and privacy require additional state intervention for their protection against violations by freedom of speech. Freedom of speech is a right, whereas dignity or privacy is an "imperfect" right. "Imperfect" liberty here means a liberty that needs additional positive government action to become effective. American judges do not see themselves as having legitimacy to limit speech to protect privacy in many cases. They refuse to restore the *status quo ante* through imposing compensatory damages in many cases. French judges consider it important to engage in restorative intervention as agents of the state. In this sense, enforcing the protection of privacy is like protecting social rights, the rights of the welfare state. Paradoxically, in the United States, the doctrine for strict protection emerged when some conceptions of positive rights, in the sense of

[124] Lauren Pech's dissertation, *La liberté d'expression et sa limitation: les enseignements de l'expérience américaine au regard d'expériences européennes: Allemagne, France et Convention européenne des droits de l'homme* (Presses Universitaires de la Faculté de Droit de Clermont Ferrand, LGDJ, 2003), constitutes an in-depth study of the legal status of the object of this study with a brief attempt to propose an interpretation of the eventual reasons that could guide the interpretation of the phenomenon. Three James Q. Whitman works inspired this study: "Enforcing Civility and Respect"; "The Two Western Cultures of Privacy"; and "'Human Dignity' in Europe and the United States: The Social Foundations," in Georg Nolte, ed., *European and US Constitutionalism* (Council of Europe Publishing, 2005), 98 ff. This book complements his approach by discussing the conceptual elements concerning the understanding of liberty around the French and the American Revolution. It provides a deeper analysis of the historical, political and social context of the elaboration of the understanding of the role of freedom of expression in France and in the United States.

rights of the welfare state, started gaining ground. Freedom of expression became at that time the emblem of distrust toward government intervention within civil society.

This, I argue, has its origins in a difference in the conception of the role of the state and the government. It is related to the acceptable degree of government intervention in civil society and in particular the determination of the content and limits of liberty. This difference in the protection of free speech in the French legal system as compared to the American, is the sign of a different "common character," this "way of thinking which is the effect of a chain of infinite causes which multiply and combine themselves from century to century."[125] It reflects a difference in the understanding of constitutionalism between France and the United States. The ideas on the role of the government that were dominant at the time of the foundation of the two democracies can guide our understanding of why the United States affords exceptional protection to freedom of speech today. It can also help understand the tendency in the French political and legal system to limit this liberty in order to protect other values.

The concept of "dignity" has been associated with various meanings in the history of ideas.[126] Alan Gewirth proposes two categories for the meanings attributed to it, one empirical and one moral.[127] According to the first, empirical category dignity is associated with some degree "of gravity or decorum or composure or self-respect or self-confidence together with various good qualities, which can justify these attitudes."[128] In this sense dignity is context-dependent. It is associated with the social recognition of these individual qualities. This conception is very close to that of the Romans. According to the moral meaning of the term, "dignity" is associated with the intrinsic value of each individual, which belongs to them only by the fact of being human. It is a permanent characteristic that constitutes the foundation of all rights.

The reference to dignity serves in France as a necessary justification for limiting freedom of expression. In the United States, it serves as a justification for protecting freedom of expression. As I argue, the concept of dignity is associated with an understanding of the concept of liberty. In a legal system that favors the protection of the negative aspect of liberty, as in the United States, dignity serves as the concept matrix of the philosophical justification for negative liberties. This helps one

125 Montesquieu, "De la politique," in *Oeuvres complètes de Montesquieu*, pres. and notes by D. Oster (Paris: Seuil, 1964), 173.

126 Ernst Bloch, *Droit naturel et dignité humaine*, trans. Denis Authier et Jean Lacoste (Paris: Payot, 2002); Catherine Lecomte, "Des dignités à la dignité," in Jérôme Ferrand, Hugues Petit, eds., *Fondations et naissances des droits de l'homme*, vol. 1, *L'Odyssée des Droits de l'homme* (Paris: L'Harmattan, 2003), 159–66.

127 Alan Gewirth, "Human Dignity as the Basis of Rights," in Michael Meyer and William Parent eds., *The Constitution of Rights: Human Dignity and American Values* (Ithaca and London: Cornell University Press, 1992), 10–28, 12.

128 The "empirical" conception of dignity associates it to the rituals and to the external aspect of manifestation of magnanimity.

understand why privacy is protected as autonomy around the fundamental personal decisions of an individual. Self-expression, in ways that are considered eccentric by a majority, is protected. Limitations on wearing conspicuous religious symbols such as headscarves are not accepted. In France and other European states, where government intervention is accepted to a greater extent, with a view to guaranteeing redistributive goals, there exists a tendency to accept government intervention around how individuals treat themselves as well, such as can be seen in the dwarf-throwing case. The French legal system is centered on the guarantee of the preconditions for the exercise of liberty and on the necessity to guarantee the very possibility of existence for every human being, that is to guarantee that life has a meaning for every individual. In this system, dignity is associated with social status and with government action in view of protecting this social status. The French legal order favors an understanding of the role of the government as the guarantor of the preconditions necessary for the exercise of liberty and for a meaningful life in community. This ex ante understanding in favor of state protectionism associates liberty with social status. It associates it with the necessity for the state to intervene to guarantee social esteem and interpersonal respect when it is violated by freedom of expression. This preconception in favor of the state to protect dignity has the implication of an acceptance of a role for the state in defining the content of liberty. This conception has further consequences for the protection of human dignity, including against the will of the holder of this dignity, as the headscarf cases and the dwarf-throwing cases show – that is, against the will of the person if it is not in conformity with the dominant conception of dignity and liberty imposed by the state. In the United States, dignity serves as a reference in view of protecting the negative aspect of liberty: the inviolable domain of the formation of personality.

The conception of human dignity in a legal order is very close to the dominant conception of liberty in the same legal order. As I analyze later, in this frame, the metaphysical universalism of the French Declaration of the Rights of Man and of the Citizen paradoxically goes together with a positivistic conception of these rights. According to this conception, rights must be derived from the quality of the citizen rather than the quality of man, to the extent that the state is considered as the institutor of society. The social sphere is considered by definition as being confounded with the political sphere. The metaphysical universalism of liberty underlying the French Declaration makes legitimate a positive conception of liberty. Positive liberty can have multiple meanings. It can mean either political liberty or welfare rights. It is legitimate for the state to guarantee the preconditions of the exercise of liberty, so that far from remaining a "formal" liberty it becomes a "real" liberty. It is also legitimate for the state to define the content and limits of liberty. It is the accomplishment of positive liberty, in the sense of political liberty and the accomplishment of the duties toward the totality, that guarantee the exercise of this liberty in the negative sense. It is the guarantee for a community created by the state that allows the recognition of the private sphere. The presumption is in favor of the legitimacy of state intervention. In the United States an inverse presumption is dominant. Even if the state intervenes, this intervention is always limited by considerations of degree. In the United States, a more important justification is required to make legitimate government action in the private sphere. The US Supreme Court submits legislation limiting rights to "exacting scrutiny." This scrutiny has three levels of intensity: rational basis review, heightened scrutiny, and strict scrutiny. Expressive freedoms are submitted to either heightened or strict scrutiny. As analyzed in Chapter 3, the doctrine of "strict scrutiny" emerged when the Supreme Court elaborated the "rational basis" review for legislation that limits economic liberties in the New Deal Era.[129] In *United States* v. *Carolene Products Co.*, the Supreme Court held that legislation that limits rights guaranteed by the Bill of Rights or violates the democratic process must submit to strict scrutiny; whereas, regulation of economic activity can enjoy a presumption of constitutionality, provided that it finds a rational foundation on the knowledge and experience of the legislator.[130]

The reference to human dignity in France serves to protect the social status of the person from violations coming from freedom of expression. The protectionist role of the state in France has led to a conception of dignity as a value transcending the individual. Dignity is not associated with individual liberty and self-definition. It depends on the approbation of the state. If the relation that everyone maintains with themselves is mediated by the general will, then it is legitimate for this will to define the content of dignity in France. It is this line of thinking that is reflected in the dwarf-throwing case as well as in the headscarf bans. In the dwarf-throwing case, the solicitor general, Patrick Frydman, suggested before the French Council of State that the activity violated not only the dignity of the person who was thrown but also the dignity of the spectators and of the dwarfism community.[131] This suggestion was accepted by the Council of State, which upheld the prohibition. A similar conception underlies the burka ban in France.[132] The public discussion that preceded the legislation indicates that the state imposes a conception of dignity against the will of the individual.[133] It treats them as operating under a "false consciousness."

129 See Richard Fallon, Jr., *The Nature of Constitutional Rights: The Invention and Logic of Strict Judicial Scrutiny* (Cambridge University Press, 2019).

130 *United States* v. *Carolene Products Co.*, 304 US 144 (1938), at 152, n. 4. In the famous footnote 4: "There may be narrower scope for operation of the presumption of constitutionality when legislation appears on its face to be within a specific prohibition of the Constitution, such as those of the first ten Amendments, which are deemed equally specific when held to be embraced within the Fourteenth."

131 Patrick Frydman, Concl., CE Ass., Oct. 27, 1995 (two cases), *Commune de Morsang-sur-Orge* and *Ville d'Aix en Provence*, *RFDA* (1995), 1204–1215; cf. the critique in Olivier Cayla, "Le coup d'état du droit," *Le Débat* (1998), 108–33; Stéphanie Hennette Vauchez, *Disposer de soi* (Paris: L'Harmattan, 2004), 396 ff.

132 See Ioanna Tourkochoriti, "The Burka Ban," 791–852.

133 Assemblée Nationale, *Rapport d'information fait en application de l'article 145 du réglement*, no. 2262, 32.

The conception of dignity that underlies the American constitutional order serves as the foundation of negative liberty.[134] The dominant idea underlying the protection of the Bill of Rights of the United States is the inviolability of moral status. In this area the relevant clauses of the Federal Constitution are the Fourth, Fifth, and Fourteenth Amendments to the Federal Constitution. The American courts interpreted these clauses as guaranteeing procedures in conformity with the "fundamental equity" and "the ordered liberty."[135] The underlying idea is the need to limit the government to ensure the protection of the inviolability of moral personality. For this reason, the concept is invoked to protect freedom of expression against limitations protecting the social status of the person, as it is the case in French law. Human flourishing is associated with the respect of a sphere of inviolability. In the United States, the archetype of the protection of this sphere is freedom of conscience. Political power should respect the dignity of the persons associated with natural inalienable rights among which is their intellectual freedom.[136]

Dignity in the United States is associated with the moral qualities of epistemic and practical rationality, which are associated with the legitimacy of political power.[137] Every limitation of a negative right therefore requires an important justification. Equality, associated with the concept of human dignity, is understood in the sense of protection in equal terms of the negative liberty of all.[138] The idea, dominant in France, that it is the mission of the state to guarantee subsistence and the preconditions for the exercise of liberty does not exist in the United States. The hierarchy of political values dominant in the constitutional system of the United States is formed on the priority of negative liberty.

Human dignity is associated equally to democratic self-government and to popular sovereignty in the American context. However, the idea of guaranteeing the preconditions of the exercise of liberty is nonexistent in the Federal Constitution. For this reason, the dominant conception of dignity is limited to the inviolability of the personal and moral sphere.[139] The idea of fraternity, omnipresent in the French conception of dignity, is nonexistent in the philosophy underlying the Constitution of the United States. Some states enacted clauses protecting social rights at the end of the nineteenth century and the beginning of the twentieth century. At the federal

[134] William Parent, "Constitutional Values and Human Dignity," in Meyer and Parent, eds., *Constitution of Rights*, 47–72, 47; William Brennan, Jr., "The Constitution of the United States: Contemporary Ratification," *University of California Davis Law Review* 19 (1985), 2–15, 8.

[135] *Palko* v. *Connecticut*, 302 US 319 (1937), *Hurtado* v. *California*, 110 US 516 (1884), *Snyder* v. *Massachusetts*, 291 US 97 (1934), *Rochin* v. *California*, 342 US 165 (1952).

[136] David A. J. Richards, "Constitutional Liberty, Dignity, and Reasonable Justification," in Meyer and Parent, eds., *Constitution of Rights*, 73–101.

[137] Ibid., 96.

[138] Martha Minow, "Equality and the Bill of Rights," in Meyer and Parent, eds., *Constitution of Rights*, 118–28, 122.

[139] Louis Henkin, "Human Dignity and Constitutional Rights," in Meyer and Parent, eds., *Constitution of Rights*, 210–228, 216; see also Louis Henkin, "Rights, American and Human," *Columbia Law Review* 79 (1979), 405–425, 409, 419.

level, following the New Deal, the normative conception of democracy was modified toward accepting a more extended role for the government. However, even according to this new normative conception, the state is not considered as having an extended paternalistic role in guaranteeing human dignity. The well-being of the individual is a personal question. The welfare state existing at the moment in the United States is the result of regulation by Congress and not an imperative inscribed in the Federal Constitution. Although some state constitutions protect positive rights today, the Supreme Court has been reducing the scope of state regulation inspired by ideas of the welfare state since the 1970s.[140]

The concept of dignity in the United States serves to justify the protection of freedom of expression. In France, it serves as a foundation of the need to limit freedom of expression. This reflects that in France it is legitimate for the government to intervene to protect the privacy and the social status of a person when it is violated by speech. In the United States, the distrust toward the government leads to protecting freedom of expression over privacy and human dignity. In France, trust toward the government legitimizes intervention to ensure that dignity as social status is protected. In the United States, the reference to human dignity is associated with a conception of negative liberty. This conception prevents limitations to the negative aspect of freedom of expression. The requirement for governmental transparency creates a presumption in favor of protecting expression. Public debate should be "robust, uninhibited and wide open."[141] The requirement for a lively public debate is also present in France and other European countries. Comparative law is a discipline of relative differences. The theory proposed in this book holds for expressive freedoms. It may not hold for all freedoms. It provides a general proposal of understanding differences in the protection of freedom of expression. Local specificities and other factors may affect the foundations of the regulation of other liberties. In France, there is a relatively greater acceptance of the role of the government to limit expression. The judges see themselves as legitimized to limit freedom of expression in order to protect competing rights. Speech is overvalued in the United States, whereas it is relatively undervalued in France. The dangers of erring on both sides are equally worthy of consideration. In the chapters that follow, I elaborate how the conception of human dignity that underlies the reasoning of the judges relates to the conception of liberty dominant in a legal and political system. This conception dictates positive obligations toward government actors. In Europe and the United States, there is a difference in the degree of government intervention that is legitimate. In the United States, the government intervenes to a greater extent to protect negative liberties, whereas in France the state intervenes to ensure the respect of positive liberties as well. As mentioned earlier, even when government

140 This is so since *San Antonio Independent School Dist.* v. *Rodriguez*, 411 US 471 (1973).

141 *New York Times Co.* v. *Sullivan*, 376 US 254 (1964), at 270.

intervention becomes acceptable in the United States in order to protect positive liberties, freedom of speech becomes a "preferred" liberty.

The approach of this study presupposes transcending the positivistic perspective. The difference in the understanding of the equilibrium of the legal regime toward freedom of expression presupposes the consideration of ideas underlying the legal structure, the ideas which inspire and transcend this structure. The study of the law as being a closed and self-referential system missed an important aspect of the legal phenomenon. The idea of legitimacy concerns rather the acceptance of the normativity of the law. It has its origins outside this structure itself, in the conception of the natural law that underlies this structure. Kelsen's attempt to reduce law to a system that derives its legitimacy only from its legality, the conformity to a formal mode of production of the law, is marked with contradictions.[142] He ultimately also accepts the idea of the social contract as the foundation of the fundamental norm. The ultimate source of the legitimacy of the law exists in the understanding of the dominant ideas of political and moral philosophy that underlie the formation of the content of the law. These ideas are submitted to the trial of time and to the variability of the political and social necessities.

1.3 HERMENEUTICS AND THE IMAGINARY

It is an understanding of the role of the government that is reflected in jurists' opinions on favoring one liberty over another. It is the political imaginary[143] that guides the ex ante understanding of all jurists in a legal system with regard to the necessity to protect one liberty to the detriment of another. Any interpretation, as an actualizing appropriation of the meaning of a text or a phenomenon, is founded upon an anticipation of meaning.[144] Interpretation is apprehension of something that is presented to us. Meaning is a dimension of existence: the interpreter projects various meanings onto the text that they are interpreting, formed by their situation in a specific context. Their ex ante understandings condition their appropriation of the meaning of the text: its very intelligibility. Among the many possibilities of projected meanings, some are adopted in the final meaning of the text by corroboration in reference to the whole text. For the current of hermeneutics, understanding the meaning of a text involves a circular process.[145] The interpreter attempts to understand the text from its parts and the elements from the whole. They arrive at

142 Hans Kelsen, *Reine Rechtslehre*, trans. Charles Eisenmann (Paris: LGDJ, 1999); Hans Kelsen, *General Theory of Law and State*, trans. Anders Wedberg (Cambridge, MA: Harvard University Press, 1949); Hans Kelsen, "Justice et droit naturel," in *Le droit naturel: annales de philosophie politique* III (Paris: Presses Universitaires de France, 1959).

143 In the sense that Cornelius Castoriadis attributes to the term in *L'institution imaginaire de la société* (Paris: Seuil, 1975).

144 Martin Heidegger, *Being and Time*, trans. John Macquarrie et Edward Robinson (New York: Harper & Row, 1962), 188 ff.

145 Ibid.

a "reflective equilibrium" between their ex ante understandings and the version that they adopt as the definitive meaning of the text. In other words, "understanding is an attitude which is not only reproductive but also and always productive."[146]

These anticipations of meaning (*Vorhable, Vorsicht, Vorgriff*), qualified as "prejudices" by Gadamer,[147] condition the very receptivity of the reader of the text. They are "legitimate prejudices." Understanding exempt of a *praejudicium* is impossible. *Praejudicium* is used here in a neutral and descriptive sense (*Vorurteil*), meaning preliminary judgment of the meaning of a text. It does not have the negative connotations of a precipitated and arbitrary judgment. As Gadamer notes, the attempt of the Enlightenment to do away with prejudice resulted in the creation of a new prejudice, the "prejudice against prejudice."[148] The type of prejudice that Gadamer discusses is not incompatible with the Kantian formula of the necessity for everyone to use their own understanding. On the contrary, it aims to describe and make explicit the factors that influence the formation of understanding. It is not incompatible with the necessity to use one's own reason. Gadamer accepts that reason allows one to critically appreciate some prejudices.

According to the Gadamer's insight, tradition re-emerges in any attempt of reason to reverse it. This conservation is an act of liberty as much as its reversal and innovation. For Gadamer, every era understands a transmitted text in a different way, as any text is part of the totality of a tradition. The prejudices and the preconceptions of the interpreter, are not always entirely at their free disposal.[149] Prejudices are formed and reformed incessantly. In the course of time, prejudices are reconsidered, often dissolved and replaced by new prejudices that form our understanding. We can reflect upon and filter a part of our prejudices, while some of them are unconscious. The interpreter's present horizon is constantly reformed. The term "horizon" denotes that the interpreter's perspective is situated in time and in space. It also denotes that they aspire to transcend their point of view and to see "beyond." Understanding is the result of the fusion of the horizon of the interpreter with the horizon of the author of the text. Therefore, the meaning of a text is the result of an infinite process of understanding. It consists in the fusion of the prejudices of the interpreter and the linguistic conventions that compose the text. It also consists in the fusion of the horizons of the text's author and of its interpreter. Both the author and the interpreter are engaged in an effort to transcend their existing situation and to assign meaning to the text. Temporal distance between the moment the text was written and the moment the text is interpreted allows for the evolution of the self-understanding of societies and of the legal actors within them. Through legal interpretations societies can actualize themselves by redefining their

146 Hans-Georg Gadamer, *Vérité et méthode*, trans. Pierre Fruchon, Jean Grondin, and Gilbert Merlio (Paris: Seuil, 1976), 318.

147 Ibid., 286 ff.

148 Ibid., 294.

149 Ibid., 317.

ideological commitments and adapting them to the requirements of their evolving sense of justice.[150] The foundations of a constitutional order are based on principles that evolve in time. The actualizing reading of interpreters of legal texts participates in this evolution of collective self-understanding by readjusting the principles of justice to resolve new cases of conflicts between rights that emerge.

A legal text, such as a constitutional text, expressing linguistic conventions, is a "conceptual context"[151] establishing a perspective, a logic, the "projection of a wish."[152] The text inaugurates a dialogue with its interpreter who carries a common sense formed in a specific context. Very often the text of a constitution is the result of a compromise between political ideas irreducible to the unitary expression of one idea. As Laurence Tribe and Michael C. Dorf note, this plural character of a constitution allows the evolution of the possible readings of a constitutional text, reflecting and forming in return the evolution of the common sense.[153] The understanding of the text of a normative proposition includes a normative judgment by reference to a world of values always external. It comes from a conception of natural law understood here as principles of morality and justice.

The specific conceptions that expressed and formed the understanding of the role of the state and of liberty in the moments of the two democratic revolutions formed the principal ideas that guide the understanding of the interpreters of the law in cases concerning freedom of expression. The recourse to these ideas justifies the protection of one type of liberties at moment *a*. The evolution of the historical context leads to the use of the same protective ideology to justify the protection of another category of liberties at a later moment β. In the United States, the distrust toward the parliament led, during the Founding Era, to a libertarian conception of the protection of some negative liberties, like economic liberty. It helped create an ideological core on the role of the government. In the twentieth century, this libertarian attitude toward economic liberty was no longer acceptable. It was then that freedom of expression became a "preferred" liberty of the US Supreme Court, which the Court justified by reference to the ideology of the Founding Era. In the twentieth century, the US Supreme Court judges reconstructed a narrative according to which a legal regime of strict protection of freedom of expression conforms better to the theory of government dominant during the Founding Era. In France, on the contrary, the

150 To some extent this is the methodological approach that Jack Balkin follows in *Living Originalism* (Harvard University Press, 2011).

151 Olivier Cayla, *La notion de signification en droit: contribution à une theorie du droit naturel de la communication* (unpublished doctoral dissertation, University Paris II, 1992), 820.

152 Laurence Tribe and Michael C. Dorf, *On Reading the Constitution* (Harvard University Press, 1991), 14. Akhil Reed Amar also invites his reader to reflect on the ideas that "support and supplement the written Constitution without supplanting it." *America's Unwritten Constitution: The Precedents and Principles We Live By* (New York: Basic Books, 2012), xi. For Amar, the written constitution cannot work without the unwritten constitution, which fills in its gaps and stabilizes it. Ibid.

153 Laurence Tribe and Michael C. Dorf, *On Reading the Constitution*, 17 ff.

trust toward the exercise of collective power led to the consideration of liberty as consubstantial to its definition by the government. Freedom of expression was never considered as a special liberty.

I argue that it was a more profound tradition that was expressed in the 1960s when the US Supreme Court issued its important decisions protecting speech. The Supreme Court expressed principles that were at stake during the foundation of the two democracies that defined the role of the government in France and the United States. Many factors can guide our understanding as to the difference in the approaches. First of these is the understanding of the role of the government, and the corresponding understanding of liberty. Second, behind the understanding of the role of the government lies the understanding of the role of the law in the two legal orders. A specific conception of natural law, of a conception of justice that permeates positive law, also lies there. The difference in the understanding of all these concepts lies in the key political problems existent at the foundation of the two democracies and their evolution. Among many other influences, a strong idealistic current marked the French revolutionary era, whereas the American revolutionaries were guided by pragmatism. This affected their respective visions as to the possibilities and duties of the government and the mission of the law. I propose an understanding for the government *lato sensu*, understood as composed by the legislative, the executive, and the judiciary.

The distrust in the United States against the government is expressed in their understanding of privacy as a right that is threatened principally by state intervention and not by the actors of civil society like the press.[154] As James Whitman notes, the starting point for understanding the right to privacy is in the idea that every citizen is a free and sovereign political actor, dominating their home, and matured in the idea of the protection against state intrusion in decisions that concern the self.[155] The French conception of the right to privacy was formed around the idea of the protection of a person's social status, against the excesses of freedom of the press. In France, the right to privacy is associated with a conception of "dignity" as social status. The protection of this equal dignity for all was among the causes of the French Revolution. As François Furet notes, this revolution aimed to a great extent at establishing a new political sociability.[156] It aimed to change political institutions and society itself. It was an attempt to abolish a society organized in concentric circles and to guarantee equal rights to all. According to a conception of dignity as social status, the person has the right to determine their public *persona*, the image that others will have of them. The state, charged with promoting and protecting this equality, can legitimately protect a person's social status, when they think that others

154 James Q. Whitman, "The Two Western Cultures of Privacy," 1171.

155 Ibid. For James Whitman it is in this spirit that the decisions of the US Supreme Court in favor of a protection against state interventions concerning searches and seizures of vehicles (*Boyd* v. *United States*, 116 US 616 [1886]), abortion (*Roe* v. *Wade* 410 US 113 [1973]) and homosexuality (*Lawrence* v. *Texas*, 123 S. Ct. 2472 [2003]) can be explained.

156 François Furet, *Penser la Révolution française* (Paris: Gallimard, 1978).

have violated it.[157] When speech is at stake, liberty outweighs equality and the reciprocal respect in the United States, whereas the French rigorously protect dignity and equality.

The difference in approach between France and the United States indicates a profound difference that concerns the "imaginary institution"[158] of society and the state on each side of the Atlantic. I propose an interpretation of the constructive representation of history and of the self-understanding of the judges, on the basis of their divergent judgments on the protection of one liberty – freedom of expression – over other competing liberties. An interpreter's subjectivity is formed in the dialectic between the self and context. The way in which the judges attribute justice is participation in a sense of justice that they form while being themselves formed in it. Legal institutions and judicial interpretation are considered through the prism of a conception that considers the social element, the functional element, and the symbolic element as complementary.[159] The three angles simultaneously define each other and interact among themselves.

Further, the imaginary element is as important as the "rationality" or "functionality" of institutions, the conquest of their symbolic logic and their progressive "rationalization."[160] The rationality and functionality of an institution do not necessarily go together: rules can have many logical consequences that are not explicit at the beginning, but that play a role in the evolution of social life. A society's self-image is formed thanks to imaginary meanings that valorize and structure ideas. The life of a society takes place in the explicit and implicit reference to the past and the future.[161] The imaginary institution of society is based on the choice of narratives, reflected among others in judicial discourse. The judicial discourse contributes to the formation of this self-understanding. French and American case law is considered in its evolution in time as carrying imaginary significances founded in the past while projecting toward the future. These narratives also have an existential dimension as they serve the role of assuring the character of a community.[162] Despite the disenchantment of the modern era, new forms of religion always re-emerge as elements that hold a society together.[163] Our societies need to be enchanted in some

157 James Q. Whitman, "Enforcing Civility and Respect," 1363 ff.

158 See Cornelius Castoriadis, *Institution imaginaire*, 8.

159 Ibid., 158.

160 Ibid., 186.

161 Ibid., 325.

162 On the law and the constitution as expressing the fundamental rules of solidarity among a people, see the classical analysis of a French constitutional law scholar in Léon Duguit, *Traité de droit constitutionnel*, vol. 2 (Paris: Albert Fontemoing, 1923). Hauriou also notes the importance of the background ideas that permeate "the puissance publique." Maurice Hauriou, *Précis de droit constitutionnel* (Paris: Sirey 1929), 35.

163 On the rejection of metaphysical schemes, see Marcel Gauchet, *Le désenchantement du monde: une histoire politique de la religion* (Paris: Gallimard, 1985); on the re-emergence of religion, see Marcel Gauchet, *La religion dans la démocratie* (Paris: Gallimard, 1998), 27. On the role of religion as part of strengthening the collective consciousness that holds a society together see the classical

way.[164] The contemporary nation states have created their own civil religions, which define their collective consciousness and hold individuals together. These elements find expression at the imaginary level of all legal actors.

In this respect, the US Supreme Court's landmark decision protecting speech, *New York Times* v. *Sullivan*, which emerged in 1964, expressed and formed the imaginary identity in the United States. At this moment, the Supreme Court judges realized that a doctrine protecting free speech fits the narrative of the Founding Era better. A doctrine of minimal government control of speech fits better with the conception of limited government formed during the Founding Era. Legal discourse expresses its own rationality. It is founded on premises whose origin is in the interpreter's ex ante understanding[165] of the meaning of the legal clauses that protect a liberty. Historically conditioned ideas guide the interpreters' understanding of a constitutional text. They also guide the self-reflections of a society.

This approach is close to Laurence Tribe's conception of the "invisible Constitution."[166] The invisible Constitution is constituted by the invariable architecture of the Constitution, its "general frames, its barriers, its models of behavior," which determine its "general form and its structure." Without the invisible Constitution, the visible Constitution could not become a supreme law, nor achieve a specific meaning. The invisible Constitution is constituted by all these elements as they are understood and applied by every interpreter. These may be the official interpreters – the courts or actors incarnating official functions – or the collective conscience. The contribution of the judges as official interpreters is decisive. For Tribe, the form of the Constitution remains more or less similar through different ideological eras. All the actors of the American constitutional order, all the interpreters who construct the invisible Constitution, work inside existing forms. Even if its meaning and its substance changes, the Constitution evolves in a recurrent architectonic model.[167] The readers of the Constitution project models upon these clauses and make judgments in the name of invisible structures that conservatives and liberals describe as the "tacit postulates of the constitutional scheme."[168] This is a constitutional structure that does not exist inside the text of the Constitution.[169]

The difference in the understanding of the content of expressive freedoms and of their limits, the exceptional value attributed to freedom of expression in the

analysis of Émile Durkheim in *The Elementary Forms of Religious Life*, [1912] trans. Karen E. Fields (New York: The Free Press 1995) and *The Division of Labor in Society* [1893] trans. Lewis A. Coser (New York: The Free Press, 1984). For an analysis of the US Constitution in the spirit of a "civic religion," see Sanford Levinson, *Constitutional Faith* (Princeton University Press, 1988).

164 Gauchet, *Le désenchantement du monde*, 27.

165 In the sense that Hans Georg Gadamer attributes to the term in *Vérité et méthode*.

166 Laurence Tribe, *The Invisible Constitution* (Oxford University Press, 2008), 9 ff., 54.

167 Ibid., 54.

168 Ibid., 73.

169 Ibid., 77.

American legal order over other values, can be understood by reference to the formation of fundamental concepts of political philosophy on each side of the Atlantic: the role of government and the understanding of liberty. Freedom of expression is a freedom from government intervention. Positive action by the state is required in order to protect its negative aspect. The protection of other values such as privacy and human dignity, when they are in conflict with freedom of expression, necessitate state action for its protection against violations by the government and private persons, arising from within civil society. Freedom of expression is an aggressive liberty whereas privacy and human dignity are imperfect liberties, necessitating additional positive state action for their protection. The analysis that follows proposes an interpretation of the differences and can only be relative: it concerns the presentation of a set of ideas that could guide the understanding of the differences. What is more, some anachronisms are inevitable in any effort to understand ideas and their historical function. The attempt to understand the present by reference to the past includes the risk of projecting onto the past concepts we use to understand the present. Aristotle had seen that the necessity of creation goes from what is consequent to what is antecedent: if it is the constructed building that confers to the materials their necessity of instruments,[170] for the genesis of ideas, the material obtains a meaning for an intellectual construction only when we turn from the present to the past.[171] We can only make sense of the past thanks to the conceptual tools we have developed to understand our present. However, unlike the Aristotelian approach, according to which every opinion as such corresponds to a horizon of truth, inside which it is necessarily constituted, the approach of this study insists that inevitably the subject-interpreter projects meaning on the historical events. If historical reality is polymorphous, every attempt to philosophically make sense of historical facts implies their organization in relation to some ideas that facilitate their reading.[172] The recourse to the foundations of the crucial concepts will provide insights that can help us understand the ideas imprinted on the collective consciousness of the Americans and the French.

170 Aristotle, *Physics*, II, 9; *Anal. Post.* II, 12.

171 Pierre Aubenque, *Le problème de l'être chez Aristote: essai sur la problématique aristotélicienne* (Paris: Presses Universitaires de France, 1962), 76.

172 Georges Gusdorf, *Les révolutions de France et d'Amérique: la violence et la sagesse* (Paris: Librairie Académique Perrin, 1988), 8.

2

Antiquity, Modernity, and Historical Imaginaries on the Role of the Government

2.1 THE ROLE OF THE GOVERNMENT: NEGATIVE AND POSITIVE LIBERTIES

Adopting the point of view of legal hermeneutics means examining the role of the government in defining human dignity and liberty. The weight of absolutism, associated with a paternalist vision, defines the understanding of the role of the state and the government in France. In the United States, where an ideology of distrust toward the government is dominant, the separation of powers serves to control the impact of the government upon liberty.[1] As Jeremy Waldron notes,[2] the strict protection of freedom of expression in the United States became possible during the twentieth century, as only a strong state can allow for liberality in the exercise of its subjects' liberty, such as freedom of expression. Adam Smith also noted during the eighteenth century that only a strong sovereign, possessing an effective power of coercion, can tolerate a degree of citizens' licentiousness.[3] Tolerance in the exercise of a liberty presupposes a strong state, and a state with effective enforcement mechanisms, which are characteristic of the modern state. Enforcement mechanisms exist in both the French and American states today. It is the ideology related to the role of the government that should guide our understanding of the difference in the protection of the content and limits of a liberty. Raymond Carré de Malberg saw in the German theories of self-limitation of the state a performative contradiction, since the state, by its very existence, is associated with coercion.[4] Carré de Malberg considered that it is through the moral value of governors and the people that one must expect the guarantee of the state's

[1] Cf. Judith Shklar, "Liberté positive, liberté négative en Amérique," in *Les usages de la liberté* (Neuchâtel: Ed. De la Baconnière, 1990), 107–135, 108.

[2] Jeremy Waldron, "Free Speech and the Menace of Hysteria," *The New York Review of Books* 55 (1998).

[3] Adam Smith associated the strength of a sovereign to military power, cf. Smith, *Wealth of Nations*, 707. Nietzsche also underlines the evolution toward a milder system of state coercion depending on the community's increase of power and trust in itself. Friedrich Nietzsche, *Zur Genealogie der Moral*, trans. Eric Blondel, Ole Hansen Love, Théo Levdenbach, and Pierre Pénisson (Paris: GF Flammarion, 2000), traité 2, § 10, 20.

[4] Raymond Carré de Malberg, *Théorie générale du droit et de l'état*, vol. 1 (Paris: Sirey, 1920), 242–43.

moderation. The law by itself would be impotent to ensure it. The degree to which the law determines individual rights, and to which rights find their foundation or reason for existence in the will of the government, depends on factors that constitute this ex ante understanding of the role of the government.

Underlying the difference in the understanding of the legitimacy of judicial intervention in relation to the limitation of the exercise of freedom of expression in the French and American legal orders is a more profound difference, concerning the understanding of the role of the government on the imaginary level. In the United States, it is rarely legitimate for the government to intervene as regulator of interpersonal respect for harm caused by speech. The understanding of the role of the government has different nuances in the United States compared to France. Harms attributed to offensive speech are not considered significant enough to legitimize the use of state coercion in order to ensure retribution. American judges rarely see themselves as legitimized to restore via compensation the *status quo ante* when speech violates privacy rights. This is the redistributive function of awarding civil damages. The harm caused by speech is not considered significant enough to make the use of state legal coercion legitimate. In this context, privacy is an imperfect liberty. When violated by actors within civil society, privacy requires additional positive action by the state for it to be protected. In the United States, it is legitimate for the state to engage in positive action to protect negative liberties. It is not legitimate for the state to engage in positive action to protect positive liberties more widely as well. Privacy in this sense is like other positive liberties that require additional positive action by the state, such as the liberties of the welfare state. The right not to be offended by hateful speech in the public sphere is similarly not protected in the United States in the absence of heavier sanctions for hate-based defamation (which exist in France).

The difference in the understanding of the role of the state corresponds to a difference in the understanding of liberty, since the two notions are by definition in a dialectical relation. The understanding of the limits of government, of public power, is antagonistic to the understanding of the limits of liberty. Liberty derives from the "sovereignty" of the individual over themselves.[5] It derives from their autonomy and the degree to which it is legitimate for the government (and the legislative, executive, or judiciary branches composing it) to limit the sovereignty of the individual over themselves in order to protect another liberty or another social value. The protection of liberty presupposes the existence of the state, as liberty is effective only when protected by law when it is sanctioned by the state.[6] A person can violate another person's liberty only when the state allows it through the law. The

[5] Hart defines recognizing rights as attributing a kind of "sovereignty" over one's moral world. H. L. A. Hart, "Are There Any Natural Rights?," *Philosophical Review* 64 (1955), 175–91. See also Richard Tuck, *Natural Rights Theories* (Cambridge University Press, 1979), 6; Léon Duguit, *Traité de droit Constitutionnel*, vol. 1 (Paris: Ed. de Boccard, 1921), 633.

[6] See also Charles Fried, *Modern Liberty and the Limits of Government* (New York: Norton & Company, 2007), 76–77.

understanding of the role of the government in protecting liberty varies in time and in space. The civil religion of the French is formed around the moralizing role of the state, the idea that there is an organic unity between the state and the citizens. This idea makes it legitimate for the state to protect citizens and to teach them how they should exercise their freedom of expression. The French conception of liberty, as it was proclaimed in 1789 and redeveloped during the postrevolutionary era, is marked by the paradox of attempting to reconcile a liberalism of the subject and liberty through the state.[7] In the United States, the conception of liberty is associated with "natural liberties" which are seen as "self-evident" and "divine gifts." It is possible to talk about a "constitutional faith,"[8] protecting these liberties as the factor that assures the cohesion of the American multicultural society. A conception of liberty as natural underlies the interpretation of constitutional rights.

The concept of liberty has been associated with various meanings and nuances in the course of the history of ideas.[9] A number of distinctions have been proposed for the term. Positive and negative liberty is one set of these distinctions. The modern understanding of political liberty as negative associates the concept with a sphere of inviolability the individual should enjoy against the state. This is the meaning of negative liberty against the state. It stresses the subjective aspect of liberty, for the accomplishment of the individual. The emphasis of the Ancients on duty and on political participation is replaced by the Moderns with the conception of liberty, understood as voluntary self-regulation.[10] One possible understanding of "positive" liberty associates it with political liberty, dominant in antiquity – the liberty to participate in political decision-making. Another understanding of positive liberty associates it with positive/social rights. This is the liberty to have the preconditions and presuppositions of political and negative liberties guaranteed so that they become meaningful. Negative liberties can remain purely formal, according to Marx's critique, unless the state guarantees the preconditions a person needs to exercise them.

Philip Pettit has suggested another understanding of liberty in the political sense beyond the negative/positive distinction. Pettit associates liberty with nondomination

7 Lucien Jaume, *L'Individu effacé ou le paradoxe du libéralisme français* (Paris: Fayard, 1997), 554.

8 Sanford Levinson, *Constitutional Faith* (Princeton University Press, 1988). On the Constitution as the "American essence" and judicial review as the way to "discern and enforce the American essence," see also Thomas Grey, "Constitution as Scripture," *Stanford Law Review* 37 (1984), 1–25, 19. Allusion is made here to the metaphysical factors of the formation of collective consciousness underlined in Émile Durkheim, *The Elementary Forms of Religious Life*, trans. Karen E. Fields (New York: The Free Press, 1995). See also Shklar, "Liberté positive."

9 A classical analysis of the various kinds of liberty can be found in Benjamin Constant, "De la liberté des Anciens comparée à celle des Modernes" in Marcel Gauchet ed., *Écrits politiques* (Paris: Gallimard, 1997), 589. See also Yildiz Silier, *Freedom: Political, Metaphysical, Negative and Positive* (Aldershot: Ashgate, 2005); Quentin Skinner, *Liberty before Liberalism* (Cambridge University Press, 1998).

10 Timothy Fuller, "Thomas Hobbes and Emergent Modernity," in Edward McLean, ed., *An Uncertain Legacy: Essays on the Pursuit of Liberty* (Wilmington, DE: Intercollegiate Studies Institute, 1997), 73–90, 79.

and noninterference.[11] Exemplary of the domination relationship is the master–slave relationship. Nondomination and noninterference need to coincide for liberty to exist. According to this conception, liberty means not to have others interfere in the worsening of someone's choice situation. Freedom as nondomination means that a party does not have the capacity to interfere on an arbitrary basis in some of the other's choices. Pettit traces this understanding of liberty in the neo-Roman tradition, starting with Machiavelli. Machiavelli's understanding of freedom as a desire "not to be ruled" is compatible with republicanism and the concern for the common good. Freedom in this sense is understood as the opposite to slavery. Elements of this theory in the sense of freedom as nondomination and noninterference exist in the understanding of liberty and republicanism in the United States against the government. The idea of freedom as not being dominated or interfered with by social actors exists within French republicanism. French republicanism accepts the positive role of the state to liberate citizens from other social actors' undue influence. The burka ban and the strict regulation of political campaigns are elements of this understanding. The same understanding does not exist in the United States to the same extent, as *Citizens United* shows.

The distinction between negative and positive liberty was also proposed for liberty in the metaphysical sense. A third meaning of positive liberty is associated with the possibility and the power of self-determination, in a reasonable way and not just a rational way.[12] Rational reason is reason oriented toward maximizing utility. Reasonable reason is accepting the requirements of justice. The latter conception is derived from the necessity to use one's liberty properly with a view to promoting self-accomplishment while respecting others. This is the sense that Isaiah Berlin gives to the term in "Two Concepts of Liberty"[13]: dominating oneself means exercising one's reason, in conformity with one's superior nature, with one's autonomous self. This self, corresponds with the "essence" of human beings, as seen by rationalist philosophy. It consists of using reason, in opposition to one's empirical weak self, carried away by passions, desires, and the "inferior" nature of the human being.[14] Positive moral liberty in the Kantian sense is associated with a positive moral content, defined by reason under the requirement of the universalizability rule.[15] Negative liberty in the moral Kantian sense is associated with a negative moral content, not respecting the universalizability rule.[16] At the same time, negative liberty tends to self-destruction as a violation of some universal principle common

11 Philip Pettit, *Republicanism: A Theory of Freedom and Government* (Oxford University Press, 1999), 22 ff.

12 According to the meaning of the terms that John Rawls uses in Rawls, *Theory of Justice*, 145 ff.

13 Isaiah Berlin, "Two Concepts of Liberty," in *Four Essays on Liberty*. Oxford University Press, 1969.

14 Berlin, "Two Concepts of Liberty," 132.

15 Immanuel Kant, *Fondements de la métaphysique des moeurs*, trans. J. Barni (Paris: Librairie philosophique de Lagrange, 1848), 86.

16 Kant, "On the Common Saying," 73. According to Kant, the Constitution of the state and the law regulates external freedom "so that it harmonizes with the freedom of everyone else."

to all human beings, such as dignity, by definition associated by Kant to humanity and its potentiality to use reason. In this it is close to Rousseau's conception of virtue, interpreted as criticizing "rational" reason and approving the use of "reasonable" reason.

Positive liberty in the moral sense is often reflected in positive liberty in the political sense: the preconception of a certain rational moral motivation inspires state action in order to guarantee positive liberty not only as participation, but also as a social right. The government sees itself as having the mission to realize the rational and reasonable reason of human beings, as it considers them incapable of realizing it by themselves. As Isaiah Berlin notes, a conception that presupposes an organic association between all members of society justifies the oppression of a part of the members of society in view of imposing this "real" conception of the self. The community or the government is the authentic interpreter of the content of positive liberty. It is also seen as the interpreter of positive liberty in the moral sense. This is seen as coinciding with the concept of dignity. According to this conception it is legitimate for the government to impose on individuals a vision of dignity that it considers appropriate, not allowing them the possibility to decide by themselves. In this sense, dignity is conceived as transcending the individual human being whose quality it is. It is seen as having a meaning that is to be enforced by the state. This conception is reflected in decisions in France that outlaw dwarf-throwing and the wearing of conspicuous signs of religious affiliation covering the face.

This approach aims to study the sociopolitical frame that led to the emergence of legal rules and challenge them in cases where it seems that there is injustice in the application of rules upon concrete cases of human rights. As I showed in the last chapter, understanding how a rule emerged should lead to a philosophical analysis on the reasons we might have to maintain a rule or not. Gadamer did not elaborate much on the possibility of transcending one's horizon. Habermas showed how by adopting a hermeneutical perspective on the origins of legal ideas it is possible to engage in a reflection on principles of justice that support them.[17] In the conclusion, I analyze how the intellectual trajectory on the emergence of legal ideas can assist critical reflection upon the same ideas.

2.2 ANTIQUITY, MODERNITY, NATURAL LAW, AND LIBERTY

The difference in the approach to freedom of expression in the two legal systems can be considered through the prism of the "quarrel between the Ancients and the Moderns."[18] The understanding of the role of government in France as defining the content and limits of freedom of expression is an amalgam of elements of Greek antiquity and modernity. It is reminiscent of the conception of the Ancients whereby

[17] Habermas, *Between Facts and Norms*.

[18] Taken from Luc Ferry's book title, *Le droit: la nouvelle querelle des Anciens et des Modernes* (Paris: Presses Universitaires de France, 1994).

the state incarnates prudence. According to this conception, human beings are social and political by nature and the state should promote essentialist-perfectionist goals. As I analyze later in the book, during the debates on the elaboration of the Declaration of the Rights of Man and the Citizen, an understanding that the natural state of man is social was dominant. The spirit of American law on freedom of expression is closer to the modern natural rights philosophy. In other words, the difference in the understanding of the concept of liberty in the two legal orders derives from a difference in the understanding of natural law. In the United States a conception of liberty as natural persists. In France, liberty is considered as a quality that exists only to the extent that it is recognized by the "general will." In the chapters that follow, I show how a tradition of state paternalism survives from some of the intellectuals who influenced the French revolutionaries and the French conception of the role of the government. In the United States on the contrary, the jusnaturalist conception of liberty present in the American Founders continues to underlie the American constitutional order, particularly in the area of freedom of speech.

The difference in the understanding of the concept of liberty in the two legal orders derives from a difference concerning the understanding of natural law. "Natural law" means here the basic ideas about justice and morality underlying what is enacted as positive law.[19] These ideas justify its obligatory force as law and make it legitimate. As Michel Villey notes, any conception of positive law is based on a valid theory of natural law.[20] Lawyers refer to conceptions of justice and morality expressed by the idea of natural law in their application of rules. Their task is to complete the written legal rules in a way so as to make them applicable in every new case arising from reality. By positivism, I mean in this context that liberty is considered to exist only to the extent that it is enacted by law.

A difference in the understanding of natural law is underlying the difference in the understanding of liberty. Natural rights theories are dominant in the United States, whereas in France liberty is considered as protected only to the extent that it is defined by the state. A conception of negative liberty as an element of human nature implies that political institutions aim at guaranteeing this negative liberty. Its foundation is transcendental and ahistorical. A conception of the natural state as social means that liberty is a quasi-artificial construction, which owes its existence to state enactment. According to this conception, as reflected in French law, liberty is

19 John Finnis uses the term "natural law" to mean (i) a set of basic practical principles that indicate the basic forms of human flourishing as goods to be pursued and realized; (ii) a set of basic methodological requirements of practical reasonableness; and (iii) a set of general moral standards. Finnis, *Natural Law and Natural Rights* (Oxford University Press, 1980), 23. My use of the term is very close to this understanding of the same concept. See also John Finnis, "Natural Law: The Classical Tradition," in Jules L. Coleman, Kenneth Einar Himma and Scott J. Shapiro, eds., *The Oxford Handbook of Jurisprudence and Philosophy of Law* (Oxford University Press, 2004), 1–60.

20 Michel Villey, "Abrégé du droit naturel classique," *Archives de Philosophie du Droit* 5 (1960), 25–72, 56.

consubstantial with its enactment by the state. The state decides in favor of the necessity to protect a liberty, taking into account considerations of general interest. Recognizing a liberty as natural or not has important implications for the legitimacy of the role of the state as regards defining its content and its limits. When judges decide on a limitation of liberty's conformity with the Constitution, if they are inspired by a jusnaturalistic conception, they are willing to restrain any attempt to define its content and to limit its exercise. If they consider liberty as a construction that owes its existence to state enactment, they are more willing to uphold legislation defining its content and its limits.

The understanding of the role of the government in France as defining the content and limits of freedom of expression is an amalgam of elements of antiquity and modernity. It is reminiscent of the conception of the Ancients that the state incarnates prudence. It is also associated with the rationalism of the individual, an idea from modernity. This rationalism, though, is to be guided, if not won over, by the state. The paternalistic role recognized in the French state is associated with the promotion of an essentialist-perfectionist goal concerning the vision of man, the citizen and the content of one's freedom of expression. It is inspired by a gnoseological hypothesis of the possibility of knowing the good as against moral relativism. The state will impose limitations on how human beings express themselves when this self-expression is not in conformity with the vision of human dignity that it takes for granted, as the cases of the burka ban and dwarf-throwing show. It will also enforce civility and respect when freedom of expression violates the privacy and dignity of other members within society. It is also legitimate for the state to limit hate speech and to impose a version of historical truth that expresses a position against moral relativism, as is made evident by the ban on holocaust denial. The legal status of freedom of expression in the United States is closer to the postulates of modernity. The Supreme Court's rejection of content distinctions is far from a paternalistic conception of the state associated with the promotion of an essentialist-perfectionist aim, concerning the vision of man, the citizen and the content of freedom of expression. In the United States, it is not legitimate for the government to protect the citizens from the danger of arriving at wrong opinions. The government will intervene only when there is a danger of disrupting the public order.[21] As the fighting-words doctrine dominant in the United States shows, the government will intervene only when there is a risk that speech "inflict[s] injury or tend[s] to incite an immediate breach of the peace."[22] This preconception in favor of government intervention to limit liberty helps understand why it is easier in the French legal order to enforce civility than it is in the United States.

The difference in the understanding of natural law between Europe and the United States can help us understand the difference in the understanding of the role

[21] See Kent Greenawalt, *Fighting Words, Individuals, Communities and Liberties of Speech* (Princeton University Press, 1995), 53.

[22] *Chaplinsky* v. *New Hampshire*, 315 US 568, 572 (1942).

of the state and the government in defining the content and limits of liberty. The jusnaturalist discourse on liberty, dominant in America, is opposed to the discourse on liberty as a quasi-artificial quality dominant in France. Although the French revolutionaries proclaimed the universal rights of every human being as a subject with material needs, they ended up accepting liberty only to the extent that the state and the government define it as such. This conception is very close to the one dominant in antiquity, with some nuances brought about by the specificities of modernity. In the United States on the contrary, the dominant understanding is that the content of liberty is not to be defined by the government. This conception of liberty as negative liberty is consistent with modern natural law theories. Modern natural law theories refer to transcendent subjective rational norms, inherent in the reason of the subject and in the natural rights of the individual. Antiquity, and in particular Aristotle, associated natural law with natural norms defined in relation to the natural end of every being, the *telos*. Every human being was conceived as having a potential that tends toward the accomplishment of its natural essence. Villey notes that ancient philosophers of physics secularize the notion of justice elaborating the notion of natural order; they discern natural law in the objective order that their philosophy discerns in the universe of the astronomers.[23] The conception underlying the notion of liberty in French law is closer to Aristotle's conception, which associates the foundation of the law with the natural evolution of each being toward its accomplishment. As I analyze later, this evolution of the individual is bound to the *polis* and the quality of the citizen according to Rousseau's conception that it is being a citizen that makes one a man.[24]

This implies that liberty is considered a quasi-artificial quality, dependent on being enacted by the state legislator. This ex ante understanding guides valuation of liberty by judges. The French Constitutional Council is less willing to declare a law limiting freedom of expression as contrary to the Constitution. The inverse ex ante understanding is dominant in the case law of the US Supreme Court. This Court operates under a presumption in favor of freedom of expression and only important justifications can legitimize upholding laws limiting it. In this context, the dominant vision of natural law is closer to the Moderns and the primacy of natural rights. This conception leads to interpretations that consider rights as "trumps," according to Dworkin's conception.[25] Rights are considered as elements having a special weight against collective goals. For freedom of expression, this means also protecting it over "personality rights," as they are called in Europe – the rights protecting the right to privacy and dignity understood as social status. The need to protect the imperfect

[23] Michel Villey, *La formation de la pensée juridique moderne* (Paris: Presses Universitaires de France, 2003), 87. See also Luc Ferry and Alain Renaut, *Système et critique: essais sur la critique de la raison dans la philosophie contemporaine* (Brussels: Ousia, 1984), 222.

[24] Jean-Jacques Rousseau, "On the Social Contract," trans. Donald A. Cress, in *The Basic Political Writings*, ed. Peter Gay (Indianapolis, IN: Hackett, 1987).

[25] Dworkin, *Taking Rights Seriously* (explaining the famous characterization of rights as "political trumps").

liberty of privacy and dignity does not always justify the intervention of the judge to compensate harm caused by speech.

The French law on freedom of expression reflects a positivism in the protection of liberty associated with a conception of ancient natural law. This conception sees liberty as the product of reason, which searches the just through cosmic nature, where the individual is only a subordinated part.[26] As deduced from the status of freedom of expression, French legal positivism is associated with a conception of classic natural law and with the limited role that this recognizes in individual liberty. The French law of freedom of expression seems to derive from a conception of this liberty as integrated in a cosmic order. State law contributes to the accomplishment of the citizens, protecting them from opinions that are harmful. American law is closer to the protection of individual will associated with modernity, concerning the formation of opinions and plans of life. The "legicentrism" of the French is associated with an ancient conception of natural law, which associates liberty with the positive act of enactment by the state. American law is characterized by distrust toward the government, especially the legislative. The judiciary controls the legitimacy of the law. The criteria that judges use reflect the modern philosophy of natural rights. The French conception of the paternalistic role of the state goes together with the acceptance of the role of the law as a command of reason. According to this conception, reflected in the status of freedom of expression, state law absorbs natural law entirely. According to the "legicentric" French conception, if individual rights "cannot be invoked against the law, neither be exercised in the absence of law, they are led to the right to be governed by the law."[27]

For Aristotle, there is a continuity between the order of the world and the effort of men to achieve what nature had left unaccomplished, while for the Moderns self-understanding goes together with the realization of the finite condition of man and the limits of reason.[28] Ancient/classic natural law was founded on the idea of a natural cosmic end, apprehending the human subject as "a mixture of reason and naturality, of liberty and necessity."[29] Human beings were seen as natural parts of their political communities, which were also seen as existing naturally. Ancient conceptions of natural law are oriented toward the good life inside the community, which is seen as natural. Modern natural law conceptions tend to focus on the

[26] Villey, *Formation*, 195.

[27] Michel Troper, "Jefferson et l'interprétation de la Déclaration des droits de l'homme de 1789," *Revue Française d'Histoire des Idées Politiques* 9 (1999), 3–23, 16.

[28] Philippe Raynaud, "Locke et les limites de la raison libérale," in Philippe Raynaud and Stéphane Rials, eds., *Une prudence moderne?* (Paris: Presses Universitaires de France, 1992) 21–33, 33; Phillipe Raynaud, "Anciens et Modernes," in Philippe Raynaud et Stéphane Rials, eds., *Dictionnaire de philosophie politique* (Paris: Presses Universitaires de France, 2003), 12–16; André Tosel, ed., *De la prudence des Anciens comparée à celle des Modernes: sémantique d'un concept, déplacement des problématiques* (Paris: Les Belles Lettres, 1995); Gil Dellannoi, *Eloge de la Prudence* (Paris: Berg International Editeurs, 1993).

[29] Bernard Bourgeois, *Philosophie et droits de l'homme, de Kant à Marx* (Paris: Presses Universitaires de France, 1990), 13. See also Villey, "Abrégé du Droit Naturel Classique."

sphere of inviolability and individual natural rights. For Aristotle, the supreme good that we pursue as such is eudemonia, psychic energy that we can only obtain inside political society, given our social nature. The ultimate aim of politics, as architectonical science, as the foundation and the presupposition for the development of any other science, is to form virtuous citizens.[30] The work of the legislator is, according to the Aristotelian conception of society, to define how someone can become good and what the best aims of life are. Also, it is to inculcate in the soul of the citizens that their perfection is identified with the perfection of their community.[31] For if man is "by nature" a political being, only the *polis* can guarantee well-being. The rationality of human beings directs them toward political life, because, even if they do not always need reciprocal help, they still aspire to live together.[32] For Aristotle the legislator should provide for the happiness of the citizens.[33] Happiness is associated with excellence and comes about by virtue or study: "an activity of the soul in conformity with virtue."[34] The task of the legislator, legitimate by virtue, is to address the reason of the citizens and to educate them in virtue.[35] It belongs to legislative prudence, the "architectonic" prudence, to discover or establish the best laws in any society.[36] The legislator concludes the search for the naturally just in a world of contingence. Written laws thus have the value of justice because they are founded on the conclusions drawn by the legislator on what is naturally just.[37] The legislator's task consists of ensuring that the citizens become "of a certain quality, in other words, honest men and capable of noble actions."[38]

The modern separation between legality and morality constitutive of the theory of law and ethics, which presupposes the state as an organism distinct from the communities of life and their ethical historical institutions, does not exist in Aristotle's thought.[39] Positive law is not different, for Aristotle, from natural law, to the extent that the former comes from *ethos*, an ethical given of the habitual and traditional order of the *polis*. Positive laws have the *polis*, with its ethical institutions, as their foundation and presupposition. The *polis* and its institutions constitute a *telos*, a live organism in motion toward its accomplishment.[40] Aristotle associates

30 Aristotle, *Ethique à Nicomaque*, 1099 b 30–33.
31 Aristotle, *Politics*, H, 1333 a 8, aussi 1333 b 21.
32 Aristotle, *Politics*, Γ, 1278 b 3.
33 Aristotle, *Politics*, H, 1324 b, 17sq. On the role of the legislator in Aristotle cf. Pierre Pellegrin, "Aristote," *in Dictionnaire de Philosophie Politique* (Paris: Presses Universitaires de France, 2003), 28–36, 31 ff.
34 Aristotle, *Politics*, H, 1333 a 9.
35 Aristotle, *Politics*, H, 1333 a 9.
36 Richard Bodéüs, *Le philosophe et la cité: recherches sur les rapports entre morale et politique dans la pensée d'Aristote* (Paris: Les Belles Lettres, 1982), 81 ff.
37 Villey, *Formation*, 94–95.
38 Aristotle, *Ethique à Nicomaque*, 1, 10, 1099 b 30, 70.
39 Cf. Villey, *Formation*, 84.
40 Aristotle, *Politics*, I, 1253a, 1 ff.

the end of any *polis* with the end of its constitution, without providing a clear criterion to judge the legitimacy of constitutions.[41]

Practical wisdom and knowledge are associated with an organic and hierarchical conception of the social bond: politics must be the work of those who have acquired experience in life.[42] Aristotle associates excellence in the political task with prudence: prudence is by excellence a virtue of political life identified with the one of *ανήρ σπουδαίος*, the citizen who is a leader. According to the close association postulated by Aristotle between ethics, morality and politics, prudence in politics is the right way to rule.[43] Prudence is associated with moral virtue.[44] Prudence is acquired late in life. Furthermore, for Aristotle, social inequalities have their origin in nature, in virtue and vice: for this reason, and under some conditions, they are useful and just.[45] Aristotle even gives legitimacy to the authority existent between husband and wife, as well as paternal and royal authority.[46] He associates with the natural possession of leadership qualities justified by the capacity to reason.[47]

For Aristotle, human beings are by nature political. This conception goes together with the idea of prudence in politics. For some modern thinkers on the contrary, the political universe is artificial. It derives from the rational capacities of the individual subject.[48] In antiquity, subjectivity was conceived as consubstantial with the cosmos, following its teleological movement. The metaphysics of modernity focuses on the human being as a subject possessing freedom of will.[49] Since Descartes, the question became how it is possible to conceive transcendent values despite their immanence in subjectivity.[50] In the domain of political thought, the question takes the form of political humanism. It means situating the foundation of political values – beginning from the legitimacy of state authority – on man and not on tradition, divine or natural. The doctrine of "natural" rights, associated with the emergence of the metaphysics of the subjectivity, suggests that rights are intrinsically attached to man, to his "nature." A human life deserving this name would be inconceivable in the absence of recognition of rights by positive law. "Natural" rights, necessary to the accomplishment of

41 Cf. Harvey Mansfield, Jr., "Les formes de la liberté: le constitutionnalisme dans la pensée politique classique et moderne," in Terence Marshall, ed., *Théorie et pratique du gouvernement constitutionnel: la France et les Etats-Unis* (La Garenne Colombes: Editions de l'Espace Européen, 1992), 23–33, 29.

42 Aristotle, *Politics*, H, 1332 b 4.

43 Aristotle, *Ethique à Nicomaque*, V1, 1144b 25, 312.

44 Aristotle, *Ethique à Nicomaque*, V1, 1145a 5, 313–4.

45 Aristotle, *Politics*, A, 1255 b 2.

46 Aristotle, *Politics*, A, 1259 a 2, XII.

47 Aristotle, *Politics*, A, 1260 a, XII, 6.

48 Raynaud, "Anciens et Modernes," 13.

49 Luc Ferry, *Philosophie politique 1: le droit: la nouvelle querelle des Anciens et des Modernes* (Paris: Presses Universitaires de France, 1984), 14–16.

50 Luc Ferry, "Actualité de la querelle de l'Aufklärung et du Romantisme," in *La Révolution française entre Lumières et Romantisme: cahiers de philosophie politique et juridique* (Centre de Publications de l'Université de Caen, 1989), 195–209, 198.

human dignity are opposed to contingent rights, to rights which would not be prepolitical.[51]

This idea emerged gradually throughout history. The crucial shift was from understanding *ius* as an objective state to associating it with the individual. An understanding of cosmic justice gives way to a doctrine of natural law as founded on the nature of man and his ability to act rationally to ensure self-preservation. According to some, the individualism associated with the idea of reflecting subject emerged after the criticism of classic subjectivity by the nominalism and the voluntarism of William of Ockham and Duns Scot.[52] For some others, the idea of individualism existed already in the Franciscans who used the term *ius* in a subjective sense even before Ockham.[53]

Social contract theories are attempts to found political authority on the individual subject in terms of equality. The thought experiment of the state of nature corresponds in the epistemological discourse of modernity to the idea of the *tabula rasa*, concerning prejudices inherited from the past and it serves to limit the power of the state.[54] In the world of the Ancients, the validity of values and intersubjective communication is founded on the immanence of the cosmic order of tradition. For Descartes, the foundation of values is in the subjectivity of each person.[55] Political humanism founds political values – beginning from the legitimacy of power – on man and not on tradition. Thanks to the mediation of rational subjectivity, the conceptualization of the difference between an *is* and an *ought*, becomes possible. This is the distinction between a state that is existent, traditional, and inegalitarian, and the ideal of equality. This equality constitutes the principal metaphysical premise of modernity. Equality presupposes and is the result of the acceptance of every individual's ability for reflection. Every human being has the ability to act in order to transform the world by reference to transcendent values. The conceptualization of the reflective subject and every subject's ability to search for meaning leads to the autonomization of a normative sphere transcending the real sphere. If government authority is entrusted to

51 Guy Haarscher, "Droits de l'homme," in Philippe Raynaud et Stéphane Rials, eds., *Dictionnaire de philosophie politique* (Paris: Presses Universitaires de France, 2003), 190–197, 190; see also Guy Haarscher, *Philosophie des droits de l'homme*, 4th ed. (Brussels: Editions de l'Université de Bruxelles, 1993).

52 Pierre Alféri, *Guillaume d'Ockham: le singulier* (Paris: Minuit, 1989); Jean-Marc Trigeaud, "Droit," in Philippe Raynaud et Stéphane Rials, eds., *Dictionnaire de philosophie politique* (Paris: Presses Universitaires de France, 2003), 163; Villey, *Formation*; Michel Villey, *Le droit et les droits de l'homme* (Paris: Presses Universitaires de France, 1983); Charles Taylor, *Sources of the Self, The Making of the Modern Identity* (Cambridge, MA: Harvard University Press, 1989); Louis Dumont, *Essais sur l'individualisme* (Paris: Seuil, 1985), 84–89.

53 Brian Tierney, *The Idea of Natural Rights, Studies on Natural Rights, Natural Law, and Church Law 1150–1625* (Michigan: Eerdmans, 1997).

54 Ferry, "Actualité de la querelle de l'Aufklärung," 199.

55 Ibid., 198. See also Emmanuel Faye, *Philosophie et perfection de l'homme, de la Renaissance à Descartes* (Paris: Vrin, 1998), 335.

another agent, then its scope is limited according to the relationship of trust. This foundation is important for the social contract theorists. As Tocqueville noted, Descartes himself did not extend his radical approach outside of philosophy to questions of politics.[56] It was the theorists of the social contract who made this step. In France, although the Jacobins attempt to express political humanism, the means they used to realize it are reminiscent of the ancient conception. Most of the French revolutionaries, and most obviously the Jacobins, trust the reason of the state to discover the good and to dictate it to the citizens over the reason of the individual.

Social contract theories situate the foundation of state authority in convention and not in prudence, as this was the case for the Ancients. According to these theories, the interpretation of natural law depends on the understanding of every subject. It is only on the basis of the social contract that someone can be designated as the person whose interpretation will count as "objective."[57] This theory has important implications concerning contemporary democratic regimes. Hobbes is a social contract thinker who expressed the idea of natural equality between men. He also expresses the opinion (contrary to the Aristotelian idea of natural prudence existing only in some people, who are thus the most competent to enunciate opinions on political action and government[58]), that every person must recognize every other person as equal in nature to themselves. For Hobbes, the division between governors and governed is founded on consensus and not on the difference of their "faculties of the mind."[59] The opposite opinion is considered by Hobbes as "a vain conceipt of ones owne wisdom," contrary to reason as well as experience.[60] For Hobbes, nobody can decide for us what is prudent for us. Nobody can assign the force of command to their discourse on the basis of their "wisdom." Each one of us is as wise as everyone else to decide what is prudent for themselves. For Hobbes, absolute liberty is unthinkable. In the struggle for self-preservation, it can lead to self-destruction. This is a proposition dictated by reason, which exists in each human

56 For Tocqueville, the philosophical method born in the sixteenth century, which became more specific and generalized during the seventeenth century, could not be commonly adopted to the extent that the political laws, the social state and the habits of spirit that derive from it were opposed to it. Equality existed earlier among the Americans than among the French. Thus Americans were applying the method on political questions. Tocqueville suggests at this point that time was necessary so that the equality postulated on the level of philosophy meets the equality postulated in political issues. Alexis de Tocqueville, *De la démocratie en Amérique*, II (Paris: Gallimard, 1961), 16–17. On the same subject, in François Azouvi et Jean-Marie Beyssade, "Descartes," in Philippe Raynaud et Stéphane Rials, eds., *Dictionnaire de philosophie politique* (Paris: Presses Universitaires de France, 2003), 155–159, the authors trace the contradictory reference to the principles of the method of Descartes, which for some give the impression of a radical political doctrine, whereas for others of a conservative preaching.

57 Thomas Hobbes, *Leviathan*, ed. Richard Tuck (Cambridge University Press, 1991), chaps. 14 and 15.

58 Aristotle, *Politique*, 1277 b 17–18 (Paris: Les Belles Lettres, 2002), 62.

59 Hobbes, *Leviathan*, chap. 15. On this difference between the Ancients and the Moderns, cf. also Blandine Barret-Kriegel, *L'Etat et les esclaves* (Paris: Payot, 1989 [1979]), 54.

60 Hobbes, *Leviathan*, chap. 13.

being. It does not have in itself the force of command.[61] It is only the social contract, the collective intentional decision, and the legal construction of representation that can create a sovereign to enforce the law.[62] However, the powers of the government are limited to the domains for which the authorization the people have invested in it is valid. For Hobbes[63] and other social contract thinkers,[64] the government is created by contract for the guarantee of self-preservation by providing an interpretation of the natural law that will count as "authoritative." It will count as such, because it is made by the entity recognized as having the capacity to assign legal force to its commands, that is to "enact" legal norms. The question that emerges in the transition from cosmic natural law to natural subjective rights, is which are the rights that would be seen as "natural." For Hobbes, it seems that they are those rights associated with life and survival. The two fundamental "faces" of modern metaphysics are reason and will, that is liberty thought of as being the capacity of the person to act by themselves according to their representation of ends. Paradoxically, in France a version of modern rationalism leads to the acceptance of a "modern prudence."

According to the paradigm dominant in modernity, there is a distinction between ethics and politics. Politics, society, and morality are conceived as three separate spheres, which overlap in some respects. The separation between these three spheres did not exist in the thought of antiquity. Paradoxically, despite the reference to universal rights, the French Declaration of the Rights of Man and of the Citizen was elaborated in circumstances where a conception of natural law, which was closer to the Ancients, was dominant. Those rights are to be realized by the state, since, according to the dominant understanding in France, human life does not make sense outside of the social and political state. The conception of natural law underlying the French Declaration and the relevant conception of liberty is close to that of antiquity and its primacy for the community against which liberty is a social construction. The French Declaration accords primacy to the community to define the rights of "men" and "citizens." This conception goes together with a rationalist understanding concerning the role of the government, seen as incarnating prudence. The government assigns meaning to the quasi-artificial construction

61 We must note in this respect that Hobbes uses the terms "natural law," in two senses. Firstly, in the epistemological sense, concerning the realization on behalf of the subject of the necessity to accept the limitation of one's liberty in view of survival. Secondly, in a normative sense, according to which there is a profound disagreement concerning the definition of right and wrong, a disagreement which will be decided definitely by the sovereign who is invested with the force of legal command.

62 See also the analysis of Olivier Cayla, *La notion de signification en droit: Contribution à une théorie du droit naturel de la communication* (Dissertation, Paris II University, 1992).

63 Hobbes, *Leviathan*, chap. 21, in which are enumerated the liberties of the subjects, liberties conceptually submitted to the contemporary understanding of the notion of liberty to self-determination.

64 Cf. John Locke, *Second Treatise of Government*, esp. chap. 9, "Of the Ends of Political Society and Government." For Locke, in the end the need for self-preservation leads us to quit the absolute liberty that we had in a "state of nature" and to submit it to the regulation of the laws of political society only to the extent that this is necessary for self-preservation ("so far forth as the preservation of himself and the rest of that society shall require"). Ibid, chap. 9, § 129.

of liberty. "The idea of the general will is at the heart of any state-enacted law and the emancipation of society must pass by the realization of principles of "pure practical reason" by the submission of the particular (interest, mores, society) under a universal (reason, law, the state)."[65] The conception of the general will in the participants in the National Assembly during the summer of 1789 debating the French Declaration is close to the essentialism of the Ancients. They are close to the Aristotelian idea that the legislator is prudent, knowledgeable, and wise, and that "the law is an intelligence without passion."[66] According to this conception, the legislator concludes the search for the content of natural law. The legislator adds to natural law specific determinations and brings into natural law something from their own will to define what is just.[67] Rousseau offers a reconstruction of all these ideas, while taking individual liberty into account. This is the reason why he was so popular among the actors of the French Revolution: conservatives, moderates, and revolutionaries.

Classic natural law could not have revolutionary implications whereas modern natural law does. The idea of natural rights and of the social contract inspired, to some extent, both the American and the French revolutions. These ideas interacted differently, however, with other ideas present in the two different settings. Through a paradoxical detour, the French conception of natural law is closer to the ancient conception, while passing from Rousseau's individualism, which has revolutionary implications. The modern democratic revolutions modified the understanding of liberty by stressing the liberty of the individual. The fictive idea of a social contract serves as an interpretative scheme to revolutionary action. The declaration of rights is the act through which natural rights were enacted as positive.[68] The political meaning of the recognition of rights is to assign limits to the powers of the government and to constitute a defense of the liberty of the individual. This meaning is antecedent to the understanding of liberty as political or "public liberty," according to the French understanding of liberty.[69]

At the moment of the two revolutions emerges the question of how to make natural law positive and how to actualize democracy. The significance of the revolutionary and declaratory task is different on each side of the Atlantic.[70]

65 Jean-Marc Ferry, "La rationalisation habermassienne de la prudence," in Raynaud et Rials, eds., *Une Prudence Moderne?*, 83 (my translation).

66 Aristotle, *Politics*; Aristotle, *Ethique à Nicomaque*; Villey, *Formation*, 93; see also Pierre Aubenque, "La loi chez Aristote," *Archives de Philosophie du Droit* 25 (1980), 147–157, 156.

67 Villey, *Formation*, 94–95.

68 On the tension between the ancient natural law and the modern natural law as it was reflected in the French declaratory text, cf. the analysis of Lucien Jaume, "Préface aux Droits de l'Homme," in Lucien Jaume, *Les déclarations des droits de l'homme (du débat 1789–1793 au préambule de 1946)* (Paris: Flammarion, 1989), 27–65.

69 Simone Goyard-Fabre, "La Déclaration des droits ou le devoir d'humanité: une philosophie de l'espérance," *Droits* 8 (1988), 41–54, 42.

70 Jürgen Habermas discusses insightfully this opposition in *Theory and Praxis*, trans. John Viertel (Boston: Beacon Press, 1973), 105.

Rousseau's ideology of the Fall provides elements for inspiration. In America, democracy should liberate and allow the operation of natural interests. In France, it should reconceptualize a unified central government as a positive power, situated in the sovereignty of the people. It would also establish, through state action, a different social order, which would be egalitarian against a hierarchical conception of society. It should moralize a corrupt society. The moralizing role of the state during the French Revolution and the intense turbulent period that followed it is reminiscent of the ancient conception of natural law, according to which ethics should be one of the principal missions of politics. In this general context, making liberty "positive" – in the sense of enacting it, in view of its recognition as a "subjective right" – and the role of the state – in view of defining its content and limits – are very important in the work that went into the French Declaration. In France, it is being a citizen that makes one a man, as Rousseau thinks. It is the declaration of political rights that leads to the emergence of the rights of man. This hierarchy established in the end of the French Declaration implies the acceptance of the role of collective power, concerning the definition of liberty. In France, the dominant conception of liberty is one that considers it a quasi-artificial construction, posed by state law. It is less seen as a natural quality of the individual, which should be left to follow their free development. The primacy of society upon the individual is associated with the moralizing role of the state. The state is seen in France as having the practical rational wisdom to define the good of the individual. All these elements, associated with the role of politics to define the good of the individual, reflect the ancient conception of natural law.

This difference in the understanding of the concept of liberty also has implications for the role of the government in realizing liberty and human dignity. Human dignity can be understood as guaranteeing the necessities of human existence, and as a moral status as defined by social morality. As such it is often associated with the government's positive moral role as the agent liberating individuals from poverty as well as from their own irrationality. The conception of the multiple facets of liberty implies different understandings of the role of the government in the protection of these facets. According to one conception, the state should guarantee only the protection of negative liberty. According to another, the state, incarnating reason, should adopt measures guaranteeing the protection of human dignity as an inherent quality of all individuals. According to Hayek's libertarian vision of liberty, which expresses the classic thesis of the Whigs and of Locke, the state should be the sole guarantor of negative liberty.[71] Its mission should be to prevent any violation of negative liberties. On this point, it is necessary to clarify that the distinction between positive and negative liberty does not necessarily correspond to a negative vision of the role of the state. The state is considered as a necessary institution to guarantee

71 Developed in particular in Friedrich A. Hayek, *The Constitution of Liberty* (Chicago: University of Chicago Press, 1960).

negative liberty through positive measures too. As liberties and obligations are correlative, the recognition of a negative liberty goes together with the recognition of an obligation of the state to provide for the protection of this negative liberty. The difference between state intervention to guarantee only negative liberty and intervention to guarantee positive liberty as well, in the sense of foreseeing the necessities of human existence to realize some conception of human dignity, is only a matter of degree.

Therefore, the limitation of property, a negative liberty par excellence, through taxation to guarantee the existence of the state is conceivable and compatible with a minimalist conception of the moralizing role of the state. In return, the state guarantees this negative liberty and acts as guarantor and arbitrator of the interests of civil society. The acceptance of the role of the state as arbitrator of the interests of civil society can go together with a minimalist conception of the degree to which it is legitimate for the state to define the content and limits of a liberty in order to accomplish a goal dictated by the conception of liberty of the agents of political power of the moment. Accepting the role of the government as arbitrator does not necessarily mean accepting government intervention to impose its conception of the good upon society. For example, Adam Smith is in favor of taxation to guarantee the existence of the state. He is also in favor of government intervention to amend, on a case-by-case basis, the negative unintended consequences of the free market. Nevertheless, he does not go as far as to accept the government's role in imposing its conception of the good upon society.[72] According to Smith, if peaceful coexistence is guaranteed by "moral sentiments," the role of the government must be limited to the degree that is strictly necessary to ensure the operation of the market. This is in opposition to Hobbes, for whom the conflict of interpretations on what is right or wrong, just or unjust, necessitates a sovereign whose interpretation counts as authoritative. This conception is also different from that of Rousseau, who thinks that the moral deprivation of humanity necessitates the moralizing intervention of the state. The difference between the three thinkers is a difference of the degree and quality of government intervention within civil society.

The moralizing conception of the government can go together with a conception of the government as regulating the economy. Nevertheless, the two conceptions can also be understood as being distinct. As I argue in the case of France, an ex ante understanding in favor of government intervention in the area of the economy goes together with accepting the government as having the role to impose a moral and comprehensive vision of the good upon society. Redistributing goods is also a moral goal. According to the Hayekian vision of liberty, if the state is necessary for guaranteeing negative liberty, this does not mean that it should also assume moral goals like redistributing goods. It is not appropriate for the state to assume the moral

[72] Smith, *Wealth of Nations*, 724, 758; see also Adam Smith, *The Theory of Moral Sentiments* (Indianapolis: Liberty Fund, 1982), 234.

obligations that the members of a society or a family have toward each other.[73] The question is therefore the recognition of the extent of the government's intervention concerning the elements of communication between law, politics, and morality. This is the interminable "quarrel"[74] in the course of the history of ideas about the point of adjustment of the role of the state in defining this communication. It concerns designing limits between the political, social, and moral spheres, which are the *acquis* of modernity. This is in opposition to Greek antiquity, when the distinction between these spheres did not exist. The conception of the legal status of freedom of expression in French and American law reflects the interminable quarrel between the Ancients and the Moderns about the distinction between the three above-mentioned spheres and their limits.

According to the conception of the role of the state, a different understanding of the concept of "human dignity" is also protected by the two legal orders. Both legal orders reflect the need to protect dignity in the moral sense, as unconditional respect that must be recognized in humanity. There is, however, disagreement as to what kind of state action this respect implies. The American legal order reflects the need to protect dignity as a negative liberty understood itself in the sense of self-determination. This conception is very close to the one that Renaissance thinker Giovanni Pico della Mirandola put forward.[75] The French legal order protects dignity in the sense attributed to the concept by the Romans: the protection of social status, or the social recognition of the individual.[76] At the same time, it dictates enforcing a view on how human beings should treat themselves, as the dwarf-throwing case analyzed earlier shows. In France, there is trust in the government to define the content and limits of liberty and to enforce civility. In the United States, it is not legitimate for the government to enforce "civility." This role is undertaken by society, as "political correctness" shows. Political correctness, as self-regulation of society, through social coercion, reflects a vision of society close to the one postulated by Locke, Hutcheson, Smith, and Hayek. Tocqueville had described the force of social morality in American society.[77] The moral bond substitutes for the loosening of the political bond. If liberty is not densely regulated on the legal level, the

73 Friedrich Hayek, "Social or Distributive Justice," in Chiaki Nishiyame, Kurt R. Leube, eds., *The Essence of Hayek* (Stanford: Hoover Institution Press, 1984), 88–89; see also Friedrich Hayek, *The Road to Serfdom* (University of Chicago Press, 1944).

74 Luc Ferry, *Le droit: la nouvelle querelle des Anciens et des Modernes* (Paris: Presses Universitaires de France, 2007).

75 Giovanni Pico della Mirandola, *De la dignité de l'homme*, trans. Yves Hersant (Paris: Editions de l'Eclat, 1993).

76 Panayotis Kondilis, *Περί Αξιοπρέπειας* (Athens: Indicto, 2000) [Greek translation of the text "Würde" in *Historisches Lexicon zur politisch-sozialen Sprache in Deutschland Geschichliche Grundbegriffe*, vol. 6 (Stuttgart: Klett-Cotta, 1984); Alain Michel, "La dignité humaine chez Cicéron," in Pierre Magnard, ed., *La dignité de l'homme – actes du colloque tenu à la Sorbonne (Paris-IV)* (Paris: Honoré Champion éd., 1995), 17–24.

77 Alexis de Tocqueville, *Democracy in America*, trans. George Lawrence, ed. J. P. Mayer (Garden City, NY: Doubleday, 1969), 262 ff.

social force of majoritarian common opinion weighs heavily in ensuring the proper exercise of liberty. In America, on the political level the majority is counterbalanced by a series of "checks and balances" for the protection of individual liberty, and this to an extent much more elaborated than in France. However, social majority is very strong, almost invincible in the United States. Institutional liberalism does not necessarily coincide with social liberalism.

In France, liberty is conceived as having a precise positive content, in the moral sense attributed to the term by Berlin. In this sense liberty must tend toward the realization of some good, the respect for oneself and for all of humanity in the exercise of liberty. Rousseau's conception of the state is dominant, according to which the political, social, and moral spheres are confounded. It is legitimate for the state to enforce a vision of the good upon society and to make sure that humans exercise their moral liberty in a positive direction. Kant maintains a distinction between external freedom, regulated by the law, and internal freedom, regulated by morality. If a person neglects their moral duties against themselves, they are violating their moral duties and thus may be morally unfree. Kant does not elaborate, however, in favor of enforcing human dignity through state action. The constitution of the state and the law regulate external freedom "so that it harmonizes with the freedom of everyone else."[78] Nevertheless, the conception of freedom of expression dominant in France accepts the enforcement by law of this positive content in the exercise of liberty. *Internal and external liberty seem to be confounded.* The burka ban, the ban on dwarf-throwing and the ban on the denial of crimes against humanity can be understood from this perspective. On the contrary, the conception of liberty, and in particular of freedom of expression, underlying the American legal order is one of negative liberty in the sense attributed to the term by Hayek. It presupposes that it belongs to the subject – holder of liberty – to define their moral content and not to the state. Therefore, in comparison with France, it is legitimate for the government to intervene to a lesser extent concerning the definition of the content and limits of freedom of expression. The mobilization of the mechanism of state coercion for imposing limits to the exercise of liberty is legitimate only when this exercise is seen as causing grave harm to others.

2.3 HISTORICAL IMAGINARIES

The understanding of the role of the government in limiting freedom of expression today reflects historical imaginaries. There are nuances between France and the United States in the understanding of the role of the government *lato sensu* – understood as including the executive, the legislative, and the judiciary branch. In the United States an attitude of distrust is dominant, whereas in France collective authority is seen as something positive. In France, the royal imaginary has played

78 Kant, "On the Common Saying," 73.

a significant role in defining the understanding of the mission of the government, whereas the imaginary of "checks and balances" dominates in the United States. Prerevolutionary conceptions of sovereignty in France affected the postrevolutionary conception and the role of the government. In the United States, conceptions of mixed constitutionalism reflect this distrust toward the government, which manifests itself during the twentieth century in the doctrine of rigid protection for free speech.

In France, under the influence of Rousseau, the dominant ideology of a strong government leads to a conception of freedom of expression as defined by the government. This vision leads to state paternalism in defining the opinions that are just and worthy of being heard and those that are harmful. It also leads to the necessity to protect the individual against themselves when they decide to express themselves in a way that violates their "dignity," or at least in a way that violates the dominant version of what human "dignity" dictates. An example of this is the ban of the Islamic headscarf as well as the refusal to attribute the French nationality to a person wearing the niqab. Although modernity is characterized by the division of three spheres – the political, the social, and the moral – Rousseau's thought underlines the primacy of the ethical and moral moment and the confusion between civil society and the state. This may lead to potentially dangerous consequences for individual liberty. The practical difficulties inherent in the realization of the general will have the potential to render the notion a legitimizing myth for government overreach. This is because the anterior historical context manifests itself and reappears in any attempt to achieve change, as the new and the old are always in a dialectical relation.[79]

Different political and social needs led to different conceptions of the role of the government. These conceptions create their own imaginary, which supports their viability and endurance in time. In France, an imaginary of an organic unity between the parliament and the people is dominant. This imaginary has its origins in the idea of organic unity that existed between the monarch and the people in the Ancien Régime. The understanding of the role of the government in France is affected by the organic vision that the Middle Ages inherited from Aristotle,[80] Bodin's and Rousseau's vision. The paternalistic role of the state in France has its origins in the attempts by the king to ensure his authority by presenting himself as the protector of the lowest social strata against the feudal lords.[81] The idea that the king was "debtor of justice" consolidated around the twelfth century.[82] The theory of the divine right of kings led to the doctrine of organic unity between the king and the

79 Cf. Hans-Georg Gadamer, *Vérité et Méthode* [originally *Wahrheit und Methode*], trans. Pierre Fruchon, Jean Grondin, and Gilbert Merlio (Paris: Seuil, 1970), 303.

80 Bernard Guenée, *States and Rulers in Later Medieval Europe*, trans. Juliet Vale (Oxford: Blackwell, 1985), 44.

81 Nannerl O. Keohane, *Philosophy and the State in France: The Renaissance to the Enlightenment* (Princeton University Press 1980), 6.

82 Bertrand de Jouvenel, *De la souveraineté: à la recherche du bien politique* (Paris: Génin, Librairie de Médicis, 1955), 219.

subjects that the French Revolution inherited. Carl Schmitt and Böckenforde noted that the significant concepts of the theory of the modern state are secularized theological concepts.[83] The omnipotent legislator became the substitute for the omnipotent God. For the political theology of the Middle Ages, the king became the physical mortal agent of God and at the same time the representative of an immortal mystic entity.[84] The same imaginary determined a conception of unified government. Jean Bodin and other French theorists contributed to the idea of a unity of government.[85] He formulated the principle of unity of public power that was influential in France. He insisted on the union of the legislative and the executive power in the hands of the monarchy. Its impact upon civil society will be manifested in a way that will not be moderated by a system of "checks and balances." Rousseau was also read in France as consistent with the idea of a strong government and of an omnipotent legislator.[86] Dominant in the French imaginary is an understanding of a strong government that has a positive impact upon society. This conception was inherited by the nation following the French Revolution. Ideas of state paternalism elaborated during the monarchy in France persist in the contemporary understanding of the government. As Marcel Gauchet notes, during the French Revolution, distrust toward agents and holders of political power was "the formidable reverse of a faith in its positive character once it was taken away from those who had usurped it."[87]

Despite the fact that after the two revolutions the people are considered sovereign on both sides of the Atlantic, there are subtle nuances in the understanding of the concept of sovereignty itself. This has implications for the understanding of the role of the government. Following the French Revolution, the nation succeeded the monarch in the understanding of sovereignty. From then on, sovereignty is seen as residing in the nation and exercised by its representatives that speak in its name. The nation's will can only express the general will, the common good which is something qualitatively different from the sum of the individual interests of the people. In the national will persists the idea of a unity of government after the revolution in France. In America, the people also participate in the imaginary of sovereignty. If in France popular sovereignty is associated with trust toward the government that speaks in the name of the nation, in America, popular sovereignty is associated with distrust toward the same role. This difference in imaginary is very important. In America,

83 Carl Schmitt, *Political Theology*, trans. George Schwab (Cambridge MA: The MIT Press, 1985), 36; Carl Schmitt, *The Concept of the Political*, trans. George Schwab (University of Chicago Press, 1996), 42. See also also Ernst-Wolfgang Böckenforde, "La naissance de l'État: processus de sécularisation," in *Le droit, l'État, et la constitution démocratique*, trans. Olivier Jouanjan, Willy Zimmer, and Olivier Beaud (Paris: Bruyland LGDJ, 2000), 114.

84 F. H. Hinsley, *Sovereignty* (London: C.A. Watts & Co. Ltd., 1966), 64; Ernst H. Kantorowicz, *The King's Two Bodies: A Study in Medieval Political Theology* (Princeton University Press, 1997 [1957]), 9.

85 Jean Bodin, *Les six livres de la République* (Paris: Jacques du Puys, Librairie Juré, 1576).

86 See Chapter 4.

87 Marcel Gauchet, *La Révolution des droits de l'homme* (Paris: Gallimard, 1989), 37.

the common good is to be discovered through representation but it is the result of the confrontation of the particular interests that exist within civil society. And it is associated with the idea of negative liberty. Émile Boutmy noted that the term "sovereignty" in Article 3 of the French Declaration of the Rights of Man and the Citizen[88] has its equivalent in the American context, in the term "power," which expresses something palpable.[89] For Émile Boutmy, latent in the phrase in the French Declaration, "sovereignty habitually resides in the Nation,"[90] which has no equivalent in the American Declaration, is the idea of a nation, a mystic entity held to be the possessor of this sovereignty. It is legitimate for the nation to define the liberties that the citizens have. This means that the collective imaginary in France accepts an active role for the government concerning the definition of the content and limits of rights. The state, considered as incarnating "prudence," is charged with the mission of ensuring the realization of liberty, despite the discourse of the theorists of the social contract and the realization of the need to protect individual rights.

Revolutions lead to a dialectic between the old and the new. Hans Georg-Gadamer notes that even when life changes suddenly, as is the case during revolutionary periods, there is "conserved under the *prima facie* change of everything a part of the past much more considerable than we think and which finds its authority by allying itself with what is new."[91] In her analysis of the two revolutions Arendt is in line with Gadamer in many respects.[92] The differences in the fundamental presuppositions of the two legal orders can be understood, among other things, in relation to the different political problems that led to the two revolutions. Historians show that if the revolutionary impulsion in America was a reaction against the legislative activity of the British parliament, one of the revolutionary impetuses in France, as in many other European countries, was the problem of mass poverty. A society structured in concentric circles around royal power made this problem difficult to resolve. In this context, political theorists note that the transfer by the Revolution, on the imaginary level, of the king's "sovereignty" to the National Assembly took place without a qualitative change in the understanding of the role of the government.[93] The French democracy and republic were formed by the rejection

88 "The principle of all sovereignty resides in the nation. No body nor individual may exercise any authority which does not proceed directly from the nation" (Engl. translation by The Avalon Project, Yale Law School).

89 Émile Boutmy, "La Déclaration des droits de l'homme et du citoyen et M. Jellinek," *Annales des Sciences Politiques* 17 (1902), 415–443, 427.

90 Article 3 of the French Declaration of the Rights of Man and of the Citizen.

91 Gadamer, *Vérité et méthode*, 303 (my translation).

92 These ideas are summarized eloquently in Hannah Arendt, *On Revolution* (London: Penguin, 1990 [1963]), 24.

93 Cf. Lucien Jaume, *Le discours jacobin et la démocratie* (Paris: Fayard, 1989), 10; Gauchet, *Révolution des droits de l'homme*, 33, Pierre Rosanvallon, *La démocratie inachevée: histoire de la souveraineté du peuple en France* (Paris: Gallimard, 2000), 70; Pierre Rosanvallon, *Le modèle politique français: ;a société civile contre le Jacobinisme, de 1789 à nos Jours* (Paris: Seuil 2004), 11.

of the monarchical order, through substitution of one form of government for another.[94] Arendt notes insightfully that Rousseau's theory of the general will, inspiring and directing the nation no longer composed by a multitude but as forming one person, became "axiomatic" for all the factions and parties of the French Revolution, being the "theoretical substitute" for the sovereign will of an absolute monarch.[95] The idea of unity of sovereignty and government persists after the revolution.

For Sieyès, the nation is the abstraction that ensures legitimacy in the exercise of power.[96] Sovereignty is institutionalized, formally vested in the people and exercised by its representatives. Reproducing the imaginary conception of the monarch, the nation should speak with "a single, unified will," which should encompass the wills of all three previously existing Estates of the Ancien Régime.[97] Sieyès clearly distinguishes the common interest from the individual interest and happiness of every citizen. And he discusses the formation of the National Assembly in a way that neutralizes individual interest so that the will of the majority cleaves to the public good. He makes clear that each deputy does not represent his constituency but "the whole association."[98] This conception is the exact reverse of the one dominant in the United States, where representation of local constituencies is very important. In France, the common interest is not the result of the confrontation of various private interests, as it is in America for Madison. It is something qualitatively different, which encompasses and harmonizes partial points of view. This means that the National Assembly should be constituted in a way that isolates individual interests, ensuring that the will of the majority will always lead to the general good. For Sieyès, the national will is the product of every individual will. The legislative will belongs thus for him entirely to the nation and the representatives that speak in its name. This conception of a unified common interest perpetuates the mentality of a unity of interest that the monarchy had created. Sieyès's conception of the power of the nation resonates with Bodin's voluntarism for the prince whose will was the origin of law. The will of the nation should from now on be the law: "The nation exists above all, it is the origin of all. Its will is always legal, it is the law itself."[99] The nation for Sieyès should not subject itself to the restrictions of a positive form. Its will is always "supreme." It is the "source" and "supreme master" of all positive law.[100] Power

94 Jaume, *Discours jacobin*, 10.

95 Arendt, *On Revolution*, 156.

96 Joseph Emmanuel Sieyès, "Qu'est-ce que le Tiers-Etat?," in *Ecrits Politiques*, ed. Roberto Zapperi (Paris, Editions des Archives Contemporaines, 1985), 160–162.

97 Ibid., 163.

98 Joseph Emmanuel Sieyès, "Views of the Executive Means Available to the Representatives of France in 1789," in *Political Writings*, ed. Michael Sonenscher (Indianapolis, IN and Cambridge, UK: Hackett, 2003 [1789]), 12.

99 Sieyès, "Qu'est-ce que le Tiers-Etat?," 160–162.

100 Ibid., 163.

belongs solely to it. Its interest is the general interest itself. Sovereignty is exercised on the basis of some ultimate conception of the general will that all identify with, and not as the interplay of interests,[101] as is the conception of *The Federalist*.

Rousseau's thought, which in many respects follows Bodin, provided inspiration to the Jacobin centralizing conception of the state as well.[102] The understanding of the role of the government in France carries the weight of an evolution of dominant ideas expressing state paternalism and an organic unity between rulers and the people. The monarch was seen as forming a unity with the people and as having the mission to protect their dignity. The people and the parliament, which by a speech act, giving itself legitimacy, became their representative,[103] would be henceforth considered as having the mission of accomplishing this paternalistic task, of considering the well-being of citizens, and guaranteeing the protection of the dignity of all. The protection of this equal dignity for all was an important element of the French Revolution, as one of its aims was to establish a new political sociability.[104] It aimed at abolishing a society organized in concentric circles and at guaranteeing equal rights for all – a real equality of rights. The need to protect the dignity of everyone, to protect the physical existence of the person, led to a consideration of the positive role of the state, in realizing this protection. In America, on the contrary, the revolution arose from a reaction against the activity of the British parliament, which was seen as oppressive and limiting liberty. The Founding Fathers implemented the separation of powers in a way that limits the government's impact upon individual liberty. The construction and the organization of the American states as well as of the federal government is characterized by a series of "checks and balances" aiming to control, filter, and generally moderate the government's power and its impact on individual liberty. Judges also operate in this general context. They think that it is less legitimate for themselves to intervene in defining the content and limits of liberty.

If French constitutionalism is founded on a positive conception and a trust regarding the exercise of collective power, the inverse attitude prevails in the American context. The conception of authority, which played an important role on the level of the imaginary in France,[105] faded in the United States because of different social and political circumstances. Historians show that Americans did not aim to regenerate a corrupt society, as was the case in France, but affirmed their independence against the legislative activity of the British parliament, which they

101 Cf. J. L. Talmon, *The Origins of Totalitarian Democracy* (Middlesex: Penguin 1952), 44.

102 Julien Boudon, *Les Jacobins: une traduction des principes de Jean-Jacques Rousseau* (Paris: LGDJ, 2006); Simone Goyard-Fabre, *Politique et Philosophie dans l'oeuvre de Jean-Jacques Rousseau* (Paris: Presses Universitaires de France, 2001), 96 ff.

103 Jaume, *Discours jacobin*, 283.

104 François Furet, *Penser la Révolution française*, 2nd ed. (Paris: Gallimard, 1985), 67–68. See also Jack R. Censer and Lynn Hunt, *Liberty, Equality, Fraternity, Exploring the French Revolution* (Pennsylvania: Pennsylvania State University Press, 2001), 3.

105 In the sense that Cornelius Castoriadis attributes to the term (see Chapter 1).

saw as oppressive.[106] If France is still under the domination of the idea of a paternalistic conception of the role of the state, which is seen as incarnating "prudence," the American founding myths are formed around the idea of an integral reconceptualization of the fundamental notions of government and of the relation between society and the state. The political and social circumstances in America led to a different conception of the role of the government and the state more generally. American society had an egalitarian structure, long before the American Revolution (with the abstraction of slavery). For this reason, many historians held the opinion that there was never a revolution *stricto sensu* in America.[107]

The distrust dominant in the United States toward the exercise of collective power led it to organize its legal order in such a way as to limit the impact of government upon liberty. The American revolutionaries saw their efforts as conceiving a new political science, as inaugurating a *novus ordo seclorum*.[108] Respect for the Constitution is associated with the ideology of American patriotism and constitutes an element of their national identity. Although the ideas of government by contract or consent, popular sovereignty, and natural rights existed both in France and in America, the distinctive work of the American Revolution was to work out a model for the realization of these ideas.[109] The role of the government is associated with a version of natural law underlining the importance of individual rights in America since the Founding Era.[110] As analyzed later in this book, natural rights discourse emerged in America shortly before the Declaration of Independence in order to delegitimize attempts by the British parliament to enact legislation limiting the negative liberties of the people in the colonies. A paternalistic conception of the role of the government, like the one that is dominant in Europe, did not become dominant there.

Freedom of speech plays an important role in this system of government as it ensures accountability and transparency. If government is created to protect natural negative rights, freedom of speech is an exemplary negative right. In fact, it is an

[106] Gordon Wood, *The Creation of the American Republic: 1776–1787* (Chapel Hill, NC: University of North Carolina Press, 1998), 173; Bernard Bailyn, *The Ideological Origins of The American Revolution* (Cambridge, MA: Harvard University Press, 1967); Eric Nelson, *The Royalist Revolution: Monarchy and the American Founding* (Cambridge, MA: Harvard University Press, 2014).

[107] See for example Wood, *Creation of the American Republic*, 3.

[108] See Forrest McDonald, *Novus Ordo Seclorum: The Intellectual Origins of the Constitution* (University Press of Kansas, 1985); Stanley N. Katz, "The American Constitution: A Revolutionary Interpretation," in Richard Beeman, Stephen Botein, and Edward C. Carter II, eds., *Beyond Confederation, Origins of the Constitution and American National Identity* (Chapel Hill: University of North Carolina Press, 1987), 23–37.

[109] R. R. Palmer, *The Age of the Democratic Revolution: A Political History of Europe and America, 1760–1800* (Princeton University Press, 1959), 214.

[110] Wood, *Creation of the American Republic*, 37; Gordon Wood, *The Radicalism of the American Revolution* (New York: Vintage, 1993); Gordon Wood, *Empire of Liberty* (Oxford University Press 2009); Louis Hartz, *The Liberal Tradition in America* (New York: Harcourt, Brace & World, 1955); Seymour Martin Lipset, *American Exceptionalism: A Double-Edged Sword* (New York: W. W. Norton & Company, 1996), 87.

important liberty that ensures the protection of all other rights serving as a check on government. It enhances the checks and balances of the American system of government. As argued in this book, the twentieth century development of a libertarian conception of free speech was the evolution of the theory of government that emerged in America during the Founding Era.

The kind of power against which Americans were revolting influenced their conception of state power in the next phase. As Arendt notes, the American Revolution was the result of a conflict with limited monarchy; the government of the king and the parliament from which the colonies emancipated themselves was not a *potestas lebigus soluta*, a power above the laws, as in France.[111] Just as the ancient order did not recognize an omnipotent power to authority, the new power established in America was understood ex ante as limited too. The French Revolution made a transfer of legitimacy from an absolute king toward an assembly of representatives without any alteration concerning the ex ante understanding of the extent of the power of the government. The American Revolution, in transferring legitimacy from the British parliament to local governments in America, presupposed an understanding of government limited by bills of rights.

The importance of freedom of speech emerges with the ideology of opposition which lead to the American Revolution.[112] Freedom of speech becomes important as it is at the same time a negative and a political liberty. The English radicals of the eighteenth century were advocating for change in the definition of seditious libel, to allow freedom of the press to criticize the government.[113] This tradition of the radical Whigs and the emerging popular ideology were part of an intellectual tradition that underlined the importance of political speech for popular sovereignty. In this context, the conception of the protection of freedom of expression in the United States can be understood by considering the wide context of the "age of democratic revolutions."[114] The ideological current that inspired the Americans of the period was the social and political thought of the Whigs of the English Civil War and the period of the Commonwealth of England.[115] Transforming Christian liberties into

111 Arendt, *On Revolution*, 157.

112 On this point, see David Rabban, "The Ahistorical Historian: Leonard Levy and Freedom of Expression in Early American History," *Stanford Law Review* 37 (1985), 795–856, 800. Rabban criticizes Leonard Levy who downplays the importance of free speech during the founding era in *Emergence of a Free Press* (New York: Oxford University Press, 1985). There are others who note that freedom of speech was a principle of the Founding Era: Zachariah Chafee, Jr., *How Human Rights Got into the Constitution* (Boston University Press, 1952); and David Kairys, "Freedom of Speech," in David Kairys, ed., *The Politics of the Law* (New York: Basic Books 1998), 194 ff.

113 Wood, *Creation of the American Republic*, 317.

114 According to the famous title of the book by Robert Roswel Palmer.

115 Caroline Robbins, *The Eighteenth Century Commonwealthman: Studies in the Transmission, Development and Circumstance of English Liberal Thought from the Restoration of Charles III till the War with the Thirteen Colonies* (New York: Atheneum, 1969, [c. 1959]), 385; Wood, *Creation of the American Republic*, 22; McDonald, *Novus Ordo Seclorum*, 66.

natural rights and political demands, their engagement with liberty of conscience was translated into support for freedom of expression and the press.[116]

The Whigs stressed the need for participation of the people in the government, political or civil liberty, the power of a civil society or state to govern itself as it deems proper by its own laws, as well as negative liberty against the government. John Trenchard and Thomas Gordon were radical Whigs famous in England, authors of the journal *Independent Whig* and the famous *Cato's Letters*, which present a comprehensive synthesis of the republican and Lockean thought that informed the American struggle for independence. *Cato's Letters* emphasizes that freedom of political expression provided the most effective means for the people to keep their sovereignty and liberties against the government. Freedom of speech was described in *Cato's Letters* as the "bulwark of liberty" and the administration of government as the "Attendance of the Trustees of the People upon the Interest and Affairs of the People."[117] In the generation of the American Revolution, the emphasis of Joseph Priestley and Richard Price on the relation between freedom of political expression and popular sovereignty was very influential.[118] During the colonial period the Americans considered the press as a fundamental tool in order to unify the people in the conflict against the threat imposed by the British crown. The structure of the Federal Constitution and the First Amendment consolidated these views.

The institutions of the contemporary American republic are founded upon a distrust toward the legislative branch and toward mechanisms of representation more generally. The conflict that led to the Declaration of Independence was due, among other things, to the enactment of legislation mostly of fiscal nature, as expressed in the motto "no taxation without representation." Taxation by the British parliament upon the colonies was legitimate in the eyes of the British government by reference to the theory of virtual representation. According to this theory, the colonies, whose people were part of the English people, were represented in the British parliament although they did not elect representatives there, for the aim of representation was to discover the common interest of the English people as a whole and not to defend the interests of social factions.[119] The American Revolution was a reaction to this theory of virtual representation.[120]

116 Anthony Handley Lincoln, *Some Political and Social Ideas of English Dissent, 1763–1800* (Cambridge, 1938), 182.

117 Thomas Gordon and John Trenchard, *Cato's Letters*, vol. I, no. 15, Gordon, "Of Freedom Of Speech: That The Same Is Inseparable From Publick Liberty" (Indianapolis: Liberty Fund, 1995 [1724]), 79–81.

118 On this influence see Dabid Rabban, "Ahistorical Historian," 824, 828, 844.

119 Wood, *Creation of the American Republic*, 173; J. G. A. Pocock, "1776: The Revolution Against Parliament," in *Three British Revolutions: 1641, 1689, 1776* (Princeton University Press, 1980); Nelson, *Royalist Revolution*, 70.

120 This was a recurrent issue in the major political thinkers and actors of the time like James Otis. James Otis, "A Vindication of the British Colonies" [1765], in Richard Samuelson ed. *Collected Political Writings of James Otis* (Indianapolis, IN: Liberty Fund, 2015), 186; Richard Bland of

A significant part of American historiography discusses the negative character of rights as dominant in the foundation of American constitutionalism.[121] Other works emphasize the "republican synthesis" as the innovation that the American revolutionaries brought about in the understanding of republicanism.[122] A comparison with the French approach can help better evaluate the subtle nuances in the understanding of republicanism between the two systems. Both legal and political systems express republican ideals. In the United States, the common good is defined as the need to protect negative liberties. In France, negative liberties are protected only to the extent that they are compatible with the common good.

In America greater weight is given to the idea of natural rights within republicanism out of a distrust toward the government that can be traced back to the Declaration of Independence. Bernard Bailyn, who studied the American intellectual movement before the revolution in the writings of pamphlets in circulation during the revolutionary period, shows that although they referred to the classical authors of Greek and Roman antiquity, the ideas that inspired them were drawn from the rationalism of the Enlightenment.[123] John Adams wrote a treaty discussing the failures of Ancient Greek and Roman democracies and how their mistakes could be instructive for Americans in their effort to construct a functioning democracy.[124] When the Americans moved to create their state constitutions and the Federal Constitution, their understanding of republicanism was influenced by the intellectual heritage of the debates around the Declaration of Independence.

Neo-Roman theories of republicanism were appealing to the Americans precisely because some idea of protecting the individual exists in them. They were also aware that they were modifying these theories, creating a totally new understanding of republicanism that would be associated with the protection of natural

Virginia, *An Inquiry into the Rights of the British Colonies* (Williamsburg: Alexander Purdie & Co., 1766), 27; Thomas Jefferson, "A Summary View of the Rights of British America" [1774], in Paul Leicester Ford, ed., *The Works of Thomas Jefferson*, vol. 2 (New York and London: G.P. Putnam's Sons, 1904), 49–89. See also Nelson, *Royalist Revolution*, 66–107.

121 Carl Becker, *The Declaration of Independence* (New York: Vintage Books 1958); Bailyn, *Ideological Origins*.

122 Michael P. Zuckert, *Natural Rights and the New Republicanism* (Princeton University Press, 1994); Michael P. Zuckert, *The Natural Rights Republic: Studies in the Foundation of the American Political Tradition* (University of Notre Dame Press, 1996). For a nuanced vision of the understanding of liberty in America see also *Aspects of American Liberty, Philosophical, Historical and Political* (Philadelphia: The American Philosophical Society ed., 1977). For an emphasis on the neo-Roman elements within American republicanism, see J. G. A. Pocock, *The Machiavellian Moment: Florentine Political Thought and the Atlantic Republican Tradition* (Princeton University Press, 1975). For an emphasis on the influence of elements of Roman republicanism upon the US Constitution, see M. N. Sellers, *American Republicanism: Roman Ideology in the United States Constitution* (London: MacMillan, 1994); M. N. S. Sellers, *The Sacred Fire of Liberty: Republicanism, Liberalism and the Law* (London: MacMillan, 1998).

123 Baylin, *Ideological Origins*, 26.

124 See John Adams, *Defence of the Constitutions of Government of the United States of America* [1778], in *The Works of John Adams*, vol. 4 (Boston: Charles C. Little and James Brown, 1851), chaps. VII-IX, 469–578.

rights.[125] The idea of a mixed constitution was also present in neo-Roman theories. Machiavelli discusses a theory of mixed government, building off Polybius' thesis through the medieval rediscovery of Aristotle.[126] Machiavelli considers the best form of government to be the one that provides institutional representation for all social classes within a republic. The social power of the various classes would be offset if it found expression in balanced political power. And this would result to the best possible protection for the freedom of the republic but also negative liberty (security). This idea evolved later into the understanding of "checks and balances" and the separation of powers dominant in the United States.[127]

Although the Americans admired the Florentine republican experience, they believed that their circumstances made possible a range of political experimentation beyond what was already known and practiced in Europe.[128] In their opinion, governments are exposed to corruption. The fear of the excessive ambition of governments, which was seen as having the potential to corrupt, is characteristic of the thought of the Whigs.[129] Eighteenth-century Americans considered humans as beings of self-interest, an idea articulated by David Hume, which means that they cannot be trusted.[130] They read in Hume that human depravity imposes the institution of forms and methods of control on any human business.[131] They considered that virtue cannot control vice, but the system of government should be organized in

125 In this respect for the governments of the states, see Adams, *Defence*, chaps. VII-IX. Similarly *The Federalist* contains criticisms of ancient republics. See for instance James Madison, "No. 63: A Further View of the Constitution of the Senate, in Regard to the Duration of Appointment of Its Members," in Alexander Hamilton, John Jay, and James Madison, *The Federalist*, ed. George W. Carey and James McClellan (Indianapolis, IN: Liberty Fund, 2001), 327. On this point, see the analysis in Chapter 3. See also Thomas L. Pangle, *The Spirit of Modern Republicanism: The Moral Vision of the American Founders and the Philosophy of Locke* (University of Chicago Press, 1988), 43.

126 Nicolo Machiavelli, *Discourses*, in *The Historical, Political and Diplomatic Writings* (Boston: James R. Osgood and Company, 1881), bk. 1, chaps. 2–6, 98.

127 Mark E. Berghausen and Skylar Albertson, "The Rise and Fall of the Separation of Powers," *Northwestern University Law Review* 106 (2012), 527–606, 534.

128 David A. J. Richards, *Foundations of American Constitutionalism* (New York: Oxford University Press, 1989), 22.

129 Wood, *Creation of the American Republic*, 21, Daniel Walker Howe, *The Political Culture of the American Whigs* (University of Chicago Press, 1979), 30.

130 Richard Hofstader, "The Founding Fathers: An Age of Realism," in Robert H. Horwitz, ed., *The Moral Foundations of the American Republic* (Charlottesville: University Press of Virginia, 1979), 73–85, 77 ff.; Forrest MacDonald, *Novus Ordo Seclorum*, 188–89.

131 David Hume, *That Politics May Be Reduced to a Science*, in Knud Haakonssen, ed., *Political Essays* (Cambridge University Press, 1994), 4–15, 11. Hume thinks that consequences may be deduced from the force of laws and of particular forms of government as any which mathematical sciences afford: the modes of government that have the form and methods of control proved stability and wisdom, while the governments of Athens and Rome resulted in the destruction of these governments because of defaults in their constitution. Good law can beget order and moderation in governments, even where manners and customs have instilled little humanity or justice into the tempers of men. On Hume's influence upon the American Founders, see Douglas Adair, "That Politics May Be Reduced to a Science: David Hume, James Madison and the Tenth Federalist," in Douglas Adair, Trevor Colbourn, eds., *Fame and the Founding Fathers* (Virginia: Institute of Early American History and Culture, 1974), 93–106.

a way that vice stops vice. Although the French revolutionaries believed that power is something positive once it is transferred from a monarch to a parliament, the Americans of this period feared the corrupting potential of power. Madison's phrase that "ambition should counteract ambition" expresses the same spirit regarding the federal government.[132]

The Federal Constitution of 1787, developed in order to overcome the crises caused by the previous Confederation, which instituted a weak federal structure, inherited principles existing within local governments.[133] The new federal government would protect the states against "foreign dangers," regulate relations with foreign nations, maintain harmony and relations among states, provide for some objects of general utility and retain the states from certain injurious acts.[134] The understanding of natural rights and of self-government during the revolution had repercussions on the constitution of the federal state. The debate on the ratification of the constitutional project of 1787 allowed them to see the political and philosophical implications of the Revolution of 1776 with greater clarity.[135] The crucial question was how to create a central power without compromising liberty or reproducing the British centralized system of government, against which they had declared independence. As Bailyn notes, many of the ideas developed during the debates on the constitutions of the states were refined and elaborated in view of their application to the Federal Constitution.[136] The need for a strong centralized government, which was taken for granted by the French revolutionaries, was feared in America. The challenge that *The Federalist* addressed was how to create a central government that would be strong enough to guarantee the subsistence of the Federal state, unlike other failed federations, while being compatible with the imaginary of a limited government that would not impede excessively upon the liberties of the

132 James Madison, "No. 51," in Hamilton, Jay, and Madison, *The Federalist*, 268. See Richard K. Matthews, *If Men Were Angels: James Madison and the Heartless Empire of Reason* (Lawrence: University Press of Kansas, 1995), 22.

133 Pauline Maier, *Ratification: The People Debate the Constitution, 1787–1788* (New York: Simon & Schuster, 2010); John M. Murrin, "A Roof without Walls: The Dilemma of American National Identity," in Richard Beeman, Stephen Botein and Edward C. Carter II, eds., *Beyond Confederation, Origins of the Constitution and American National Identity* (Chapel Hill and London: University of North Carolina Press, 1987), 333.

134 James Madison, "No. 41," in Hamilton, Jay, and Madison, *The Federalist*, 208. On security, see Alexander Hamilton, "No. 11," in Hamilton, Jay, and Madison, *The Federalist*, 49; and Alexander Hamilton, "No. 16," in Hamilton, Jay, and Madison, *The Federalist*, 76.

135 Michael Klarman, *The Framers' Coup, The Making of the United States Constitution* (Oxford University Press, 2016), 12. Under the Articles of the Confederation, Congress lacked the power to impose taxes and regulate interstate and foreign commerce. Ibid., 15. The national government lacking the power to impose taxes could not fund itself and the states seeing themselves as fully sovereign engaged in economic policies that from a national point of view were damaging to other states See Mark Tushnet, *The Constitution of the United States of America: A Contextual Analysis* (Oxford: Hart, 2015), 10. See also Carl J. Friedrich and Robert G. McCloskey, *From the Declaration of Independence to the Constitution: The Roots of American Constitutionalism* (New York: The Liberal Arts Press, 1954).

136 Baylin, *Ideological Origins*, 228.

citizens.[137] The Federalists had to persuade people that the new central government would protect from external dangers like every other government known at the time, while respecting liberty internally.

Those who objected to the creation of a federal government were making anew the democratic and libertarian arguments that had led to the Declaration of Independence. "Natural rights" discourse emerged again to stress the need to limit the sphere of the federal government.[138] Strengthening the central power would have the potential to result in a monarchy-like regime.[139] Creating a centralized legislative power contained the danger of "legislative despotism," should this power remain unrestrained.[140] The need to protect freedom of the press was mentioned with great emphasis in the writings of those who were critical to a Federal Constitution.[141] Freedom of the press – "the right of the people to express their sentiments upon every public measure" – was seen as an important element for a "free nation."[142] The distrust toward the government was associated with the "checking function" of the press. Freedom of the press was to figure as an "invaluable personal right" in a bill of rights according to a conception of limited government.[143] The press was considered to be the factor of "greatest part of the liberty that exists" to the extent that it informs the public on politics.[144] Liberty of conscience was discussed as a "natural right" that is not among those that are surrendered for the good of society.[145]

137 See for instance Alexander Hamilton, "No. 23," in Hamilton, Jay, and Madison, *The Federalist* 115–16: "A government the constitution of which renders it unfit to be intrusted with all the powers which a free people *ought to delegate to any government*, would be an unsafe and improper depository of the NATIONAL INTERESTS." See also Alexander Hamilton, "No. 26," in Hamilton, Jay, and Madison, *The Federalist*, 126–27; James Madison, "No. 37," in Hamilton, Jay, and Madison, *The Federalist*, 181.

138 See for instance Brutus, "To the Citizens of the State of New-York," N in Herbert Storing and Dry Murray, eds., *The Complete Anti-Federalist*, vol. 2 (Chicago University Press, 1981), 372 ff.

139 For the relevant discussion in relation to the powers of the executive see George Mason, "Opposition to a Unitary Executive," in Max Farrand, ed., *The Records of the Federal Convention of 1787*, vol. 1 (New Haven, CT: Yale University Press, 1911), 113.

140 James Wilson, "Intervention to the Debate of June 16, 1787," in Farrand, ed., *Records of the Federal Convention of 1787*, vol. 1, 266.

141 George Mason, "Objections to the Constitution of Government Formed by the Convention (1787)," in Herbert Storing and Dry Murray eds., *The Complete Anti-Federalist*, vol. 2. (Chicago, Chicago University Press, 1981), 13; Brutus, "To the Citizens of the State of New York," in Storing and Murray, eds., *Complete Anti-Federalist*, vol. 2, 375; Centinel I, "To the Freemen of Pennsylvania," in Storing and Murray, eds., *Complete Anti-Federalist*, vol. 2, 142; Centinel I, "To the People of Pennsylvania," in Storing and Murray, eds., *Complete Anti-Federalist*, vol. 2, 143–44; Essays of an Old Whig I, in Storing and Murray, eds., *Complete Anti-Federalist*, vol. 2 (Chicago University Press, 1982), 20–21; Aristocrotis, "The Government of Nature Delineated or an Exact Picture of the New Federal Constitution," in Storing and Murray, eds., *Complete Anti-Federalist*, vol. 3 (Chicago University Press, 1981), 198.

142 Centinel I, "To the People of Pennsylvania," 143–44.

143 Ibid.

144 Essays of an Old Whig I, 20–1.

145 Essays of an Old Whig, V, in Storing and Murray, eds., *Complete Anti-Federalist*, vol. 3, 34.

Responding to the Anti-Federalists' concerns, *The Federalist* is permeated with passages that show how creating a central government does not necessarily mean tyranny. The Federalists insisted that the American Constitution would bring about a government of "a mixed nature," which had no precedent. The centralized government would be organized in such a way as to distribute power, forming a self-correcting system so that no body or institutional center would win a monopoly of force or influence that would dominate the nation. The limitation of government by the division of powers in "checks and balances" would not be seen as a concession to weakness nor as a refusal of democracy but as the best possible guarantee of liberty.[146] Madison noted more insightfully than Montesquieu himself how difficult it is to distinguish between the legitimate authority of the three branches of government.[147] He takes even further Montesquieu's conception of the separation of powers.[148] Although for Montesquieu it was enough that the various branches are incarnated by different agents, Madison insinuates that Montesquieu has not denied that the various branches should control one another.[149] Madison believed that they could serve as a check on one another in case one of them would usurp power beyond what would be constitutionally apportioned. For both Hamilton and Madison, a large republic would ensure better the protection of negative liberty against the irrational tendencies of popular majorities.[150]

Steve Pincus notes that the American revolutionaries' conception of the role of the government aimed to spur growth and to create the preconditions for a solid commercial society.[151] Indeed, *The Federalist* indicates a concern in favor of a government, which would project strength abroad in order to defend the nation's commercial interests. The same government would make sure that commerce operated smoothly across states. This is in conformity with Adam Smith's conception of the role of the government as promoting a free market economy.[152] And just as Smith was being critical of the interventionist state of the monarchies of Europe upon free commerce, Hamilton was motivated by a concern to establish government intervention to the extent that is strictly necessary for the same purpose. Government

146 Alexander Hamilton, "No. 9," in Hamilton, Jay, and Madison, *The Federalist*, 38. See also Michael Kammen, *A Machine That Would Go of Itself: The Constitution in American Culture* (New York: Knopf, 1987); Henry Steele Commager, *The Empire of Reason* (New York: Anchor Press, Doubleday, 1977), 234.

147 James Madison, "No. 37," in Hamilton, Jay, and Madison, *The Federalist*, 182.

148 James Madison, "No. 47," in Hamilton, Jay, and Madison, *The Federalist*, 251.

149 Ibid.

150 Alexander Hamilton, "No. 9," in Hamilton, Jay, and Madison, *The Federalist*, 39 ff. Madison discusses the same passage from Montesquieu James Madison, "No. 43," in Hamilton, Jay, and Madison, *The Federalist*, 227.

151 Steve Pincus, *The Heart of the Declaration: The Founders' Case for an Activist Government* (New Haven, CT: Yale University Press, 2016), 96.

152 On Smith's influence upon the understanding of the formation of the commercial society in America in the post-independence era see also Caroline Winterer, *American Enlightenment: Happiness in the Age of Reason* (New Haven, CT: Yale University Press 2016), 209.

intervention is a matter of degree. Guaranteeing the preconditions of the operation of a free market economy does not necessarily go together with imposing a comprehensive vision of the good upon society and aiming to form virtuous citizens.

Interpretations of the debates between Federalists and Anti-Federalists stress their concern to create a government that would be strong in order to project military power abroad.[153] Projecting strength abroad in order to protect the interests of a commercial republic does not legitimize a strong government inward. The imaginary of limited government that should protect the natural rights of the citizens was present in the supporters and the opponents of the Federal Constitution. The Federalists did aim to create a strong government that would project military power abroad because only this kind of government can protect negative liberty effectively internally.

A first challenge to the First Amendment emerged during the debates on the Sedition Act. It showed that free speech was seen as a value important for democracy already since the Founding Era.[154] The Act was enacted by Congress in 1798, on the brink of a war with France, by a weak Federalist majority.[155] It criminalized the action of printing, expressing, or publishing any "false, scandalous and malicious writing or writings against the government of the United States, or either house of the Congress of the United States, or the President of the United States, with intent to defame the said government, or either house of the said Congress, or the said President, or to bring them, or either of them, into contempt or disrepute."[156] Seen as a temporary emergency measure, it was set to expire on March 3, 1801, the last day of Adams's term of office. The Federalists claimed that the excesses of the republican press threatened the nation's existence by spreading falsehoods. In their opinion the Act was a legitimate exercise of the powers of the parliament. The parliament was exercising power delegated by the people. The Anti-Federalists criticized the Act, referring to radical Whig arguments. They saw in the Federalists' attempt to reconcile popular sovereignty with federal government an inappropriate application of antirepublican principles. Thomas Jefferson and James Madison secretly authored the Kentucky and Virginia Resolutions in the fall of 1798, which declared that the

153 See Max Edling, *A Revolution in Favor of Government: Origins of the U.S. Constitution and the Making of the American State* (Oxford University Press, 2003).

154 Gordon Wood, "The Democratization of Mind in the American Revolution," in Horwitz, ed., *Moral Foundations*, 102–128, 123.

155 The Federalists enacted the Sedition Act in a sensitive political context: the failure of the diplomatic negotiations with France, which was seen as threatening to divide the American people from its government via the French party. When the Republicans who had opposed the domestic and foreign programs refused to cooperate, the Federalists enacted the Sedition Act. J. Smith, *Freedom's Fetters: The Alien and Sedition Laws and American Civil Liberties* (Ithaca, NY: Cornell University Press,1956), 425, cited in Rabban, "The Ahistorical Historian," 850.

156 "An Act in Addition to the Act, Entitled 'An Act for the Punishment of Certain Crimes Against the United States,'" July 14, 1798, Yale Law School Avalon Project available at: https://avalon.law.yale.edu/18th_century/sedact.asp [accessed 26 July 2019].

Sedition Act violated the First Amendment because it impeded the right to examine public figures.[157] The Kentucky and Virginia legislatures invited other states to join them declaring the Sedition Act void. Madison notes the importance of the liberty of the press as a "bulwark of liberty," adding that some "licentiousness" in the exercise of the liberty of the press is "an evil inseparable from the good with which it is allied; perhaps it is a shoot which cannot be stripped from the stalk without wounding vitally the plant from which it is torn."[158] In the same speech, Madison notes the detrimental consequences for intellectual and religious freedom that result from the regulation of freedom of speech by "arresting reason in her progress toward perfection."[159] The debates on the Act showed the importance of freedom of speech in the American system of government. Libertarian theorists rejected Blackstone's conception on the permissibility of limiting speech by the parliament which is sovereign.[160] Under the Act the government could limit any criticism of its policies.[161] This would be incompatible with popular sovereignty. They also rejected that there can be false political opinions under the First Amendment. Almost two centuries later the Supreme Court discussed the same ideas in some of its decisions affirming its doctrine of robust protection of freedom of speech.[162] In a context of popular indignation toward the law, which threatened the very existence of the Federalist Party, when Jefferson succeeded Adams in the presidency, he pardoned all sentences.[163]

The creation of the Federal Constitution led to constitutional changes at the level of the states too, which weakened their governments.[164] In fact, most of the current state constitutions were introduced after the Federal Constitution and influenced by it. Thirty-seven new state constitutions were adopted between 1800 to 1860.[165] Many contemporary state constitutions disperse power in a way that goes even beyond what the federal government does.[166] This dispersion has the form of dividing the executive branch among multiple officials each independently elected and the form of a stricter horizontal separation of powers among branches of state government. State

157 Geoffrey Stone, *Perilous Times: Free Speech in Wartime, From the Sedition Act of 1798 to the War on Terrorism* (New York, Norton, 2005), 34.

158 James Madison, "Address of the General Assembly to the People of the Commonwealth of Virginia" [1799], in *The Writings of James Madison*, vol. 6 (New York: G.P. Putnam's Sons, 1906), 336.

159 Ibid., 337.

160 Rabban, "The Ahistorical Historian," 852; Stone, *Perilous Times*, 75.

161 Stone, *Perilous Times*, 39.

162 "Under the First Amendment there is no such thing as a false idea. *Gertz* v. *Robert Welch, Inc.*, 418 US 323, 339 (1974).

163 Leon Whipple, *The Story of Civil Liberty in the United States* (Westport, CT: Greenwood Press, 1927), cited in David Kairys, *The Politics of the Law* (New York, Basic Books, 1998), 196. Forty years later on July 1840 Congress repaid all of the fines paid under the Sedition Act with interest. Stone, *Perilous Times*, 73.

164 Robert F. Williams, *The Law of American State Constitutions* (Oxford University Press, 2009), 75.

165 G. Alan Tarr, *Understanding State Constitutions* (Princeton University Press, 1998), 94.

166 James A. Gardner, *Interpreting State Constitutions: A Jurisprudence of Function in a Federal System* (University of Chicago Press, 2005), 169.

constitutions also contain limitations in the use of affirmative state powers such as the taxing and spending powers.[167] They also contain strong democratic checks, in the form of referenda. Some contemporary state constitutions provide that legislative bodies should operate part time and should have term limits. Some state constitutions provide that legislatures should meet only biennially.[168]

The hypothesis advanced here on the role of the government to limit speech is supported by writings that attempt to interpret why government intervention in the economy is only moderate in the United States. Louis Hartz and Martin Lipset propose that moderation in government and the rejection of the state as having the mission to protect dignity and material subsistence can be understood in relation to the fundamental sociocultural realities of America.[169] The sociological background in America led to a system of values that expresses pure rationalism. It is not inhibited by traditional values of rigid social classes derived from feudalism.[170] Louis Hartz argues that the idea of an omnipotent state and government is missing in America, as Americans only aimed to create a new political order in the absence of a feudal ideology in a world which was always liberal.[171] The absence of an aristocratic or feudal past, which is akin to the absence of a tradition of state paternalism, cannot legitimize the efforts of the least privileged social classes to mobilize government action to improve their situation. Socialism is strong where monarchical statism legitimized strong government and where elitism generated reaction from the least privileged. John Dewey also notes that in America the absence of feudalism gave less leverage to the Benthamite system of legal and administrative reform.[172] The individualist premises in America prevented the appearance of a tyranny of the nation, because the logic of liberalism led to a perception of the dangers of coercion.[173]

Its critics note that the New Deal, just like other movements in Europe during the same period, was to a great extent "a contradictory mix of pre- and post-capitalist elements" that could be described as being close to social-democratic planning.[174]

167 The Michigan Constitution forbids the Michigan legislature from imposing annual property taxes in excess of "15 mills on each dollar of the assessed valuation of property."

168 These are the legislatures of Arkansas, Kentucky, Nevada, North Dakota, Oregon, and Texas.

169 Hartz, *Liberal Tradition*; Lipset, *American Exceptionalism*.

170 The conception of life which was called "Americanism" in Antonio Gramsci, "The Intellectuals," in *Selections from the Prisons Notebooks* (New York: International Publishers, 1971), cited in Lipset, *American Exceptionalism*, 87.

171 Hartz, *Liberal Tradition*, 173. For this author there is an association between the Bourbons and Babeuf, exemplified by Rousseau. The civil war and the rejection by the South of the liberalism of the Founders and the acceptation of servitude does not mean for this author that the American liberal idea is weak. The feudal reaction of the South was theorized by an organic conception of society marked with such a hyperbole that it was impotent to destroy the dominant Lockean spirit, being just a logical farce in the general frame of the enlightenment. Ibid.

172 John Dewey, *Liberalism and Social Action* (New York G.P. Putnam's Sons, 1935), 17.

173 Hartz refers to the New Deal period as a period aiming only to the resolution of problems where ethics was forgotten. Hartz, *Liberal Tradition*, 231.

174 See Cass R. Sunstein, *The Second Bill of Rights: FDR's Unfinished Revolution and Why we Need it More than Ever* (New York: Basic Books, 2004) for a criticism of this thesis. See Wolfgang Schivelbusch,

Nevertheless, even critics accept that the absence of class consciousness in the United States prevented the emergence of socialism.[175] The New Deal and other periods of crisis indicate that there has been vacillation in the degree of government intervention that is necessary to ensure a well-functioning market. Government action is deployed in degrees. Ensuring the proper functioning of the market during a crisis does not mean accepting government intervention in other areas such as limiting speech or economic redistribution.

Even in periods during which the normative understanding of democracy changes in the United States, such as the period of the New Deal, a paternalistic vision of the state did not become dominant. The distrust toward the role of government was never converted into trust. The role of government limits itself to what is strictly necessary to help the country out of the economic crisis. The change in the normative conception of democracy did not provide the basis for a comprehensive plan of intervention in civil society. In this sense, the radicalism of the New Deal prevented the appearance of socialism in the profound anchoring of liberalism in American society. The New Deal was rather a "Great Exception" in the understanding of the role of the government in the United States.[176] Bruce Ackerman developed a theory founded on a "dualist" conception of the American constitutional order.[177] According to this conception, the actualizing interpretation of the constitutional clauses in the United States allowed for a change in the role of the government during the New Deal period as a response to the socioeconomic crisis that the country was facing. This change was equal to a "constitutional revolution." Ackerman also accepts a general tendency of distrust toward the government. Important though it was, government intervention in the economy was short-lived and limited to saving the economic system consistently with a limited conception of the role of the government.

Natural rights discourse, omnipresent in America during the Founding Era, is reflected today in the protection of freedom of speech.[178] The tradition of French republicanism is based on the idea of a unified state that is trusted to provide for the

Three New Deals: Reflections on Roosevelt's America, Mussolini's Italy, and Hitler's Germany, 1933–1939 (New York: Metropolitan Books 2006), 11.

175 Schivelbusch, *Three New Deals*, 187.

176 See Jefferson Cowie, *The Great Exception: The New Deal and the Limits of American Politics* (Princeton University Press, 2016).

177 In the book of capital importance for American constitutional theory, *We the People*, vol. 1, *Foundations* (Cambridge, MA: Harvard University Press, 1991), vol. 2, *Transformations* (Cambridge, MA: Harvard University Press, 1998).

178 Thinkers that articulated a natural rights discourse to justify the rupture with the British parliament during the Founding Era were among others James Otis and Samuel Adams. See James Otis, *The Rights of the British Colonies, Asserted and Proved* (Boston & London: J. Almon, 1764), 29, 31, 42; James Otis, *A Vindication of the British Colonies* [1765], in Samuelson, ed., *Collected Political Writings*, 186; Samuel Adams, "The Rights of the Colonists: Report of the Committee of Correspondence to the Boston Town Meeting" [November 20, 1772], *Old South Leaflets* No. 173, available at: https://memory.loc.gov/service/gdc/scd0001/2009/20090211001ri//20090211001ri.pdf; Thomas Jefferson, "A Summary View of the Rights of British America" [1774], in Ford, ed., *Works of Thomas Jefferson*, vol. 2, 49–89.

good of the citizens.[179] Modern French republicanism contains more elements from antiquity associated with a deep trust toward the government. As I argue, this form of republicanism makes denser state regulation of expressive freedoms legitimate in France. Freedom of expression is protected in the case law of the US Supreme Court as a negative liberty, as the absence of state interference and as liberty associated with self-government. A conception of freedom of expression as collective liberty also underlies its protection,[180] since one of the principal causes of the movement for independence was the violation of the colonies' self-government by the British parliament. The ex ante understanding in favor of negative liberty and of the special importance of freedom of expression as a liberty promoting self-government gives rise to a tendency among American judges to overprotect this liberty to the detriment of other values. French judges, on the contrary, inspired by a conception that it is legitimate for the state and the government to define the content of liberty and its limits, and to ensure the preconditions for the exercise of liberty, see themselves as obliged to limit this liberty in order to protect other values. Human dignity understood as social status and the understanding of the role of the government as having legitimacy to define the content of liberty are elements that justify limiting freedom of expression to protect other values in France.

2.4 DECLARATIONS AND THEIR SPIRIT

The Americans invented a political theory that would be in position to reconcile republicanism with natural rights. The differences relating to the political theory of the French and the American revolutionaries are visible in the texts declaring liberties. These texts can offer very important insights on the understanding of liberty within a legal system. The French aimed, among other things, to establish during their revolution a new political sociability, to reaffirm on the ideal level the principles and individual qualities that make a human life worthy of being called human.[181] This advanced idealism of the French Declaration of the Rights of Man and the Citizen, along with the political problems of mass poverty and the conception of the role of the state as the agent that will provide for the guarantee of this dignity in all possible senses of the term, contributed to the conception of republicanism of a different nature in France. The recognition of liberty would depend on the position given to it by the state, its enactment by the law. In other words, as Hannah Arendt notes, the rights consecrated by the Declaration of the Rights of

179 On a discussion of French republicanism as based on the idea of a unified strong government which is trusted to realize the liberties of the citizens see Jaume, *Discours jacobin*, Gauchet, *Révolution des droits de l'homme*; Rosanvallon, *La démocratie inachevée*; Rosanvallon, *Le modèle politique français*.

180 Richard Primus, "An Introduction to the Nature of American Rights," in Barry Alan Shain, ed., *The Nature of Rights at the American Founding and Beyond* (Charlottesville and London: University of Virginia Press, 2007), 15–24, 23.

181 For an analysis of these ideas, see Chapters 2 and 3.

Man and the Citizen were not conceived as indications of the limits of all legitimate government but as its foundations.[182]

Declarations of rights are speech acts whose pragmatic meaning can be illuminated by reference to the general context of their enunciation. They respond to concrete political problems.[183] Instead of looking only at the locutionary meaning of a declaration, we need to focus on its illocutionary and perlocutionary sense: their importance for intellectual history and the progress that they express and bring in their respective contexts. The two peoples on each side of the Atlantic constitute themselves through the performative of their declarations. With the American Declaration the people declare themselves independent by inventing an identity.[184] The French people in their own context perform through their Declaration a new structure of society. They institute a new political sociability against a past structured in concentric circles around royal power. The French Declaration became part of the "bloc of constitutionality" in France since the Constitution of 1958 and the 1971 decision of the French Constitutional Council on freedom of association.[185] Still, as Georges Vedel notes, it has always constituted a sort of "quasi-existential belief in a rule,"[186] as the knowledge of the text has always been part of the formation of citizenship in France. The political life of the Third Republic was formed under its influence and the administrative courts were applying it for a long time, although the constitutional value of the text had not been declared. The American Declaration has always played a similar role in the collective consciousness.

Although the two declarations are the result of a common intellectual evolution, they point toward two different conceptions of constitutionalism. The difference can be described as that between negative and positive constitutionalism.[187] Both declarations aim to protect the negative rights of citizens. In France, the protection of negative rights goes together with a conception of an interventionist state that can

182 Arendt, *On Revolution*, 148.

183 The analysis of declarations as speech acts is based on the insights of John Austin, *How to Do Things with Words?* (Cambridge, MA: Harvard University Press, 1975). On declarations as performative, see also Jacques Derrida, "Declarations of Independence," *in Negotiations: Interventions and Interviews 1971–2001* (Redwood City, CA: Stanford University Press, 2002), 47; Alain Trognon, "La déclaration en tant qu'acte de discours," in François Borella, ed., *Les valeurs de la Révolution devant la science actuelle* (Presses Universitaires de Nancy, 1990), 79–96; Danielle Allen, *Our Declaration: A Reading of the Declaration of Independence in Defense of Equality* (New York: Norton 2014), 92 ff.

184 Jacques Derrida, *Otobiographies: l'enseignement de Nietzsche et la politique du nom propre* (Paris: Galilée, 1984), 25. See also, Alain Trognon, "La déclaration," 79–96.

185 71–44 DC, Rec. 29, RJC I-24.

186 Georges Vedel, "Intervention in the Debate on the Presentation by Michel Troper, 'La Déclaration des droits de l'homme et du citoyen en 1789,'" in *La Déclaration des droits de l'homme et du citoyen et la jurisprudence* (Paris: Presses Universitaires de France, 1989), 27; see also Georges Vedel, "Place de la Déclaration dans le 'bloc de constitutionnalité,'" in *La Déclaration des droits de l'homme et du citoyen et la jurisprudence* (Paris: Presses Universitaires de France, 1989), 35–64.

187 For the distinction between negative and positive constitutionalism, see Martin Loughlin, "The Constitutional Imagination," *The Modern Law Review* 78 (2015), 1–25.

assure that citizens can exercise these rights. In this respect, the French understanding reflects a conception of positive constitutionalism. The concern to make sure that citizens can enjoy "real" liberty and not just "formal" liberty affects the understanding of constitutionalism in France. This is associated with a degree of greater state intervention in defining the content and limits of rights. This applies to freedom of expression to the extent that it is legitimate for the state in France to define its content and its limits. It is also legitimate for it to protect individuals from modes of self-expression that are considered as dictated by a "false consciousness" as the burka ban and the dwarf-throwing shows.

The "*legicentrism*" (centrality of the law) of the French Declaration indicates this trust toward the legislator in defining the content and limits of the rights proclaimed.[188] The prestige of the law comes from a triple equivalence, to the extent that the law expresses the generality of the rule as origin (product of the parliament) the generality as form (impersonal character of the norm), and generality as mode of administration.[189] According to the internal logic of the French Declaration of the summer of 1789, state-enacted law has an important role in defining the content and limits of rights of man.[190] The idea dominant in France is that the law, instead of threatening rights, gives them an effective reality.

The wording of Article 11 of the French Declaration, which protects freedom of expression, is exemplary of the centrality of the law that helps realize liberty. It foresees that the law may define what constitutes an "abuse" of the free communication of ideas and opinions.[191] In the same spirit, Article 10 of the same Declaration provides that freedom of religion should not "disturb the public order defined by law."[192] The law is the instrument of collective sovereignty, which allows the accomplishment of the liberty of each citizen through the power of all, while allowing independence.[193] In America during the Founding Era, many state constitutions contained clauses protecting freedom of the press against the legislative branch. This inspired the First Amendment to the Federal Constitution. During the nineteenth century, on the federal level, the regulation of freedom of expression

188 Stéphane Rials, *La Déclaration des droits de l'homme et du citoyen* (Paris: Hachette, 1988).

189 Rosanvallon, *Modèle politique français*, 85; see also Carré de Malberg, *Théorie générale du droit et de l'Etat* I, 293. Rousseau stresses this point in his "Lettres Écrites de la Montagne," in *Oeuvres Complètes* (Paris: Gallimard, 1964), 842–43. He states very clearly that freedom is only possible under a government of laws. Even the worse of laws is more valuable than the best leader, for while every leader has some preference, the law has no preferences. Ibid., 843.

190 Lucien Jaume, *La liberté et la loi: les origines philosophiques du libéralisme* (Paris: Fayard, 2000), 331.

191 According to which: "The free communication of ideas and of opinions is one of the most precious rights of man. Any citizen may therefore speak, write and publish freely, except what is tantamount to the abuse of this liberty as shall be defined by Law." (English translation by the Avalon Project, Documents in Law, History and Diplomacy, Yale Law School.)

192 "No one shall be disquieted on account of his opinions, including his religious views, provided their manifestation does not disturb the public order established by law." (English translation by the Avalon Project, Documents in Law, History and Diplomacy, Yale Law School.)

193 Gauchet, *Révolution des droits de l'Homme*, 177.

was sparse. On the level of the states, there were limitations to freedom of expression, due to the importation and application of the English common law.[194] There was already incompatibility between this common law and the theory of sovereignty adopted at the moment of the Declaration of Independence. This incompatibility became obvious to legal actors during the twentieth century.

The "legicentrism" of French constitutionalism stands in opposition to the distrust toward the legislator dominant in American constitutionalism. This distrust can be traced back to the ideas that led to the Declaration of Independence. The American Declaration of Independence is characterized by the recognition of the necessity of power and distrust toward power. The Americans declared their independence against the oppressive activity of the British parliament.[195] Facing an economic crisis, the British Empire decided to impose taxation on the colonies. A series of acts by the British parliament (the Sugar Act of 1764, the Stamp Act of 1765, and the Tea Act of 1773) caused agitation in the colonies, as they violated negative liberty through taxation that was seen as arbitrary. They drove those that emerged later as the major political actors of the early years of the republic to engage in "natural rights" discourse.[196] Whereas the first article of the French Declaration places liberty and equality on the same level,[197] the American Declaration does not express a concern to affirm equality separately but makes it a corollary of liberty and independence.[198] Among the acts enacted by the British parliament, the Stamp Act had a direct impact upon freedom of speech, as it concerned the freedom of the printers., The American bills of rights aim to guarantee rules that transcend the legislative branch.

A tradition of constitutionalism was already emerging in the American colonies in the seventeenth century. The charters accorded to the colonies as a matter of privilege and grace were seen as the written source of their basic freedoms. The colonists were quick to oppose any infringements upon their charter rights.[199] Even before independence, colonial legislation was subject to review for its compatibility with norms of a "higher status."[200] Since 1775 in America, the various historical

194 David Rabban, *Free Speech in Its Forgotten Years* (Cambridge University Press, 1997); Norman L. Rosenberg, "Another World," *Reviews in American History* 16, no. 4 (December 1988), 554–559; Alexis J. Anderson, "The Formative Period of First Amendment Theory," *The American Journal of Legal History* 24, no. 1 (January 1980), 56–75.

195 See Section 2.3.

196 See Chapter 5.

197 "Men are born and remain free and equal in rights. Social distinctions may be based only on considerations of the common good."

198 Men "are by nature equally free and independent."

199 Bernard Schwartz, *The Bill of Rights: A Documentary History* (New York: Chelsea House Publishers, 1971), 50–51. The First Charters were the Virginia Charter of 1606, the Fundamental Orders of Connecticut 1639, and the Maryland Act for the Liberties of the People 1639.

200 See William Michael Treanor, "Judicial Review Before Marbury," *Stanford Law Review* 58 (2005), 455–562, 468; Mary Sarah Bilder, *The Transatlantic Constitution: Colonial Legal Culture and the Empire* (Cambridge, MA: Harvard University Press, 2004), 73–90; Joseph Henry Smith, *Appeals to the Privy Council from the American Plantations* (New York: Columbia University Press, 1950).

charters of the colonies "were understood as documents that proved the existence of a pact concluded between an English king and his American subjects."[201] Before the Declaration of Independence, the idea emerged that an act of parliament can be contrary to fundamental law and should be judged void. James Otis contributed to the doctrine that it is the duty of the judiciary to declare unconstitutional statutes void. Otis made a case in February 1761 in his oration for the Writs of Assistance case, in favor the duty of the judiciary to declare unconstitutional statutes void.[202]

Many of these bills of rights of the American states contain implicitly the idea of a state of nature that is egalitarian and where everyone enjoys equal negative natural rights. Most of the revolutionary declarations contain guarantees against *ex post facto* laws as well as protecting freedom of the press and religion.[203] The first state constitutions also protected freedom of speech and of the press.[204] Many state constitutions in the eighteenth and early nineteenth centuries contained more extensive bills of rights than the federal bill of rights.[205]

The variety of constitutionalism that was established in France and the United States after the two revolutions is also obvious in the constitutional design of the judiciary branch. In America, texts declaring the rights of the colonies had created the consciousness of the constitutional character of these texts associated with "judicial review." The doctrine of judicial review became a part of the living law during the decade before the Federal Constitution. Courts began to assert their authority to hold unconstitutional legislation void in the area of negative rights

201 Bernard Schwartz, *Bill of Rights*; Wood, *Creation of the American Republic*, 317.

202 "John Adams's Notes on the First Argument of the Case, February 1761," in Samuelson, ed., *Collected Political Writings*, 6. See also James Otis, "Essay on the Writs of Assistance Case," in Samuelson, ed., *Collected Political Writings*, 15–18, noting the absence of checks and restrictions in the colonies of the activities of the custom house officers, unlike what is the case in England.

203 The constitutional development during the Revolutionary period was characterized as "a movement from the British conception of the protection of rights to the American Conception." Schwartz, *Bill of Rights*, 180. The Declaration of Rights and Grievances, 1765 refers to the right of taxation only through representation (III), to the need to protect the property of the citizens, and to the trial by jury, reprinted in Schwartz, *Bill of Rights*, 197. It also refers to the "full and free enjoyments of the rights and liberties" of the colonies. Reference to freedom of the press and freedom of religion and to a general conception of limited government, clauses which by their nature concern the executive and the legislative branch, exist in the Virginia Declaration of Rights 1776, the Pennsylvania Declaration of Rights of 1779 (having Thomas Paine as one of its authors), the Delaware Declaration of Rights of 1776 (section 23), the Maryland Declaration of Rights of 1776 (religion XXXIII, press XXXVIII), the North Carolina Declaration of Rights 1776 (press freedom art. XV), the Georgia Constitution of 1777 (religion art. LVI, press LXI), the New York Constitution 1777 (religion in XXXVIII), the Vermont Declaration of Rights 1777 (religion III, press XIV), the Massachusetts Declaration of Rights 1780 (religion II, press XVI), the New Hampshire Bill of Rights of 1783 (press XXII, religion V). The Connecticut Declaration of Rights refers to the protection of "Civil and religious Rights and liberties." A number of these texts refer to "natural, essential and inherent rights preventing the legislature from making laws limiting them and foreseeing judicial review by Supreme Courts." Ibid. An exception to this rule is the New York Constitution of 1821, which did foresee that citizens would be responsible for "abuse" of that right.

204 Schwartz, *Bill of Rights*.

205 Gardner, *Interpreting State Constitutions*, 173.

against the government, referring to colonial charters and state bills of rights.[206] When the necessity to create a federal government emerged, the debate on the Federal Constitution revived the discussion on the need to control the operation of legislative majorities. Madison insisted on the role of the judiciary for the protection of negative rights against the partiality of factions which can win over legislatures.[207] Hamilton noted the need for an independent judiciary to protect liberty.[208] As the "least dangerous branch to the political rights of the constitution," it can be "an excellent barrier to the encroachments of the representative body."[209] During the discussion of the Amendments to the Constitution, Madison emphasized again for the judiciary the role of limiting the majorities to guarantee the liberty of minorities.[210] He noted the need to protect against the legislative, which he saw as the "most powerful and most likely to be abused" branch of government.[211] He underlined the importance of protecting freedom of speech, a freedom that he thought was "unguarded" in the British Constitution.[212]

For the French revolutionaries, the abuses of political power under the Ancien Régime could be addressed by laws that would be general and would apply equally to all. In the United States, the principal political problem was, for Madison, the tyranny of the generality of the law as a product of the social and political majority to the detriment of minorities.[213] Even before *Marbury* v. *Madison*, lower federal courts invalidated state legislation found to be at odds with the Federal Constitution.[214]

With the First Amendment, the American Framers aimed to prevent federal legislation or federal officials' action from violating freedom of conscience, of the press and of association: they aimed to protect autonomy and not to proclaim abstract rights.[215] The First Amendment aimed to guarantee social peace in a context of religious difference against the predominance of various religious sects within the states. It concerned the transposition at the level of the federal

206 See for example *Holmes* v. *Walton*, New Jersey (September 7, 1780), ruling in favor of a right to "constitutional jury" (delivered orally – no surviving copy exists), cited in Austin Scott, "Holmes v. Walton: The New Jersey Precedent," *American Historical Review* 4 (1899), 456; The Ten-Pound Act Cases (1786–1787) (trial by jury in actions for debt and actions for trespass not involving title to land referring to the New Hampshire Bill of Rights art. xx) (New Hampshire); *Commonwealth* v. *Caton*, 4 Call 5 (1782) (Virginia), *Trevett* v. *Weeden* (1786) (trial by jury, Rhode Island), *Bayard* v. *Singleton*, 1 NC 5 (1787) (trial by jury in suits involving property) (North Carolina).

207 James Madison, "No. 10," in Hamilton, Jay, and Madison, *The Federalist*, 42 ff.

208 Alexander Hamilton, "No. 78," in Hamilton, Jay, and Madison, *The* Federalist, 401.

209 Ibid., 402.

210 James Madison, "Amendments to the Constitution" (speech of June 8, 1789), in A *Century of Lawmaking for a New Nation: U.S. Congressional Documents and Debates, 1774 – 1875*, Annals of Congress, House of Representatives, 1st Congress, 1st Session, 457.

211 Ibid., 454.

212 Ibid., 453.

213 According to the famous enunciation in *The Federalist* No. 51.

214 *Hamilton* v. *Eaton*, 11 F. Ca. 336 (CCDNC 1792), *Vanhorne's Lesse* v. *Dorrance* 2 US (2 Dall.) 304 (CCD Pa. 1795) (right to property referring to "natural rights").

215 Émile Boutmy, *Etudes de droit constitutionnel: France, Angleterre, Etats-Unis* (Paris: Plon, 1888), 95.

government of protection that already existed against the governments of the states. At the time of founding, the Amendments to the Constitution were not considered to be the "fundamental safeguards of liberty" that they are understood to be today.[216] It was the role of the Supreme Court over the following centuries, especially after the incorporation of the Amendments by the Fourteenth Amendment, making them applicable to the states, which led to them adopting the meaning that they have today.[217]

In France, the control of constitutionality of legislation is a very recent development compared to the United States. Overall, the judiciary in France evolved in such a way that is indicative of the general spirit of trust toward the government. The control of constitutionality was established only in 1958, during the Fifth Republic, with the creation of the Constitutional Council. The French Declaration obtained constitutional validity following the Constitutional Council's decision of July 16, 1971 on freedom of association.[218] The Constitutional Council intervened until recently only in the middle of the debate on the opportunity of enacting a legal norm. Until 2008, a referral to the Constitutional Council had, as an *a priori* control, the form of an interinstitutional deliberation. It was limited to the actors who cooperated in the creation of the law, including the president of the republic, the prime minister, the president of the National Assembly, the president of the Senate, and a group of sixty members of the parliament and sixty senators.[219] The citizens could not appeal to the Constitutional Council concerning the application of a law in a concrete case. This was an incomplete system because laws enacted before the creation of the Council had escaped control.[220] What is more, during the application of a law new cases of interpretation appear that have an impact on citizens' rights and cannot be foreseen in advance. The Constitutional Law of July 23, 2008 introduced considerable modifications concerning referrals to the Council.[221] The

[216] Klarman, *The Framers' Coup*, 595.

[217] Amar, *Bill of* Rights, 280.

[218] 71–44 DC, Rec. 29, RJC I-24. From 1959 till 1971 the Constitutional Court gave its opinion on the conformity to the Constitution of twenty two laws declaring many of them unconstitutional. The novelty introduced by this decision consists in the proposal of a new foundation concerning the control of constitutionality of the law which limits a liberty: the Constitutional Councilaffirmed the constitutional value of the Declaration of the Rights of Man and of the Citizen. Louis Favoureu and Loïc Philip, *Les Grandes Décisions du Conseil Constitutionnel*, 10th ed. (Paris: Dalloz, 1999), 252–71. Louis Favoureu, "La Déclaration de 1789 et le juge: une problématique Américaine?," *La Revue Tocqueville* XIV (1993), 147–155. Georges Vedel, "L'incorporation de la Déclaration de droits de l'homme dans la Constitution française," *La Revue Tocqueville*, XIV (1993), 157–63.

[219] Art. 61(2) of the French Constitution.

[220] Denis Lacorne, "Le débat des droits de l'homme en France et aux Etats-Unis," *La revue tocqueville* XIV (1993), 5–31, 22; Jean Rivero, "Intervention in the Debate on 'Les Libertés,'" in Louis Favoureux, ed., *La continuité constitutionnelle en France, de 1789 à 1989* (Presses Universitaires d'Aix-Marseille, 1990), 162; François Luchaire, *Le juge constitutionnel en France et aux Etats-Unis: étude comparée* (Paris: Economica, 2002).

[221] Loi constitutionnelle 2008–724 du 23 juillet 2008 de modernisation des institutions de la V République [Constitutional Law 2008-724 of July 23, 2008 on modernizing the institutions of the Fifth Republic], JO, July 24, 2008.

law widened the possibility to refer to the court. Article 29 of this law establishes the possibility to make a referral to the Constitutional Council in a case pending before a court, when a citizen contends that a law violates a constitutional right. The Constitutional Council examines the case only if the Council of State (supreme jurisdiction of the administrative branch of the French judiciary) or the Court of Cassation (supreme jurisdiction of the civil branch) have decided within a specific deadline whether they will refer the case or not.[222]

The Constitutional Council did not have the opportunity to examine a priori the constitutionality of numerous laws limiting speech as none of the political actors having the authority to make a referral used this option. For instance, the "Gayssot Law," which criminalizes the denial of crimes against humanity, was not referred to it. Following the modification of the referral procedure to the Constitutional Council, the Court of Cassation refused to refer an application for a constitutionality ruling for the "Gayssot Law" as it considered that the application did not raise any legal issue of "a serious nature" because the limitation of the denial of the relevant crimes "is not violating the constitutional principles of freedom of expression and opinion."[223] In another case where the Constitutional Council evaluated the constitutionality of the law following the change in the referral process, it held that the law is in conformity with the French Constitution as it aims to repress "an abuse of freedom of expression."[224] Similarly, the Constitutional Council never had the opportunity to evaluate the constitutionality of the Law on the Presumption of Innocence, which outlaws the publication of elements of identification of victims of sexual aggression and suspects of crimes.[225]

France maintains a distinction between "ordinary" and "administrative" justice. Tocqueville noted in *Democracy in America* that this distinction emerged from the necessity to ensure to the state the status of privileged litigant.[226] The state's privileged role in transforming civil society led to the creation of special jurisdictions which judge the legality of acts emanating from public power in litigation between the state and the citizens.[227] The Council of State, the supreme court of the administrative jurisdiction, emerged from the transformation into a judge of the pre-existing Royal Council. The transformation of administrative courts – and principally of the Council of State into guarantor of the protection of liberties called "public" – took place later in the history of the institution.

222 According to the new art. 61(1) of the French Constitution inserted by article 29 of Constitutional Law 2008–724.

223 Cour de Cassation [Cass.] [supreme court for judicial matters], May 7, 2010, no. 12008.

224 CC, Decision 2015–512, QPC, Jan. 8, 2016.

225 See Chapter 1.

226 Tocqueville, *Democracy in America*, 683–84. See also H. S. Jones, *The French State in Question: Public Law and Political Argument in the Third Republic* (Cambridge University Press 1993), 85.

227 Tocqueville, *Democracy in America*, 683–84.

To conclude, the institutional design in France and in the United States indicates the degree of trust or distrust toward the law to define the content and limits of liberty. The French Declaration is situated "on the level of the law."[228] The American texts declaring rights, state and federal, provided institutional guarantees for the protection of the negative aspect of these rights against legislation from an early stage. A conception of negative constitutionalism emerged in America even before independence. This conception of constitutionalism as distrust toward the government, contributed to the doctrine for freedom of expression which emerged in the twentieth century. According to this conception, freedom of speech is part of the checks and balances that compose the American system of government. References to the press as the "fourth branch" of government express this mentality. Legislation limiting speech is rarely upheld by the US Supreme Court. In France, it is frequently not even referred to the Constitutional Council. The tradition of positive constitutionalism, dominant in France, trusts the legislative power with the mission to realize liberty. The need to establish control of constitutionality of the law as a mechanism that limits the legislative branch emerged late in French constitutional history. In the United States, the free speech doctrine emerged thanks to the role of judicial review within the constitutional system. In France, courts have not assumed a similar role in the area of speech.

Ideas do not remain static in the course of time as societies evolve. Even elements of distrust toward the government predominant in the American tradition were moderated by the current of progressivism at the beginning of the twentieth century. As analyzed in the following chapters, an attempt to reconcile republicanism with natural rights echoing the neo-Roman thought is present in America since the Founding Era.[229] Throughout American constitutional history there was a fluctuation in the understanding of where greater weight should be given: on the side of the common good or on the side of individual rights? During the Founding Era the balance would lean toward individual rights. During the second half of the nineteenth century the American states tended to weigh the common good more heavily in some respects. During the New Deal and under the influence of progressivism, weight was given to the need for redistribution. Toward the end of the twentieth century the balance leans toward the protection of natural rights anew. Since the New Deal Era and to date, the protection of expressive freedoms has won significant grounds. This relates to the natural rights tradition, the distrust toward the government and to the dominant understanding of democracy existing at the Founding Era. As analyzed in the next chapter, the

228 V. Marcaggi, *Les origines de la Déclaration des droits de l'homme de 1789* (Paris: Fontemoing, 1912), 36.

229 Rogers M. Smith's work criticizing Louis Hartz's insistence on Locke can be understood as part of the scholars who note the innovations that the American Founders brought to constitutionalism. See Rogers M. Smith, *Liberalism and American Constitutional Law* (Harvard University Press, 1985).

combination of all these factors led to the very protective regime of free speech today.[230] The American tradition formed in the Founding Era formed the genes of the ideas that manifested during the twentieth century in the United States as free speech libertarianism. In France a tradition of trust toward the state to realize liberties was always dominant. This tradition is visible today in the regulation of freedom of speech.

230 Unlike interpretations like Charles Beard's in the *Economic Interpretation of the Constitution* (New York: MacMillan, 1913), which focus on the economic interests the American Founders were aiming to protect, this study makes an argument on political ideology, informed by the need to protect an economic system too.

3

The Underlying Ex Ante Understanding of Liberty

The difference in the protection of freedom of expression between France and the United States can be understood in reference to the understanding of liberty that is considered worth protecting in a legal system. Freedom of expression can be seen as a negative liberty, a liberty against the government. It can be seen as a positive liberty too, in the sense of having met the preconditions that are necessary to exercise this liberty. More generally, having other needs met, which ensure survival and enable a person to be able to express themselves, are aspects of liberty understood in a positive sense. Having the state ensure that citizens obtain access to a variety of currents of opinion can be seen as the positive aspect of freedom of expression. Having access to the media is another aspect of seeing freedom of speech as a positive liberty. In the United States, freedom of expression is protected in the negative sense. In France, some of its positive aspects are protected too. This attitude relates to the legitimacy of the government to define the content and limits of liberty. Even the protection of negative liberties requires positive action from the state. The state needs to make sure that itself and other parties do not infringe the citizen's negative sphere of inviolability. The protection of positive liberties requires something more. It requires even more extended government intervention. It requires the state to engage in redistributing goods to make sure that the citizens will be able to exercise their negative liberties. The state should make sure that negative liberties do not remain empty forms, according to the famous Marxist critique. The state should help citizens realize their liberty.

In the area of freedom of expression, this means willingness of the state to make sure that citizens have access to the media in the form of a right to respond to publications. It also means that the state intervenes by limiting the rights of some people in order to enable others to be heard. This is relevant in the area of political campaign funding. The rejection of limits upon independent political campaign expenditure by the US Supreme Court in *Citizens United*[1] means that the Court refuses to see the distinction between formal and real freedom of speech during

[1] *Citizens United* v. *FEC*. 558 US 310 (2010).

political campaigns. The Court overlooks that not everyone has the same ability to be heard. Similarly, restrictions upon hate speech in France are dictated by a comprehensive protectionist approach toward the role of government. The state intervenes to protect vulnerable groups from hate. It also intervenes to prevent the creation of stereotypes against social groups. These stereotypes mean in the long term that these groups are not heard when they speak. The burka ban in France can also be understood as part of a general effort of the state to make sure that citizens enjoy "real" liberty. The ban was justified in reference to the need to protect women from the oppression of their families. It was seen as a measure to help them realize their liberty against social pressure. It was also seen as a measure that helps women liberate themselves. Their willingness to wear a burka, when not formed under social pressure, was seen as part of a "false consciousness."[2] The state is invested with the task to realize the reason of the citizens because they are incapable of realizing it themselves.

American constitutionalism during the Founding Era was formed on the understanding of liberty as negative. Liberty described in the constitutional texts of the era implied that the state would not intervene in the sphere of inviolability that individuals should enjoy. Although this understanding of liberty has changed throughout the centuries, the idea that freedom of expression is a negative liberty par excellence survives in the United States. Contemporary law on freedom of expression protects the negative facets of this liberty against government intervention. There is unwillingness within the American legal system to protect this liberty as a positive liberty. The French revolutionaries considered that it is the mission of the state to help human beings realize their liberty. A similar discourse did not exist with the same acuteness in America during the Founding Era. The progressives' ideas, which emerged in the United States at the beginning of the twentieth century, underlined the importance of free speech for individual development and self-government. Their ideas survived only to the extent that they were compatible with distrust toward the government in regulating expressive freedoms. The understanding that it is the mission of the state to help citizens realize their liberty in relation to freedom of expression is still missing today.

Therefore, the difference in the understanding of the role of the government between France and the United States corresponds with a difference in the understanding of liberty. Sovereignty as a facet of the modern state is relational, in that it expresses public power and creates the rights that the citizens have.[3] A study of the understanding of liberty in the two legal orders reveals some subtle but present differences in the conception of the aspects of liberty that should be protected by the state. Americans are more inclined to protect negative liberty. The French, on the other hand, favor the protection of positive liberty, understood as governmental

[2] See Tourkochoriti, "The Burka Ban," 791–852, 844.

[3] See Martin Loughlin, *The Idea of Public Law* (Oxford University Press, 2003), 73.

intervention to ensure the preconditions for the exercise of liberty. This conception is associated with a particular conception of human dignity. The debates in the National Assembly during the summer of 1789 indicate that the French Declaration of the Rights of Man and the Citizen aimed at proclaiming the necessity of guaranteeing a dignified life for every human being. By that they meant a life where every human being has the possibility to exercise their liberty. The texts declaring liberties, elaborated in contexts characterized by different political problems, have different illocutionary effects.[4] The American Declaration of Independence and the Bills of Rights of the states were the product of a new conception of republicanism, which associated the necessity of protecting the public good with the need to protect the rights that were proclaimed as "natural." These were essentially negative rights. The conceptual distinction between liberty rights and social rights had not appeared at the moment of the French Revolution. However, in the spirit of the French revolutionaries, the two notions were confounded. The reference to the universality of the rights of the human being as such in the French Declaration implied the protection of their physical existence. Negative rights are at the same time the rights of the citizen and this reflects a positive conception of the state as guarantor of the preconditions of liberty. The question of "assistance" was omnipresent in the discussions that led to the Declaration of 1789, and in thinkers such as Sieyès and Mably.[5] During the discussions of the Constitutive Assemblies in France, there was a very animated debate on the "duties" of human beings toward other human beings. In the United States, the ultimate aim of the government is to guarantee and protect negative rights and liberties. In France, it is to ensure the preconditions for exercising any right associated with human dignity and to intervene to limit the content and limits of liberty and by extension to provide for the guarantee of rights that are now called "social."

The concern to provide for "social rights," in association with the conception of the "rational republic," contains the danger of an "overdetermination" of the conditions of the realization of liberty, as the case of freedom of expression shows. This tendency to overdetermine the content of liberty is due to the philosophical background to the role of the state analyzed in the previous chapter. It can be traced back to the concrete political problems that the French revolutionaries were facing. The revolutionary legislators who dominated the political sphere from 1789 saw themselves as having the authority to entirely redefine the structures of the new state. Their legal optimism was characteristic of the era of the Enlightenment. It allowed them to hope that human reality would conform without resistance to a new "rational" legal ordering in conformity with everyone's interests.

[4] According to John Austin's use of the term. Austin, *How to Do Things with Words*, 100. Austin calls illocutionary force the force of a speech act in a specific context of communication.

[5] Cf. Luc Ferry and Alain Renaut, *Philosophie politique 3: des droits de l'homme à l'idée républicaine* (Paris: Presses Universitaires de France, 1992), 186.

The French revolutionaries' high level of idealization was justified by the search for a new meaning for the world, for life and for its political organization.[6] The idealistic point of view expressed the need to transcend the oppressive immanence of the Ancien Régime. In this effort to radically reverse all ancient values, the sanction of positive law was necessary. The revolution posed the principle of liberty in the rights of man and of the citizen. The French revolutionaries understood liberty as the possibility of realizing one's being as human, of being oneself, and of leading a human life.[7] They considered that they were realizing Rousseau's idea that it is only by affirming oneself as a citizen that someone can affirm oneself as being human.[8] The affirmation of human rights can condition their realization only if they are articulated together with the rights of the citizen. Human rights would be realized by including in their essential content the rights of the citizen. In the French Declaration of 1789, the rights of man are conditioned upon the rights of the citizen. Hegel saw in the Declaration the conservation of natural rights, but which are by definition social, as they associated with the idea of equality.[9] By a paradoxical inversion the identification between power and society in the French context leads to a conception of authority as the medium by which to realize liberty. According to the French conception, the rights of the citizen are the reason why the rights of the individual exist.

For French republicanism, liberty is consubstantial with the public good. This version of republicanism recognizes the practical effectiveness of the rights of the citizen by conceiving them in a "legal horizon of coercion and of legitimacy."[10] According to American republicanism, private liberty is protected exactly because it promotes this republicanism, as this republicanism makes indispensable the distinction between the private and the public. As Georges Gusdorf has noted, the French revolutionaries intended to construct an ideal republic according to ideas dictated by reason, the pure spirit inspiring human rights.[11] Their constitutional schemes collapsed "under the weight of their own immaturity."[12] The American revolutionaries, on the contrary, showed a democratic liberalism. In America, the Declaration of Independence was the legal and constitutional affirmation of an existing situation.[13]

6 On the close association between the search for meaning, the orientation toward the good and the is–ought distinction, see Charles Taylor, *Sources of the Self: The Making of the Modern Identity* (Cambridge, MA: Harvard University Press), 28–29.

7 Joachim Ritter, *Hegel et la Révolution française* (Paris: Beauchesne, 1970), 26 ff. See also Simone Goyard-Fabre, "Les Lumières ont-elles préparé la Révolution?," *Cahiers de Philosophie Politique et Juridique* 16 (1989), 23–43, 23.

8 Jean-Jacques Rousseau, *Du contrat social (première version, manuscrit de Genève)*, in *Oeuvres complètes*, vol. 3 (Paris: Gallimard, 1967), 281–346.

9 G. W. F. Hegel, *The Philosophy of History*, trans. J. Sibree (New York: Dover, 1956), 444 ff.

10 Rials, *La Déclaration*, 395.

11 Gusdorf, *Les révolutions*, 48–49.

12 Ibid.

13 Ibid., 48–49. See also Robert R. Palmer, "The European Enlightenment in Its American Setting," in *Aspects of American Liberty, Philosophical, Historical and Political* (Philadelphia: The American Philosophical Society, 1977), 47–55.

The Americans had been practicing self-government for generations. They aimed to protect the negative aspect of their self-government. They also aimed to protect their negative liberty against infringement by the British parliament. Discourse on the need to protect social rights emerged much later in the United States (at the end of the nineteenth century) and mostly at the level of the states.

The French Revolution – guided by an idea regulating reality – aimed to regenerate humanity, and thus to establish a new idea of reason and justice among men reforming society. The American Revolution aimed to constitute a new form of independent government breaching the link of allegiance to the British crown, not modify the established social structure. The American Revolution brought change on the international level through the illocutionary force of the Declaration of Independence. The historical trajectory of the emergence of republicanism in the United States is different. This difference depends essentially on the imaginary level,[14] on the evolution of the understanding that human beings have of themselves and of their quality as citizens on each side of the Atlantic. In the United States, the power of the government is considered as an instrument that society needs to preserve security and negative liberty. It is not legitimate for the government to intervene in what society is capable of doing by itself.

In the United States at the beginning of the twentieth century, the progressives supported government intervention in the economy so that everyone could have the same starting point. They also criticized the discourse on negative natural rights. Many state constitutions also enacted clauses protecting positive rights. Although they catalyzed the New Deal, the progressives' ideas did not lead to an entire reconceptualization of the role of government. Arguably, the New Deal served as a catalyst toward protecting expressive freedoms in the United States. When government intervention in the economy became accepted, American libertarianism found expression in the protection of speech rights. Regardless of the political party in power, the philosophy undergirding the federal guarantee of a competitive market shifted from more government intervention to less. Wide government intervention in the economy was short-lived. In the area of economic freedoms, courts in the United States started invalidating legislation related to the protection of positive rights in the 1970s. In addition, since 1970, the newspaper industry has enjoyed an exemption from the application of antitrust laws enacted by legislation.[15] Government libertarianism won over anew.

3.1 METAPHYSICAL UNIVERSALISM VERSUS PRAGMATIC PROCLAMATION

The understanding of liberty that underlies the French Declaration of the Rights of Man and of the Citizen encompasses all the kinds of liberty, later distinguished as

[14] Gusdorf, *Les révolutions*, 48–49.

[15] On the basis of the Newspaper Preservation Act, see Lebovic, *Free Speech and Unfree News*, 195.

political liberty, negative liberty, and positive liberty (in the sense of rights of the welfare state). The French Declaration aimed to proclaim principles on the metaphysical level concerning every human being, whereas the American declarations of rights were less ambitious. The French Ideologues, operating in a vacuum, and not very adapted to the concrete realities of political life, called for a radical innovation dictated by reason.[16] On the contrary, the Americans already had parliamentary and administrative experience in the local assemblies of the colonies. They were engaged there in developing structures appropriate to each one of the states before the Declaration of Independence and the Federal Constitution of 1787. The French revolutionaries appealed to the most universal principles, to the very foundations of the law. As Marcel Gauchet notes, the French revolutionaries had to appeal to universal principles as a substitute for the absence of legality that the Assembly suffered from, when it proclaimed itself as "national" and "constituent."[17]

The question of realizing the rights proclaimed as being universal, associated with the human being as such, and of the need to ensure the preconditions that make liberty effective, was omnipresent during the French declaratory work. "The Americans had already acquired the dignity of prototype in the eyes of the French," even before independence.[18] The representatives of the people in France were proclaiming universal and intemporal principles that concern all aspects of the existence of humanity.[19] The French Declaration proposes the manifesto of an ideological radicalization for the entire human universe.[20] The French revolutionaries aimed at defining the frame inside which any future legislation should take place. More specifically, they believed that a democratic Constitution is valid only if it respects and promotes the imprescriptible and inalienable rights of the human being. The American Declaration of Independence of 1776 bears the imprint of Anglo-Saxon empiricism. The French Declaration is inspired by a different intellectual sensibility, having a highly idealistic project, "the demand of the impossible."[21] In this sense, the French Revolution is seen by Hegel as the result of the work of thought upon itself, the "child of philosophy," an event in the history

16 Gusdorf, *Les révolutions*, 198–99.

17 Marcel Gauchet, *La révolution des pouvoirs: la souveraineté, le peuple et la représentation 1789–1799* (Paris: Gallimard, 1995), 55.

18 Georges Gusdorf, *Les sciences humaines et la pensée occidentale*, vol. 8, *La conscience révolutionnaire des idéologues* (Paris: Payot, 1978), 214, 210. Even if Jefferson collaborated closely through intermediaries to the French Declaration, the two texts have different performative effects though their placement in different illocutionary circumstances. The American colonies had long benefited from the rights that the French were claiming in 1789. The Mayflower Compact of the Pilgrim Fathers had since 1620 attested to the conviction among the new colonizers that they were entering a land where religious liberty would be saved, thus pulling along other liberties.

19 Pierre Bouretz, *La république et l'universel* (Paris: Gallimard, 2000), 46.

20 Tocqueville also attributed the high level of idealization of the French revolutionary discourse to the work of the intellectuals and to the fact that in France, in opposition to the United States, had not practiced political liberty before its revolution. Alexis de Tocqueville, *L'Ancien régime et la Révolution*, bk. 3, chap. 1 [1856] (Paris: Gallimard, 1967), 232–33.

21 Gusdorf, *Les révolutions*, 245.

of the entire world.[22] It is seen by Kant as an element of moral progression of humanity.[23] Kant credits the revolution for establishing republicanism, expressing the idea that it is the republican constitution that guarantees the liberty for a people in the sense that it has "the faculty to obey only laws to which he gave its assent."[24] But this need to protect self-government went together with the need to respond to the question of mass poverty. The French Declaration appears as the expression of a true intellectual necessity, the result of a long process of the maturity of thought. Its proclamation of liberty in abstract terms responded to the needs of all social classes: those of the bourgeoisie to have its negative liberties protected against arbitrary government, and those of the popular movement against poverty.[25]

Following the revolutionary movement, positive law is seen as expressing the ideal of justice, thereby justifying a radical rupture with the past.[26] The French revolutionaries saw themselves as accomplishing a regeneration, an exit from the state of "lethargy" they were in to organize themselves entirely anew.[27] They were operating a transvaluation of values,[28] a new evaluation of values that confirmed the is–ought distinction, the distinction between facts and norms. The search for a new meaning for the world, life, and its political organization made necessary the idealist point of view. Idealism would help them transcend the oppressive immanence of the Ancien Régime. As Tocqueville noted, the French revolutionaries needed to reimagine

22 Hegel, *Philosophy of History*, 446–47; Alfred Stern, "Hegel et les idées de 1789," in E. Barker et al., eds., *La Révolution de 1789 et la pensée moderne* (Paris: Presses Universitaires de France, 1940), 225–35; Jacques d'Hondt, "Le Parcours hégélien de la Révolution française," in *Hegel et les français* (New York: Georg Olms Verlag Hildesheim, 1998), 139–54.

23 Emmanuel Kant, *Le conflit des facultés en trois sections*, trans. J. Gibelin (Paris: Vrin, 1935), 101–2. Kant's judgment concerning the revolution is ambivalent. He judges positively the content of the revolution, political humanism, and negatively its form, the revolutionary process. Kant thought that the revolutionary state as such was a state of public injustice. Kant's condemnation of the right to resist is associated with the necessity to affirm the superiority of a legal order, even unjust, upon anarchy, cf. Luc Ferry, "Kant" in François Furet et Mona Ozouf, eds., *Dictionnaire critique de la Révolution française: interprètes et historiens* (Paris: Flammarion, 2007), 157–64, 161; Alexis Philonenko, *Théorie et praxis dans la pensée morale et politique de Kant et de Fichte en 1793* (Paris: Vrin, 1968). Kant is hesitating between the denunciation of the absurdity of the right to revolution and his support of the French Revolution to the extent that it is founded on principles which unite theory and practice under the guidance of theory, while condemning the empirical realization, practical and pragmatic of the "revolutionary theory." Benjamin Delannoy, *Burke et Kant: interprètes de la Révolution française* (Paris: L'Harmattan, 2004), 52.

24 Immanuel Kant, *Projet de paix perpétuelle*, trans. Jean Darbellay (Paris: Presses Universitaires de France, 1958), 91.

25 Roger Barny, *Le droit naturel à l'épreuve de l'histoire: Jean Jacques Rousseau dans la Révolution (débats politiques et sociaux)* (Paris: Les Belles Lettres, 1995), 21. As such it expresses the complexity of the needs of the political conditions of the moment.

26 The Decree abolishing feudal privileges was enacted on August 11, 1789. *Archives Parlementaires*, vol. 7, 397.

27 Roger Barny, *Les contradictions de l'idéologie révolutionnaire des droits de l'homme, droit naturel et histoire* (Paris: Les Belles Lettres, 1993), 135.

28 Friedrich Nietzsche, *Zur Genealogie der Moral* [1887], trans. Eric Blondel, Ole Hansen Love, Théo Levdenbach, and Pierre Pénisson (Paris: GF Flammarion, 2000).

entirely an ideal society "above real society, whose Constitution was still traditional, confused and irregular, where the laws remained diverse and contradictory, the social classes strictly separated, the conditions fixed and the obligations unequal."[29] "There was no interest any more in what was, in order to consider what could be, and in the end everybody lived in spirit in this ideal city, which the writers had created."[30] As a great historical originality, this "domiciliation of utopia on the land of the humans" was the result of the effort to begin history anew through law according to the requirements of "reason" alone.[31] For this reason, and as a result of the dramatic succession of events that led to the Terror, it was the object of criticism and interpretations of thinkers as varied in their approaches as Hegel, Fichte, Burke, and Bentham.

For Hegel, the ideality and universality of the discourse of human rights in France arises from the necessity to negate the particular "non-law" of privileges in order to obtain the form and the affirmation of universal right in the discourse, which negates the reality of these privileges.[32] Some elements of empirical rationalism, the heritage of the eighteenth century, were present in the French Declaration. German idealism, providing an ideal, metaphysical foundation to liberty by disengaging it from any empirical blending, sees in the natural rights proclaimed in the Declaration the objective conditions of the realization of liberty in the interaction of individuals.[33] Indispensable to this regeneration effort, and the radical inversion of any of the old values, was the sanction of positive law.[34]

The law conditioning the empirical realization of liberty for the French revolutionaries expressed a normative conception of liberty understood in the metaphysical sense. This understanding included the various types of liberty that emerged later in constitutional thought. As the metaempirical foundation of the law, it includes all rights, the rights understood in the negative sense, the "positive," "civic," and political rights.[35] For German idealism and for the French revolutionaries, affirming oneself as being free in the world means affirming oneself as a metaempirical or metaphysical subject having universal rights. Associating the universality of rights with practical and theoretical reason leads to making the rights of man concrete in a progressive development from liberty rights to social rights.[36]

29 Alexis de Tocqueville, *L'Ancien Régime et la Révolution*, bk. 3, chap. 1, 238–39 (my translation).

30 Ibid.

31 Gusdorf, *Conscience révolutionnaire*, 116.

32 G. F. Hegel, *The Philosophy of History*, trans. J. Sibree (New York: Dover, 1956), 446–47; Bourgeois, *Philosophie et droits de l'homme*, 82; see also Bernard Bourgeois, "Hegel," in Philippe Raynaud et Stéphane Rials, eds., *Dictionnaire de philosophie politique* (Paris: Presses Universitaires de France, 2003), 313–20.

33 Bourgeois, *Philosophie et droits de l'homme*, 55; Jean Hyppolite, "La signification de la Révolution française dans la 'Phénoménologie' de Hegel," in E. Barker et al., *La Révolution de 1789 et la pensée moderne* (Paris: Presses Universitaires de France, 1940), 193–224.

34 Alexis de Tocqueville, *L'Ancien Régime et la Révolution*, 238–39.

35 Bourgeois, *Philosophie et droits de l'homme*, 17.

36 Ibid.

Hegel notes that the particular interest cannot be preserved but in the interest and ends of another, that is the state, which has the mission to provide for the welfare of the citizens.[37] The concern for ensuring the preconditions for the exercise of liberty was omnipresent during the French Revolution. It is this conception that later led to the emergence of the new category of rights, the category of social rights understood as the rights protected by the welfare state.

Numerous declarations of rights and constitutional texts discussed in the National Assembly during the summer of 1789 indicate that the French revolutionaries' understanding of liberty encompasses all three meanings of liberty: political, negative, and positive (in the sense of rights to state redistribution). In the preamble to the Constitution read by Sieyès on July 21, 1789 in the National Assembly, this conception of liberty, understood in universal terms, appears clearly. This text reflects an understanding of liberty as negative, political, and positive in the sense of the right to have the preconditions met that enable a person to exercise their liberty.[38] The idea that liberty is amplified in society is omnipresent too. Sieyès discusses the right to property upon one's person as the first right. Real property is merely an extension of personal property. Human work has the ability to transform things. A human being may appropriate through work objects that they need to survive. Private property is to be protected by the social state. Sieyès emphasizes that liberty makes sense only in a society that guarantees happiness. The preamble states explicitly that those citizens who cannot provide for their needs have the right to be assisted by their fellow citizens. Target, another member of the Committee of the Constitution, presented a draft for a "Declaration of the Rights of Man in Society" a few days later.[39] This draft included an article according to which, "the political body owes to everyone the means of subsistence, either by property, or by work, or by the work of his fellow men (*semblables*)."[40] The discussions on the text that became the Declaration of 1789 indicate a concern among the principal political actors for ensuring the means of subsistence to those who do not have them. "Work and subsistence" are "obligations of society" toward those who do not have it.[41] The Charter containing the French Constitution proposed by Charles-François Bouche contains a clause referring to compassion and generosity and "the obligation of the members of society to assist one another in times of need."[42]

37 G. W. F. Hegel, *Elements of Philosophy of Right*, § 265–68, trans. H. B. Nisbet (Cambridge University Press, 1991), 287–88.

38 *Archives Parlementaires*, vol. 8, 256–61.

39 Presented during the meeting of the National Assembly of July 27, 1789, *Archives Parlementaires*, vol. 8, 288.

40 Art. 6 of the "Project of Declaration of the Rights of Man in Society" by M. Target, Presented during the meeting of the National Assembly of the July 27, 1789, *Archives Parlementaires*, vol. 8, 288.

41 Malouet, Speech in the National Assembly, Monday, August 3, 1789, *Archives Parlementaires*, vol. 8, 339.

42 "Charte contenant la Constitution française dans ses objets fondamentaux," art. 8, proposed to the National Assembly by Charles-François Bouche on 12 August 1789, *Archives Parlementaires*, vol. 8, 400.

In this sense, Hegel's interpretation of the French Revolution was particularly insightful. He saw in the French Revolution the elevation on the level of the law, of the liberty that a human being has to be a human being: the revolution elevated the principle of liberty to the intelligible level of the state and posed the possibility of the realization of one's being as human and of living a human life in the rights of man and of the citizen.[43] The affirmation of being a citizen leads to affirming oneself as being human. For Hegel, in opposition to the world of antiquity and the absorption of moral individuality in the cosmos, the emergence of subjectivity as reflective interiority and the manifestation of subjectivity in civil society is as important as political liberty.[44] He applauds the French Revolution as the triumph of liberty and the affirmation of self-government.[45] Hegel sees in the French Revolution the realization of political liberty and its elevation on the level of the law. The power that man has to be oneself becomes universal and for all a principle of the purpose of society and the state. For the first time, human beings become human beings independently of any other characteristic, religion, or origin. By consecrating political liberty, the French Revolution poses the foundation of the abstract ahistorical character of the human being. This abstraction is associated with a conception of human existence as a social existence and with the satisfaction of human needs through work.

Fichte's thought and his interpretation of the French Revolution can serve as an intermediary step in this respect in regard to the conceptualization of human dignity as associated with the right to work.[46] His scheme of thought was associated later with socialism.[47] He takes Sieyès's conception in the preamble further. Fichte turns the understanding of negative liberty and its instantiation par excellence, the right to property, into a positive liberty. All human beings have a property on themselves since the pure self, which is reason dominating our sensibility, can use property as means for its goals, he notes. Around us, there are things that are not their property in themselves, because they are not free, but that are not originally ours as they do not belong immediately to our sensible self. We have the right to apply our own sensible forces to all the aims that we would like to achieve, and that the law of reason does not forbid, and thus turn things into our objects.[48] So far his reasoning is very close to Locke's. Fichte continues that, therefore, if a particular constitutional situation,

43 Hegel discusses the French Revolution in many of his works analyzed later in the chapter. There is significant secondary French literature on Hegel's interpretation of the French Revolution. See in particular Ritter, *Hegel et la Révolution française*, 26; Bourgeois, *Philosophie et droits de l'homme*, Goyard-Fabre, "Les Lumières ont-elles préparé la Révolution?," 23–43, 23.

44 G. W. F. Hegel, *Introduction to the Philosophy of History*, trans. Leo Rauch (Indianapolis and Cambridge: Hackett, 1988).

45 G. W. F. Hegel, *The Philosophy of History*, trans. J. Sibree (New York: Dover, 1956) 444 ff.

46 J. G. Fichte, *Considérations destinées à rectifier les jugements du public sur la Révolution française*, trans. Jules Barni (Paris: F. Chamerot, 1859).

47 See Otto Friedrich von Gierke, *Natural Law and the Theory of Society 1500 to 1800*, 1913, trans. Ernest Barker (Cambridge University Press, 1934), 104.

48 Fichte, *Considérations*, 145.

a specific state of the law, prevents us from realizing ourselves by giving to something the form of a medium for our goals, this state of the law is unjust and a people has the right to reverse it. The French Revolution aims to restore this state of reality where it is possible for every human being to develop their abilities and to work properly in order to satisfy their needs against an inegalitarian reality that is favorable to the prodigality of some but represents a situation of distress for others.[49] We have a right for the state to ensure that we can exercise our liberty to work in order to sustain ourselves. This was for Fichte the central requirement of the French Revolution and this is where all the rights of man and of the citizen meet: in the obligation of the state to make sure that all citizens have the possibility to sustain themselves: that they would have the necessary preconditions to exercise their liberties. This is consistent with Fichte's thesis that freedom and rights are possible only in community with others. Human flourishing is possible only under laws that allow the same possibilities for everyone under a new state in France. As analyzed in Chapter 5, the French went even further in their conception of rights. They considered that rights by definition do not make sense outside of society.

The French Declaration confirms in principle the reconceptualization of the role of the state, founded from then on upon political rights, which are the accomplishment of the rights of man. The affirmation of the rights of man can lead to their realization but only by including in its essential content the rights of the citizen as founded on the rights of man. The declaration of the rights of man is conditioned by the declaration of the rights of the citizen. Hegel noted insightfully that the Declaration of the Rights of Man and of the Citizen conserves a conception of natural rights as social, associated with the idea of equality by definition.[50] Bernard Bourgeois has insightfully noted that the French declarations express the articulation of the rights of the person, the rights of the social individual defined by common utility, and the rights of the citizen realized by legislation.[51] The first category of rights protects, for every person, the liberty that belongs to them as a person: their capable will. The second category protects the rights to realize this liberty, the social rights associated with the realization of liberty measured by "common utility." These rights can only be realized and constitute effective rights that everyone can have if everyone accepts the definition of their content and their limits by the law.

Hegel applauded this conception as in his opinion the rational state is the space and the absolute agent of the realization of the rights of man. This is because the individual has truth and moral reality only as a member of the state, which is the best possible instantiation of reason.[52] The state ensures the bond between individuals and the substantive universal good that makes the existence of individual liberty

49 Fichte, *Considérations*, 220–25.
50 Hegel, *The Philosophy of History*, 444 ff.
51 Bourgeois, *Philosophie et droits de l'homme*, 17.
52 Hegel, *Elements of Philosophy of Right*, § 259, 281.

possible.[53] This means that in the state, duty and right are united in one and the same relation.[54] Hegel also thought that the constitution of a state reflects the level of maturity of reason of a people. The proclamation of rights in France reflected a conception that did not correspond to the level of maturity of reason within French society. For Hegel, the French aimed to impose upon reality the politics of human rights as an exaltation of pure will and of pure thought. The realization of the irrationality of privilege and the agitation of spirit resulting from oppression led to the elaboration of a Constitution, which expressed the law in abstract terms. The French Revolution and the Declaration of the Rights of Man and of the Citizen are the result of the work of thought upon itself, the result of philosophy.

Hegel's work represents a decisive step in the philosophical understanding of the French Revolution because it linked three problems that have dominated all the great interpretations of the event ever since: the relations between the revolutionary events, the internal logic of the "abstractions of 1789," and the political instability, which characterizes the revolutionary process.[55] For Hegel, this abstract humanism of the revolution led to the Terror because it contributes to the idea that human beings do not find their essence by their inscription in reality but by cutting themselves off from any naturalization. This ahistorical conception of humanity includes the claim that individuals can define themselves by reference to this abstract conception of humanity and transcend their limitations.[56] The Jacobin government aimed to incarnate universal will and to express absolute liberty, a liberty that conceives its object a priori by elevating it to the level of concept. This abstract conception, being absolute and expressing the universal, attempts to modify reality according to its a priori representations. This government action could only result in "negative action," the "fury of destruction,"[57] Hegel notes, given that it was impossible for reality to correspond to this abstract representation. These internal contradictions between ideas and reality are inherent in any abstract beginning, in its attempt to become concrete.[58]

Postulating teleological evolution toward a realization of reason in history, Hegel stresses the role of contingency for political institutions, in the long trajectory of this realization. As he notes in his *Principles of Philosophy of Right*, the effective spirit of a people expresses itself in its institutions on every step of historical evolution.

53 Hegel, *Elements of Philosophy of Right*, § 268, 288.

54 Hegel, *Elements of Philosophy of Right*, § 261, 283–84. See Pierre Hassner, "Georg W.F. Hegel," in Leo Strauss and Joseph Cropsey, eds., *History of Political Philosophy*, 3rd ed. (University of Chicago Press, 1987), 732–60.

55 Philippe Raynaud, "Révolution française," in Raynaud and Rials, eds., *Dictionnaire de philosophie politique*, 669–76, 675.

56 G. W. F. Hegel, *Phenomenology of Spirit*, trans. A. V. Miller (Oxford University Press, 1977), § 585–95. See Robert Legros, "Hegel entre Lumières et romantisme," in *La Révolution française entre Lumières et romantisme, Cahiers de Philosophie Politique et Juridique* 16 (1989), 143–57, 156.

57 Hegel, *Phenomenology of Spirit*, § 589, 359.

58 See Jacques d'Hondt, "Le parcours hégélien de la Révolution française," in d'Hondt, *Hegel et les français*, 146.

> The constitution of a specific nation will in general depend on the nature and development of its self-consciousness; it is in this self-consciousness that its subjective freedom and hence also the actuality of the constitution lie. The wish to give to a people a Constitution *a priori*, even if its content were more or less rational, is an idea [Einfall] which overlooks the very moment by virtue of which a constitution is more than a product of thought. Each nation accordingly has the constitution appropriate and proper to it.[59]

The state, contingent in the long march toward the realization of reason, is only a manifestation of the life of a people, contained in the culture of this people. If this is the case, then a constitution, fabricated a priori, cannot be implanted in a people whose historical evolution has not yet reached the degree of rationality that corresponds to it.[60] Postulating that the legal constitution is effective only to the extent that it theoretically expresses the constitution, in the organic sense of the term, in which a people have historically fabricated its real practice, Hegel aimed to underline the dialectic of the injustice associated with abstract moralism.[61] The French Jacobins are exemplary of this abstract moralism.

For Hegel, the abstraction of the Constitution of 1791 and of the Declaration of the Rights of Man and of the Citizen are moments of the dialectic movement of history. Similarly, the Jacobin dogmatism and its abstractions are the intermediate steps toward the progression of the realization of reason in history.[62] "World history is the world's court of judgment":[63] this highly idealistic character of the proclamation of liberty costed the French Declaration the possibility of its realization. The historical revolution did not conform with the goals of the Ideologues, the renewal of the established order. Appalled by the Terror, they placed their hopes in Bonaparte. These hopes were not fulfilled either: "if the future reactionaries will accuse the Ideologues of having gone too far, the future revolutionaries will accuse them of an insurmountable bourgeois mentality which prevented them from going far enough."[64] The need to guarantee the social conditions for the exercise of individual liberty – conceived as liberty of the social human being – the concern to limit liberty and define its content through the conception of liberty as the relationship with the self and, by extension, with others through the medium of the will of the rational state, was omnipresent in the French revolutionaries.

59 Hegel, *Elements of Philosophy of Right*, § 274, 371.

60 As noted in Bernard Bourgeois, "Hegel," in Raynaud and Rials, eds., *Dictionnaire de philosophie politique*, 314. On the necessity to "situate" the rational "in the movement of the real" in order to "save" it, so that it is not "reduced to the contingency of the real," see Marcel Gauchet, *L'avènement de la démocratie*, vol. 1, *La Révolution moderne* (Paris: Gallimard, 2007), 142 ff.

61 Hans-Georg Gadamer, "Hegel's Philosophy and Its Aftereffects until Today," in *Reason in the Age of Science*, trans. Frederick G. Lawrence (Cambridge, MA: MIT University Press, 1986), 21–37, 30.

62 Jacques d'Hondt, "Hegel et Napoléon," in d'Hondt, *Hegel et les français*, 203; Jürgen Habermas, "*Theory and Practice*, trans. John Viertel (Boston: Beacon Press, 1973), 138 ff.

63 As Hegel notes in his *Elements of Philosophy of Right*, § 340, 371.

64 Georges Gusdorf, *Les sciences humaines et la pensée occidentale*, vol. 8, *La conscience révolutionnaire et les idéologues* (Paris, Payot, 1978), 22.

Aiming too high, they failed and led to a new consolidation of power and understanding of liberty.

Hegel's criticisms point toward the internal logic of the abstractions of the declarations of rights and the political instability that characterized the revolutionary project.[65] He furnished a model of interpretation of the character of the French Revolution. Using the law to reform humanity and to establish an abstract idea of rights will fail if social circumstances are not ready. In other words, using government *dirigisme*, which derives from a long tradition of trust toward the positive character of the government in France, to implement abstract principles is bound to fail. It will lead to a new consolidation of power and to a different understanding of the possibilities of government action to realize liberty. The French Revolution was only one step in the progressive realization of reason in history. The channels of its movement were defined by an understanding of the role of the government that had preceded it, and the solution to the impasses that it led to were implemented by a similar understanding. Paradoxically, this state action to realize liberty leads to an association with legal positivism in the French context like Fichte's and Rousseau's, where liberty is to be meaningful only if recognized by the state.

This "metaphysical" character of the rights proclaimed by the French Declaration was the object of Edmund Burke's critique.[66] Burke insists on the role of tradition, of experience and of prejudice concerning the protection of a liberty. His views on the French Revolution are not necessarily inscribed in a conservative framework as Joseph de Maistre's are.[67] Burke condemns the abstraction of the principles proclaimed in 1789 and the obsession with reason. The French revolutionaries, who think that they can design an ideal republic on paper a priori, lack experience, he notes.[68] This is what justifies the difference in his reaction to the French and the American revolutions. In his opinion, the universalism of the proclaimed rights in France is an abstraction from reality. It establishes an unrealizable relation between theory and practice. For Burke,

65 Philippe Raynaud, "Révolution française," in Raynaud and Rials, eds., *Dictionnaire de philosophie politique*, 669–76, 675.

66 Edmund Burke, *Reflections on the Revolution of France*, in L. G. Mitchell, ed., *The Writings and Speeches of Edmund Burke*, vol. 8 (Oxford University Press, 1989), 53. For secondary bibliography, see Philippe Raynaud, *Trois révolutions de la liberté: Angleterre, Amérique, France* (Paris: Presses Universitaires de France, 2009); Ernest Barker, "Edmund Burke et la Révolution française," in E. Barker et al., *La Révolution de 1789 et la pensée moderne* (Paris: Presses Universitaires de France, 1940), 1–32; Cecil P. Courtney, "Burke et les Lumières," in *La Révolution française entre Lumières et romantisme*, 53–64; Franc Lessay, "Burke et la nationalisation de la raison," in *La Révolution française entre Lumières et romantisme*, 65–82; Gérard Gengembre, "La contre-révolution et le refus de la constitution," in Michel Troper and Lucien Jaume, eds., *1789 et L'Invention de la Constitution* (Paris: LGDJ et Bruylant, 1994), 55–74; Gerard Gengembre, "Burke," in François Furet et Mona Ouzouf, eds., *Dictionnaire critique de la Révolution française: interprètes et historiens* (Paris: Flammarion, 2007), 51–61.

67 De Maistre, *Considerations on France*, trans. Richard A. Lebrun (Montreal and London: McGill-Queen's University Press, 1974).

68 Burke, *Reflections*, 111–12.

practice must follow the continuity of history, which separates it from theory.[69] It is circumstances that give any political principle its "distinctive color and effect." He accepts a positivistic approach to rights, considering that if civil society is the result of a convention, this convention must be the law. The law limits, modifies, and gives sense and content to any prescription and affirmation of liberties and to the role of the state concerning the definition of their limits. The practical science of government must be guided by practical utility, which provides a "dense medium" in which "are refracted from their straight line" the "metaphysical rights – rays of light."[70] He also insists that the necessity to protect one liberty over another is relative in time and in space. "To the proportion according to which rights are metaphysically true, they are morally and politically false," submitted to the prudential judgment of political reason.[71]

However, Burke's analysis on the French Declaration overlooks the role assigned to the law and the preconception of the role of the state as legitimized to define the content and limits of liberty. In this sense, Hegel seems to better capture the events surrounding 1789 with his dialectical approach to theory and practice.[72] As Hans Georg-Gadamer notes, even when life changes suddenly, as it is the case during revolutionary periods, there "is conserved under the *prima facie* change of everything a part of the past much more considerable than we think and which finds its authority by allying itself to what is new."[73] The critical spirit of the revolution leads to a dialectical inversion. This inversion comes out from its own moralizing impasse and its incapacity to revolutionize the world. Burke seems to accept Hegelian elements as he admits the idea of the work of tradition, of the operation of collective mentality through generations constructing a system of political and social values, as an objective spirit, the "sovereign reason of the world." This is accumulated by the human spirit, which directs the process of history and the life of the states. However, he does not reason in a way that is comparable to the Hegelian dialectic. For Burke, it is the past that must be respected in the present. Hegel would respond that it is precisely the past that traces the way that the present follows in a dialectical movement, in which the present inevitably carries some signs and traces of the past whatever its ambition to irrevocably abolish the past might be.

69 Benjamin Delannoy also notes this point in his *Burke et Kant: interprètes de la Révolution française*, 46.

70 Burke, *Reflections*, 112.

71 Ibid.

72 Cf. Jacques Aumètre, "La Révolution: réalisation et révélation de la raison," *in* Jacques Aumètre et al., *Les Lumières et la Déclaration des droits de l'homme: rupture ou continuité?* (Québec: Presses de l'Université de Québec, 1990), 11–29; Philippe Raynaud, "Lumières et Anti-lumières: de la Révolution française au romantisme politique," in *La Révolution française entre Lumières et romantisme, Cahiers de Philosophie Politique et Juridique* 16 (1989), 179–92, 192.

73 Gadamer, *Vérité et méthode*, 303.

This highly idealistic character of the French Declaration was also the object of Bentham's critique.[74] From his utilitarian perspective, human happiness cannot be defined by reference to an objective good or to "natural" rights. Politics should be engaged in promoting the greatest good for the greatest number and must not be justified in relation to some individual or group. He defends social action in order to scientifically improve the general well-being, which will have the consequence of ensuring the self-fulfillment of individuals.[75] For Bentham, there are no "natural rights" that could be opposed to legal rights. Declaring the existence of "imprescriptible" rights would incite resistance against the law. He sees in the clause of Article 4 of the French Declaration, according to which the limits of liberty would be determined by the law, a contradiction and an insoluble confusion. If the limits of liberty are determined by the law, this means that liberty can be conceivable as valid only from the moment that the law has determined its limits. It does not make sense to say that liberty is valid before the legislator gives it force and validity by determining its limits. The same applies for Bentham concerning the clauses of the French Declaration on freedom of opinion. According to Article 10, "No one shall be disquieted on account of his opinions, including his religious views, provided their manifestation does not disturb the public order established by law."[76] Bentham notes that in any case, it is the law that defines this "public order." The evaluation of when such a violation occurs depends on circumstances. Thus, it is impossible, Bentham thinks, that any legislator could enunciate inflexible and adamantine rules concerning what is a violation of public order. For Bentham the concept of "natural rights" is an "imaginary identity," a "chimera," as rights are only the "children" of the law on the basis of its diverse operations and its functions.[77] Bentham's critique stresses the internal contradictions of the French conception of liberty as it is drawn from the declaratory texts that followed the revolution. Despite the references to natural law, the role foreseen for the state by the French Declaration in relation to the determination of liberty means conceiving liberty as posed by the law. The law has an important role in defining the content of liberty, its limits, and the very possibility of the realization of liberty. Even the discourse on "natural rights" of the French Revolutionaries associates them with the natural character of society and its role in making liberty meaningful as analyzed in Chapter 5.

74 Jeremy Bentham, *Anarchical Fallacies; Being an examination of the Declaration of Rights issued during the French Revolution*, in Jeremy Waldron, ed., *Nonsense Upon Stilts: Bentham, Burke and Marx on the Rights of Man* (London and New York: Methuen, 1987), 60–61. It would be absurd in his opinion, to presuppose an entity which would have legal effects but which would subsist not only in law but against the law.

75 Timothy Fuller, "Jeremy Bentham and James Mill," in Leo Strauss and Joseph Cropsey, ed., *History of Political Philosophy*, 3rd ed. (University of Chicago Press, 1987 [1963]), 710–31, 715–16.

76 English translation by the Avalon Project, Documents in Law, History, Diplomacy, Yale Law School, http://avalon.law.yale.edu/18th_century/rightsof.asp.

77 Bentham, *Anarchical Fallacies*, 73.

The highly idealistic aims of the French Revolution and its tendency to regenerate humanity as well as to reform France, led Tocqueville to draw a parallel between its force and significance with that of a religious revolution comparable to the Protestant reformation.[78] It provided a unificatory ideological scheme on the basis of principles, just like the reformation had done before, above any other previous unificatory element such as language or nation. Hegel also insisted on the radical character of the French Revolution, studying the opposition between the Protestant states and the Catholic states like France, stressing the role of religion for the understanding of subjectivity and liberty.[79] For Hegel in the Protestant states, following the reform and the introduction of the principle of subjectivity, which generates religious emancipation and internal harmony, humans are recognized in their real existence as free singularities. The Protestant world is advanced in reflecting in such a way as to realize the absolute highest point of self-consciousness.[80] The abstractions of the French revolutionaries reflected the division between two types of conscience admitted by the Catholic world, the religious conscience and the conscience of the abstraction of thought. This division does not exist in Protestantism.[81] Hegel thinks that the French established an intellectual principle as the foundation of the state. This principle does not find its origin in the religious sentiment, as the principle of divine selection of state power does. It is a principle of certitude, the identity of self-conscience with itself. For Hegel, a separate declaration of rights for the Catholic world was necessary, compared to the Protestant world, as human subjectivity is vulnerable to the oppression of the politico-religious "objectivity." This also made its realization impossible to the extent that the internal rejection of religion condemns to failure the external affirmation of this rejection, as realized during the Terror. This is how Hegel comes to the conclusion that human rights can only be realized in the context of an existence that is first religiously reformed.[82] For Hegel, it was this abstract humanism of the French Revolution that led to the Terror. Luther liberated the Christian from the bonds of canonic law and made them master of themselves, at least in the religious sphere, having discovered the *Innerlichkeit*, dear to the Germanic thought and to the normative competence of the free subjectivity, according to Michel Villey.[83] The Protestant state is by essence capable of recognizing human rights in practice as its legitimacy derives from reason, contemplating the law, justice, and the good of the community.[84] On the contrary, in Catholic states like France, the interference of the

78 Tocqueville, *Ancien Régime*, 68–72.

79 Hegel, *Philosophy of History*, 438 ff., Pierre Hassner, "Hegel," 740–41, Bernard Bourgeois, "Hegel," 314.

80 Hegel, *Philosophy of History*, 44 ff., Jacques d'Hondt, *De Hegel à Marx* (Paris, Presses Universitaires de France, 1972), 132.

81 Bourgeois, *Philosophie et droits de l'homme*, 84.

82 Bourgeois, *La raison moderne et le droit politique* (Paris: Vrin, 2000), 119.

83 Villey, *Formation*, 287.

84 Hegel, *Philosophy of History*, 445.

spiritual power with the law encouraged by the church provides a divine foundation to the arbitrary will of the political power. The state negates the formal emergence of subjectivity and rights can exist only by being proclaimed – they must be proclaimed in order to revolutionize the law.[85]

Agreeing with Hegel, Georg Jellinek attributes Lutherian origins to the religious conceptions that inspire the Mayflower Compact and through it the American Declaration of Independence.[86] The association of Protestantism with Lockeanism, facilitated by the religious elements in Locke's thought, seems to be a plausible hypothesis, which can guide the understanding of liberty in the American context.[87] This metaphysical foundation leads to a negative conception of natural rights. God is seen as prescribing through natural law moral duties to individuals, among which self-preservation, which can be accomplished by the use of rights or moral powers, by the exercise of which moral duties are imposed on others to allow the beneficiaries of rights to act free from any interference.[88] The reference to the moral sentiments as the justificatory ideology of the American Declaration and the necessary recognition that follows from liberty as generalizable did not aim to justify the role of the state in guaranteeing the preconditions of the exercise of liberty, but insisted on the necessary universalization of negative liberty for all members of the moral community.

If the highly idealistic character of the proclamation of liberty in France is inscribed in a radical break from the past, the American Revolution sought to re-proclaim the liberties long enjoyed by the Americans.[89] The French Declaration is inscribed in the necessity to regenerate a French nation according to the requirements of idealistic reason. As analyzed in Chapter 2, John Austin's theory of speech acts is relevant to declarations of rights.[90] They are speech acts and have what he calls "illocutionary force" in a specific context of communication. The illocutionary

85 Bourgeois, *Philosophie et droits de l'homme*, 82. The alliance between the monarchic authority and the divine authority, which Bossuet had theorized in the *Politique tirée de l'écriture sainte*, led to the consideration of catholicism as a threat of civic liberties. It is only in this frame that can be understood, as Tocqueville had noted in *Democracy in America* the animosity of the French toward religion, the dissolution of the ecclesiastical order by the revolutionary power and the persecutions of the priests. From now on, the religious element is seen as conservative and reactionary by the "true democrats"; this antagonism between the Church and the state always renewed despite some attempts of reconciliation perverts the political life of the nation throughout the centuries. Cf. Gusdorf, *Les Révolutions de France et d'Amérique*, 103.

86 Georg Jellinek, *La Déclaration des droits de l'homme et du citoyen, contribution à l'histoire du droit constitutionnel moderne*, trans. Georges Fardis (Paris: Albert Fontemoing, 1902), 79.

87 See the analysis of Michael Zuckert, in *The Natural Rights Republic: Studies in the Foundation of the American Political Tradition* (University of Notre Dame Press, 1996), 148–201.

88 James H. Hutson, "The Emergence of the Modern Concept of a Right in America: The Contribution of Michel Villey," in Barry Alan Shain, ed., *The Nature of Rights at the American Founding and Beyond* (Charlottesville and London: University of Virginia Press, 2013), 48.

89 Gusdorf, *Les Révolutions de France et d'Amérique*, 47 ff.

90 According to John Austin's conception in *How to Do Things with Words* (Cambridge, MA: Harvard University Press, 1862).

force of the American Declaration consists in breaking the link with the metropolis, inscribed in the necessity to justify the reasons for independence before the whole world.[91] Among the aims of the American Revolution was the proclamation of the protection of the British liberties as liberties of the subjects in the colonies. The American Revolution challenged the prerogatives of the British sovereign to limit liberty. The American bills of rights pre- and post-revolution refer to a conception of transcendental liberty formed by modern natural law theories. In the Founding Era, they aimed at affirming mostly negative rights. They also aimed at affirming the negative aspect of political liberty. Political liberty can have a negative aspect in the sense of not being interfered with in the exercise of political liberties. This negative aspect of political liberty has an impact upon negative liberties themselves as they are affected by the exercise of political liberties. Therefore, the need to affirm the negative aspect of political liberty at the moment of the American Revolution had a repercussion upon negative liberties themselves. Hegel's analysis attributes to the French Revolution the capital importance on the idealistic level of guaranteeing human liberty par excellence, the liberty that each human being has to be a human being by the affirmation of being a citizen. This political liberty of participation was a liberty practiced in America.[92] The American Declaration of Independence aimed to reaffirm the "negative" protection of this liberty of self-government practiced in the communities of the colonies against the British government. It aimed to protect self-government from external interference by the British parliament. It aimed to protect a "collective" liberty as a "negative" liberty – in its negative aspect. It responded to the political problem of defining the scope of state power to protect "administrative decentralization," or local self-government.

In Europe, a hierarchical social organization and the hereditary immunities of the nobility were an important obstacle to the establishment of equal liberties of participation. Social distinctions of this type had faded in America. Some historians note that life in some communities of the first colonies, seventeenth-century Virginia and New England, for example, had led to a communitarian ethic dictated by some common religious beliefs, which was unfavorable to rights individualism.[93] It should not be underestimated that the communitarian spirit in some American cities commonly limited liberty at the communal level, as

91 Aiming to provide to the world the reasons for independence, it provided inspiration to a world of Declarations see David Armitage, *The Declaration of Independence: A Global History* (Cambridge, MA: Harvard University Press, 2007).

92 Hutson, "Emergence," 25–24, 40–41. The author insists on the communal nature of the life in 19th century North America, which resulted in the "subordination of the person to the collectivity" and denounces the "individualist illusion" citing also Barry Shain, *The Myth of American Individualism: The Protestant Origins of American Political Thought* (Princeton University Press, 1994). On the same idea Richard Primus, "An Introduction to the Nature of American Rights," in Shain, ed., *The Nature of Rights*, 15–24, 23.

93 Hutson, "Emergence," 45.

historians note.[94] The Glorious Revolution and the Bill of Rights of 1689 introduced the necessity to affirm the concept of rights in the self-consciousness of the colonies and led them to find the necessary conceptual elements in thinkers such as Locke. The conflict with the British parliament led the American political actors to affirm a conception of negative rights, which was up to then vague and imprecise. American thought matured around the idea of inherent rights, which led to a wave of bills of rights elaborated in the new states after 1776 with safeguards against the government. As analyzed later, simultaneously the need to ensure peaceful coexistence among various religious communities led them to realize that all religious communities should enjoy equal negative liberty.

The concern to protect the negative aspect of self-government together with negative liberty was reaffirmed during the construction of the federal state. The Americans realized the need to protect the negative aspect of any liberty on the federal level as well as on the level of the states. The Declaration of Independence aimed to defend the negative aspect of the liberty of self-government and to remind the British that they were violating traditional English liberties in relation to the colonies.[95] The necessity to protect the political liberty of the communities negatively against encroachments by the British, inscribed in the Declaration of Independence, and the experience with self-government, led to a conception of limited government both at the level of the new states and at the federal level. The liberties that the American Framers aimed to protect against the government were negative liberties, the ones they saw threatened by democratic, majority decision making. They elaborated a conception of republicanism that they considered superior to any other practiced in history until then, because they had learned from the mistakes of republicanism as practiced in antiquity and medieval Europe.[96] They drafted a Constitution that would protect their system of government from self-harm. The American declarations of rights, state and federal, motivated by a sense of moderation toward republicanism, sought to limit majorities.

94 Barry Alan Shain, "Rights Natural and Civil in the Declaration of Independence," in Barry Alan Shain, ed., *The Nature of Rights at the American Founding and Beyond* (Charlottesville and London: University of Virginia Press, 2007), 116–62, 131.

95 See John Phillip Reid, "The Authority of Rights at the American Founding," in Shain, ed., *Nature of Rights*, 68–115, 83 ff.; see also, John Phillip Reid, *Constitutional History of the American Revolution: The Authority of Rights* (Wisconsin: University of Wisconsin Press, 1986); John Philip Reid, *The Concept of Liberty in the Age of the American Founding* (Chicago and London: The University of Chicago Press, 1988), 77; Graig Yirush, *Settlers, Liberty and Empire: The Roots of Early American Political Theory, 1675–1775* (Cambridge University Press, 2011).

96 See for instance John Adams, "A Defence of the Constitutions of Government of the United States of America," in *The Works of John Adams*, vol. 4, 469–588, vol. 5, 3–478. See also Richard Hofstadter, "The Founding Fathers: An Age of Realism," in Robert H. Horwitz, ed., *The Moral Foundations of the American Republic* (Charlottesville: University Press of Virginia, 1979), 73–85, 79 ff.

The French declarations referred to "natural, negative rights" in a context that indicated trust toward the government to realize rights. These are liberties against the state, which the state should realize. This was because, as Hegel noted, they understood liberty *in abstracto*, as englobing all the possible meanings of the term: negative and positive. This meant positive liberty in the sense of political participation, and in the sense that the state would provide to the citizens the preconditions for the exercise of their liberty. The American declarations did not appear to commit a performative contradiction, as the context of their enunciation, characterized by distrust toward the state, coincides with their content, the enunciation *expressis verbis* of this distrust. This libertarian conception of rights was considered as compatible with republicanism and the pursuit of the common good. The exercise of negative rights was seen as facilitating the common good.[97] In America, interest in political affairs was dictated from a concern that state action would sooner or later limit negative liberties. Tocqueville had underlined the importance of the guarantee of negative liberties and the close link that exists between negative and political liberties. In his eyes, American institutions were exemplary, as through the recognition of negative and political liberties they ensured consensus for state action and vivid interest in political affairs.[98] Citizens are interested in political affairs, because political decisions will affect their negative liberties, sooner or later.

The Declaration of Independence had the effect of affirming through a speech act a real situation acquired throughout generations in America.[99] The Americans had experienced self-government and were aware of the potential of the law to limit liberty. Far from being a "leap into the unknown," the American democracy had a past in the daily life of the colonies.[100] Burke emphasizes this reluctance of the British parliament to adhere to the principles of British constitutional law by not respecting the natural liberties of the colonies.[101] This is the reason why he was sympathetic to the American revolutionaries and critical toward the French.[102] In his opinion, the rights-claims of the former took place in the name of the protection of the British rights by citizens conscious of the legitimacy of their cause. The proclamation of liberty of the latter took place "on the pretext of human rights," a "charming delusion, which falsified them afterwards by the worst exaggerations

97 Hutson, "Emergence," 53.

98 Tocqueville, *Democracy in America*, 242, 509–13.

99 Ibid., 48–49; see also Robert R. Palmer, "The European Enlightenment in Its American Setting," *in Aspects of American Liberty, Philosophical, Historical and Political* (Philadelphia: The American Philosophical Society, 1977), 47–55, 52.

100 Gusdorf, *Les Révolutions de France et d'Amérique*, 48–49; see also Robert R. Palmer, "The European Enlightenment in Its American Setting," in American Philosophical Society, *Aspects of American Liberty*, 47–55, 52.

101 Edmund Burke, *On Conciliation with America* [1775], in Paul Langford, ed., *The Writings and Speeches of Edmund Burke*, vol. 3 (Oxford University Press, 1996), 120, 127.

102 Burke notes that "abstract liberty, like other mere abstractions, is not to be found" in America. Ibid., 120.

in a *vacuum* of humanity."[103] Burke notes that the British Empire should protect the liberties of the colonies if it wanted to preserve its unity.[104] According to Burke, the "truth" of a people is always defined by its historical precedents, which can be agitated by crises and disequilibrium leading to the restructuring of the established order. Thus, the goal to formulate a political and social order from zero by legislating under the invocation of the universal man is an ambitious initiative. The French revolutionaries renounced their past in order to replace it with ideals dictated by pure reason, which led them to the Terror. The Americans invoked precedents to support their cause. Those precedents existed in principles already legitimate for the people of Great Britain. The French revolutionaries aimed to reconstruct an ideal republic on the basis of abstract principles and their constitutional schemes "collapsed under the weight of their own immaturity."[105] On the contrary, the American revolutionaries voiced ideas dictated by a democratic liberalism permeated by pragmatism.

Suggesting an association between the American Declaration of 1776 and the English Declaration of 1689 was useful to the movement of independence. The Americans claimed that they were proclaiming the liberties of the "English."[106] At the same time they moved even further the conception of liberty that existed in previous texts. The English Declaration is not permeated by a conception of rights and liberties that have a "divine" or "natural" origin. It crystallized a balance of powers between the parliament and the king at the time it was proclaimed.[107] It also expressed a vision of modernizing the English society of its time, which was opposed to the centralizing vision dominant in France at the time.[108] Therefore, despite some similarities between the English Declaration of 1689 and the American Declaration of 1776, there are significant differences in the underlying conception of liberty. These differences concern the five principal doctrines of the American Declaration of Independence: equality, the conception of government as an artificial element, natural rights as the foundation and the aim of politics, consensus, and the right to revolt.[109] The doctrine of "natural rights" as the limitation of the power of

103 As Georges Gusdorf notes in *Les révolutions*, 166. See also Jaume, *Individu effacé*, 550; Raynaud, "Révolution française," 669–83.

104 Burke, *On Conciliation with America*, 165. See also Edmund Burke, "Second Speech on Conciliation, 16 November 1775," in Langford, ed. *Writings and Speeches*, vol. 3, 198.

105 Gusdorf, *Les révolutions*, 166.

106 John Phillip Reid, "The Authority of Rights at the American Founding," in Shain, ed., *Nature of Rights*, 67–115; Reid, *Constitutional History of the American Revolution.*

107 Geoffrey Lock, "The 1689 Bill of Rights," XXXVII, Political Studies, 540–61; Martin Loughlin, *The British Constitution: A Very Short Introduction* (Oxford University Press, 2013), 44; Lois G. Schwoerer, "The Bill of Rights: Epitome of the Revolution of 1688–89," in J. G. A. Pocock, . *Three British Revolutions: 1641, 1688, 1776* (Princeton University Press, 1980), 225–43.

108 See Steve Pincus, *1688: The First Modern Revolution* (New Haven, CT: Yale University Press, 2009).

109 For an analysis of the similarities and differences between the English Declaration of 1689 and the American Declaration of 1776, see Michael P. Zuckert, *Natural Rights and the New Republicanism* (Princeton: Princeton University Press, 1994), 6; Michael Zuckert, *Natural Rights Republic*, 99 ff.

government is absent from the text of the English Declaration. Even if the latter attempted to limit the royal power, the protection of rights was not considered the principal aim of government. This is a meaning that the Declaration obtained later. The rights mentioned in the English Declaration are not the negative and complementary rights of life, liberty, and the pursuit of happiness, but rather the requirement that the king should not commit some acts without the authorization of parliament. This philosophy of negative natural rights aimed to provide the elements of legitimacy to any governmental agency, to limit state coercion and to establish the "rule of law," as general rules – limits on state action. Even during the debates on the construction of the federal government, the Americans referred to the English Bill Rights of 1689 as constitutive of a social contract between individuals and power.[110]

Another factor that must be considered on the symbolic level is the message that the movements aimed to transmit to the rest of the world. The Americans sought to justify their separatist movement, using English constitutional history as well as theories of international law as points of reference.[111] John Adams justifies the rupture by reference to the absence of royal protection, which discharged them from their allegiance, a reflection inspired by Vattel.[112] The Americans sought to persuade people of the legitimacy of their separatist cause. The reference to natural rights rather than to civil rights aims to underline that the British parliament was violating political norms that were the object of international consensus.[113]

The American revolutionaries had parliamentary and administrative experience gained in the colonies' local assemblies. This experience led them to the elaboration of the structures of constitutionalism within each state even before the establishment of the Federal Constitution of 1787. They were also conscious of their aims and their possibilities.[114] By 1776, they had elaborated a notion of a constitution that was different from the one of eighteenth-century Englishmen, as a superior law that would serve to measure any other law.[115] The realization of the necessity to protect liberties against the British parliament during the Founding Era caused and

110 "A Maryland Farmer, 15 February 1788 (Baltimore), Maryland Gazette," in Storing and Murray, eds., *The Complete Anti-Federalist*, vol. 5, 11.

111 Especially Emer de Vattel's, *Le droit des gens ou principes de la loi naturelle appliqués à la conduite et aux affaires des nations et des souverains* (Neuchâtel: Abraham II Droz, 1758), translated into English as *The Law of Nations or Principles of the Law of Nature, Applied to the Conduct and Affairs of Nations and Sovereigns* (London, J. Newbery et al., 1760); Barry A. Shain, "Rights Natural and Civil," 116–62, 125; Armitage, *Declaration of Independence*, 38.

112 John Adams, *Thoughts on Government* [1776] repr. in *The Works of John Adams*, vol. 4 (Boston: Little, Brown & Co., 1856), 197, a thought inspired by Vattel's *Law of Nations*, bk. 1, chap. 17; see William Ossipow and Dominik Gerber, "The Reception of Vattel's Law of Nations in the American Colonies: From James Otis and John Adams to the Declaration of Independence," *American Journal of Legal History* 57 (2017), 521–55, 538.

113 Shain, "Rights Natural and Civil," 124.

114 Gusdorf, *Les révolutions*, 198–199; Wood, *Creation*, 257.

115 Wood, *Creation*, 260.

perpetuated a conception of the necessity to protect negative liberty against state governments. On this point, the decisive legal step happened prior to the period of the Declaration of Independence. The American Revolution and the reconstruction following the American Civil War equally impacted upon the history of the Bill of Rights in the United States. The incorporation of the Bill of Rights thanks to the Fourteenth Amendment of the Federal Constitution following the Civil War and its applicability on the level of the governments of the states contributed decisively to the protection of negative liberty.[116] Akhil Reed Amar's federalist reading of the Bill of Rights emphasizes that, beginning in the 1830s, the early abolitionists developed theories of natural rights, individual liberty and higher law consistent with a "declaratory" interpretation of the Bill of Rights.[117] Instead of seeing the Bill of Rights as creating new rules facilitating the federal structure of the state – applicable to the federal government and delimiting its competences against the states – the abolitionists read it as a norm of a pre-existing superior value applicable to all governments, state and federal.[118] The images of the imperialist British government and of local heroism had inspired the Bill of Rights. A spirit of national heroism against slavery inspired the Fourteenth Amendment during the reconstruction after the Civil War. The First Amendment aimed initially at delimiting the Federal Congress's enumerated powers of regulation. It posed as a rule that Congress did not have the power to regulate freedom of expression over the states. When the First Amendment became applicable against the states thanks to the Fourteenth Amendment, no limitation of freedom of expression was acceptable, whether it comes from the federal government or the states. The textual foundation, which initially sought to protect the states' autonomy in relation to religious questions, became, after the reconstruction, the foundation for invalidating, at the federal level, any state policy that would violate the individual rights of citizens to free speech and freedom of religion.[119] The individualist vision, which insisted on the need to protect minority rights centered on the power of the judges against the abuses of local governments, became dominant after the Civil War. It is at that moment that Americans realized that they ought to strengthen the federal government in this respect. This interpretation by Amar needs complement. As I argue, this evolution can be seen as a rediscovery and adaptation of the principles of the Founding Era to the new circumstances. During the reconstruction, the Americans realized the implications of the natural rights discourse that existed during the era that preceded the American Declaration of Independence. A discourse against slavery in reference

116 Akhil Reed Amar, "The Creation, Reconstruction and Interpretation of the Bill of Rights," in Shain, ed., *Nature of Rights*, 163–80, 165, see also Amar, *Bill of Rights*, 280.

117 Amar, *Bill of Rights*, 161.

118 Ibid.

119 Amar, "Creation," 166. For Akhil Reed Amar, Madison's vision – the protection of individual liberty and of minority rights – was very progressive for its time, whereas a local spirit was largely dominant. Ibid., 172.

to natural rights, which already existed in some of the thinkers of the Founding Era, led them to proclaim more emphatically these rights during the reconstruction.

According to the conception of American republicanism, private liberty is protected exactly because it promotes this republicanism, because this republicanism makes indispensable the distinction between the private and the public, whereas for French republicanism, liberty is consubstantial with the public good. If the American Revolution was principally political, the French Revolution owes its exemplary character to the fact that it wanted to create a new order through a speech act. As analyzed in Section 3.2, this conception has significant implications for freedom of expression.

3.2 RECONCEPTUALIZATION OF THE ROLE OF THE GOVERNMENT VERSUS DEFINITION OF THE LIMITS OF THE ROLE OF THE GOVERNMENT

As Michel Villey stresses, every comprehensive conception of the world, when it becomes dominant in a social group, has repercussions upon the legal world.[120] Religious ideas or the philosophy of sciences, morality, history, politics, or political economy all have a considerable importance for the history of philosophy of law.[121] The law reflects and crystallizes any difference of *Weltanschauung* posed at the moment of the foundation of a democracy and evolving in time. Behind the highly idealistic discourse of the French revolutionaries is hidden a conception of the state as being charged with the mission of instituting the social sphere in conformity with its will, according to the great political revolutionary principles, or later, under Bonapartisme, according to the grand administrative principles.[122] This is opposed to the "empirist" conception of the state as having functions of a considerably less ambitious scope in the United States. The difference between this abstract vision and this empirical vision of the state corresponds to different conceptions of liberty.

The difference in the conception of the role of the state finds its origin in the political problems with which the two declaratory movements were confronted. If in America, the Declaration of Independence was itself the expression of "common sense," of "self-evident truths," the French Declaration needed itself to form public opinion. The American revolutionaries were aiming to apply ideas of limited government. The philosophically oriented members of the National Assembly in France aimed to create a new society. Given the dialectic between theory and practice, the subtle differences in the understanding of the concept of liberty are due to the difference in the social conditions in which the two declaratory movements refer to the same principles.

120 Villey, *Formation*, 278.
121 Ibid.
122 Jaume, *Individu effacé*, 283.

The French Declaration is marked by universalist idealism. The French revolutionaries were fascinated by collective power, which they aimed to recompose. They thought that once its usurpers were removed, collective power could not do harm. They postulated an identification between government and society. The French conception of liberty tends to make the general absorption of powers in the unity of the collective sovereign the instrument of the "positive amplification" of the rights of the individual.[123] Although the French Declaration is inspired by some elements of the individualist current guaranteeing the imprescriptible rights of the individual, these rights are seen as having a social basis. It binds the powers of the person to those of the political subject. Rights flourish only in collective democratic politics in terms of equality. As Marcel Gauchet notes, the French Declaration expresses a logic of correspondence between the rights of the individual and social authority and not of sharing between the two; he stresses "the irreducibility of individual resistance and the irresistibility of social power."[124] The idea of solidarity as a principle to be realized by the state was omnipresent in the thought of the French revolutionaries.[125]

This fascination with the exercise of collective power is visible even in the current of the Physiocrats that influenced the spirit of the revolution.[126] Their thought seems to be a paradoxical amalgam of economic libertarianism associated with political absolutism.[127] "The best of governments is the one that resembles the most the one of the sky, which maintains everything and is never seen. . . . It is forgetting the first result of experience, that is that what is nicely done is what is done by itself, and without being ordered . . . ."[128] At the same time, they consider that legal monarchy is the best possible government to the extent that it guarantees the reunion of wills:

> What we call republic, considered as government could never be anything else than an attempt of transition from a state of disorder to the restoration of order . . . . The common interest, which is the standard of the republic, is the interest of nobody: it is only in monarchy that this interest has a proprietor, someone who is truly interested in maintaining it. In fact, the true government is only the direction of the social force, and this force consists in the union of wills. . . . This Republic must be subordinated, free and sovereign, under the teaching of legal despotism."[129]

123 Gauchet, *La révolution des droits de l'homme*, 46–47.

124 Ibid., 124.

125 Patrice Higonnet, *Sister Republics: The Origins of French and American Republicanism* (Cambridge, MA: Harvard University Press, 1988), 148. Patrice Higonnet attributes the bourgeois individualism of the French in 1789 to their disappointment toward the guardians of the inherited corporate order like the king, the church, the nobility and the parlements and less to a spirit of a possessive individualism as such.

126 Georges Weulersse, *La physiocratie à l'aube de la Révolution: 1781–1792* (Paris: EHESS, 1985).

127 Marquis de Mirabeau letter to Marquis Longo, 10 January 1788, cited in Weulersse, *Physiocratie*, 190. See also James Kloppenberg, *Toward Democracy: The Struggle for Self-Rule in European and American Thought* (Oxford University Press, 2016), 206.

128 Marquis de Mirabeau letter to Marquis Longo, 190.

129 Marquis de Mirabeau, 1785, vol. 3, 26–27, cited in Weulersse, *Physiocratie*.

The individualistic elements from the ideas of the Physiocrats did not persuade French society in the 1780s, which continued to aspire for institutions that would protect individuals against misfortune and economic upheaval.[130]

Although the French Declaration is marked by Locke's thought, aiming to promote the guarantee of individual rights, it indicates trust in state power concerning the definition of the content and limits of rights. It expresses a compromise between the affirmation of the imprescriptibility of human rights and the essential protection of the rights of the citizen as forming a *continuum*. It recognizes the practical effectiveness of the rights of the citizen by conceiving them within a constraining legal horizon.[131] For the French, the rights of the individual exist only thanks to society. In opposition to the spirit that would be dominant in the American political development, private liberty is for the French to be affirmed and realized only through its recognition by public authority. The powers of the individual find their frame of expression and expansion in political society. This means that personal liberty and social authority belong together. The fact that the rights of man were declared at the same time as the rights of the citizen is not a simple coincidence. It affects their Declaration and the meaning of engagement for them: the Declaration of the Rights of Man and of the Citizen is an essentially civic or political act.[132]

The preamble to the Constitution read by Sieyès in the National Assembly on the July 21, 1789 expressly mentions that the aim of any social unity is to "manifest, amplify and ensure the rights of the man and the citizen."[133] It offers a narrative on the social origins of rights, associating the mission of society with the protection of these rights. It mentions that a human being is subject to their needs by nature and possesses by nature the means to confront them. The preamble notes that nothing is more important in the life of a human being than the relationships with their "*semblables*." Even if there are inequalities of means between human beings, this does not mean that there should be inequality of rights.[134] The text emphasizes that the citizens who by misfortune are not able to provide for their needs have "just rights" to the assistance of their fellow citizens. The text emphasizes that

> the advantages that we can draw from the social state are not limited to the effective and complete protection of individual liberty; citizens have a right to all the goods of the association .... We know that those of the citizens that bad fortune condemns to inability to provide for their needs have on the basis of justice rights to the assistance of their fellow citizens.[135]

130 Higgonnet, *Sister Republics*, 158–59.

131 Stéphane Rials, *La Déclaration*, 395.

132 Bourgeois, *Raison moderne*, 122.

133 "Préliminaire de la Constitution, reconnaissance et exposition raisonnée des droits de l'homme et du citoyen," read on the July 21, 1789 by Sieyès, *Archives Parlementaires*, vol. 8, 256–61.

134 Ibid., 257.

135 Ibid., 259 (my translation).

The social order is for Sieyès complementary to the natural order. Its object is the happiness of all members. For Sieyès, it is the mission of the social state to protect equality of rights against the natural inequality of means. Sieyès notes that the aim of the laws of society is to protect the weak from the strong. Covering the universality of the citizens, it guarantees to all the plenitude of their rights. Even conservative members of the National Assembly like Malouet expressed concerns about realizing rights.[136] If America enjoys real effective equality, this is not the case in France, he notes. He urges the members of the National Assembly to create "wise institutions," which will bring together the "happy" and the "unhappy" classes of society. A declaration of rights makes sense only within a constitution that equalizes those who are deprived of enlightenment and means with those that are the most fortunate, he notes. Thus, it is important to unify all rights, natural, civil, and political, and to bring any declaration of rights into a close alignment with the human beings that it concerns.

Among the drafts of declarations of rights developed during the various phases of the French Revolution, two drafts that present rights and duties in the balance enumerate "assistance" as one of the rights of man. Thirteen drafts on the whole – or one in two – consecrate rights that would be later called "social" rights or rights to social benefits from the community in which a person belongs. A close study of the debates around the elaboration of the Declaration of 1789 confirms that the concern to guarantee the preconditions of the exercise of liberty was omnipresent among the relevant political actors even then. The 1789 Declaration was conceived among an intense debate in the Constituent Assembly on the question of subsistence. It was elaborated amid social unrest caused by the crisis of subsistence, which led to constitutional change in France. Political actors discussed the idea of duties as preceding rights and of the need to discuss those first before any discussion on the Constitution. Dupont, a liberal, notes that it is important to fix through duties the links that hold the social contract.[137] Although this option did not win over in the text of 1789, it did prevail later. Marcel Gauchet is right in emphasizing that the opposition between the supposed bourgeois liberal orthodoxy of 1789 and the social or popular spirit of 1793 is exaggerated.[138] In the French context a widespread understanding existed at the time that "a society that wants to think of itself as composed of individuals cannot remain indifferent to the circumstances that allow a member to realize their autonomy."[139] Otherwise, it is bound to fail in achieving its own goal to produce individuals by being attentive to their potential for independence.[140] The doctrinal conflict between liberalism and socialism, which

136 Speech to the National Assembly, August 1, 1789, *Archives Parlementaires*, vol. 8, 323.

137 Speech in the National Assembly on the August 4, 1789 by Dupont, *Archives Parlementaires*, vol. 7, 340; and by Abbée Grégoire, ibid., 340–41.

138 Gauchet, *La révolution des droits de l'homme*, 99.

139 Ibid. (my translation).

140 Ibid.

emerged later, concerns questions that were obvious to the French revolutionaries: the principle of individual independence presupposes that a person has the material preconditions that allow them to exercise their liberty.

From early on the idea of a declaration of rights was present in the minds of the participants in the Constituent Assembly in the summer of 1789, who came from a wide ideological spectrum including Jacobins, Girondins, and Thermidorians.[141] The Declaration of 1789 did not include a reference to solidarity rights as was elaborated in a hurry in response to the urgent constitutional question to situate in the nation the *locus* of legitimacy of the government's power.[142] Nevertheless, it did include, in its preamble, a reference to the duties that "all members of the social body" have.[143] A reference to duties toward others exists in numerous other texts proposed in the summer of 1789 such as the Charter containing the French Constitution proposed by Charles-François Bouche.[144] The extensive debates on the need for the state to provide for the subsistence of the citizens that preceded the Declaration of 1789 indicate that its meaning was not purely to guarantee negative rights – rights of nonintervention. The negative rights in the text of the Declaration itself were proclaimed in a general context of concern about how citizens would have means of subsistence. The Declaration of 1793 emphasizes even further the requirement of solidarity. It extends the list of protected rights and explicitly mentions a right to assistance by the state for the citizens to whom the state cannot provide work.[145] The Declaration of 1795, written immediately after the Terror, explicitly proclaims the duties of citizens toward one another. It refers to the duty to defend society and motherland,[146] to obey the law,[147] to do good,[148] and to respect liberty, equality, and property. The inclusion of a list of duties indicates that the Thermidorians of the revolutionary left were at the time anxious about not only guaranteeing the rights of "man."[149] Although the idea to create a declaration of duties was new in 1795, the duties themselves were not. They existed in the preamble of 1789 and in many of the previous declarations of rights by reference to the idea that duties derive from rights.[150] The Constitution of 1848 constituted a synthesis of

141 Michel Troper, *Terminer la Révolution: La Constitution de 1795* (Paris: Fayard, 2006), 94.

142 Gauchet, *La révolution des droits de l'homme*, 100–01. See also Maurice Duverger, *Les Constitutions de la France* (Paris: Presses Universitaires de France, 1944), 38–39. Duverger notes that the Declaration of 1789 was written in a hurry and in the midst of disorder. The reference to duties was omitted at the time as the principal aim was to react against despotism.

143 See English translation by Constitutional Council, www.conseil-constitutionnel.fr/conseil-constitutionnel/root/bank_mm/anglais/cst2.pdf.

144 "Charte contenant la Constitution française dans ses objets fondamentaux," proposed to the National Assembly by Charles-François Bouche on August 12, 1789, *Archives Parlementaires*, vol. 7, 400.

145 Article 21 in Duverger, *Constitutions de la France*, 44.

146 Articles 3 and 9.

147 Articles 3, 5, 6, 7.

148 Articles 2, 4, 8, 9.

149 Troper, *Terminer la Révolution*, 95.

150 Ibid., 97.

all these texts and once again included duties in its preamble. It states that "the Republic must, through fraternal assistance, assure the existence of the citizens in need," but also that "duties reciprocally oblige the citizens toward the Republic and the Republic toward the citizens."[151]

As Georges Gusdorf notes, through a paradoxical inversion, the identification of power and society in the French context leads to a conception of authority as the medium to realize liberty.[152] The revolutionary legislators since 1789 saw themselves as having authority to entirely redefine the structures of the new state. This legal optimism, proper to the Enlightenment, gave them hope that human reality would adapt itself to the new legal orders, which were more "rational" than those of the Ancien Régime and in greater conformity with everyone's interest.[153] If the Ancien Régime subsisted through privileges and habits, the new regime must proceed to a rational design of the human domain.[154] The neologism "adunation," invented by Sieyès, refers to the attempt to bring about unity in all domains and the transition from the irrational multiplicity to the uniformity imposed by reason.[155] The king had eliminated other bonds of allegiance toward creating individuals in the past and then the nation, as Tocqueville notes in his 1856 work *L'Ancien régime et la Révolution*. The revolutionary government reproduced this mentality, imposing a new normalization of life. Uniformity of standards of measurement and uniformity of language upon the diversity of local languages were among the measures adopted at the time. Collective power was seen as the agent par excellence in a position to realize effective equality and thus effective liberty in French society. Although in the United States equality was a reality, slavery aside, in the French context the egalitarian theme is in conformity with the norm of unification, the plan of "adunation," which dominated the entire political and social space. The abolition of feudal rights and privileges of any kind decreed on the night of August 4 to 5, 1789 are measures in this direction. Even if the idea of equality is limited in its applications, it proposes a kind of myth in the more radical revolutionaries of a regulatory principle of a utopian republic.[156]

Criticisms from the left pointed to the limits of the efforts of the French revolutionaries in their attempts to realize liberty. Proudhon and Marx saw in the French texts that declared liberties the proclamation of the necessary liberties for the emergence of bourgeois society founded on the "illusion of democracy." Not all of these criticisms were fair. Proudhon criticizes the French declarations for not arriving at a fully satisfactory conception of human rights. Following these declarations, the law appears as the "right of man against man," the "right to the respect of

151 Constitution of 1848, preamble (my translation).

152 Gusdorf, *Conscience révolutionnaire*, 257.

153 Ibid.

154 Ibid., 103.

155 Ibid., 183 ff.

156 Therefore the vote on the basis of income was preserved by the Constitution of 1791, to be surpassed by the Constitution of 1793 and its consecration of the principle of universal suffrage.

human dignity." This is contrary to previous conceptions, which placed this respect in the fear of God and ended by humiliating this dignity through the theme of the Fall.[157] For Proudhon, if the declarations placed the cause of the respect of human dignity at the center of society's interests, they also contributed to negating this principle by destroying "the *conditio sine qua non*, inneity, immanence," of man as such. They should, in his opinion, found the right of man against man upon justice, the sovereign and constitutive faculty of man as he feels himself in solidarity with other members of the same collectivity.[158] For Proudhon, justice is the faculty to feel our dignity in others as in ourselves. It is also the willingness to engage in action to protect it.[159] Proudhon insists on the necessity to protect the physical existence and the fundamental needs of human beings, anticipating the concept of social rights. From his anarchic point of view, it is only the abolition of the state that can facilitate the task of public conscience, which solely can guarantee all liberties.

Marx thinks that the French declarations are full of paradoxes. They affirm negative liberties, as they are the product of a "bourgeois" revolution. They distinguish, in his opinion, between man and the citizen, the "member of the bourgeois society," the "egoistic" man separated from man and from the collectivity.[160] For Marx, the French Revolution contributed to the separation of state and civil society, and thus to the domination of private interests in a general frame of relations of force, which tend to separate human beings. The emphasis on the "man," distinct from the "citizen," indicates for Marx that the French Revolution destroyed the previous feudal bonds without substituting other bonds among individuals. The liberty to do everything that does not harm others is for Marx the liberty of man as an isolated monad, folded upon himself. Property, for example, would be the right to have and dispose of one's fortune at will without caring about others, independently from society.[161] The so-called human rights would be those of "private caprice," of the individual separated from the community and society. The citizen, as conceived in the French Declaration, would be the servant of the egoistic man. Marx criticizes the abstract conception of natural rights that exists in some of the articles of the French Declaration. He thinks that, along with Rousseau's conception of citizenship, they perpetuate a fictive distinction between the natural man, the man of civil society, and the political man. For Marx, Rousseau's conception of the citizen, founded on the idea of the transformation of the perfect and solitary individual into a part of a greater whole from which this individual receives their life and being, also reflects an artificial distinction. Marx thinks that Rousseau presupposes a distinction between the social man and the man as a political subject. This conceals for Marx

157 Pierre Joseph Proudhon, *De la justice dans la Révolution et dans l'église*, vol. 1 (Paris: Libraire de Garnier Frères, 1858), 171.

158 Ibid., 172.

159 Ibid., 173.

160 Karl Marx, "The Jewish Question," in Robert Tucker, ed., *The Marx-Engels Reader* (New York: Norton, 1978), 42–45.

161 Ibid., 48.

the fact that man is by definition social and political. Marx understands humans as "species-beings" characterized by creativity that is possible because human consciousness is by definition social. For Marx, human emancipation is the complete identification between the individual, real man, and Rousseau's abstract citizen. Political emancipation is not enough – it must go together with human emancipation.

For Marx, the political spirit established by the French Revolution is the mystificatory expression of civil society. Behind the "appearance" of the legal form of rights are hidden social inequalities between those who can exercise their liberties effectively, as they possess the necessary means, and those for whom the exercise of rights is utopic.[162] The Declaration is a fiction covering social reality, the oppression by the bourgeoisie – owners of the means of production – of the inferior classes, forced by their conditions of existence to submit themselves to their direction. This fiction is perpetuated through the distinction between the social and the political sphere. In the political sphere there is equality, but in the social sphere there is class oppression. Political emancipation is not enough as it does not protect from the material impossibility to exercise rights. The distinction between "formal" liberty and "real" liberty persists and is perpetuated by the abstraction in the conception of citizenship. Despite the claim to universality, rights are only legal constructions that make sense in relation to a specific phase of the social and economic organization.[163]

Marx's criticisms of Rousseau are not entirely just. Rousseau thinks that the political state is what makes a human being a human being. "It is being a citizen that makes one a man," says Rousseau in the Geneva manuscript of *The Social Contract*.[164] For Rousseau it is society through language that makes a being a human.[165] In this respect he agrees with Marx's formation of consciousness.[166] For both Rousseau and Marx, consciousness is social as it is created by language. Rousseau's thought experiment of the natural man in his *Discourse on the Origin of Inequality* does not aim to legitimize society as being something different from political society. On the contrary, Rousseau uses it to prove that it is only in the ideally constructed society that he envisions in *The Social Contract* that the positive qualities of the human being can flourish. Rousseau refers *in passim* to natural rights only to make the point that rights do not make sense outside of society. It is only in political society that humans can exercise their liberty. There is an existential undertone in Rousseau's understanding of liberty and of the mission of society to

[162] See also Karl Marx, *Capital*, vol. 1, trans. Ben Fowkes (New York: Vintage, 1977), 719, for a criticism of the "liberty" of the workers to sign into a "legal fiction of" a contract of employment written with great lyricism.

[163] Jeremy Waldron, "Karl Marx's 'On the Jewish Question'," in Waldron, ed., *Nonsense Upon Stilts*, 119–36, 127.

[164] "We begin to become properly men only after having been citizens." John-Jacques Rousseau, *Du contract social: manuscrit de Genève* in *Oeuvres complètes* (Paris: Gallimard, 1967), 287.

[165] Jacques Derrida, *De la grammatologie* (Paris: Minuit, 1967).

[166] Karl Marx, "The German Ideology," in Tucker, ed., *Marx-Engels Reader*, 158.

realize it. If by giving up all their liberty human beings lose nothing, but on the contrary they win more than they had before, as he notes in *The Social Contract*, this is because it is political society that makes liberty and life meaningful. As analyzed in Chapter 5, these ideas were present among the political actors of the French Revolution.

Furthermore, a close reading of the debates in the National Assembly related to the elaboration of the French declarations of rights indicates that Marx' interpretation of the purpose of the French declarations of rights overlooks the context of their elaboration. Some historians have also noted that discussing the bourgeoisie as the motor of social change in France during the French Revolution is an oversimplification.[167] For François Furet, Marx has not interpreted correctly the chaotic and polymorphous political life of the French Revolution and its aftermath.[168] While social class struggle was at the heart of the French Revolution, the discussions held at that time on liberty and equality offer an extraordinary view of the alliances and conflicts between social classes.[169] Furet notes that Marx underestimated the importance of the contribution of the mass of the people living in extreme poverty. He saw it only as an instrument that the bourgeoisie was able to appropriate for its own struggle for emancipation. Thus, he did not succeed in explaining the wide range of events that followed the French Revolution, principally the Terror.[170] Marx provides contradictory interpretations of the Terror, first, considering it as an instrument of the realization of bourgeois interests and of liberalism, then as incarnating the interests of the mass of *sans-culottes*, when, in fact, the revolution continued well beyond liberalism.[171] He subordinates the "proletarian" Terror to the realization of its opposite, the bourgeois moment of the French Revolution. He overlooks the social movement of the peasants of July–August 1789, which ran parallel to the urban revolution.[172] Alfred Cobban shows that to a great extent the reference to broad categories like the "bourgeoisie" does not accurately describe the social movement that led to the French Revolution, because the bourgeoisie had already substituted itself for the feudal seigneurs.[173] The interests of these two social classes were identified at the moment of the revolution. Cobban argues that the social groups that led to the radical proclamation of values, composed mostly of the urban middle classes and the better-off peasantry, cannot be reduced to the category of the "bourgeoisie."[174] Even these classes had cleavages.

167 François Furet, *Marx et la Révolution française* (Paris: Flammarion, 1986); Alfred Cobban, *The Social Interpretation of the French Revolution* (Cambridge University Press, 1964).

168 Furet, *Marx et la Révolution française*, 48.

169 François Furet et Mona Ozouf, "Préface," in *Dictionnaire critique de la Révolution française: acteurs*, 2nd ed. (Paris: Flammarion, 2007), 9–24, 10.

170 Furet, *Marx et la Révolution française*, 55.

171 Ibid., 56.

172 Furet, *Marx et la Révolution française*, 58.

173 Cobban, *Social Interpretation*, 47.

174 Ibid., 120.

The grievances of the lowest social strata in town and country were actually against the coming of a capitalist order.[175] The National Assembly abolished seignorial dues on August 4, 1789, out of a fear of a peasant revolt in the same spring and summer. It was this fear that led the members of the Assembly to adopt the idealized discourse of the Declaration of the Rights of Man and the Citizen.

Proudhon and Marx may be correct in noting the French Revolution did not go far enough. Nevertheless, it was exactly the struggle against inequality of wealth that led to the loss of the orientation of the general will and to the Terror in the late stages of the French Revolution.[176] The integral democracy, as applied during the Terror, was the antithesis of what it claimed to be, a totalitarian regime. It completely absorbed the private man in the citizen in its attempt to assure transparency and to resolve the social question. The social question of mass poverty and the necessity to provide for the equal dignity of all caused the revolutionary movement and the succession of turbulent events that led to the destruction of individuality in the absorption of the individual into the citizen. The social discomfort that followed during the entire nineteenth century in France can be attributed to the failure to find a solution to the problem of guaranteeing effective equality for all. The French Revolution attempted to proclaim not only negative liberty but also positive liberty in the political sense. It expressed the need to protect liberty in a universal sense, including all positive understandings of liberty as negative and positive. And it was inspired by the need to make liberty "effective" for all. The revolutionary motive transcended simple class interest and the words "Liberty," "Equality," and "Fraternity" designated an attempt to transcend the society of classes.[177] By cutting men off from their attachment to particular social groups and by making them parts within the metaphysical unity of the "nation," the French revolutionaries created a situation that elevated individuals above themselves through the festive feeling of their fraternity.[178]

Furthermore, Marx has not considered the importance of another parameter: the significance of the affirmation of positive liberty in the sense of political liberty, as participation. Marx thinks that the conceptual apparatus of democracy and its promise remain unrealizable to the extent that liberty remains an empty form. It is deprived of meaning for the greatest part of human beings to the extent that they do not have the material possibility to exercise it. Political rights are the rights explicitly constitutive of the forms of common action that valorize the human being as a social being and tend toward the realization of the human species being, as Marx conceives it. Formally at least, they constitute the type of community that Marx envisions as

175 Ibid., 167.

176 Hegel, *Dokumente zu Hegels Entwicklung*, cited in Jean Hyppolite, "La signification de la Révolution française dans la 'Phénoménologie' de Hegel," in Barker, ed., *La Révolution de 1789 et la pensée moderne*, 193–224, 219–20.

177 Ernst Bloch, *Droit naturel et dignité humaine*, trans. Denis Authier and Jean Lacoste (Paris: Payot, 2002), 208–9.

178 Bourgeois, *Raison moderne*, 87–88.

result of human emancipation.[179] Claude Lefort notes that Marx, trapped in his ideological critique of rights, overlooked that the French Declaration brought about the recognition of the free communication of thoughts and opinions, which opens the possibility for a true public space transcending the interests of the bourgeoisie.[180] The rights of the French declarations are not purely formal and ahistorical, masking the formal interests of the bourgeoisie. In order to truly understand the purpose of the rights of man, some "indetermination" is indispensable to their critical scope.

Far from promoting the "man separated from man," according to the Marxist formula, the French declarations allow for a conception of liberty as "liberty of relations," which projects a representation of human bonds instituting the social domain.[181] Although the revolutionary government did not realize a collectivist egalitarianism, as Proudhon notes, it did redefine the mission of the state as being the realization of the rights of man and the citizen. The social question, the need to confront mass poverty, was omnipresent during the French declaratory work. The ideal and rational republic would be charged with the task of assuring "universal felicity," which would encompass the "happy citizen and all his co-citizens in a global design."[182] The fascination with collective power, once liberated from its usurpers, and the reconceptualization of the role of the state, went together with the conception of public power as having the mission to ensure collective happiness. The French Revolution did not succeed in realizing one of its major objectives, the reconciliation between reality and principle. Nevertheless, it did express the will to bring a rupture with an inegalitarian social reality and a social order marked by arbitrariness and privilege. It expressed the principle that individuals would relate to their community in terms of effective equality.

This overall conception is visible in relation to the question of happiness in the revolutionary moment on the two sides of the Atlantic: the Americans make happiness a right and pose it as belonging to the person, whereas the French make it an end and envision it as related to the community.[183] The American Declaration of Independence and the bills of rights of several states reflect a conception of happiness according to which it is the right of each person to define for themselves a project of existence.[184] Everyone can have their own conception of happiness and, what is more, the search for private well-being is doubled by public happiness,

179 Jeremy Waldron, "Karl Marx's 'On the Jewish Question'," 127.

180 Claude Lefort, *L'invention démocratique* (Paris: Fayard, 1981), 77 ff. See also Pierre Manent, *Cours familier de philosophie politique* (Paris: Gallimard, 2001), 177–81.

181 Pierre Bouretz, "Egalité et liberté," *Droits* 8 (1988), 71–82, 76.

182 Gusdorf, *Conscience révolutionnaire*, 257.

183 For the American perspective, see Richard Bland, *An Inquiry into the Rights of the British Colonies, Intended as an Answer to the Regulations Lately Made Concerning the Colonies, and the Taxes Imposed upon Them Considered* (Williamsburg: Alexander Purdie and Co., 1766), 10. For the French perspective, see for instance Babeuf, "Manifeste des Plébéiens: 9 frimaire an IV," in Maurice Dommanget ed., *Pages choisies de Babeuf* (Paris: Armand Colin, 1935), 250–64, 257.

184 The novelty in the conception of the Americans of the Revolutionary Era was the idea that "individual happiness was a natural right not to be violated by the government." See Cecelia

which stems from participation in public affairs. The French approach expresses a different perspective: happiness becomes a collective value first and then an individual one. The parliamentary debates since June 1789 indicate the concerns of all political actors that happiness is to be attained collectively. Mounier, for instance, a moderate, stated explicitly that the aim of society is the common happiness in a discussion related to the question of subsistence.[185] From these debates it emerges that equality was understood as social. The emphasis is not on the sphere of autonomy of the person, protected by law. It rather focuses on the condition of an integration of the individual in the community. While the American revolutionaries also officially recognized the right of each individual to their share of happiness, the French conception is different in that the nation was seen as charged with the mission to take specific measures to assure this share to those who did not possess it.[186]

The French revolutionaries were aware of the distinction between real liberty and formal liberty.[187] The concern to guarantee the necessary preconditions for the exercise of liberty was omnipresent during the declaratory work in France. This was the case already before the first declaration, the Declaration of 1789. In the weeks before the Declaration, the members of the Assembly were struggling to respond to the solution to famine and poverty.[188] Hernou, representative of Saint-Jean-de Losne advocated in favor of a declaration of "the rights of the nation," which would impose a form of taxation proportional to the property and to the ability of each individual.[189] His suggestion already sounds like Marx's later well-known phrase "from each according to his abilities to each according to his needs." The reference to property does not only aim to protect its negative aspect but also to guarantee the means necessary for subsistence. Political actors across the ideological spectrum referred to the need to protect the most impoverished. Even aristocrats such as Lally Tolendal insisted on the urgency to respond to the question of human suffering. He associated the Declaration of Rights in 1789 with the need to provide "real assistance" to alleviate suffering.[190] The Declaration should have the mission to reaffirm the unity among the people of France and their common happiness, he noted.

M. Kenyon, "Constitutionalism in Revolutionary America," in J. Roland Pennock and John W. Chapman, eds. NOMOS XX, *Constitutionalism* (1979), 84–120, 87; Thomas G. West, *The Political Theory of the American Founding: Natural Rights, Public Policy and the Moral Conditions of Freedom* (Cambridge University Press, 2018), 34.

185 M. Mounier, Speech in the National Assembly, Thursday, July 9, 1789, *Archives Parlementaires de 1787 à 1860*, vol. 8, 216.

186 Cf. Gusdorf, *Conscience révolutionnaire*, 254.

187 For an extensive analysis of the distinction between "real" and "formal" liberty, see Raymond Aron, *Essai sur les libertés* [1967] (Paris: Hachette, 1998).

188 The debates of the summer of 1789 right before the Declaration of 1789 indicate this concern. See in particular the debates on Monday, July 6, 1789, *Archives Parlementaires de 1787 à 1860*, vol. 8, 194–99.

189 Discourse of Tuesday, July 7, 1789, *Archives Parlementaires de 1787 à 1860*, vol. 8, 200.

190 Speech in the National Assembly, July 11, 1789, *Archives Parlementaires de 1787 à 1860*, vol. 8, 222. See also Keith Michael Baker, "The Idea of a Declaration of Rights," in Dale Van Kley, ed., *The French*

Even though there are opinions defending property as a negative liberty, such as Condorcet's, there is no universal consensus on this understanding. Roger Barny notes that many of the bourgeois Ideologues refused to consider all the implications of their thought, enticed by the theme of equality that the necessities of the revolutionary struggle brought to the forefront.[191] In the relevant debates, the idea that property is not a natural but a social right associated with the idea of equality is present.[192] Brissot, a leading Girondin, wrote in 1787 that property is the necessary means to provide for the good of the citizens.[193] The aspiration for a profound transformation, which would create the social conditions of justice and of happiness, is omnipresent in his works. In parallel, the protest against the disequilibrium that the concentration of property introduces into society is the object of constant references since Rousseau. The discourse of popular egalitarianism of the period subordinates the right of property to the right to life. For some, the conception of liberty and property underlying the Declaration expressed the physiocratic doctrine according to which the Declaration consecrates the liberty to assure one's preservation and to provide for everyone's well-being through the use of a person's natural faculties.[194] For others it finds its doctrinal source in the literature of opposition to the Physiocrats accentuated by 1789 and the crisis of the means of subsistence in 1790.[195] According to this literature, property, far from being an absolute right, must be limited each time that the superior interest of the community or human existence makes it necessary. This conception of property as artificial, traced back to some of Rousseau's basic conceptions, gains ground in a general discussion on the meaning of equality and the requirement of social justice. Whichever the doctrinal foundation of the conception of property, its consideration as a good subjected to limitations for the protection of subsistence was dominant in France in relation to confronting the social question of mass poverty. At the time, the same question was not under consideration in America to the same extent. In France, Rousseau is interpreted as reformist. He will become revolutionary with the deepening of the political and social crisis.[196] Rousseau's theory of property becomes an ideology used by the partisans of the law on land redistribution, who invoke the idea of an egalitarian share between individuals. The discussion on the reform of inheritance

Idea of Freedom: The Old Regime and the Declaration of Rights of 1789 (Stanford University Press, 1994), 174.

191 Roger Barny, *Le droit naturel à l'épreuve de l'histoire*, 32.

192 Ibid., 33.

193 See the debates presented in Roger Barny, *Le triomphe du droit naturel: la constitution de la doctrine révolutionnaire des droits de l'homme* (1787–1789) (Paris: Les Belles Lettres, 1997), 45. "Without property, wrote Brissot, the people has no homeland . . . therefore before trying to give an education to the people we will need to assure property for them." While monarchy persists it would be impossible to assure property for the people as its abuses entirely "rob" the people. Ibid., 45.

194 Vincent Marcaggi, *Les origines de la Déclaration des droits de l'homme de 1789* (Paris: Fontemoing, 1912), 212.

195 Roger Barny, *Le droit naturel à l'épreuve de l'histoire*, 126 ff.

196 Ibid., 127.

law is a sign of the fact that the legal equality proclaimed by the bourgeois revolution comports as its ultimate end the equality of properties, as the only conceivable form of real equality.[197]

Even before the revolution, the ideological spectrum in France also contained voices in favor of utopian communism, such as Abbé Mably, Étienne Gabriel de Morelly, and Gracchus Babeuf. Mably, in his *Rights and Duties of the Citizen*, expresses his ideal of a utopian republic whose first law would be not to own anything. The product of the work of each citizen would be the "treasure of the state and the patrimony of each citizen."[198] Morelly, in his *Code de la Nature*, written well before the Declaration of 1789, develops his conception of an ideal society where everyone would work for the common good and would receive all that they need for their subsistence from the community.[199] Babeuf stresses the idea of a community of land and an equal distribution of its products between all citizens by designing a revolutionary communist program excluding private property.[200] He saw a medium for perfect equality in a law on land redistribution. The distinction between "formal" liberty and "real" liberty also exists in Condorcet. In his

197 Ibid., 129. The interpretation of the social contract that became prevalent was that the only measure that could be derived was not collectivization, but the sharing of properties. Ibid., 134.

198 Gabriel Bonnet de Mably, *Des droits et des devoirs du citoyen* (Paris: Librairie Marcel Didier, 1972 [1789]), 111. See also Fernanda Mazzanti Pepe, "Mably pour une démocratie à la mesure de l'homme," in Peter Friedemann, Florence Gauthier, Jean-Luc Malvache, Fernanda Mazzani Pepe, eds., *Colloque Mably: la politique comme science morale*, vol. 1 (Bary: Palomar Casa Editrice, 1995), 65–83; Florence Gauthier, *Triomphe et mort du droit naturel en Révolution, 1789–1795-1802* (Paris: Presses Universitaires de France, 1992); cf. Judith Casali de Babot and Guillermo Salvatierra, "Mably: utopie ou réalisme dans la pensée pré-révolutionnaire?," in Friedemann et al., *Colloque Mably*, 85–99. See also Michael Oakeshott, *Morality and Politics in Modern Europe* (New Haven, CT: Yale University Press, 1993), 97.

199 Étienne Gabriel de Morelly, *Code de la Nature* (Paris: Paul Masgana, 1841 [1755]).

200 "Lettre à Dubois de Fosseux, Roye après le 1er juin 1786," in V. Daline, A. Saitta, and A. Soboul, eds., *Oeuvres de Babeuf, Tome I, Babeuf avant la Révolution* (Paris: Bibliothèque Nationale, 1977), 107; Gracchus Babeuf, "Manifeste des plébéiens: 9 frimaire an IV," (November 3, 1795) in Maurice Dommanget, ed., *Pages choisies de Babeuf* (Paris: Armand Colin, 1935), 250–64. See also, François Furet, "Babeuf," in François Furet et Mona Ozouf, eds., *Dictionnaire critique de la Révolution française: acteurs*, 25–35, 33. Babeuf's thought concerned the structures of agricultural production, exchange, the persistent feudality, and the emerging rural capitalism as well as commercial capitalism. Albert Soboul sees a clear association between Babouvism and Blanquism and then between Blanquism enriched by the experience of the Parisian Commune of 1871 and the doctrine and the Leninist practice of the dictatorship of the proletariat in "Babeuf et le babouvisme," in *Oeuvres de Babeuf*, vol. 1, 21. The claim of the community of goods, exceeding the claim of the sans-culottes of "equality of happiness," the conspiracy of the equals, daughter of the utopia but made more precise during the revolutionary period, supposed a radical transformation of society. See Claude Mazauric, *Babeuf et la conspiration pour l'égalité* (Paris: Editions Sociales, 1962), 11. For Claude Mazauric, the Jacobine dictatorship was an attempt at compromise between the contradictory interests of the revolutionary bourgeoisie and those of the popular masses of the faubourgs and of the country, with the aim of realizing the revolutionary unanimity necessary to external victory and annihilating the aristocratic counter-revolution. The conspiracy of the Babouvists followed the famine of the years 1795–1796.

Esquisse d'un tableau historique des progrès de l'ésprit humain, Condorcet warns about the "destruction of liberty" by the "inequality of wealth."[201]

Jean Jaurès is one of the historians who underlines the universal significance of human rights that are equally valid for the proletariat and whose realization can only be accomplished within a social democracy.[202] It was a later reading of the Declaration by French intellectuals in the nineteenth century, such as Benjamin Constant and François Guizot, which particularly attributed to it the meaning of protecting only the negative aspect of liberty.[203]

Arguably, in France the impossibility of ensuring the preconditions of the exercise of liberty in 1789 and its aftermath led to a more explicit proclamation in 1848. Tocqueville, speaking before the Constituting Assembly of 1848, criticized the discourse in favor of the "social republic." This discourse associated with the tradition of 1789 a moral duty of the state to provide assistance through redistribution.[204] In Tocqueville's opinion, what sanctifies the French Revolution in the eyes of the people was the desire to introduce Christian charity into politics. He stresses that the social aim of the Revolution, to do away with social classes, was as important as its emancipatory purpose, namely the consecration for every citizen of the possibility to judge thanks to their "enlightenment and their liberty." Nevertheless, according to Tocqueville's individualist perspective, the aim of politics is not to realize the happiness of human beings in society through state action. It is to guarantee to individuals the liberties to seek happiness as they understand it. For Tocqueville, the socialism of 1848, which discussed the idea of a right to work, compares to the Ancien Régime. In socialism, he sees state intervention that is equally dangerous for both individual property and intellectual freedom. Just like the Ancien Régime, the social state expresses a paternalistic vision, that wisdom resides only in the state and that the subjects are weak beings who must be submitted to its guardianship.[205]

The establishment of concrete real liberties and determined existing rights was conditioned by the practical affirmation of liberty as universal, with the state assuming the responsibility of realizing liberty. The content of the affirmation of the rights of man proclaimed liberty in absolute terms for the French

201 Manuscript finished in October 1793. Marie-Jean-Antoine-Nicolas de Caritat, Marquis de Condorcet, *Esquisse d'un tableau historique des progrès de l'esprit humain*, ed. Monique and François Hincker (Paris: Editions Sociales, 1966).

202 Jean Jaurès, *Histoire socialiste de la Révolution française* (Paris: Jules Rouff, 1900). For Jaurès the revolutionary bourgeoisie exceeded itself announcing thus the emergence of a new law. The work of the revolution was universal, and it is precisely this element, which turned the weapons of the sovereign against the winner, that is itself. The only medium for France to animate the universal revolution was to give a universal formula to its own movement (Paris: Editions Sociales, 1969), 422.

203 Tony Judt, "Rights in France," *La Revue Tocqueville* 1 (1993), 67–108, 73–74.

204 "Discours prononcé à l'Assemblée constituante dans la discussion du projet de Constitution (12 septembre 1848) sur la question du droit au travail," in *Oeuvres complètes d'Alexis de Tocqueville*, vol. 9 (Paris: Michel Lévy Frères, 1866), 551.

205 Ibid., 543.

revolutionaries, as the highest ideal for humanity.[206] Nevertheless, in the French context, this realization is marked by the paradox that the agent of realization of the rights is the coercive structure of the state. For the French revolutionaries, the claim of essential universal liberty identifies all men with an abstract idea of "man," whose liberty is defined by the state. The state by definition mediates between the citizens and realizes their rights.

Freedom of expression is considered as a liberty to be realized in France. The state is charged with the mission to ensure that the freedom of the person expressing themselves and the freedom of the receivers of information are protected. The legislation on pluralism and transparency in the domain of the audiovisual aims to prevent the formation of oligopolies that would reduce the variety of the currents of expression. This is a major priority for the French state, as indicated by the decisions of the Constitutional Council.[207] At the same time, the state protects access to the media and defines the content of freedom of expression in relation to opinions that seem harmful. This is part of the same conception of the role of the state as providing to the citizens the preconditions for the exercise of their liberties.

The concern to provide for "social" rights that was omnipresent at the revolutionary moment, in association with the conception of the "rational republic," contains the danger of an "overdetermination" of the conditions necessary for the realization of liberty, as is the case regarding freedom of expression. Providing the necessary preconditions for the exercise of liberty goes together with accepting that the state has the mission to transcend the distinction between "formal" liberty and "real" liberty. The conception of the need to protect human dignity as a guarantee of the necessities of human existence as well as moral status within society is associated with the positive moral role of the state, which should liberate individuals from poverty as well as from their own "irrationality." The French Revolution reveals a conflicting structure of rationality, which, by assigning to the idea of liberty an "objective" value, negates the fundamental philosophical presuppositions of modernity: the possibility of the subject to judge for themselves and by themselves. The state, seen as incarnating reason and prudence, integrally absorbs the reason of the individual.[208] This distinction is relevant for cases of self-expression too. Outlawing the spectacle of dwarf-throwing can be understood as assuring that the distinction between "real" and "formal" liberty does not exist for the person concerned. The person who participates in the spectacle is considered as not having the possibility to realize their freedom. They treat themselves in a way that violates their "dignity." In this situation, the state projects a vision of "dignity" that the individual must meet in

206 Bourgeois, *Raison moderne*, 134.

207 CC, Decision 84-181DC, Oct. 11, 1984, Rec. 73 RJC I-199, concerning the written press and of July 29th 1986 concerning the audio-visual sector and Decision 88–248DC, Jan. 27, 1989, Rec. 18, RJC I-339, concerning the French Superior Audiovisual Council.

208 The "cult of reason" during the Jacobin Era confirms this general attitude. See François Alphonse Aulard, *Le culte de la raison et le culte de l'être suprême (1793–1794), essai historique* (Paris: F. Alcan, 1892).

order to realize their liberty. The state, through the prohibition, dictates how they should exercise their liberty.

The prohibition of the wearing of conspicuous religious symbols in France can also be interpreted by reference to this conception. The prohibition can be understood as part of a wider conception of top-to-bottom secularism that dictates to individuals that they should not manifest their religious convictions conspicuously.[209] The 1905 French legislation on secularism can be understood as part of this wider perspective of state-imposed secularism that expresses disregard for individual reason. The state helps individuals to realize their liberty as they cannot realize it by themselves. The state aims to help liberate women from the oppression of their families in the cases when the burka is not self-imposed. In the cases where it is, the state treats women as having a false consciousness of what it means to be free. It is trusted to help them realize their freedom. In the United States, similar limitations are not accepted. There, an understanding of secularism as having emerged from the bottom to the top is dominant. The links with the philosophy of natural rights make a compelling case against government limitations to the manifestation of religious conscience.[210]

The French revolutionaries aimed, among other things, to regenerate humanity, guided by an idea of regulating reality, and to establish a new idea of reason and justice among men by reforming society. The American revolutionaries sought to constitute a new form of independent government in rupture with the bond of allegiance with the British crown and not to reconstruct society. The American revolutionaries aimed to establish a new republic at the international level through the illocutionary force of the Declaration of Independence. The historical trajectory of the emergence of republicanism in the United States is different from France. It is affected by the evolution of the understanding on the imaginary level that human beings have of themselves and of their quality of being a citizen. The origin of this self-understanding in France comes from the public domain, and went through various metamorphoses during the centuries, passing from the domination of a king to that of an assembly. In this context, the need to affirm human liberty on the ideological level and to guarantee its material realization through the guarantee of the preconditions for its exercise implies a conception of liberty whose exercise is associated with the public good, a quality whose content and limits can be defined by state action. In France the idea of an organic unity between the state – which would from then on be democratic – and its citizens was perpetuated. In America, the individual is the starting point and every new small community of colonies saw itself as composed by individuals conceiving themselves as participating fully in the community.

209 For an analysis of the ban on wearing conspicuous signs of religious affiliation in France dictated by conception of secularism from the top to the bottom, see Ioanna Tourkochoriti, "The Burka Ban."

210 Ibid., 831 ff.

In colonial America the separation between the public and the private sphere followed a slow process. The communitarian spirit associated with the widely spread practice of self-government in the first communities of the colonies legitimized limits to individual liberty in order to promote community goals.[211] The absence of a state mechanism independent from the communities led to the assignment of intersubjectively shared aims to private actors (the concept of the public good was not yet formed at that level). According to Gordon Wood, intersubjectively shared goals were accomplished by private persons *contra* benefits accorded by administrators, such as various immunities. The revolution and the movement of independence reversed this situation because by creating "republics," it contributed to the introduction of the concept of the "public good" through the introduction of the neo-Roman thought of the Whigs, which stressed public collective liberty. At the same time, the emphasis on republican power led to the realization of the need to protect individual rights as opposed to the public good. Governments progressively became independent from communities, employing their own personnel.[212] The revolutionaries underlined the primacy of the public good upon private individual interests and sought to separate the public sphere from the private. With this emergence of the concept of *res publica*, promoting a unitary public good, which would from then on be superior to the private interests, emerged a conception of the public sphere as independent from the private sphere. This new republican state power was not considered as the exercise of the authority of one person, as the exercise of particular prerogatives or the rights of persons having an economic or social superiority. The prerogatives of the British crown were either eliminated or allocated to state legislative bodies. As the fusion of the public and private spheres was taking place, the need emerged to protect the public good and to ensure its realization independently from private actors who were until then employed for its materialization. This led state legislative bodies to legislate on questions of general interest such as economic development, and to refrain from regulating activities of the private sector such as morality and religion.

In the Founding Era, there were some American voices discussing the importance of ensuring the preconditions for the exercise of negative liberties. Madison discusses the "unequal faculties of acquiring property" as leading to "different degrees and kinds of property."[213] Both Madison and Jefferson discuss the need for a society to confront poverty. It seems though that the underlying consideration was political stability as social inequality would be a danger to public peace and security. Madison is critical of what he called an "immoderate" and "unmerited" accumulation of wealth. He notes the need for "a state of comfort" for the poor as a guarantee

211 Gordon Wood, "The History of Rights in Early America," in Shain, ed., *Nature of Rights*, 233–57, 239 ff.

212 Wood, "History of Rights," 239 ff.

213 James Madison, "No. 10," in Hamilton, Jay, and Madison, eds., *The Federalist*, 43–44.

for stability of government.[214] He considers both "extreme wealth" and "extreme indigence" as threats to democracy, as they would lead to the emergence of factions in government.[215] At the same time, he considers that the natural differences in men's ability to acquire and accumulate wealth would lead to the emergence of factional interests that could threaten republicanism.[216] Jefferson, writing to Madison from France in 1785, notes the enormous inequality in the division of property that he saw in France.[217] "The laws of property have been extended as to violate" the Lockean "natural right" to appropriate what they need in order to survive, he notes. He expresses a concern that an equal division of property is impracticable. He advocates for tax exemption for those whose income fell below a certain point and taxation for owners of higher portions of property in a geometrical progression. He believes that the small landholders are "the most precious part of a state." More generally, in America social conflict did not lead to the emergence of class consciousness and thinkers like Gracchus Babeuf did not emerge there.[218]

Starting at the end of the nineteenth century, a movement in favor of enacting social rights in legislation and state constitutional texts emerged in the United States.[219] Some state constitutions were amended to include provisions protecting workers' rights. Those included child labor restrictions, maximum hours provisions, and minimum wage and worker safety guarantees. State legislation amplified these rights. Similarly, some states have since 1868 enacted provisions in relation to the needs of the poor, persons with disabilities, and the elderly. In the 1830s, state constitutions required legislatures to intervene in order to mitigate the negative effects of capitalism.[220] These measures included limits upon monopolistic railroads and relevant protection for their employees and customers. They also attempted to establish social safety nets. Between 1864 to 1940 state constitutions added protective labor provisions.[221] This intervention can be seen as compatible with Adam Smith's approach. Smith was in favor of government intervention to ensure the functioning of the free market against monopolies. He was also in favor of minimum redistribution to redress the negative unintended consequences that emerge from free markets

214 The Papers of James Madison, ed. R. Rutland and W. Rachal (Charlottesville: University of Virginia Press, 1975) 14, 197–98.

215 See Cass Sunstein, *The Second Bill of Rights: FDR's Unfinished Revolution and Why We Need it More than Ever* (New York, Basic Books, 2004), 116.

216 Madison, "No. 10," 44.

217 Letter to James Madison, October 28, 1795 (letter misdated; the actual date of this letter is ten years earlier, Jefferson having written 1795 instead of 1785) in *Political Writings*, ed. Joyce Appleby and Terence Ball (Cambridge University Press, 2012), 105–7.

218 See Higonnet, *Sister Republics*, 185.

219 See John J. Dinan, *The American State Constitutional Tradition* (University Press of Kansas, 2006), 194; Emily Zackin, *Looking for Rights in All the Wrong Places, Why State Constitutions Contain America's Positive Rights* (Princeton University Press, 2013).

220 Ibid., 34.

221 Ibid., 112.

and the division of labor. He was in favor of providing public education for everyone. Smith does not discuss what are understood today as welfare rights and many state constitutions have gone beyond what he considered necessary government intervention to ensure the functioning of the market.

Despite these efforts at state level, the US Supreme Court was not familiar with the distinction between "real" liberty and "formal" liberty until 1937 and its famous "switch." The Court invalidated legislation imposing maximum working hours[222] and minimum wages for women and children[223] in the name of an abstract conception of contractual freedom. The Court also invalidated legislation that would have prevented interstate commerce in the products of child labor, referring to the need to protect federalism in relation to a matter that was reserved for state and local control.[224] These decisions were reversed after 1937 and the Supreme Court started upholding minimum wage laws allowing New Deal policies to be implemented.[225]

In the 1930s, the idea that capitalism can have consequences that can endanger democracy itself gained ground at the federal level too. The ideological current of progressivism contributed to a modification of the dominant understanding of the role of the government.[226] The progressives suggested that poverty can be an "unintended consequence" of a weak economic system. It should not be considered as a consequence of personal inactivity and vice. The progressives did not accept the protection of property as negative liberty to the detriment of the public good. The currents of Legal Realism and Sociological Jurisprudence raised awareness about the profoundly unjust character of the legal forms of freedom of contract.[227] They noted how the reference to a formal freedom of contract can conceal the power imbalances on the two sides of the contract relationship.

222 *Lochner* v. *New York*, 198 US 45, 56 (1905) (invalidating legislation imposing maximum working hours for employees in a bakery); see also Gary Peller, "The Metaphysics of American Law," *California Law Review* 73 (1985), 1152–290.

223 *Adkins* v. *Children's Hospital of the District of Columbia*, 261 US 525 (1923). Reversed by *West Coast Hotel Co.* v. *Parrish*, 300 US 379 (1937).

224 *Hammer* v. *Dagenhart*, 247 US 251 (1918) (invalidating the Child Labor Act of 1916, which would have prevented interstate commerce in the products of child labor). The case was overruled by *United States* v. *Darby*, 312 US 100 (1941).

225 *West Coast Hotel Co.* v. *Parrish*, 300 US 379 (1937).

226 Morton J. Horwitz, *The Transformation of American Law, 1870–1960* (Oxford University Press, 1992); Duncan Kennedy, *The Rise and Fall of Classical Legal Thought* (Washington, DC: Beard Books, 2006); Frank Michelman, "Possession v. Distribution in the Constitutional Idea of Property," *Iowa Law Review* 72 (1987), 1319, 1334. For the relevance to freedom of speech, see Mark Graber, *Transforming Free Speech: The Ambiguous Legacy of Civil Libertarianism* (Oakland: University of California Press, 1991), 75 ff.; Laura Weinrib, *The Taming of Free Speech* (Cambridge, MA: Harvard University Press, 2016), 66–67.

227 For American Legal Realists see Oliver Wendell Holmes, "The Path of the Law," *Harvard Law Review* 10 (1897), 457. For the current of sociological jurisprudence, see Roscoe Pound, "Mechanical Jurisprudence," *Columbia Law Review* 8 (1908), 605–23; Roscoe Pound, "Liberty of Contract," *Yale Law Journal* 18 (1909), 454–87.

The pragmatist philosopher John Dewey also criticized the idea of original and fixed "natural rights."[228] Dewey stressed the importance of context and accident as defining the possibilities that persons have to exercise their liberty.[229] Skeptical about the Soviet experiment of his time, Dewey nevertheless advocated for social control of the economic forces in order to ensure the protection of "civil liberties." He defined those as the liberties of the citizens as opposed to the liberties of a hypothetical "state of nature."[230] Dewey's pragmatist approach was qualitatively different from the one dominant in France. He did not go as far as the French revolutionary idealists had gone in advocating an organic vision of society that manifests an ultimate cosmic unity. As analyzed earlier, Kant, and Hegel in some respects, applaud the idealism of the French Revolution. Dewey, as a pragmatist, did not entirely adopt Hegelian conceptions of the state as expressing the spirit and the will that holds individuals together. He did note that liberalism in his time should mean liberation from material insecurity.[231] The economic reality of capitalism created a gap between the ideals of liberalism and the possibility to realize them.

In the New Deal Era, Franklin Roosevelt adopted measures that echoed those of liberal European reformists. These interventions were ambitious rather than an attempt to provide compensatory redistribution, such as fulfilling a social minimum after the fact.[232] Historians have criticized the New Deal policies as being vague and deprived of a clear ideological orientation.[233] Although it was inspired by European style planning policies, it was to a great extent a response to a global trend in favor of protectionism that would allow domestic markets to survive.[234] As such it was in line with the Founders' vision of ensuring the survival of a "commercial republic."[235] The New Deal was not Keynesian, fluctuating instead "between fiscal conservatism and pump priming."[236] It offered policies, such as social security, collective bargaining and fair labor standards, national regulation of child labor, minimum wages, universal retirement, overtime compensation, and welfare benefits for the poor and

228 John Dewey, *Liberalism and Social Action* (New York: G.P. Putnam's Sons, 1935), 33.

229 John Dewey, "Philosophies of Freedom," in *On Experience, Nature and Freedom*, ed. Richard J. Bernstein (Indianapolis/New York: Bobbs-Merrill, 1960), 270; John Dewey, "Philosophy and Democracy," in D. Morris and Ian Shapiro, eds., *Political Writings* (New York: Hackett, 1993).

230 John Dewey, "Liberalism and Civil Liberties," *The Social Frontier* (February 1936), 137–38. See also James Kloppenberg, *Uncertain Victory: Social Democracy and Progressivism in European and American Thought 1870–1920* (New York: Oxford University Press, 1986), 329 ff.; Robert Westbrook, *John Dewey and American Democracy* (Ithaca, NY: Cornell University Press, 1991), 431.

231 John Dewey, *Liberalism and Social Action* (New York: G.P. Putnam's Sons, 1935), 17.

232 Samuel Moyn, *Not Enough: Human Rights in an Unequal World* (Cambridge, MA: Harvard University Press, 2019), 71.

233 See Jefferson Cowie, *The Great Exception: The New Deal and the Limits of American Politics* (Princeton University Press, 2016), 96–97; Kiran Klaus Patel, *The New Deal: A Global History* (Princeton University Press, 2015), 49.

234 Patel, *New Deal*, 59, 61, 65.

235 See Chapter 2.

236 Patel, *New Deal*, 80.

the disabled. The National Resources Planning Board founded in 1933 was a government consultation body that elaborated concepts of social rights such as unemployment relief, fair wages, safeguards against accidents and illness, and education. Some major acts enacted at that time were the National Labor Relations Act (1935), guaranteeing collective labor rights and the Fair Labor Standards Act (1938), guaranteeing minimum wage and safety in the workplace. The ideology behind these acts was less to guarantee labor rights as a social good and more to provide increased wages to boost consumer demand to save the market from collapsing.[237] Generally, in the United States, working people's social identities as consumers trump their identities as workers.[238]

When the New Deal was fading, Roosevelt elaborated in his 1944 State of the Union address his famous economic bill of rights.[239] He referred explicitly to a right to a "useful and remunerative job"; a right to earn enough to provide adequate food, clothing and recreation; the right of every farmer to raise and sell his products at a return that will give him and his family a decent living; the right of every businessman, large or small, to trade in an atmosphere of freedom from unfair competition and domination by monopolies at home or abroad; the right of every family to a decent home; the right to adequate medical care and the opportunity to achieve and enjoy good health; the right to adequate protection from the economic fears of old age, sickness, accident and unemployment and the right to good education. Roosevelt's economic rights were part of a pragmatic approach, an experiment that was necessary to save the economic system. They were not part of a comprehensive government plan to regulate the economy inspired by a conception of liberty as "universal" in the sense understood by the French political tradition.

Government intervention is a matter of degree. Some positive government action is also necessary for citizens to be able to guarantee their negative liberties (e.g., policing). Roosevelt's analysis of these liberties was part of a vision of government intervention for guaranteeing negative liberties. It was not part of a wider vision of state paternalism driven by a comprehensive theoretical scheme. This is in conformity with Adam Smith's conception in favor of a government that guarantees the functioning of the market. Adam Smith was in favor of government intervention in a way that would guarantee free competition and he was thus in favor of government action to prevent monopolies. Similarly, Hayek was in favor of a minimum wage, which he saw as an important medium for the survival of the economic system. The insight he expressed was that deep social inequalities threaten the operation of the

237 See Steve Fraser, "The Labor Question," in Steve Fraser and Gary Gerstle, eds., *The Rise and Fall of the New Deal Order, 1930–1980* (Princeton University Press, 1990), 78.

238 See James Whitman, "Producerism and Consumerism," *Yale Law Journal* 117 (2007–2008), 340.

239 See Sunstein, *Second Bill of Rights*, 13. For Sunstein, Roosevelt did not envision creating a system of relief, which would go against American ideals of self-reliance. See also William E. Forbath, "The New Deal Constitution in Exile," *Duke Law Journal* 51 (2001), 165, 207.

free market. Historians agree that the American reformers were not as successful as the Europeans in implementing principles of distributive equality.[240] Roosevelt's approach was not motivated by a comprehensive philosophical conception of the role of the government.[241] Although the progressives tried, through the interpretation of the Constitution as a "living" document, to implement some redistributive imperatives,[242] they did not succeed in creating a robust conception in favor of social rights. The conception underlying many of those measures is one of a shared contribution to risks. The minimal conception of social rights implemented in the New Deal did not manage to survive against a general approach of distrust toward extended government intervention in the market in regard to redistribution.

Both political developments[243] and judicial enforcement of rights[244] stopped the expansion of the welfare state. This was a result of the joint operation of various institutional actors, including the executive, the legislative, and the judiciary. The paradigm of "collaboration" of various institutional actors, which describes at a metalevel how the various branches operate, helps to make sense of these institutional developments.[245] The limits to the expansion of the welfare state were an unintended consequence of the action of various institutional actors motivated by the same ideology of distrust toward the government. For a short period of time, it seemed that the Supreme Court might be moving in the direction of reading the Constitution as implying some commitment to redistribution.[246] By 1937, some measures of protection against poverty were implemented. The Warren Court contributed to the flourishing of this conception.[247] This conception did not survive for long at the federal level despite parallel movements at state level.

240 See Moyn, *Not Enough*, 71; Ira Katznelson, *Fear Itself: The New Deal and the Making of Our Time* (New York: Norton 2014).

241 See Patel, *New Deal*, 64, in which the author distinguishes the New Deal from "radical utopias in other parts of the world." Unlike the situation in Germany or the Soviet Union, the United States "did not use its massive apparatus to control the lives of individuals" especially those who disagreed with New Deal policies. Ibid., 64–65. Patel notes that prohibition, one effort of moralizing regulation, failed in the 1920 as the New Deal expanded, and this failure, along with resistance toward social engineering projects, reaffirmed the American spirit against extended government intervention within civil society. Ibid., 119.

242 William E. Forbath, "Constitutional Welfare Rights: A History, Critique, and Reconstruction," *Fordham L. Rev.* 69 (2001), 1821.

243 Moyn, *Not Enough*, 84.

244 Sunstein, *Second Bill of Rights*, 169.

245 See Aileen Kavanagh, 'Beyond Silence and Censure in the Collaborative Constitution', Symposium on Constitutional Silence, Trinity College Dublin, August 2016 (paper on file with author).

246 The Court ruled that a law enacted by the state of California that made it a misdemeanor for anyone knowingly to bring or assist in bringing into the state a nonresident "indigent person" was unconstitutional in reference to the commerce clause of the US Constitution. *Edwards* v. *California* 314 US 160 (1941).

247 Lucas A. Powe, Jr., *The Warren Court and American Politics* (Cambridge, MA: Harvard University Press, 2001). The Court held that the equal protection clause requires that states provide trial transcripts to poor people appealing their convictions for free. *Griffin* v. *Illinois*, 351 US 12 (1956). It also held that the Constitution requires that everyone receive the assistance of counsel in criminal cases in *Gideon* v. *Wainwright*, 372 US 335 (1963), as well as on their first appeal of a criminal

President Nixon's election in 1968 and his Supreme Court appointees significantly immobilized the expansion of social benefits.[248] Judicial review, conceived as imposing limits to the action of the legislative, contributed to preventing the current in favor of expanding socioeconomic guarantees. Nixon's four appointees to the Supreme Court[249] did not read the Federal Constitution as protecting social and economic rights. The American conception of the separation of powers prevented the entrenchment of welfare rights within American constitutional discourse.[250] Later, President Carter, a moderate liberal Democrat, was elected in order to accomplish serious deregulation with bipartisan support.[251] Since the 1970s, few state constitutions have included provisions in favor of eliminating poverty and inequality.[252] In some states, they do guarantee the right to an eight-hour day, a minimum wage, and protection from blacklisting practices, as well as education rights in line with international developments in the area.[253] Those developments in the area of the economy affected the emergence of a doctrine of free speech.

Historians have proposed various interpretations as to the concrete political and social circumstances that led to the emergence of the free speech doctrine in the United States. These theories, which focus on various historical events as having led to the emergence of the doctrine, need to be complemented with the theory proposed in this book, which associates the importance of freedom of expression with the theory of government dominant in the United States. Historical circumstances led to the affirmation of a doctrine that was supported by the political theory of the Founding Era. Historians may disagree as to the facts that led to the emergence of the doctrine. Independently of which interpretation is most persuasive, the approach in this book suggests that the origins of the doctrine are deeper.

conviction in *Douglas* v. *California*, 372 US 353 (1963). The Court further accepted in *Boddie* v. *Connecticut*, 401 US 371 (1971) that in the context of divorce, the state would have to pay for a person's court fees and costs. In *Memorial Hospital* v. *Maricopa County*, 415 US 618 (1969), the Court further held that a state cannot impose waiting periods before new arrivals could receive welfare benefits. "The durational residence requirement, in violation of the Equal Protection Clause, creates an "invidious classification" that impinges on the right of interstate travel by denying newcomers "basic necessities of life."" Finally, in *Goldberg* v. *Kelly* 397 US 371 (1971), the Court held that a state cannot take away a person's welfare benefits without "due process," without a hearing,

248 As argued in Sunstein, *Second Bill of Rights*, 169.

249 Chief Justice Burger and Justices Harry Blackmun, Lewis Powel, and William Rehnquist.

250 The Burger Court held that there is no discriminatory effect in a Maryland law that set maximum limits per month on welfare grants and discriminated between children in small and large families. *Dandridge* v. *Williams*, 397 US 471 (1970). It also held that there is no discriminatory effect in a system of financing public schools that administers funds on the level of taxable wealth, which meant that per pupil expenditures were higher in wealthier areas. *San Antonio School District* v. *Rodriguez*, 411 US 1 (1973).

251 William Eskridge, Jr. and John Ferejohn, *A Republic of Statutes: The New American Constitution* (New Haven, CT: Yale University Press, 2010), 151.

252 These are the states of Louisiana and Hawaii. The New York Constitution as amended in 1938, also provides for the care of the needy. The New York Constitution, the Alaska Constitution, and the Louisiana Constitution provide that the local legislature can establish systems of public health.

253 Zackin, *Looking for Rights*, 108.

A comparative approach can assist our understanding of the emergence of a legal doctrine in one part of the world by focusing on the broader context of ideas that led to the emergence of this doctrine and evaluating how it compares with ideas existing elsewhere.

Arguably, the New Deal served as catalyst for the emergence of a robust free speech doctrine. The change in the understanding of the role of the government during the New Deal Era contributed to a doctrine of strict protection for freedom of expression.[254] At that moment, economic liberty was seen as leading to an unequal distribution of power and wealth and thus as a liberty that should be limited. It is then that the idea emerged that freedom of expression should be a constitutionally exceptional liberty. The newly recognized legitimacy of the federal government to regulate the "free market" went together with the increasing consideration of the political aspects of freedom of expression. Speech should remain beyond government intervention. In the area of economic liberties, it became legitimate for the government to intervene. This intervention followed a step-by-step approach, which aimed to ensure the survival of the market. This made the regulation of the "marketplace of ideas" illegitimate. The famous dissents by Justices Holmes and Brandeis, expressing a conception in favor of free speech in reference to Mill's marketplace of ideas a few decades earlier, won over the majority of the Supreme Court.[255] From then on government regulation of economic liberties became legitimate. Freedom of speech became the emblem of the American conception of limited government. Ideas of the Founding Era, like distrust toward the government, found expression in the protection of freedom of expression.

In 1937, the Supreme Court unanimously reversed the indictment of a Communist Party organizer convicted under Oregon's criminal syndicalism statute.[256] In its opinion, the Court discusses the right to free speech as implied by "they very idea" of republican government.[257] The idea of republican freedom as independence dominant in the Founding Era emerges anew. So does the emphasis on the negative aspect of freedom of association. Shortly thereafter the same idea appears in the reasoning of the court in relation to the negative aspect of the right to

[254] G. Edward White, "The First Amendment Comes of Age: The Emergence of Free Speech in Twentieth-Century America." *Michigan Law Review* 95 (1996), 299–392, 308; Bruce Ackerman, *We the People*, vol. 1, *Foundations* (Cambridge, MA: Harvard University Press), 124 ff. In Jeremy Kessler, "The Early Years of First Amendment Lochnerism," *Columbia Law Review* 116 (2016), 1915, the author focuses on the economic aspects of the protection of freedom of expression, which received emphasis during the period of the New Deal. First Amendment libertarianism emerges in the form of opposition to taxation of press corporations. Sam Lebovic makes a similar argument associating free speech to economic freedom in Lebovic, *Free Speech and Unfree News*.

[255] See the famous dissent by Justice Oliver Wendell Holmes joined by Louis Brandeis in *Abrams* v. *United States*, 250 US 616 (1919); also in *Gitlow* v. *New York*, 268 US 652 (1925).

[256] *De Jonge* v. *Oregon*, 299 US 353 (1937).

[257] Ibid., 364, discussing *United States* v. *Cruikshank*, 92 US 542 (1875). Cruikshank discusses the right of the people peaceably to assemble for lawful purposes as existing "long before the adoption of the Constitution." *United States* v. *Cruikshank*, 92 US 551.

freedom of association to holding a public meeting in public places and to distributing leaflets in relation to the National Labor Relations Act.[258] In the meantime, case law emerges that reaffirms the negative aspect of the freedom of expression in the form of freedom of religion. The Supreme Court emphasizes the freedom to distribute religious tracts against local ordinances that impose requirements of a priori licensing.[259] The Court refers to leaflets as "historic weapons in the defense of liberty," citing "the pamphlets of Thomas Paine and others" in American constitutional history.[260] The same Court held that legislation that is applied in a way that limits the religious freedom to impart one's religious views to others violates the due process clause of the Fourteenth Amendment.[261]

During the New Deal Era, the acceptance of government intervention in the economy had an impact on the mechanisms of judicial review.[262] The Supreme Court began to distinguish between "economic" and "political" liberties, assuring greater protection to the latter. At this moment, the doctrine of "preferred" liberties for the First Amendment freedoms emerged, including the freedom of speech, assembly, and religion. Despite accepting state intervention to limit economic liberties, political liberties are protected by reference to the idea of liberty that existed at the moment of the Declaration of Independence. That is, as political liberties and negative liberties against the state. This conception is reflected in the doctrine established in the famous Footnote 4 of *United States* v. *Carolene Products Co.*[263] According to this doctrine, legislation that limits the rights guaranteed by the text of the Bill of Rights or that, in one way or another, violates the democratic process must go through "more exacting judicial scrutiny," whereas economic regulation enjoys a presumption of constitutionality. It should be upheld on a rational basis review, if it is rationally justified by reference to the knowledge and the experience of the legislators.

The Supreme Court first referred to freedom of speech and freedom of religion as being in a "preferred position" against "discriminatory attempts to wipe them out" in *Jones* v. *City of Opelika.*[264] The opinion was written by Justice Stone, the author of Footnote 4 in *Carolene Products Co.* The case concerned a city ordinance imposing a license to the distribution of religious leaflets, which was itself conditional upon payment of a designated annual tax and issuance fee. Justice Stone notes that the license was dependent upon the whim of the administration, which thus exercises

258 *Hague* v. *CIO* 307 US 496 (1939).

259 *Lovell* v. *City of Griffin*, 303 US 444 (1938).

260 Ibid., 452.

261 *Cantwell* v. *Connecticut*, 310 US 1940.

262 Richard H. Fallon, Jr., *The Nature of Constitutional Rights: The Invention and Logic of Strict Judicial Scrutiny* (Cambridge University Press, 2019), 16.

263 *United States* v. *Carolene Products Co.*, 304 US 144, 152, n. 4 (1938). According to the footnote: "There may be narrower scope for operation of the presumption of constitutionality when legislation appears on its face to be within a specific prohibition of the Constitution, such as those of the first ten Amendments, which are deemed equally specific when held to be embraced within the Fourteenth."

264 *Jones* v. *City of Opelika*, 316 US 584, 608 (1942).

a power of censorship prohibited by the Constitution. The same Court repeated the same idea in cases following this related to other city ordinances requiring licenses for the distribution of religious materials. The Court notes that taxing the exercise of the religious practice of distributing materials can make its exercise so costly as to deprive it of the resources necessary for its maintenance.[265] It also affirms the doctrine of "preferred position" of freedom of speech against enforcing criminal legislation protecting the right to property of a company-owned town.[266]

Historians have discussed the contribution of the New Deal to the emergence of free speech doctrine from various perspectives. For Adam Lebovic the emergence of a robust First Amendment doctrine coincides with a return to Lochner era libertarian ideas.[267] Lebovic associates the movement with the emergence of the big business press at the beginning of the twentieth century. Big newspaper corporations were among those that criticized the New Deal as a threat to the traditional understanding of liberty in the United States.[268] The regulatory activity of the administrative agencies during the New Deal was in this context illegitimate, as a threat to freedom of expression as corporate freedom. In conflicts between socially liberal visions of press freedom and classical libertarian visions, the latter won out.[269] Publishers were successful in using liberal arguments for press freedom to insulate themselves from government regulation. This theory can be understood within the general framework on the role of the government suggested in this study in relation to the political theory dominant in the United States since the Founding Era. This interpretation holds due to the dominant ideology in the United States that the government exists to protect the negative aspect of the natural rights of citizens.

Another historian, Laura Weinrib, sheds light on the emergence of a robust First Amendment doctrine as a compromise between liberals and conservatives at a moment of intense social struggle in the United States around the New Deal Era.[270] Liberals focused on the need to protect the expressive rights of workers and conservatives and those of business interests against the government. For Weinrib, up to the New Deal Era, judges were predisposed in favor of protecting business interests to the detriment of employees' free speech. This was the case even in states that had constitutions containing free speech clauses similar to the First Amendment. Boycotts by workers were held to be impediments to interstate commerce.[271] These views went together with a dominant vision of the judiciary as the institution that would protect rights against majorities. Both currents saw the

265 *Murdock* v. *Pennsylvania*, 319 US 105 (1943).
266 *Marsh* v. *Alabama*, 326 US 501 (1946) 509.
267 Adam Lebovic notes the importance of press freedom as corporate freedom against the attempts of the New Deal administrative agencies to regulate the newspaper industry. Lebovic, *Free Speech and Unfree News*, 3, 18; see also Kessler, "The Early Years," 116.
268 Lebovic, *Free Speech and Unfree News*, 54.
269 Ibid., 87.
270 Weinrib, *Taming of Free Speech*, 38.
271 *Loewe* v. *Lawlor*, 208 US 274 (1908); *Gompers* v. *Buck's Stove and Range Co.*, 221 US 418 (1911).

judiciary as the protector of the rights that would lead to an extended protection for free speech. Before the First World War conservatives saw the judiciary as the agent that would protect their negative property rights. After the war liberals saw the judiciary as the institution that would protect against conservative majorities restricting workers' rights to free speech.[272] Before the war, the conservatives were the ones expressing distrust toward the government. After the war, it was the liberals who saw threats to free speech in government action. The corporate media feared the increased intervention of the administrative state. Workers feared that, were the government to intervene with their expressive interests, this would result in protecting the interests of their employers. Press corporations feared government regulation of their corporate interests. The reference to democratic theory in order to protect speech was also a theory on which both liberals and conservatives would agree.

These interpretations may be complemented with an analysis on the role of the government and its mission to realize liberty. This analysis can help us understand why from a comparative perspective only the United States reached an exceptionally protective legal regime for freedom of speech. The theories of Lebovic and Weinrib, which discuss the context of the emergence of free speech, may be complemented by an approach looking at the broader context of distrust toward the government dominant in the United States. All political and social actors, New Deal liberals, conservatives, the corporate media, and workers expressed views that can be seen as different facets of the need to protect the negative aspect of free speech against the government. Class conflicts such as the ones described by Weinrib existed in other parts of the world. If it was only in the United States that a robust doctrine of free speech emerged, her interpretation needs to be complemented by focusing on some deeper philosophical ideas that have defined the understanding of the role of the government by political and social actors. Moreover, these approaches focus on the political aspects of freedom of expression only. When the focus is enlarged to include freedom of religion, then the state's need to protect the negative aspect of freedom of expression becomes more obvious. The Supreme Court's decision to focus on expressive freedoms around the New Deal Era indicates the revival of a conception of distrust toward the government to regulate expressive freedoms consistent with the natural rights conception of the Founding Era.

This distrust went together with the re-emergence of democratic conceptions in favor of free speech, which also existed at the Founding Era. The progressives in America at the beginning of the twentieth century noted the importance for freedom of speech for democracy. Their conception survived to the extent that it was consistent with the protection of negative rights and with an understanding of democracy as the best regime to protect negative freedom dominant in America

[272] Weinrib, *Taming of Free Speech*, 120–211. Though this development was far from being straightforward and advocates of workers' rights long saw the judiciary as an institution that would dismantle labor protection. During the class struggle for labor rights in the first decades of the twentieth century, the courts did not protect workers' rights but gave the advantage to the employers' business interests.

since the Founding Era. In the 1930s, Dewey discussed intelligence as a "social asset."[273] He notes the difficulties that the masses of men with precarious economic conditions face to develop freedom of thought. A conception of liberty as independence from need and social power underlies his thought. The progressives appealed to government regulation of economic life in order to ensure that the press is not controlled exclusively by one social class. Dewey defends free speech for political dissenters.[274] Although the progressives did not succeed in bringing about a comprehensive change in the understanding of the role of the government, they did contribute to the establishment of a doctrine of free speech. Their democratic arguments in favor of free speech were successful to the extent that they were re-elaborating ideas dominant in the Founding Era. Brandeis's concurring opinion in *Whitney* v. *California* is indicative of this approach. Brandeis reads elements of progressive thought on the importance of self-development for self-government as compatible with the conception of liberty dominant in the Founding Era.[275] *Whitney* did not overturn the conviction of one of the founders of the Communist Labor Party for "criminal syndicalism." Nevertheless, it did pave the way to the articulation of a robust free speech doctrine that came later. Brandeis articulated that the danger justifying limits on speech should be "imminent." This criterion was used to protect speech later on in *Brandenburg* v. *Ohio*.[276]

Theories of civil libertarianism that emerged within the current of progressivism associated freedom of speech with the idea of negative liberty better protected thanks to self-government. Zechariah Chafee makes a case in favor of free speech libertarianism, associating it with democracy, while he subscribes to pragmatism and sociological jurisprudence.[277] Chafee also emphasizes the social interest in free speech, associating it with an expansive reading of negative constitutional guarantees. His thought combines deference to the legislative branch for economic and social policy with judicial protection of speech. Chafee presents his libertarian defense of free speech as transcending partisan political debate. In this respect, he succeeds in

[273] John Dewey, *Liberalism and Social Action* (New York: Capricorn Books, 1935), 67.

[274] John Dewey, *Characters and Events: Popular Essays in Social and Political Philosophy*, vol. 2, ed. Joseph Ratner (New York: Henry Holt and Company, 1929), 571, 575.

[275] *Whitney* v. *California*, 274 US 357 (1927). "Those who won our independence believed that the final end of the State was to make men free to develop their faculties, and that, in its government, the deliberative forces should prevail over the arbitrary. They valued liberty both as an end, and as a means. They believed liberty to be the secret of happiness, and courage to be the secret of liberty. They believed that freedom to think as you will and to speak as you think are means indispensable to the discovery and spread of political truth; that, without free speech and assembly, discussion would be futile; that, with them, discussion affords ordinarily adequate protection against the dissemination of noxious doctrine; that the greatest menace to freedom is an inert people; that public discussion is a political duty, and that this should be a fundamental principle of the American government." Ibid., 375. Brandeis's social thought was very close to the progressive reformers in favor of the protection of positive liberties. See Graber, *Transforming Free Speech*, 119–20.

[276] *Brandenburg* v. *Ohio*, 395 US 444 (1969).

[277] See his work Zechariah Chafee, *Free Speech in the United States* (Cambridge, MA: Harvard University Press, 1941).

rearticulating a libertarian theory for the content of free speech, presenting it as compatible with economic regulation. He extends his free speech libertarianism to legislation limiting the expressive use of private property by economically privileged speakers. Similar ideas underlie Alexander Meiklejohn's *Free Speech and Its Relation to Self-Government*.[278] Meiklejohn refers explicitly to the principle of self-government existing in the framers of the American Constitution. By underlining the essential value of freedom of speech for the democratic debate, Meiklejohn's approach facilitates the protection of subversive advocacy and the rejection of content distinctions for political speech. Later Meiklejohn even includes artistic and literary expression in the domain of expression, which should be protected for the development of individual personality and citizenship.[279] As analyzed in other parts of the book, during the Founding Era, the idea was dominant that self-government is a better guarantee for the protection of negative liberties. These ideas survived within the American constitutional tradition to the extent that they reflected a conception of negative freedom. Another conception that gained ground at the time was that America should be a society founded on liberty and democracy, but also a society that should be opposed to tyranny and arbitrariness, representing the hope for rationality and truth in the world.[280] Ideas of freedom of speech as negative liberty interacted with other ideas leading toward a vision of America as the exemplary global defender of freedom against the excesses of government.

Legislation imposing expenditure limits during political campaigns that was invalidated by the US Supreme Court in *Citizens United* v. *Federal Elections Commission*[281] reflects some of the ideas of the progressives. Robert Post notes that the progressives' effort to master the importance of business interests that were corrupting policies led them to enact statutes that would preserve representative integrity by prohibiting corporate campaign contributions and expenditures.[282] Relevant legislation, Post explains, sought to create institutional forms that would assure possibilities for the expression of public opinion. The distrust toward democratic majorities of the Founding Era was moderated in the 1830s, when the pressing issue became the need to give expression to public opinion through the American party system. Jacksonian egalitarianism led to the emergence of a new party system, which would connect voters directly with their representatives. By the beginning of the twentieth century, Americans realized that parties, instead of representing public opinion, were "misrepresentative" as they lacked popular discipline because they fell under the sway of professional politicians.[283] Public

278 Alexander Meiklejohn, *Free Speech and Its Relation to Self-Government* (New York: Harper, 1948).

279 Alexander Meiklejohn, "The First Amendment is an Absolute," *The Supreme Court Review* (1961), 245–66.

280 G. Edward White, "The First Amendment Comes of Age," 328.

281 *Citizens United* v. *Federal Elections Commission*, 558 US 310 (2010). See Chapter 1.

282 Robert Post, *Citizens Divided: Campaign Finance Reform and the Constitution* (Cambridge, MA: Harvard University Press, 2014), 29.

283 Ibid., 27.

opinion was seen by the progressives as the institution that would connect the people to their government anew at a moment when distrust toward political parties and toward representative government was widespread.[284] From this perspective, First Amendment jurisprudence emerged at a moment when faith in representative government was fading. Contemporary First Amendment doctrine since *Citizens United* has reversed this conception, renewing the older tradition of distrust toward the government.

The Cold War crisis and the McCarthyism period were backward steps for the protection of freedom of expression. Subversive advocacy was not protected in this period of crisis, despite the dissents of Hugo Black and William Douglas.[285] Nevertheless, the Supreme Court soon interpreted the category of political speech broadly and adopted a system of control that justices like Black and Douglas called "absolute." This system resulted in the protection of defamatory speech related to public officials[286] and false light privacy.[287] In the 1970s, Thomas Emerson strengthened the rationale of personal fulfillment for protecting freedom of expression.[288] He contributed to a theory that became dominant around the ideal of autonomy as an element of an ongoing process of collective self-determination.[289] He also suggested that funds expended for expression should be protected as expression itself. Later cases protecting symbolic speech such as flag burning,[290] speech against obligatory conscription,[291] and the permission for neo-Nazi groups to march,[292] indicate that the justification for freedom of expression is the protection of individual autonomy. All these cases can be understood in reference to the idea that the American political system is founded on the metaphysical postulate of distrust toward the government together with the need to respect the natural rights of the person against the state. Throughout American history, various social groups referred to this rationale. Underlying all these considerations was always an understanding that freedom of speech is to be protected as a negative liberty.

A conception of negative natural rights persists in relation to freedom of expression to the extent that in the United States this liberty is not considered as a positive

284 Ibid., 33.

285 *Dennis* v. *United States*, 341 US 494 (1951). See Mark Tushnet, "United States of America," in Markus Thiel, ed., *The Militant Democracy Principle* (Farnham, UK: Ashgate, 2009), 357; Geoffrey R. Stone, *Perilous Times* (New York, Norton, 2004). For a detailed presentation of measures enacted then, see also Paul Franz, "Unconstitutional and Outlawed Political Parties: A German-American Comparison," *Boston College International and Comparative Law Review* 5 (1982), 51–89.

286 *New York Times Co.* v. *Sullivan*, 376 US 254 (1964).

287 *Time Inc.* v. *Hill*, 385 US 374 (1967).

288 Thomas Emerson, *The System of Freedom of Expression* (New York: Random House, 1970).

289 As Robert Post notes, "First Amendment jurisprudence uses the ideal of autonomy to insulate the processes of collective self-determination." Robert Post, *Constitutional Domains: Democracy, Community, Management* (Cambridge, MA: Harvard University Press, 1995), 278.

290 *Texas* v. *Johnson*, 491 US 397 (1989); *United States* v. *Eichman*, 496 US 310 (1990).

291 *Cohen* v. *California*, 403 US 15 (1971).

292 *Collin* v. *Smith*, 578 F.2d 1197 (US 7th Cir. 1978); *Village of Skokie* v. *National Socialist Party of America*, 69 III. 2d 605; 373 NE 2d 21(1978), cert. denied, 439 US 916 (1978).

liberty,[293] as a liberty that necessitates state intervention to see its content realized, as is the case in France. The decisions of the French Constitutional Council on freedom of expression assign a teleology in the exercise of this right. Upon examining constitutionality of a law limiting media concentration and ensuring financial transparency and pluralism, the Council held that this freedom is effective when citizens have a sufficient number of publications of different trends and characters.[294] For the Council, "ultimately the objective to be achieved is that readers who are among the essential recipients of the freedom proclaimed by Article 11 of the 1789 Declaration should be able to exercise their free choice without either private interests or public authorities being able to substitute their own decisions for it or making it the subject of a market."[295] The Council sees it the mission of the state to ensure the "pluralism of sociocultural currents of expression" against oligopolies arising in the market. The state assigns an end to the exercise of the liberty, which needs to be made effective.

Considerations around having the media respect standards of fairness existed in the United States until the 1980s when resources were scarce. Denser regulation of the broadcast media was accepted in the United States at the time. The technical limits on broadcasting frequencies led to national caps on the number of radio and TV stations. The state had to make sure that various social groups had access to them. Decisions like *Red Lion Broadcasting*[296] ensured that both sides in a controversy had access to the media. This decision recognized an obligation to respect standards of fairness to be supervised by the Federal Communications Commission in a world of limited frequencies. Apart from these minor interventions justified by the scarcity of resources, the system of freedom of expression is seen as a "laissez-faire" system, which "must tolerate differences in the economic capacity of the various participants."[297] When these technical limitations were overcome, thanks to the emergence of cable and digital media, the regulation loosened. The arguments in favor of distinguishing broadcasting media from a libertarian approach that had protected the press from economic regulation evaporated too.[298] France maintains limitations on media concentration, which do not exist in the United States. In the United States, the newspaper industry was granted an exception from antitrust laws, which led them to follow the business model of maximizing

293 For a critical appreciation and a call in favor of a New Deal for freedom of expression in favor of rights of access to the media, see Cass R. Sunstein, "Free Speech Now," in G. Stone, R. Epstein and C. Sunstein, eds., *The Bill of Rights in the Modern State* (University of Chicago Press, 1992), 255–316.

294 CC, Decision 84-181DC, Oct. 10–11, 1984, Rec. 73.

295 Ibid., §38. English Translation by Charles Girard, "Equal Freedom of Expression and Intra-Right Conflicts," unpublished manuscript on file with author. See also CC, Decision 86–217DC, Sept. 18, 1986.

296 *Red Lion Broadcasting Co., Inc.* v. *FCC*, 395 US 367 (1969).

297 Thomas Emerson, "The Affirmative Side of the First Amendment," *Georgia Law Review* 15 (1981), 823.

298 Lebovic, *Free Speech and Unfree News*, 196–97. See also Lee C. Bollinger, *Images of a Free Press* (University of Chicago Press, 1991).

monopoly profits. This model led to a significant crisis with the evolution of new platforms of communication on the Internet.[299]

Furthermore, the US Supreme Court has rejected the conception of a right to respond.[300] For the Court, a statute recognizing this right operates as "government compulsion" upon a newspaper to publish what "reason tells it."[301] The statute operates as a command forbidding the paper to publish content.[302] And it imposes additional printing, composing, and material costs and takes up space that could be devoted to other material the newspaper might like to print.[303] The Court saw this right as constituting government compulsion, which affects the content of the paper and its treatment of public issues and officials.[304] French law provides for the possibility for a right to respond to publications which concern a person's honor and reputation.[305] This right limits the freedom of editors and obliges them to insert "at the head of the next issue of the periodical or newspaper, all the corrections that are instructed by an agent of public authority in relation to facts that have been mentioned inaccurately by the newspaper or periodical."[306]

The First Amendment served as a "powerful engine of deregulation" in many areas where government regulation is accepted in Europe such as data privacy.[307] The relevant decisions can also be understood as part of this general spirit of distrust toward the government to help the citizens realize their liberty. The same holds for *Citizens United* v. *Federal Elections Commission*,[308] which invalidated federal legislation imposing limits to independent expenditures that usually come from corporations, deeming it to be a violation of speech rights. This decision has been criticized as significantly overlooking the distinction between "real" freedom and

299 Lebovic, *Free Speech and Unfree News*, 213.

300 *Miami Herald Publishing Co.* v. *Tornillo*, 418 US 241 (1974). The Supreme Court held that a Florida statute on the right to respond to a candidate for a public office violates the guarantee of freedom of the Press of the First Amendment.

301 *Miami Herald Publishing Co.* v. *Tornillo*, 418 US 241 (1974), 256.

302 Ibid., 256.

303 Ibid., 256–57.

304 Ibid., 258.

305 Article 6 of Law of July 29, 1982, available at www.legifrance.gouv.fr/affichTexte.do?cidTexte=LEGITEXT000006068759&dateTexte=20110808; Michel Friedman, *Les droits de réponse* (Paris: Editions du Centre de formation et de perfectionnement des journalistes, 1994); Yves Mayaud, "L'abus de droit en matière de droit de réponse," in Jean-Yves Dupeux and Alain Lacabarats, eds., *Liberté de la presse et droits de la personne* (Paris: Dalloz 1997), 5; Martine Coisne and Jean Collin, "Le droit de réponse dans la communication audiovisuelle," in Dupeux and Lacabarats, eds., *Liberté de la Presse*, 17; Jean-Paul Levy, "Pratique du droit de réponse dans la presse écrite et la communication audiovisuelle," in Dupeux and Lacabarats, eds., *Liberté de la Presse*, 31.

306 Article 12 of the Law of July 29, 1881, as modified (my translation). The right can be exercised within a deadline of three months following publication and by the same medium of communication. It can be enforced through preliminary injunction.

307 *Sorrell* v. *IMS Health Inc.*, 131 S. Ct. 2653, 2672 (2011). See Chapter 1. Robert Post and Amanda Shanor, "Adam Smith's First Amendment," *Harvard Law Review Forum* 128 (2015).

308 *Citizens United* v. *Federal Election Commission*, 558 US 310 (2010). See Chapter 1.

"formal" freedom to participate in political debates and to affect electoral results.[309] Under the ruling, any corporation can engage in independent expenditures favoring a political candidate of their choice. The decision gives an advantage to those members of civil society who have the material resources to enjoy real freedom of expression. It gives an advantage to those that already have the material possibility to make themselves heard within the public debate.

In a previous decision, *Buckley* v. *Valeo*, the Court stated that "the concept that government may restrict the speech of some elements of our society in order to enhance the relative voice of others is wholly foreign to the First Amendment," which was designed to secure "the widest possible dissemination of information from diverse and antagonistic sources" and "to assure unfettered interchange of ideas for the bringing about of political and social changes desired by the people."[310] *Citizens United* has also been criticized for referring to principles created to protect the emergence of public opinion and thus self-government while concluding that "neither equality, nor distortion, nor eliminating corruption, can count as constitutionally compelling interests capable of justifying legislation prohibiting corporations from making independent campaign expenditures directly from their corporate treasuries."[311] Robert Post, in his criticism of the decision, notes how the legislation invalidated in *Citizens United* sought to protect the integrity of public opinion against corporate interests and misrepresentation.[312] *Citizens United* is beyond the ideas dominant in the Progressive Era, which aimed to ensure that representatives are more responsive to public opinion than to personal and corporate wealth.[313] The decision seems to renew the older libertarian tradition of distrust toward governmental intervention with expressive and corporate interests. In a later decision, the US Supreme Court applied the principles of *Citizens United* and held that electoral integrity cannot justify limitations on independent corporate campaign expenditures.[314] France regulates the funding of political campaigns strictly and maintains ceilings on campaign expenditures.[315] French legislation gives the possibility to submit a request to the urgent applications judge to suppress allegations of facts that are "inexact or deceiving" and of a nature to alter the sincerity of the voting process.[316] The law applies to online media.

309 Kathleen M. Sullivan, "Two Concepts of Freedom of Speech," *Harvard Law Review* 124 (2010), 143; Samuel Issacharoff, "On Political Corruption," *Harvard Law Review* 124 (2010), 118, Lucian Bebchuk and Robert Jackson, Jr., "Corporate Political Speech: Who Decides?," *Harvard Law Review* 124 (2010), 83.

310 *Buckley* v. *Valeo*, 424 US 1 (1979), 48.

311 See Post, *Citizens Divided*, 52.

312 Ibid.

313 Ibid., 62–63.

314 *Am. Tradition P'ship, Inc.* v. *Bullock*, 132 S. Ct. 2490 (2012).

315 See Chapter 1.

316 Loi 2018-1202 du 22 Décembre 2018 relative à la lutte contre la manipulation de l'information [Law 2018-1202 of December 22, 2018 on the fight against fake news], OJ, Dec. 23, 2018, art. 1, modifying the Code electoral [Electoral Code], art. L. 163-2-I.

Hate speech regulation in France can also be seen as part of the positive mission of the state to make sure that some groups are protected from hateful expression.[317] This protection has a purpose. It is part of broader measures equalizing who can exercise an effective liberty of speech. Eliminating the discriminatory effects of hate speech allows targeted groups to be heard when they speak within the public debate. In other words, it protects the social standing of the targets of hate speech.[318]

As I argued in this chapter, the difference in the understanding of the role of the government corresponds with a difference in the understanding of liberty, given that there is by definition a dialectic between the two notions. The French revolutionaries had an understanding of liberty in a universal sense. According to this conception, liberty should be protected in all its manifestations, as a political liberty and negative liberty, but also as positive liberty. According to the latter sense, the state was seen as having the mission to provide for the preconditions for the exercise of liberty according to a conception of positive liberty later associated with the idea of the rights of the welfare state. The question of assistance was omnipresent during the declaratory work in France. A reference to solidarity rights was missing in the Declaration of 1789, which was written urgently to respond to the constitutional question. This omission was amended in later declaratory texts amid the search for the best possible way to define the founding principles of the new French democracy. The understanding of liberty was so highly abstract in the French revolutionaries that they were unable to realize it. Aiming to impose upon reality an ideal, while reality was not ready yet to implement this ideal, meant that they were bound to fail in their efforts. As Hegel notes, the attempt to impose an ideal upon reality led to the Terror, the fury of the destruction of anything that did not correspond to this ideal vision. The conception that it is the mission of the state to help the citizens realize their liberty is an element that survives within the French constitutional tradition up to date.

The Americans on the other hand had a more pragmatic vision of liberty. They proclaimed it in the negative sense, as liberty against the government. They were reminding the British Empire that they were not protecting the liberties of the English in the colonies, while providing a new understanding for these liberties. The Americans read the philosophy of natural rights in the English parliament's 1689 Declaration of Right. The doctrine of natural rights included the idea of negative rights. The sociopolitical needs that led to the American Declaration of Independence led to the invention of a new theory of republicanism, which attempted to reconcile the public good and "natural" liberties. The American revolutionaries had parliamentary and administrative experience from the colonies'

317 See Ioanna Tourkochoriti, "Should Hate Speech be Protected? Group Defamation, Party Bans, Holocaust Denial and the Divide between Europe – U.S.A.," *Columbia Human Rights Law Review* 45 (2014), 552–622.

318 For an approach favor of limiting hate speech to protect the social standing of its targets, see Jeremy Waldron, *The Harm in Hate Speech* (Cambridge, MA: Harvard University Press, 2012).

assemblies. By 1776, they had elaborated a notion of a constitution different from any existing in Europe at the time.

In the French political order, the state is seen as having the mission to guarantee the preconditions for the exercise of liberty. The metaphysics of rights in the French political context associates rights with governmental intervention in order to guarantee their preconditions and to realize liberty. This action of the state is expressed as primacy of public power. This primacy leads to the legitimacy of the action of a paternalistic state, which is based, following the French Revolution, on democratic consensus. The concern to provide for social rights, which was omnipresent at the revolutionary moment, in association with the conception of the "rational republic," contains the danger of an "overdetermination" of the conditions necessary for the realization of liberty, as is the case regarding expressive freedoms. The reconceptualization of the role of the state in France leads to the formation of institutions, which are seen as having the mission to guarantee the primacy of this paternalistic "public power," from then on democratically legitimate. This is expressed in the law of freedom of expression, where it is legitimate for the state to intervene to ensure that citizens are able to exercise their liberty. The philosophy that it is the mission of the state to help the citizens realize their liberty is reflected in the burka ban and the ban on dwarf-throwing. The same conception is reflected in attempts to ensure rights of access to the media in the form of protecting a right to respond. It is reflected in the legislation that imposes limits upon media concentration and independent expenditures in political campaigns. It is also reflected in limiting cases of harmful speech like hate speech.

On the contrary, in the United States, the affirmation of the protection of the public sphere went together with the emphasis on the necessity to guarantee the private sphere. Institutions were designed to perpetuate and assure this primacy of the private sphere. American republicanism is associated with giving primacy to the protection of the natural negative rights of the citizens. When this conception was moderated and increased government intervention within civil society was accepted, expressive freedoms became "preferred" freedoms. Acceptance of economic regulation during the New Deal served as a catalyst for the protection of freedom of speech. The progressives were successful in contributing to the doctrine of freedom of expression to the extent that their theory was compatible with an understanding of negative liberty dominant since the Founding Era. Freedom of expression is still protected in its negative facet in the United States. It is not legitimate for the state to intervene help the citizens realize their liberty, the protection of religious expression, the protection of the freedom of the press, and the protection of corporate speech in the area of independent expenditures in political campaigns can be traced back to the distrust toward government intervention in civil society dominant in the Founding Era. These rights are negative rights par excellence against the government.

4

The Moralizing Rational Republic versus the State Arbitrator of the Free Play of Interests

France has enacted legislation limiting viewpoints that run the risk of leading citizens to "wrongful" opinions. As discussed earlier, hate speech is limited in France and so is the denial of crimes against humanity. The state has legitimacy to limit modes of self-expression that are against the dominant conception of the "dignity" of the person expressing themselves, as the dwarf-throwing case shows. It is also legitimate for the government to protect citizens when they operate under a "false consciousness" as to whether their decisions are free or not. The burka ban indicates that it is legitimate for the state to dictate to the citizens how they treat themselves, if the state believes that they treat themselves wrongfully. All these forms of expression are protected in the United States. As I argue in this book, the balancing of freedom of expression and other values in France and in the United States can be understood in reference to the broader historical, social, and philosophical context in which jurists operate. The libertarian conception for the protection of freedom of speech in the American legal system can be understood by reference to the general distrust toward the government. This distrust, along with a general spirit against state paternalism, permeates legal discourse. It affects how jurists define the content and limits of a liberty and strike a balance between liberties in conflict. The trust toward the government dominant in France leads jurists to an overdetermination of the content of freedom of speech. It is legitimate for the government *lato sensu* in France to protect citizens from the danger of arriving at erroneous opinions and from expressing themselves in a way that harms their dignity. The difference in the definition of the role of the government depends, among other things, on the practical necessities to which institutions aimed to respond at the moment of their conception.

Rousseau's moralizing discourse for the role of the state was particularly attractive to the French revolutionaries who aimed, among other things, to establish a new political sociability and regenerate a corrupt human nature. The optimism of Locke and the Scottish Enlightenment focuses on the self-regulating potentialities of civil society. It legitimizes the minimal impact of the political sphere upon the social. These ideas were more inspiring for the Americans' own political needs. Inversely, the thought of Locke and of the thinkers of the Scottish Enlightenment can assist our understanding of the ideas of government that the American revolutionaries had in mind.[1] In France, the state has the task of regenerating humanity. In the United States, the state should be limited to arbitrating the differences that emerge inside civil society. Normative conceptions of the role of the government as being minimal are expressed today in the law of freedom of expression. As analyzed previously, government intervention in the economy today is accepted also in the United States. Elements of distrust toward the government that the Founders were expressing under the influence of Locke and the Scottish Enlightenment are reflected today in the case law on freedom of expression.

Contemporary law on freedom of expression in France expresses trust toward the state to moralize citizens. The burka ban and ban on the dwarf-throwing and the legislation against "manipulation of information" and "fake news" all express this tradition. Hate speech regulation in France can be seen as protecting the targeted persons from harm and as protecting the citizenry more generally against the danger of reaching false opinions. Bans on the denial of crimes against humanity also express a vision that it is the mission of the state to take position on what is inherently wrong. The terrible atrocities that took place within European society, including the Holocaust, the transatlantic slave trade and the Armenian genocide are to be remembered. The legal regime, which is protective of all these instances of expression in the United States, reflects the understanding of minimal government that exists in Locke and Smith. The liberty to burn the national flag in the United States also expresses the mentality that it is not the mission of the state to engage in a moralizing role toward protecting national identity.[2] National identity in the United States consolidates around the idea of protecting negative liberty.

Historians have shown that the French Revolution was to a great extent a political and a social revolution. It aimed to create new institutions and to eliminate political and social hierarchy. It sought to respond to the question of mass poverty. Rousseau's thought was a valuable point of reference in this respect. He was read and misunderstood by most political actors, who were able to draw the conclusions they considered the most appropriate to their political needs and to the conception of the government they considered necessary. The question of "assistance" – of social rights – omnipresent in the discourse of the French revolutionaries, presupposes a conception of the "natural" state and the prepolitical state, as a social state. A bond of organic unity among its members legitimizes state action to realize this "assistance." This idea of organic unity among the members of a society can justify state action to guarantee positive liberty in the sense of social rights and to guarantee the preconditions of the exercise of negative liberty.[3] In France, it is legitimate for the

[1] Cf. Gary Gerstle, Liberty and Coercion: The Paradox of American Government from the Founding to the Present (Princeton University Press, 2015), 20.

[2] *Texas* v. *Johnson*, 491 US 397 (1989).

[3] See also Worms, "Introduction," in Frédéric Worms, ed., *Droits de l'homme et philosophie: une anthologie (1789–1914)* (Paris: Agora, 1993), 21.

government *lato sensu* to intervene within civil society to ensure the preconditions of the exercise of liberty. This means that it is legitimate for the state to intervene to protect the citizens from poverty, as well as their own immaturity.

The difference in the protection of freedom of speech can also be understood in association with the interplay between positive law and natural law within a legal system. A legal system characterized by trust in the self-regulating potentialities of civil society tends to regulate the content of liberties, and in particular, freedom of expression, less densely. A system characterized by trust toward the government tends to regulate more densely. Locke and the Scottish Enlightenment were influential upon the American conception of government as they express trust in the reason of the individual to discover the rules of justice and morality that apply to social interaction. Rousseau is less optimistic toward individual reason and is in favor of a stronger role for the state in educating its citizens in developing a moral stance. In his opinion, natural law is to be absorbed by positive law. There are stronger elements of state paternalism in Rousseau's thought. In this respect, his ideas were very influential upon the French revolutionaries.

Rousseau's thought meets the Ancients in many respects, particularly in relation to the close association that he sees between morality and politics, civil society, and political society. According to Rousseau's ideal, there must be continuity between the internal dialogue a person has with themselves and the external dialogue concerning political action. For Rousseau, it is the quality of citizenship that conditions the quality of man.[4] It is only in society (which in his thought is confounded with political society) that man attains human dignity. It is the general will that mediates the relationship of everyone with themselves. If it is only conceiving oneself as a member of the general will that elevates humanity to its proper level, to its dignity, and any disagreement with the general will means that the dissonant individual is wrong, that they have not succeeded in adopting the impartial point of view. However, even if Rousseau was very careful to keep his discourse on the normative level and not to confound the level of *is* with the level of *ought*, passing from his theory to its practical application runs the risk of leading to this confusion. The attempt to realize the idea in the French political context led to accepting the state as being legitimized to intervene to decide even on the relation that any person has with themselves, the definition of one's plans and life projects, and thus to outlaw speech on ideas or visions of the good that are supposed to be harmful not only to social coexistence but also to the relation that each person has with themselves. The modern distinction between natural rights and positive law, where the former would serve as limits for the latter, vanishes in Rousseau. In parallel, Rousseau's analysis of the legislator in *The Social Contract* is reminiscent of the ancient conception: Rousseau recognizes an extensive pedagogical role for the

4 "We begin to become properly men only after having been citizens." Rousseau, *Du contract social (première version, manuscrit de Genève)*, 287.

legislator, which is close to paternalism. Even if subjectivity is important to Rousseau, French rationalism, whichever might be the role recognized to the subject, leads to the acceptance of a strong role for the government. This role invokes the antique conception of the *polis*, supposed to accomplish what the immaturity of subjectivity does not allow the subjects to know by themselves. With rationalistic individualism as a starting point, Rousseau's thought can be interpreted as accepting the absorption of this individuality into the general will, with the imaginary and transcendent instance supposed to have its origins in this same individuality.

The French legal and political order is dominated by an ex ante understanding of an organic unity between the government and civil society, which has its origins in the metaphysical conception of unity between the royalty and its subjects. The substitution of this royalty for another imaginary and transcendent entity, the general will, which is supposed to express "reason," is equivalent to accepting the role of this will as *par excellence* competent to define the limits and content of liberty. It is equivalent to accepting it as having the mission to define the relation that each person has with themselves, according to an inverse conception of the autonomy of the subject. The French conception of liberty, as it was enunciated in 1789 and redeveloped during the constitutional continuity of the postrevolutionary period, is marked by the paradox of attempting to find a liberalism for the subject as well as a liberty by the state, according to Lucien Jaume's phrase.[5] This paternalism has the form of the state substituting its judgment for the judgment of the citizens by banning speech it considers harmful. It also means that it is legitimate for the government to limit the content of freedom of expression to protect other concurrent rights. Despite Rousseau's precautions around the is/ought distinction, his thought was understood in the French revolutionary context, especially by the Jacobins, as justifying rational dogmatism and legal positivism.[6]

Locke and the Scottish Enlightenment provided theories that corresponded to the American revolutionaries' political needs. These needs found expression in the optimism of these theories in relation to the self-regulating potential of civil society which legitimizes the minimal impact of the political order upon the social. The state should be limited to arbitrating differences that emerge within civil society. As Lucien Jaume has analyzed, the autonomy of civil society, taken for granted by the Scottish Enlightenment and Locke, "is admitted only with hesitation" in France, since the law tends to dominate opinion.[7] The Scottish conception of moral sentiments as the element that holds society together without a coercive mechanism is an idea that does not fit in the French context. Rousseau was influential upon American thinkers only to the extent that he considers that sociability is natural. The

5 Jaume, *Individu effacé*.

6 Jaume, *Discours jacobin*, 271, 299.

7 Jaume, *Individu effacé*, 64.

Americans, distrustful toward government, did not draw the same implications from his thought for a strong moralizing government.

4.1 ROUSSEAU'S CONCEPTUALIZATION OF THE MORALIZING REPUBLIC

The tendency to overregulate freedom of expression in France can be understood by reference to a conception of the moralizing role of the government, which was reaffirmed at the moment of the French Revolution. This role reflected an older tradition of state paternalism. This conception of the role of the government in relation to freedom of expression brings France closer to antiquity than to modernity. Rousseau's thought also played a part in this, to the extent that he combines ideas of antiquity and modernity that the French revolutionaries were struggling with. The modern foundation of politics is articulated in three spheres – the political, the social, and the moral – which were confounded in the ancient conception of the cosmos. Rousseau's innovation consists in giving a new meaning to their relation by posing as a normative ideal the rationality of politics as such, by subordinating the social existence to the moral.[8] This innovation brings him very closely to the Ancients, and influenced the French revolutionaries' conception of the role of the state. Other elements in Rousseau's thought that contributed to the French revolutionaries' understanding of the role of the government are the identification between civil and political society and the absorption of natural law by positive law. Furthermore, the pedagogical role that he attributes to the legislator, the organic conception of society, and the relation between political power and the members of the social body are equivalent to the absorption of individuality in the transcendental entity of the general will. This is in spite of the reference to the social contract, which for Rousseau is a necessary conceptual tool to provide a theory of political legitimacy.

Whatever might have been the contribution of the royal power to the equalization described by Tocqueville in *L'Ancien régime et la Révolution*, the French revolutionaries felt obliged to reform a corrupt and decadent political and social state. In order to establish a new political sociability, they saw themselves charged with the mission to entirely reform society. They aimed to remodel the human domain according to the requirement of pure reason.[9] The revolution attempted to implement an order of values and to modify the order of the human world. While attempting to change life, both collective and individual, it deployed a pedagogy destined to produce a "new humanity."[10] Incarnating the constitutive values of man

8 Bourgeois, *Raison moderne*, 34.

9 Gusdorf, *Conscience révolutionnaire*, 121.

10 Ibid., 142. See also Mona Ozouf, *L'homme régénéré* (Paris: Gallimard, 1989). Discussions on wealth and the idea of the role of the government as to promote economic growth were not very popular in France on the eve of revolution. See Daniel Mornet, *Les origines intellectuelles de la Révolution française 1715–1787* (Paris: Armand Colin, 1954), 63; Jeremy Jennings, *Revolution and the Republic:*

and the citizen in the social environment, the revolutionary culture formed a whole that invades everyday life, establishing a kind of "civic catechism."

In the context of this effort to form a new reality in the image of thought, Rousseau and his "Thought of Misfortune"[11] constituted a major source of inspiration. His *Discourse on the Origin of Inequality* exposes the decadence of humanity, which is how the French revolutionaries saw the Ancien Régime.[12] The *Social Contract*, presenting the question of human destiny as a work to be accomplished, constitutes the "Charter of the new world," proposing fundamental principles applicable to politics.[13] Rousseau's concern for inequality in *Discourse on the Sciences and the Arts* leads him to a genealogy of morality and vice. He discusses its problematic implications in the *Discourse on the Origin of Inequality*. This knowledge appealed to the French revolutionaries, who aimed to reconstruct their political order and to re-establish an ideal of virtue upon humanity. The idea of virtue is predominant in Rousseau's ethics. Through the fiction of the state of nature, he describes a situation of innocence and ideal purity. When man is trapped in the circuit of exchange, pity is buried deeply in the human soul. "It is thus that the usurpations of the rich, the robberies of the poor, the wild passions of all suffocating natural pity, and the even weaker voice of justice made men miserable, ambitious and bad."[14] The establishment of property constituted a decisive point in the way toward corruption.[15]

Henry Gouhier insightfully traces a parallel between the history described by Rousseau and the Judeo-Christian Fall, where man conserves the power to correct its effects.[16] Alexis Philonenko proposes that in Rousseau's thought there is a correspondence between the "transcendental past," the isolated man of the state of nature characterized by a natural goodness and pity, the "pragmatic history," the

A History of Political Thought in France since the Eighteenth Century (Oxford University Press, 2011), 9.

11 "Pensée du Malheur," which is the title of the famous work by Alexis Philonenko. Alexis Philonenko, *Jean-Jacques Rousseau et la pensée du malheur*, 3 vols. (Paris: Vrin, 1984). More generally, on Rousseau's influence upon the French Revolution, see François Aulard, "Les philosophes et la Révolution," in *La Révolution française: revue historique* (Paris: Siège de la Société de l'Histoire de la Révolution Française, 1892), 193; Roger Barny, *Prélude idéologique à la Révolution française: le rousseauisme avant 1789* (Paris: Les Belles Lettres, 1985); Roger Barny, *Les contradictions de l'idéologie révolutionnaire des droits de l'homme, droit naturel et histoire* (Paris: Les Belles Lettres, 1993); Roger Barny, *Le droit naturel à l'épreuve de l'histoire: Jean Jacques Rousseau dans la Révolution* (Paris: Les Belles Lettres, 1995); Roger Barny, *Le triomphe du droit naturel: la constitution de la doctrine révolutionnaire des droits de l'homme (1787–1789)* (Paris: Les Belles Lettres, 1997); Higgonnet, *Sister Republics*, 140; Norman Hampson, *Will and Circumstance: Montesquieu, Rousseau and the French Revolution* (London: Duckworth, 1983).

12 Philonenko, *Jean-Jacques Rousseau et la pensée de malheur*, vol. 3, *Apothéose du désespoir* (Paris: Vrin, 1984), 21.

13 Ibid., 21.

14 John-Jacques Rousseau, *Discours sur l'origine et les fondements de l'inégalité parmi les hommes* [1754], in *Œuvres complètes*, vol. 3 (Paris: Gallimard, 1964), 176.

15 John-Jacques Rousseau, Discourse on the Origin of Inequality, trans. Donald A. Cress (Indianapolis/Cambridge: Hackett, 1987), 76–77.

16 Henri Gouhier, *Les meditations métaphysiques de Jean-Jacques Rousseau* (Paris: Vrin, 1984), 32.

Fall, and a transcendental future that he sees for humanity.[17] Rousseau inverses the theme of the Encyclopaedists, just like the one of the Scottish Enlightenment, by seeing sociability as the "immoral emergence of morality."[18] The passage from the amorality of the solitary state of nature toward morality carries the negation of the positive content of morality. If the *Discourse on the Origin of Inequality* describes what man became, *The Social Contract* exposes what man could be. Man can be regenerated in the free citizen of *The Social Contract*. The pragmatic history of Rousseau exposes the self-destruction of the human being, their alienation.[19] The civil man has become a stranger to himself.[20]

Rousseau postulates a unity between morality and politics that evokes the thought of antiquity. By the social contract, humans succeed in reconciling their social nature and liberty.[21] He implies that the natural condition of humanity is social as it is only in society that they can exist as humans and develop their conscience, which is by definition social, as mediated by language. If Rousseau's thought contains elements of methodological individualism, it also contains elements that justify the idea that he considers the social state as natural.[22] He engages with the thought experiment of the state of nature in order to prove that society is the natural state of humanity. In his thought, the social contract plays the role of providing a theory of legitimacy for the government. For Rousseau, language, which is by definition social,[23] and the mental representations that it generates makes a person a human being. Thanks to language, human beings are in a position to fully realize their capabilities, to know themselves and to develop their reflective conscience. Outside society, a human being is "a limited and stupid animal." Social relation and the development of language leads to the transition from the amoral state to the moral state, through the development of mental representation, abstract thought, and conscience. Reflexivity, the conception of oneself as a thinking subject, as well as

17 Philonenko, *Jean-Jacques Rousseau et la pensée de malheur*, vol. 1, *Le traité du mal*, 93 ff.; In Judith Shklar, *Men and Citizens: A Study of Rousseau's Political Theory* (Cambridge University Press, 1969), the author also sees in Rousseau one of the "last utopians," a thinker "pointing the awful distance between the possible and the probable by showing in great detail how men could live, even though they always refuse to do so." Ibid., 1–2.

18 Bourgeois, *La raison moderne*, 34.

19 Rousseau *Discours sur l'origine*, 192.

20 Ibid., 193.

21 He writes in *Emile* that "Those who will want to treat politics and morality separately will never understand anything concerning either of them," John-Jacques Rousseau, *Emile*, in *Œuvres complètes*, vol. 4 (Paris: Gallimard, 1969), 524 (my translation); Bourgeois, *La raison moderne*, 43; Olivier Cayla, "Rousseau Jean-Jacques, Du contrat social," in Olivier Cayla and Jean-Louis Halpérin, eds., *Dictionnaire des grandes oeuvres juridiques* (Paris: Dalloz, 2008), 495–505, 499; Catherine Larrère, "Rousseau," in Raynaud and Rials, eds., Dictionnaire *de philosophie politique*, 687–95, 692.

22 Rousseau, Emile, 600. Cf. Raymond Polin, La politique de la solitude: essai sur la philosophie politique de Jean-Jacques Rousseau (Paris: Sirey, 1971), 15; Victor Goldschmidt, Anthropologie et politique: les principes du système de Rousseau (Paris: Vrin, 1974). Cf. Pierre Manent, Naissances de la politique moderne: Machiavel-Hobbes-Rousseau (Paris: Payot, 1977), 154.

23 Jacques Derrida, *De la grammatologie* (Paris: Minuit, 1967).

the development of a sense of time, presuppose language. It is thus society through language that allows a human being to develop abstract thought, a sense of time, and aesthetic and moral criteria.[24] Subjectivity is the result of a process of socialization. There is a continuation between internal reflexivity and external reflexivity. The emergence of conscience is equivalent to the internalization of the mirror.

The reflection upon oneself and the conversation with oneself is conditioned by the situation in a community in time and in space. Reason is conditioned by its situation inside a specific society because the very possibility to conceive oneself as a subject having a conscience is conditioned by one's situation in time and in space. Individual conscience derives from society. It is society that is primary, in a conception according to which it is being a citizen that allows one to become a man: "we do not begin to become men but only after having been Citizens."[25] For Rousseau, it is thanks to the social contract that persons become capable of living according to their true nature, as it is only inside civil society that they can develop their moral being. It is society that elevates a person to the dignity of a human being. Fichte, writing much later than Rousseau and the French Revolution itself, is also very close to Rousseau on this point. Fichte notes that "if there are to be human beings at all, there must be more than one."[26]

For Rousseau, the internal dialogue that a person has with themselves or their conscience must be in continuity with the external dialogue that a person should be engaged in on political action. Morality emerges in the relation to the other. Unfortunately though, it degenerates immediately into immorality,[27] as comparison with others leads human beings to bury deep in themselves their pity. This leads to an immoral situation of generalized exploitation and loss of liberty.[28] The new social contract that Rousseau proposes responds to the necessity to save the social condition, that is morality and liberty, by obedience to self-imposed law. It is the legislator that helps humans realize their potential. The legislator elevates a people who are still minors to the knowledge of the general interest, "for otherwise, they would run the risk of 'making a mistake' and of adopting a partial point of view and not general which would mean that the people would consider something other than themselves."[29] In the ideal social contract, the transcendental future that Rousseau envisions for humanity, the continuity between the internal dialogue and the external dialogue is assured. The internalization of the mirror and the emergence of reflexivity can have obvious authentic results in the hypothetical participation of

24 Rousseau, *Discours sur l'origine*, 146–50.

25 Rousseau, Du contract social (première version, manuscrit de Genève), 287, 293.

26 Johann Gottlieb Fichte, *Foundations of Natural Right According to the Principles of the Wissenschaftslehre*, trans. Michael Baur, ed. Frederick Neuhouser (Cambridge University Press, 2000), 37.

27 Bourgeois, *Raison moderne*, 34.

28 John-Jacques Rousseau, *Discours sur les sciences et les arts* [1751], in *Œuvres Complètes*, vol. 3 (Paris: Gallimard, 1964).

29 Cayla, "Rousseau Jean-Jacques," 504.

everyone in the formation of the law in politics. However, Rousseau's theory allows for readings and interpretations that attribute a significantly "paternalistic" role to the state, which leads to a negation of the possibility for each human being to be autonomous.

For Rousseau, two characteristics anterior to reason, self-preservation and pity, allow human beings to deduce natural law. It is feeling that conditions humanity and allows perfect reason.[30] For Rousseau, pity, a prereflective human sentiment, which he defines as the "natural repugnance to see every sensible being perish or suffer, and principally one's same species," allows humanity to deduce the rules of natural law.[31] This feeling must guide reason and make it willing to accept the constraints of justice, instead of focusing on a narrowly conceived egocentric self-interest. If we follow the Rawlsian terminology and distinction between the "rational" and the "reasonable" use of reason,[32] Rousseau incites the use of the latter. The rational use of reason points toward thinking about a person's own good. Rousseau is critical of the reason of the philosophers that led them to over-emphasize the rational aspect of humanity.[33] The reasonable use of reason points toward taking everybody else into consideration when a person is defining their own good. Rousseau insists on the necessity for a person to reflect in order to impose limits upon themselves to respect others; he stresses the justness of our actions.[34] Human beings followed the wrong path as they buried their possibility for pity deep in themselves. Using only their rational reason they were led to the impasse of social inequality. Pity can help moderate the use of "rational" reason and orient it toward a "reasonable" use of reason. And, it is the mission of the state to help the citizens to bring their pity back into the surface.

Such a system presupposes a close association between the general will, the will of the state, morality, and ethics – to the extent that the human being obtains their notion of just and unjust once they have become a citizen. It does not allow for the traditional distinction between positive law and natural law. For Locke, "the state of nature has the law of nature, which must regulate it and to which everyone is obliged to submit oneself and to obey. Reason, which is this law, teaches all humans, that if they want to consult it, by being all equal and independent, nobody must harm another, in relation to his life, his health, his liberty and his good."[35] Rousseau describes the state of nature as a state where a human in the primitive stages is a "stupid and limited animal" and where in the later stages they wrongly use their reason. The human being finds their humanity anew once the conclusion of the

30 Rousseau, *Discours sur l'origine*, 143.

31 Ibid., 154.

32 John Rawls, *A Theory of Justice* (Oxford University Press, 1973), 18–19.

33 Rousseau, *Discours sur l'origine*, 156. Rousseau criticizes philosophers in his *Discours sur les sciences et les arts*.

34 Rousseau, Du contract social: (première version, manuscrit de Genève), 329.

35 John Locke, *The Second Treatise of Government*, ed. David Wootton (London: Penguin Books, 1993), 263–64.

ideal social contract that he envisions for humanity has taken place. Human reason, a virtual faculty at the state of nature, needs the social state to develop itself and attain its proper level of development.[36] Natural law, which, for Rousseau, has its origins in the reasonable faculty of a human being and their sensibility, pity, appears in order to become positive immediately. It is absorbed entirely by the general will, which mediates the relation of all with all, and the relation of every individual with themselves, given that there is no distinction between the social state and the political state for Rousseau.

In this sense natural law could not be anterior to civil laws, although Rousseau refers to it in works such as *Émile*,[37] or *Letters Written from the Mountain*.[38] Rousseau writes in *The Social Contract* that: "the crucial question is thus to distinguish well between the respective rights of the Citizens and of the Sovereign, and the duties that the first have to fulfill in their quality of subjects of natural law which they must enjoy in their quality of men."[39] He also insists that "if alienation is done without reserve, the union is as perfect as it can be and none among the associates has anything more to claim."[40] Natural law becomes almost entirely positive, since it is only positive law legislated by the general will that can guarantee the protection and the moral equality of all citizens. It ends the competitive and immoral natural state, which prevents human beings from developing themselves on their proper level and deprives humanity from its dignity. Retaining natural rights, reserving a sphere for natural law, is equivalent to altering the general will. In this sense, the book became "the gospel of a Revolution which betrayed it all the time," to the extent that the social contract was the "new" element that the revolutionaries were looking for.[41] Politics will allow the development of individual conscience and strengthen authority in a way identified with the general will. As I analyze in Chapter 5, the conception of rights as existing to the extent that they are recognized by the general will, which stresses the social foundations of rights, is the idea that can help us to understand the greater willingness to regulate freedom of speech in the French context. In the American context, a "natural rights philosophy," together with a conception of distrust toward the government makes jurists reluctant to accept limitations on speech.

Rousseau's analysis of the legislator in *The Social Contract* is close to the conception dominant in antiquity. Rousseau sees the legislator as a man of genius charged

36 Robert Dérathé, *Jean-Jacques Rousseau et la pensée politique de son temps* (Paris: Presses Universitaires de France, 1950), 164.

37 Rousseau, *Emile*, 448.

38 John-Jacques Rousseau, *Lettres écrites de la montagne*, in *Œuvres complètes*, vol. 3 (Paris: Gallimard, 1964), 842.

39 Rousseau, *Du contrat social*, in *Oeuvres complètes*, vol. 3 (Paris: Gallimard, 1974), bk. 2, chap. 4, 373 (my translation).

40 Rousseau, *Du contrat social*, bk. 1, chap. 6, 361. See also Ernst Cassirer, *The Question of Jean-Jacques Rousseau*, trans. Peter Gay (Bloomington: Indiana University Press, 1963) 52 ff.; and Martin Loughlin, *Foundations of Public Law* (Oxford University Press, 2010), 110–11.

41 Philonenko, *Apothéose du désespoir*, 18.

with the mission of transforming every solitary individual "into part of a larger whole, from which this individual receives their life and their being; to alter the Constitution of man in order to strengthen it; to substitute a moral existence for the physical and independent existence that we have all received from nature."[42] Bearer of "sublime reason," capable of "making the Gods speak," Rousseau's legislator "must have the characteristics of God's envoys."[43] Henry Gouhier sees many similarities between Rousseau's conception of the legislator and the Ancients' conception.[44] Just like the legislator of the Ancients is an educator, because his work supposes the knowledge of what is good, beautiful, and just, incarnating practical prudence, Rousseau's legislator is an agent of extraordinary qualities. Rousseau recognizes an extended pedagogical role for the legislator to ensure obedience to the law. The legislator has the authority to "make the citizens" such as "he needs that they should be," exercising "the most absolute authority . . . which penetrates until the most internal part of man and is not exercised less on the will than on actions."[45] The very justification that Rousseau proposes for the legislator comes from a paternalistic conception. He will illuminate the people, who "always want the good, but do not always see it by themselves."[46] This element survives in the contemporary understanding in favor of the role of the law in regulating the content of freedom of expression in France.

Although Rousseau borrows the idea that politics is not limited to institutional problems and that education has a priority in achieving the "good life" from Plato's *Laws* and the *Republic*, the ancient elements in his thought are peripheral. They concern "borrowed elements more than impregnations, happy encounters more than preestablished harmony, annexations more than assimilation."[47] Despite his proximity to antiquity, Rousseau remains a philosopher of modernity. If, according to antiquity, man is harmoniously integrated in a universe where order, reason, and harmony are dominant, everyone having their place and their function determined by their proper nature, the notion of autonomy in Rousseau and the acceptance of the artificial character of inequality differentiate him significantly from the Ancients. Rousseau's return to antiquity in the search for meaning, in a context of moral degradation, was not inscribed in a reactionary attempt but in an attempt to find lessons for humans in modernity.[48] Virtue, for Rousseau, is inseparable from equality. He expresses the idea, which already existed in Hobbes, that by an act of legislation coming from oneself and respecting the criterion of generalization, liberty is preserved and accomplished by obeying only ourselves. We subscribe

42 Rousseau, *Du contrat social*, bk. 2, chap. 7, 381 (my translation).

43 See Rousseau, Lettres écrites de la montagne, 728; Rousseau, Du contrat social (première version, manuscrit de Genève), bk. 1, chap. 2, 317; John-Jacques Rousseau, Discours sur l'économie politique, in Œuvres complètes, vol. 3 (Paris: Gallimard, 1964), 248.

44 Gouhier, *Méditations métaphysiques*, 143 ff.

45 Rousseau, *Discours sur l'économie politique*, 251–52, 260.

46 Rousseau, *Du contrat social (première version, manuscrit de Genève)*, 311.

47 Gouhier, *Méditations métaphysiques*, 149.

48 Leo Strauss, *Natural Right and History* (University of Chicago Press, 1950) 252 ff.

only to that which promotes our liberty and individuality. For Leo Strauss, the ultimate result of this attempt was the substitution of liberty for virtue or rather the vision that it is not virtue that liberates the human being but liberty that makes the human being virtuous in a conception where natural liberty, civil liberty, and moral liberty are confounded.[49]

The rationalism that Rousseau sees in man is faithful to a fundamental idea of ancient philosophy, the consideration that man is a "reasonable animal."[50] In this sense, if Rousseau's general will can never be wrong, an idea repeated by the French revolutionaries, this is because it expresses the universal reason to which the universality of the free individual responds. "Universality" means the intellectual generality of their reason.[51] The individual considered in themselves, according to Rousseau's idealized vision of the citizen in the ideal social contract, can already consider in themselves the point of view of the general will. In this association, it is reason manifested both in the general will and in the individual that has primacy and not the general will itself, nor the individual.

As analyzed earlier, the metaphor of the infinitesimal calculus discussed by Leibniz assists our understanding of what Rousseau means with the concept of the general will. According to this visual metaphor, every citizen has their point of view in relation to a topic.[52] There may be a perspective that sees everything from above, and that can harmonize all other partial points of view. Visual perception is like the law: if we consider a legislative assembly, for Rousseau the whole people, the problem of the formation of the general will is analogous to the problem posed by the fact that the universe is one, but that it seems infinitely multiple to the individual points of view. We must consider the political body as an entity forged by the integration of small differences – the differences between individual wills. These wills are identical in their common evaluation of the general will. In short, the general will, which defines the law, does not consist of an accumulation of common opinions that Rousseau calls "the will of all" in an accumulation of identical elements, but in a harmonious integration, in an accordance of points of view. The general will can be described as having each individual as its starting point. From the point of view of the whole, it is the integral of all individual points of view. From the point of view of the individual, according to Rousseau's formula:

> The general will is in every individual a pure act of understanding which reasons in the silence of passions, on what can man ask from his fellow men and what can his fellow men ask from him.[53]

49 Ibid., 281.
50 Gouhier, *Méditations métaphysiques*, 20.
51 Philonenko, *Apothéose du désespoir*, 52 ff.
52 Luc Ferry and Alain Renaut discuss this metaphor in *Philosophie Politique* 3: *Des droits de l'homme à l'idée républicaine* (Paris: Presses Universitaires de France, 1992), referring to Gottfried Wilhelm Leibniz, *La Monadologie* (Paris: C. Delagrave, 1881).
53 Rousseau, Du contrat social (première version, manuscrit de Genève), 286 (my translation).

In other words, the general will is the conscience of autonomy. It is the result of the continuation between the internal dialogue and the external dialogue on political action. And this will be possible, Rousseau seems to imply, if human beings are able to use both their emotions and their reason. If human beings activate their potential for pity and use their reason reasonably. According to one interpretation, Rousseau's thought has the potential to lead to "dogmatic rationalism."[54] Rousseau's understanding of liberty can lead to a confusion between morality and politics.[55] Certainly, the idea of the subject remains dominant in his thought. It seems though that French rationalism, whichever might be the role recognized to the subject, leads to an acceptance of a strong role for the state, which is reminiscent of the ancient conception of political action in the *polis*, thought to accomplish what the immaturity of subjectivity does not allow the subjects to know for themselves. The general will, as a normative ideal, is always right in Rousseau. "The most general will is always the more just."[56] This can lead to the idea that the more general the will becomes, the less the citizen or the subject can be conscious of the choice that it expresses.[57]

Rousseau accepts majority decision-making, whereas it is conceivable that a quantitative minority might express the substantive point of view of the general will. Is Rousseau founding a qualitative idea on a quantitative, as Philonenko asks?[58] Rousseau was careful to establish the general will as a substantive criterion.[59] As I analyze below, his thought can be misread in a way that makes legitimate extended government intervention, in the form of legislative action, dictated by majority decision-making. Since, according to Rousseau, the legislator has the duty to adjust and make sure that the laws are expressed in conformity with the general will, the legislator occupies the function of mediator in the state guaranteeing the spirit of the community. If liberty as autonomy is a way of acting that supposes a rational choice, the knowledge of what is just or unjust, it is expressed in the reason of the law, which is alone in a position to teach the point of view of the whole to the individual.[60]

There are elements in Rousseau's thought that bring him very close to the conception of a very strong role for the state. For Rousseau, the social contract coincides with the political contract. This is equivalent to accepting the total absorption of natural law by positive law. For Locke, the role of the legislator does not consist in absorbing the totality of natural law, but in deciding limit cases for which disagreements can emerge. For Rousseau, the legislator contributes to the

54 Georges Gusdorf, *Naissance de la conscience romantique au siècle des Lumières* (Paris: Payot, 1976), 32.
55 Bourgeois, *Raison moderne*, 44.
56 Rousseau, *Discours sur l'économie politique*, 246.
57 Philonenko, *Le traité du mal*, 248.
58 Ibid.
59 Rousseau, *Du contrat social*, bk. 4, chap. 2, 441.
60 Jean-Fabien Spitz, "Jean-Jacques Rousseau et les droits de l'individu," in Gian Mario Cazzaniga and Yves Charles Zarka, eds., *L'individu dans la pensée moderne: XVIe-XVIIIe siècles* (Pisa: Edizioni, 1995), 659–74, 664.

formation of the human subject as human, to the elevation of the human being to their proper level. This idea can be interpreted as implying extended state paternalism concerning the definition of the limits and content of liberty. For Rousseau, if liberty and will cannot be conceived independently from its mediation by the general will, if the state makes a human being a human being, the state is recognized as the instance legitimized to intervene to decide on the relation that every person has with themselves. Thus, it can outlaw speech expressing ideas or conceptions of the good, judged as prejudicial not only to social coexistence, but also to the relation that every person has with themselves. The general will can be understood as the condition of the possibility of the community, and also as synonymous with autonomy.[61] The general will and autonomy can be understood as reciprocal concepts. The general will can be understood as moral universality which coincides with ethical universality.

> Whoever refuses to obey to the general will, will be forced to do so by the entire body. This means merely that he will be forced to be free. For this is the sort of condition that, by giving each citizen to the homeland, guarantees him against all personal dependence.[62]

The individual will be "forced" "to be free": they will be assisted to elevate themselves to the dignity of citizen. If the general will is legitimized to use "force," it is because it expresses the integral of interests existing in society, the impartial point of view that the individual is incapable of seeing. The underlying idea is that the more the general will wins over the consciousness of men, the less coercive it is. If the general will is understood according to the visual metaphor discussed earlier, it excludes oppression by definition. However, the phrase can be read and understood as implying a conception of liberty that is consubstantial with the definition of its content by the state. It makes the use of coercion legitimate because everybody accepts it when they go wrong. That is, when they are incapable of adopting the point of view that someone can have from above, according to the previously analyzed visual metaphor. The question always remains pending: who expresses and who decides what is this point of view that expresses impartiality? The difficulties in realizing the idea of the general will can lead to a strong paternalistic state that overlooks the possibility of citizens' reason. Rousseau explicitly accepts censorship, as he thinks that it can "maintain the morals by preventing the corruption of opinions, by conserving their honesty, by wise applications and even by fixing them when they are still uncertain."[63]

The problems of interpretation and of application upon political action of the notion of the "general will" are due to the coincidence in Rousseau's thought

[61] Alexis Philonenko, *Apothéose du désespoir*, 38 ff.

[62] Rousseau, "On the Social Contract," in *The Basic Political Writings*, trans. Donald A. Cress, ed. Peter Gay (Indianapolis: Hackett, 1987), bk. 1, chap. 7, 150.

[63] Rousseau, *Du contrat social*, bk. 4, chap. 7.

between civil society and political society, accepted by the French revolutionaries. The impossibility of conceiving the political state independently from the social state, which has its origins in the doctrine of incorporation of the subjects in the king, is characteristic of the political thought of Rousseau and has marked the conception of liberty within the French legal order. The relation that every person has with themselves is mediated by the general will. Although Rousseau defines the formation of the general will as an ideal, his interpretation by the political actors of the French Revolution led to a conception that is equivalent to admitting that the relation with oneself is mediated by the will of the state, as the instance thought to be incarnating the general will. The French representatives in the National Assembly considered themselves, by a speech act, as the instance incarnating the general will par excellence, having legitimacy to speak in the name of the people and to mediate the relation that every person has with themselves. It is this conception that makes the outlawing of eccentric ways of self-expression, such as dwarf-throwing or wearing a burka, legitimate in the French context. Outlawing these activities is seen as liberating individuals from themselves. According to the dominant understanding, individuals who engage in these activities are operating under a "false consciousness," and it is legitimate for the state to force them to be free.

Having individualistic rationalism as its point of departure, Rousseau's thought can be interpreted as accepting the absorption of this individuality in the imaginary and transcendent instance, which is thought as having its origins in this very individuality. In France, where an ex ante understanding of an organic unity between power and civil society is dominant, having its origins in the metaphysical conception of such a unity between royalty and its subjects, the substitution for this royalty of another imaginary and transcendent entity, the general will, thought to express pure rationalism, means accepting the role of this will as having the authority par excellence to define the limits and content of liberty, the relation that everyone maintains with themselves.

4.2 THE FRENCH REVOLUTIONARIES' ATTEMPT TO REALIZE THE RATIONAL REPUBLIC

A paternalistic state, which constitutes the incarnation of the prudence of the Ancients in relation to freedom of expression, negates the possibility for citizens to decide which opinions are worthy of being heard and appreciated and which are not. In France, judges are more willing to limit offensive speech and to protect the privacy rights of individuals. Furthermore, the French paternalistic state substitutes its judgment for the one of its citizens, forbidding opinions that seem harmful and limiting the content of freedom of expression to protect other concurring rights. Limits on hate speech and on the denial of crimes against humanity can be understood from this perspective. The ban on dwarf-throwing and on wearing headscarves can be understood in reference to accepting a paternalistic mission for the state. On the contrary, the conception of freedom of expression dominant in the case law of the US Supreme Court indicates a vision of the state that accepts the possibility of the subject to judge for and by themselves which opinions are worthy of being heard. This overvaluation of the necessity to protect the autonomy of individual judgment makes judges unwilling to accept a compensating role for the state when speech is offensive or violates other rights, such as the right to privacy for public figures. The idea of state paternalism was omnipresent in the thought of the French political thinkers around the moment of the French Revolution. The key ideas that led to this conception in the thought of the French revolutionaries were a conception of society as being natural, a conception of natural law close to the one dominant in antiquity, a conception of natural solidarity and a conception of the role of the state as having the mission to moralize citizens. These elements, in combination with readings and misreadings of Rousseau's thought, contributed to the French approach.

Although Rousseau tried to distinguish the *is* from the *ought*, in the French revolutionary context, his thought was read by the Jacobins as justifying rational dogmatism and legal positivism. The elements of his thought that favored this conception in a context of an ex ante understanding of a rigorous statism, and which are reminiscent of Aristotelian positivism, are those that lead to deducing the *ought* from the *is* of the sovereign: "The Sovereign by the fact alone that he is, he is always what he should be."[64] Rousseau construed the sovereign, taking into consideration normative elements, so that he cannot be blamed for committing an error of reasoning by deducing the *ought* from the *is*.[65] As Pierre Manent notes, Rousseau's conception of liberty does not distinguish between liberty in the philosophical sense and political liberty.[66] A human being is free only if they are a free citizen. The same conception was omnipresent in the discourses of the French revolutionaries during the summer of 1789. Heteronomy is masked by the idea that the obedience of the citizen is founded on a free act of will, their own will.[67]

Isolating some elements of his thought, combined with a wider ex ante understanding in favor of the positive character of the state, led to this positivistic French conception of liberty. The dogmatic rationalist Jacobin reading can distort Rousseau's idea by considering itself as the expression par excellence of this general will. The analysis of Sieyès – the intermediary between Rousseau and the Jacobins – contributed to this

64 Rousseau, *Du contrat social*, bk. 1, chap. 7, 363 (my translation).

65 According to the famous beginning of the first book of *Du contrat social*, "man is born free and everywhere he is in chains." Rousseau, *Du contrat social*, 351. Rousseau is careful to trace analytically the legitimacy of the general will through the idea of obedience to oneself, by virtue of the thought experiment of the social contract, conceived as free convention of free men: "I want to search if in the civil order there can be some rule of legitimate and sure administration, by taking men as they are and the laws as they can be: I will try to bind always in this research what the law allows with what interest prescribes, so that justice and utility are not divided." Rousseau, *Du contrat social*, 351.

66 Pierre Manent, *Naissances de la politique moderne*, 182.

67 Ibid., 194.

interpretation: "the national will ... needs only its reality to be always legal, it is the origin of all legality."[68] The law is the true guarantor of the protection of rights because, being the expression of the general will, it is the exercise of the "principle of sovereignty" that "essentially resides in the nation." Although Rousseau distinguished between the normative and the descriptive conception of the sovereign, Sieyès did not. The unity and infallibility of the general will presuppose an enemy of the political body, external and internal. Rousseau's conception was read as implying that the "internal" enemy can be within every citizen, if the citizen focuses on their private interest and love of self. This conception led the French revolutionaries to the Terror.

The great power of the state, which is always at play in the ex ante understanding of the role of the state and the government in France, is obvious in the interpretation of Rousseau's thought since the revolution as well.[69] For Rousseau, the constitution of a political body presupposes the alienation of the "natural" rights of the individual and the restitution by the state of equal rights for everyone. The alienation of the rights of the sovereign people is thought to be for their own benefit and in their favor. This can mean extended government intervention in defining and redistributing the rights that citizens have. Even if Locke also influenced the French Declaration of Rights, the European context is more favorable to a different understanding of the declaratory clauses in relation to those of America. The French Declaration of Rights does not have the mission only to define limits for the will that expresses popular sovereignty. It has the mission to define the very purpose of the state and the government.[70] Rousseau's political philosophy can have as its implications the acceptance of a paternalistic state, aiming to impose upon individuals a specific idea of well-being. This may concern the level of ideas as well as the economy. In this way, the paternalism of the Ancien Régime can be continued and perpetuated in many domains of state activity. This becomes evident in the use that the revolutionaries make of Rousseau's conceptual tools and the reference to the terms of will and rationality.

The intellectual debates around the French Revolution reactivate the essentialism of ancient Greek conceptions of natural law, according to which the just laws are written in eternity in the *cosmos* of ideas.[71] The counter-revolutionaries expressed

68 Sieyès, "Qu'est-ce que le tiers état?," 162. However, Sieyès, concerned with the difficulties in the application of the general will, associates it to plurality. In his opinion there is something like an intermediate unanimity: there can be a unanimous agreement concerning the formation of society just like the necessary mediums to provide for oneself for the advantages of society: the choice of the means however is left to the plurality. "Préliminaire de la Constitution: reconnaissance et exposition raisonnée des droits de l'homme et du citoyen, lu les 20 et 21 juillet 1789 au comité de constitution," 200.

69 Émile Boutmy, who attempts to defend Rousseau and the character of the Declaration, only expresses the same idea in a significant manner. See Émile Boutmy, "La Déclaration des droits de l'homme et du citoyen et M. Jellinek," *Annales des Sciences Politiques* 17 (1902), 415–43, 417.

70 In this respect, Arendt's analysis is very insightful, see *On Revolution*, 148.

71 For an analysis of the various discourses on natural law in the relevant debates see Barny, *Triomphe du droit naturel*. See also Sieyès, "Préliminaire de la Constitution." "There are two ways to present big

conceptions of ancient Greek natural law, in order to criticize the attempts to revolutionize the world. Those in favor of the revolution expressed Rousseau's conception of natural law which, without excluding reason, allows for the role of the sentiment and implies the autonomy of will. However, the mediation of autonomy by the general will, the discourse on virtue, and the conception of the moralizing role of the state led to the absorption of this autonomy in the discourse on the role of the legislator in defining the content and limits of liberty. Even the revolutionaries' conception of the relation between the general will and reason is close to the ancient conception of natural law. According to this conception, natural law is associated with the harmony of the cosmos and can be known thanks to reason.

The revolutionaries attached the primacy of the general will to pure abstract rationalism. Servan defined the law as a "declaration of common reason," which implied deliberation, choice, and, finally, an act of the general will.[72] Servan proposed to the National Assembly of 1789 a draft for a Declaration of the Rights of the Man and the Citizen that defined the general will as the only "law."[73] Reference to the general will is omnipresent in this declaration, which provides that the citizens should be free to communicate their opinion in all these objects "which are not forbidden by the law."[74] Sieyès's approach is somewhere between ancient and modern natural law theories. Natural law serves for Sieyès to "enlighten and guide" the general will "toward the great end of the social union."[75] Sieyès accepts that the content of the general will should be defined by majority decision-making.[76] The approach of the revolutionaries went from the acceptance of Aristotle's natural law to the affirmation that it could be developed only in the largest democracy and by a conception of the general will as expressing reason. The general will became the only criterion that the governors have at their disposal to recognize a just application of natural law: it is concrete reason in politics.[77]

truths to men. The first is to impose them on them as articles of law and to fill their memory more than their reason. . . . When this will be done, a *Declaration* of the rights of the citizen is not a continuation of law, but a continuation of principles. The second way to offer truth is not to deprive it from its essential character, reason and evidence. We truly know what we know with reason. I think that it is in this way that the representatives of the French of eighteenth century must talk to their mandators." Sieyès, *Ecrits politiques*, 191 (my translation).

72 "Citizens are men who meditate on the basis of common reason in order to make laws to which everyone obeys." *Avis salutaire au tires état sur ce qu'il fut, ce qu'il est, ce qu'il doit être par un jurisconsulte allobroge*, 1789 (Servan d'après Barbier), cited in Barny, *Contradictions de l'idéologie révolutionnaire*, 192.

73 "Projet de Déclaration des droits de l'homme et du citoyen par M. de Servan," *Archives parlementaires*, vol. 8, 306.

74 Article 12 of "Projet de Déclaration des droits de l'homme et du citoyen par M. de Servan," *Archives Parlementaires*, vol. 8, 307.

75 See Emmanuel Joseph Sieyès, "Views of the Executive Means available to the Representatives of France in 1789" [1789] in *Political Writings*, ed. Michael Sonenscher (Indianapolis, IN: Hackett, 2003), 13.

76 Ibid., 37.

77 Cf. Roger Barny, *Contradictions de l'idéologie révolutionnaire*, 195.

The revolution substitutes the despotism of legislative reason for monarchic despotism. By concentrating all power in itself, the National Assembly inaugurated in France a time of "radical enlightened despotism."[78] Its members saw themselves as "regenerating the nation."[79] And they saw themselves as educating public opinion on the rights of man in society. In the pamphlets circulated shortly before the revolution, ancient themes are recurrent: some reaffirm society as "natural" and discuss the idea of a harmony founded on the natural hierarchy of beings.[80] These ideas are associated with bourgeois conceptions of the social contract as the foundation of government. The Pamphleteers refer to social harmony to support the most diverse political attitudes. The image of natural solidarity is omnipresent in those who support bourgeois social contract theories, in those who are in favor of a monarchical government, and in those who defend the least privileged. In the early stages of the revolution, the imaginary of a mystic union between the monarch and the people is preserved by some on all sides of the ideological spectrum. At the first stages, the revolutionaries aim to abolish the legal structure of a feudal society. Later on, they elaborate the structure of a constitutional monarchy and toward the spring of 1791 republicanism becomes dominant. Even the privileged members of the Assembly adopt the discourse of universal rights associated with a positive conception of the state.

The revolutionaries refer to social harmony to justify limits to the privileges of the Ancien Régime. Thouret, one of the fathers of the Constitution of 1789 and the first strategist of the bourgeoisie, shows exemplary ideological ambiguity.[81] He aims to win over the privileged using the discourse of fraternity, expressing the need for a harmonization of interests under the general will. He attempts to persuade them that their loss of privileges will be counterbalanced by a life of security and social peace in the union against despotism. At the same time, he needs to win over the popular masses. The idea of a natural order and of fraternity helps to transcend the class struggle toward the need to compromise. The struggle of social classes, the necessity of compromise and the ex ante understanding of the role of the state are factors that equally influence the various ideological nuances among the French revolutionaries.

In the preamble to the Constitution of 1789, read by Sieyès to the Constituent Assembly, there are obvious connections with elements of antiquity. Sieyès expresses Aristotelian elements to the extent that he sees the social state as the state that tends to the perfection of the social members.[82] The social state, he notes, is what makes

78 Gusdorf, *Conscience révolutionnaire*, 119.

79 See for instance the Discourse by Bailly pronounced in the National Assembly on the July 31, 1789, *Archives Parlementaires*, vol. 8, 313.

80 See for instance "Catéchisme national, en France de l'imprimerie des bons citoyens," p. 4, cited in Barny, *Triomphe du droit naturel*, 134 ff.

81 "Avis des bons Normands à leurs frères tous les bons français de toutes les provinces et de tous les ordres, sur l'envoi des lettres de convocation aux Etats-Généraux" [February 1789], cited in Barny, *Triomphe du droit naturel*, 137–38.

82 Sieyès, "Préliminaire de la Constitution," *Archives parlementaires*, vol. 8, 257.

human beings "noble." Following Rousseau, Sieyès notes that it is the mission of the social state to help human beings develop their physical and moral faculties through public assistance.[83] The social state is a consequence of natural law. The contribution that every citizen makes to the public is just a form of restitution, since it is society that helps a human being become a human being in the first place. In his thought more generally, Sieyès proposes a framework that unifies elements from the thought of Rousseau and Smith toward his own theory on the role of the government.[84] He associates Rousseau's popular sovereignty with the idea of representative government. In this respect, he borrows from Smith's idea of the division of labor, an idea that Constant elaborates later in his distinction between the liberty of the Moderns as opposed to the liberty of the Ancients. Rousseau's influence is also visible upon the Charter containing the main object of the French Constitution proposed by Charles-François Bouche.[85] The text reproduces the key ideas of the social contract almost word for word. The mission of political society is to amplify liberty and the common good must be the measure of all actions. The text explicitly refers to the moralizing role of the state. The duties it imposes upon the citizens are to be enforced by the law.

The French Revolution meant to reconceptualize government and radically change society. For François Furet, it was a political and a social revolution.[86] Robespierre saw it as "the best revolution that humanity had been honoured with …, the only one that had an object worthy of man, that of founding political societies in the immortal principles of equality, of justice and reason."[87] "A wonder unique in the annals of mankind,"[88] the revolution was lived as the theater of recreation of the world, thanks to the manifestation of absolute ideas in history.[89] The totality of the human life should be revolutionized through legislation. All those who are opposed to this enterprise exclude themselves from the nation, constituting a threat to "the universal idea of man which became in 1794 an idea of the universal man."[90] Robespierre's self-ascribed legitimacy was an extension of the self-ascribed authority of the original Constituent Assembly.

The debate within the National Assembly in France concerns the opposition between the individual and society, particular interests and the general interest. The greater part of the French revolutionaries accepted egoism as an anthropological

83 Ibid.

84 Sieyès, "Qu'est-ce que le Tiers Etat?"

85 "Charte contenant la Constitution française dans ses objets fondamentaux," *Archives parlementaires*, vol. 7, 400.

86 François Furet, *Penser la Révolution française*, 2nd ed. (Paris: Gallimard, 1985), 67–68.

87 Robespierre, *Oeuvres*, vol. 2 (Paris: Laponneraye, 1840), 77 (my translation).

88 Ibid., 335. "The *Declaration* of rights is not the light of sun which illuminates all men at the same instant […] It is easier to write it on paper or to engrave it on bronze than it is to establish in the heart of men these sacred characters erased by ignorance, by the passions and by despotism," Robespierre, *Œuvres*, vol. 1, 238.

89 Bourgeois, *Raison moderne*, 61.

90 Tony Judt, "Rights in France," *La Revue Tocqueville* 14 (1993), 67–108, 73–74.

postulate and as foundation of their politics, seen as a negative moral quality.[91] Contrary to Adam Smith's morally neutral conception of self-interest as principal motivation of human action in view of self-improvement,[92] or Rousseau's "self-love," a morally neutral element, the French revolutionaries associated self-interest with clearly negative connotations, those that Rousseau associates with the concept of "*amour propre*," deviating from what would be morally acceptable.[93] They saw signs of egoism in the psychology of the individualist morality of the Enlightenment: the individual as a self-sufficient entity. Sieyès is one of those who believed that self-interest is not to be feared: instead it is to be neutralized by the proper constitution of the National Assembly.[94] However, even if the theme of individualism is central for the French revolutionaries and the American revolutionaries, the former mobilized Rousseau's opposition between love of self and "*amour propre*" in order to justify the moralizing role of the state to reform and regenerate humanity. This moral pessimism goes together with an idealized image of society; a dark vision of man is associated with an optimism toward the possibility to harmonize individual interests.[95] Sieyès notes that virtue should become a national requirement.[96] Following Rousseau, he attempts to shield the formation of the national will from the interests of corporate bodies.[97]

This conception reached its peak in the Jacobins' discourse. The aim of the revolutionary legislation for the Jacobins was to realize liberty in mores.[98] Saint-Just and Robespierre were its most eloquent advocates. Saint-Just expresses Rousseau's idea of an original purity of mores that society has "denatured."[99] In Saint-Just's opinion, a free constitution is a constitution that restores this original purity of mores in men. Serving as Rousseau's echo, he notes that freedom and independence are possible only in political society, which can civilize a person on the basis of principles.[100] His thought reflects Rousseau's conception of the pragmatic history, the wrong social contract that men signed as described in *Discourse on the Origins of Inequality*. Just as Rousseau criticizes the exploitative real social contract, Saint-Just criticizes it as being the result of a fraud that provides security by annihilating human beings and depriving them of the possibility to develop

91 Barny, *Les contradictions de l'idéologie révolutionnaire*, 89.

92 Adam Smith, *The Theory of Moral Sentiments* (Indianapolis, IN: Liberty Fund, 1976 [1759]), 173–74; See also Smith, *Wealth of Nations*.

93 See for instance the discussion of "*amour propre*" in Louis de Saint-Just, "Ésprit de la Révolution et de la Constitution de France" [1790], in *Œuvres complètes*, vol. 1 (Paris: Charpentier et Fasquelle, 1908), 283.

94 Emmanuel Joseph Sieyès, "What is the Third Estate?," trans. Michael Sonenscher, in Sieyès, *Political Writings*, 154.

95 Barny, *Contradictions de l'idéologie révolutionnaire*, 91.

96 Sieyès, "What is the Third Estate?," 146.

97 Ibid., 155.

98 Saint-Just, "Ésprit de la Révolution," 283.

99 Ibid.

100 Ibid., 303.

themselves fully.[101] For him, slavery consists in preferring one's own individual happiness over one's own conservation.[102] He expresses trust toward political power eloquently, noting that the expansion of the political is not something negative in itself. For Saint-Just, legislation was necessary to reorganize political institutions, the civil state, and economic life itself. In fact, taxation is for Saint-Just a "fundamental law of government" because it has a moralizing role.[103] It can influence the "mores of the civil state" according to the "new maxims of France," following the revolution.[104] In his opinion, the French people needed a public virtue, trust in the law, a morality, to replace their habitual prejudices.[105] The mission of institutions is to guarantee public liberty but also to moralize the citizens by making them just and stimulating their sensibility.[106] In his writings during the Jacobin rule, Saint-Just considers that only stoicism as a virtue of the spirit and the soul can prevent the corruption of a commercial republic or a republic that does not have mores.[107] And he considers that it is the mission of the state to create mores inspired by stoicism. Saint-Just thinks that the sovereign is composed of "all hearts oriented toward virtue."[108] In this respect the state should practice censorship upon the citizens and the public official by magistrates who should provide examples of mores.[109]

The French were confronted with the task of reconceptualizing a coercive sovereign into a sovereign who would guarantee liberty and equality. They considered that the establishment of these values would be possible only by the citizens' virtue, as well as by this political power. In Robespierre, an attempt to achieve this is reflected in the quasi-clerical culture of the "Supreme Being."[110] Robespierre's appeal to metaphysical foundations for the action of the revolutionaries, the formal divinization of his voluntarism, was another sign of absolutization of his idealism, justifying political interventionism.[111] It was an attempt to unify the various social classes of the revolution (Montagnards, Jacobins and *sans-culottes*) motivated by the belief in the omnipotence of ideas and the appeal to virtue. The monarchy had attempted through the doctrine of the Divine Right to solidify its domination by

101 Louis de Saint-Just, "Fragments sur les institutions républicaines" [10 Messidor–9 Thermidor An II], in *Œuvres complètes*, vol. 2 (Paris: Charpentier et Fasquelle, 1908), 497.
102 Saint-Just, "Ésprit de la Révolution," 303.
103 Ibid., 329–30.
104 Ibid., 325–26.
105 Ibid., 329.
106 Saint-Just, "Fragments sur les institutions républicaines," 492.
107 Ibid., 504.
108 Ibid., 509.
109 Ibid., 530.
110 Maximilien Robespierre, "Discours sur les rapports des idées religieuses et morales avec les principes républicains et sur les fêtes nationales" [May 7, 1794], in *Œuvres de Maximilien Robespierre*, vol. 10, ed. Marc Bouloiseau and Albert Soboul (Paris: Presses Universitaires de France, 1967), 442 ff. Cf. Habermas, *Theory and Praxis*, 105–6.
111 Bourgeois, *Raison moderne*, 72.

ensuring allegiance over other important loyalties. The quasi-religious allegiance to the Supreme Being would remind the citizens of the principles of justice by stimulating in man an instinct toward virtue that would win over the negative sentiments of egoistic self-love.[112] It would ensure allegiance toward citizenship. The Decree establishing the Supreme Being associated with its cult "the practice of the duties of man," and the national celebration of numerous virtues such as friendship, frugality, selflessness, stoicism, paternal love and motherly tenderness, children's piety.[113]

Although in Robespierre's *Discourse on the Freedom of the Press* in 1791[114] he denounced government indoctrination as propagating untruth, he ended up putting forward an official version of the truth of the French Revolution that would allow him to annihilate his political opponents during the Terror. In the same text Robespierre denounces despotism as having to cede before "public opinion" or the "general will."[115] Robespierre argues in favor of the right of every citizen to illuminate the general will about the "eternal laws of reason" that positive law should express.[116] Two years later, in the name of the rights of man, he would be in favor of measures (including the death penalty) that limited "any conspiracy based on freedom of the press," such as speech against the "indivisibility of the Republic" or speech in favor of the reestablishment of the monarchy.[117] The "Thermidorian Reaction," which took over after Robespierre's fall, also attempted to impose their version of the truth, expressed by a government of the "best" of the citizens under the 1795 Constitution, which allowed for no legitimate political disagreement.[118]

The revolutionaries aim to reconstruct the ideal city and claim Descartes as their source of inspiration.[119] According to this vision, the ideal *polis* will be constructed by "the will of some men using reason."[120] Although Descartes rejected authorities in metaphysics, he was against the idea of a total remodeling of the Constitution of the state. He professed respect for the established authorities in the area of politics. Condorcet's *Esquisse d'un tableau historique des progrès de l'ésprit humain*[121]

[112] Robespierre, "Discours sur les rapports des idées religieuses," 452–53.

[113] Maximilien Robespierre, "Décret sur l'Être suprême," in *Œuvres*, vol. 10, 462.

[114] Maximilien Robespierre, Discours sur la liberté de la presse, prononcé à la Société des Amis de la Constitution le 11 Mai 1791 (Imprimerie Nationale, 1791). See also Eugène Maron, Histoire littéraire de la convention nationale (Paris: Poulet Malassis et de Broise, 1860), 224–25.

[115] Robespierre, *Discours sur la liberté de la presse*, 2.

[116] Ibid., 11.

[117] Maximilien Robespierre, *Discours sur la liberté de la presse*, in *Œuvres de Maximilien Robespierre*, vol. 8, ed. Marc Bouloiseau, Georges Lefebvre, and Albert Soboul (Paris: Centre Nationale des Recherches Scientifiques, 2007), 452–53.

[118] Kloppenberg, *Toward Democracy*, 557–58.

[119] Gusdorf, *Conscience révolutionnaire*, 36.

[120] René Descartes, *Discours de la méthode*, in *Œuvres* (Paris: Gallimard, 1937), 133.

[121] Jean-Antoine-Nicolas de Caritat, Marquis de Condorcet, *Esquisse d'un tableau historique des progrès de l'ésprit humain*, ed. Monique and François Hincker (Paris: Editions Sociales, 1966). Ironically, this essay was written when Condorcet was charged with conspiracy against the revolution in the fall of 1793. See Kloppenberg, *Toward Democracy*, 540.

proposes an association between the progress of the physical sciences and an optimist rationalism inspired by Descartes in order to entirely reconstruct political life. The French revolutionaries aimed to recreate the political and social domain.[122] They aimed to extend the ideas of the Enlightenment in the positive sciences to the sphere of politics. The programme of the Encyclopaedists was also an inspiration to them. If the disorder of the institutions is responsible for the social disorder and inequality among men, the transformation of institutions will cause the transformation of man. Therefore, it would be necessary to reform the law according to an ideal definition of the status of man and of the citizen. If the Ancien Régime was founded on habits, rites, customs, and immemorial practices, the new order should proceed on the basis of rational axioms concerning humanity. To the extent that their conception was based on this a priori vision of man, the totalitarian implications of their philosophy are grave.[123] Regimes that claim to realize rights and to "exorcize" unhappiness have this tendency.

The spirit of pure rational constructivism expressed by the French declarations has the Terror as an inevitable consequence. The "political *aporia* to which led the French Revolution, transforming the rational certitudes of the Enlightenment into self-destruction of reason," poses the question of whether there really is a politics of the Enlightenment.[124] It seems that the French Revolution is the proof of the possibility only – difficult to realize – of an emancipation for man. This is due to the contradictory structure of rationality that it revealed an "authoritarian rationality," which aimed at imposing order to assure the "rationality of liberty." It assigned an "objective" value to the regulating idea of liberty, in this way negating the fundamental philosophical presuppositions of modernity for the political domain: the possibility of the subject to judge by and for themselves.

The change takes place in the revolutionary assemblies using illocutionary force, the "performative" aspect of the constitutional discourse engaged in an enormous legislative work. During this period of intense experimentation with politics, the revolutionary constitutions, as constructions of pure reason claiming eternal validity, appear outdated immediately after having been elaborated, negated by the events that followed them.[125] The change must concern the existence of man and his conscience, his style of life and the order of predominant values. These claims come, in order to be realized, against the resistance of the time and of men. Thus, the revolution ends in a military despotism and an imperialism, which will mobilize the entire continent of Europe against its claims to hegemony.[126]

[122] See Gusdorf, *Conscience révolutionnaire*; François Azouvi, *Descartes et la France: histoire d'une passion nationale* (Paris: Fayard, 2002), 133; Marc Sadoun, ed., *La démocratie en France 1: idéologies* (Paris: Gallimard, 2000), 30; Kloppenberg, *Toward Democracy*, 472.

[123] See J. L. Talmon, *The Origins of Totalitarian Democracy* (Middlesex: Penguin 1952), 35.

[124] Simone Goyard-Fabre, "Les Lumières ont-elles preparé la Révolution?," *Cahiers de Philosophie Politique et Juridique* 16 (1989), 23–43, 37–43.

[125] Gusdorf, *Les révolutions de France et d'Amérique*, 170–71.

[126] Ibid.

Fiat justitia, pereat mundus? The tension between theory and practice and the claim of the French revolutionaries to construct reality according to their rational idealism is met with Kant's ambivalence. Kant recognizes that the French Revolution inaugurates a phase in history in which theory wins over practical reality. He clearly defines that we should not understand by the principle *fiat justitia pereat mundus* that we are allowed to use our own rights extremely rigorously – that would be contrary to the duty of virtue.[127] On the contrary, Kant aims to underline that this principle presupposes an internal constitution of the state, "in accordance with pure principles of right," and "should be seen as an obligation of those in power not to deny or detract from the rights of anyone out of disfavour or sympathy for others."[128] He considers the Jacobin radicals to be "despotic moralists," who "sin in various ways against political prudence by taking or advising some measures with too much precipitation,"[129] "blinded by an enthusiasm for practical reason which risks to lead it astray" and which experience "must soon bring back to nature."[130] He criticizes the counter-revolutionaries as moralizing politicians, partisans of the *status quo* who are "trying to cover up political principles which are contrary to right, under the pretext that human nature is incapable of attaining the good which reason prescribes as an idea. They thereby make progress impossible and eternalise the violation of right."[131] If the despotic revolutionaries violate nature, the conservative despots violate the right.[132]

Adam Smith criticized the blind enchantment of the revolutionaries before their ideal plan of government – which prevented them from imagining the slightest deviation – and the claim of the French revolutionaries to realize utopia by using the chess metaphor:[133] "in the great chessboard of human society, every single piece has a principle of motion of its own."[134] Wanting to impose a vision of the good upon society is equivalent to considering society as a chessboard, whose pieces have no other movement than the one that the hand of the revolutionaries imposes upon them. This utopian approach of the French revolutionaries, this claim by the

127 Immanuel Kant, *On Perpetual Peace*, trans. H. B. Nisbet (Cambridge University Press, 1970), 123.

128 Ibid.

129 Ibid., 119.

130 Cf. Benjamin Delannoy, *Burke et Kant: interprètes de la Révolution française*, 94. More generally, for an interpretation of Kant's thought as implying reform through existing institutions as compatible with self-rule through general laws that are self-imposed rather than as some number of individuals imposing their own interpretation of justice on everyone else, see Christopher Meckstroth, *The Struggle for Democracy: Paradoxes of Progress and the Politics of Change* (Oxford University Press, 2015), 117.

131 Kant, *On Perpetual Peace*, 119.

132 Cf. André Tosel, *Kant révolutionnaire: droit et politique* (Paris: Presses Universitaires de France, 1988), 21.

133 Adam Smith, *Theory of Moral Sentiments* (Oxford University Press, 1976), 233–34.

134 Ibid., 234. Adam Smith uses the metaphor of chess in view of criticizing the utopian moral approach of politics, dominant during the French Revolution, and suggests its replacement through an approach on a case-by-case basis. Knud Haakonssen, *The Science of a Legislator: The Natural Jurisprudence of David Hume and Adam Smith* (Cambridge University Press, 1981), 90 ff.

government to impose a systematic, perfectionistic vision of politics and the law, is, for Smith, a sign of arrogance. Imagining oneself as incarnating such prudence and trying to apply a total and highly idealist vision can inevitably lead to disorder.[135]

Admiring the French revolutionary movement, pleading for an antitraditional interpretation of the philosophy of the Enlightenment, in opposition to Burke, and interpreting the revolutionary movements on each side of the Atlantic as expressing the same profound values, Thomas Paine did not consider the inherent contradiction of the revolutionary undertaking marked by the weight of absolutism that preceded it. Reading in the French Declaration the attempt to proclaim only negative liberty, he insists on the community of the metaphysical foundation of the two revolutionary enterprises, the claim of the subjects to choose for and by themselves.[136] However, the claim to remodel the human world according to the requirement of pure reason results in a rational totalitarianism that marks the French conception of liberty. This conception negates the possibility of the individual to define its content and makes it legitimate for the state to be the knowledgeable entity capable of defining even the relation that the individual maintains with themselves. Progressively, the idea of state rationalism prevails over that of the rationalism of the individual. The state sees itself as charged with the mission to protect the individual and to ensure the emancipation of the human person by the law in the sphere of exercise of public force.[137]

The rationalism of the Enlightenment and the projection of an order upon the natural world leads to seeing the discord between the order projected upon nature and the observation of disorder in the social world as an accidental phenomenon and a consequence of the wrong use that men make of their liberty.[138] The state claims to absorb natural law entirely within positive law just like Rousseau had advised. The claim to construct *ex nihilo*, to aim at the implementation of absolute ideas, to initiate a universe without precedent, inevitably leads to extremes. It can only lead to a negation of subjectivity, of the possibility of the subject to choose and decide for themselves. The attempt of the revolutionaries is equivalent to substituting for the despotism of tradition, consolidated by divine law, a despotism of reason, a conception of state power as incarnating reason. The state thus has legitimacy to define the content and limits of liberty – and, in particular, freedom of expression.[139]

135 For Knud Haakonsen, this critique of excessive rationalism or utopias in politics is not for Smith the abdication of reason, but rather a rational appreciation of its limits; Smith denounces the pretention to apply, in a sacred way, utopian principles that nevertheless have educative and intellectual functions. Haakonsen, *The Science of a Legislator*, 92.

136 Thomas Paine, "The Rights of Man, Part I," in *Political Writings*, ed. Bruce Kuklick (Cambridge University Press, 1989).

137 Jaume, *Individu effacé*, 447.

138 Gusdorf, *Conscience révolutionnaire*, 118.

139 On the repeated attempts to limit freedom of expression itself during the French Revolution, see Charles Walton, *Policing Opinion in the French Revolution: The Culture of Calumny and the Problem of Free Speech* (Oxford University Press, 2011); Jeremy Jennings, *Revolution and the Republic* (Oxford University Press, 2013), 17.

This conception is the enlightened version of the sacralized conception of the sovereign as possessing the monopole of truth and thus detaining the highest and strongest legitimacy of the Ancien Régime. Charged with this weight of absolutism, the French revolutionaries are confronted with the difficult task of reconciling liberty with power, authority, and responsibility, a tension which permeates the clauses of the Declaration of 1789.

The law is seen as operating this reconciliation between rationalism and voluntarism, or as filtering voluntarism through "universal" rationalism. Bergasse's *Discours sur la manière dont il convient de limiter le pouvoir législatif et le pouvoir exécutif dans une monarchie*[140] is a step between the political rationalism of the French Enlightenment and the liberal doctrines of "sovereignty of reason," which would be developed under the Restoration. "The law, writes Bergasse in its most true acceptance, is only the expression of the universal reason. There is only universal reason, which has the right to command; it is in it alone that resides true sovereignty . . . . The law is the opposite of simple will. Everywhere where there is only will, there is despotism; everywhere where there is an agreement of reason and will, there is law."[141] This text, part of the debate on absolute royal veto, which aims to legitimize the limitation of the powers of the Assembly in favor of the royal veto, is indicative of the association between ancient and new elements in the conception of the law within the French legal order.

Madame de Staël, in her *Considérations sur la Révolution française* also criticizes the Ideologues' determinist conception of a government of reason.[142] She offers an analysis of the impasses and the contradictions of the various stages of the French Revolution, which, attempting to establish constitutionalism against an Ancien Régime, ended up violating the very liberties it purported to proclaim. Purporting to respect humanity, they ended in total disregard of humanity in the name of implementing abstract values. Benjamin Constant also criticizes this very strong tendency in France to consider that society must be instituted by power in reference to the general will as a "legitimizing myth."[143] Constant points out some of the difficulties in Rousseau's conception of the General Will which ends up suffocating liberty. Constant's liberalism of the subject goes together with the concern to guarantee individual liberties. "Creating opinion, regenerating opinion, illuminating opinion are words that we meet on every page as attributes of the government in all brochures in all books in all political projects, and, during the French revolution we meet them in all acts of authority."[144]

140 *Archives parlementaires*, vol. 9, 109–22.

141 Ibid. 114.

142 Madame de Staël, Considérations sur les principaux évenements de la Révolution française (Paris, 1818).

143 Benjamin Constant, *Manuscrit des principes*, in *De la liberté chez les modernes*, ed. Marcel Gauchet (Paris: Pluriel, 1980). See also Jaume, *Individu effacé*, 64.

144 Constant, *Manuscrit des principes*, 77.

This claim to revolutionize the totality of human existence by the radical negation of the existing world led to the total affirmation of the Terror, as Hegel notes. The discourse on individual rights fades before the necessity to create individuals worthy of enjoying the rights that the government, the nation, and the law establish in their name. It was the failure of the revolution to change the mores of the people that motivated Tocqueville to visit America forty years later and to study why the American Revolution led to a functioning democracy whereas the French Revolution did not.[145] His analysis of the American democracy emphasizes that democracy is based on social facts as much as on political institutions. Adopting a Hegelian point of view, according to which there is a dialectic relation between egalitarian social state and democratic mores, he notes that in America egalitarian institutions emerged upon egalitarian mores. He aimed to study whether the mechanism could be reversed: if in America egalitarian mores lead to egalitarian institutions, can egalitarian institutions lead to egalitarian mores in France?

According to the American conception of the rights of man, freedom of expression is exemplary of the philosophy of the subject in the American political order and the idea that it belongs to each individual subject to act and choose for themselves the ideas that they will or will not listen to. The prudence of the Ancients, associated with rationalism, is reflected in the conception in French law of the role of the state in defining the content and limits of liberty. A specific essence of man seems to be promoted by a particular use of freedom of expression in France. Just as it is legitimate for the paternalist state to guarantee existence, through social rights, and to compensate for harms caused by accident, it is legitimate for it to intervene to compensate for harm attributed to offensive viewpoints. The French law on freedom of expression is marked by a paternalist spirit as it is legitimate for the state to define the content of this liberty in relation to the speakers. It is also legitimate for the state to protect its "receivers" from the danger of forming opinions judged as pernicious, "false," or dangerous. Bans on hate speech and the denial of crimes against humanity are such examples. On the contrary, the case law of the US Supreme Court is clearly marked by an antipaternalist spirit, as under the First Amendment "there is no such thing as a false idea."[146] According to the same Court, "the First Amendment means that government has no power to restrict expression because of its message, its ideas, its subject matter, or its content."[147] Even if the harm attributed to provocative or offensive viewpoints is considered to be important, the consideration of freedom of expression as an exceptional liberty along with the antipaternalistic approach of the state delegitimizes the state's compensatory role.

The difference in the understanding of the concept of liberty pertains to a difference in the understanding of natural law and the interplay between natural law and positive law. Modern natural law express ideas that redefine the relationship

145 See his *Democracy in America*, vol. 1 of which was published in 1835 and vol. 2 in 1840.

146 *Gertz* v. *Robert Welch, Inc.*, 418 US 323 (1974).

147 *Police Dept. Of City of Chicago* v. *Mosley*, 408 US 92 (1972), at 95.

between individuality and sociability. According to the conception of ancient-classic natural law, sociability is an objective implication of a cosmic natural end. If modern natural law is in conformity with the idea of a separation between the three spheres – the political sphere, the social sphere, and the moral/ethical sphere – it seems that the French Declaration was elaborated in the context of circumstances where a conception of natural law closer to the ancient was dominant. The conception of natural law underlying the French Declaration and the French conception of liberty is close to that of the Ancients, concerning the primacy of the community against which liberty would be a quasi-artificial construction. This conception runs parallel to a rationalist conception of the role of the state, which is supposed to incarnate wisdom and thus assign meaning to the quasi-artificial construction of liberty. To the extent that the idea of the general will is at the heart of the device of the state and the emancipation of society must go through the realization of the principles of pure practical reason by the submission of the particular (the interest, the mores, the society) under a universal (reason, the law, the state), this conception is very close to the essentialism of the Ancients. It is very close to the Aristotelian idea that the legislator is prudent, wise, and well informed and that "the law is intelligence without passion."[148] According to this conception, the legislator works on the basis of natural justice by concluding the search for what is naturally just, which otherwise would be endless, while at the same time adding precise determinations according to his own will in order to accomplish what is just.[149] Of course, classical natural law could not have revolutionary implications, while modern natural law does. By a paradoxical detour, however, the French conception of natural law meets the ancient conception, passing by Rousseau's individualism, which has revolutionary implications.

Habermas has noted that in America the revolution aimed to liberate the spontaneous forces of self-regulation in harmony with natural law, whereas in France it attempted to affirm a constitution in conformity with natural law, against a deprived society and the corruption of the Ancien Régime.[150] Rousseau's ideology of the Fall provided the French revolutionaries with elements of inspiration. In this same line of thought, the question of "social rights" presupposes a conception of the state of nature, of the prepolitical state as a social state, whose members are bound by an organic unity, in order to see the action of government legitimized in the political state to realize these social rights. It is this idea of an organic unity between the members of a society that can justify state action in order to guarantee positive liberty in the sense of social rights, of the guarantee of the preconditions of the exercise of negative liberty.[151]

148 Aristotle, *Politique*; see also Aristotle, *Ethique à Nicomaque*; Villey, *Formation*, 93; Pierre Aubenque, "La loi chez Aristote," *Archives de Philosophie du Droit* 25 (1980), 147–57, 156.

149 Villey, *Formation*, 94–95

150 Habermas, *Theorie und Praxis*, 105.

151 Cf. Worms, "Introduction," 21.

In this respect, certain elements in Rousseau's thought were particularly inspiring to the French revolutionaries. Rousseau's thought meets the Ancients in many respects, particularly the close association that he sees between morality and politics, civil society, and political society. According to Rousseau's ideal, there must be continuity between the internal dialogue and the external dialogue on political action. His normative vision, as far as political decision-making is concerned, is finding an opinion that is as close to unanimity as possible. For Rousseau, it is the quality of citizenship that conditions the quality of man.[152] It is only in society, which is confounded in his thought with political society, that man attains human dignity and it is the general will that mediates the relationship of everyone with themselves. If it is only by conceiving oneself as a member of the general will that elevates humanity to its proper level, to its dignity, any disagreement with the general will means that the dissonant individual is wrong, that they have not succeeded in adopting the impartial point of view. However, even though Rousseau was very careful to keep his discourse on the normative level and to not confound the level of the *is* with the level of the *ought*, the transition from his theory to its application runs the risk of leading to this confusion. Therefore, for example, the attempt to realize the idea in the French political context led to accepting the state as the instance legitimized to intervene in order to decide even on the relation that any person has with themselves, the definition of one's plans and life projects. Thus to regulate any discourse that would express an idea or a vision of the good considered to be harmful not only to social coexistence but also to the relation that each person has with themselves.

Also, Rousseau's analysis of the legislator in *The Social Contract* is surprisingly reminiscent of the ancient conception. Rousseau recognizes an extensive pedagogical role for the legislator, which is very close to paternalism. Even if subjectivity is important to Rousseau, French rationalism, whichever might be the role recognized in the subject, leads to the acceptance of a strong role for the state, which invokes the ancient conception of the *polis* as an element of the continuity of the *cosmos*, supposed to accomplish what the immaturity of subjectivity does not allow the subjects to know by themselves. With a starting point of rationalistic individualism, Rousseau's thought can be interpreted as accepting the absorption of this individuality into the imaginary and transcendent instance, which is supposed to have its origins in this same individuality. This paternalism expresses itself as a substitution of the judgment of the state in place of the judgment of the citizens, banning opinions that seem harmful and limiting the content of freedom of expression in order to protect other concurrent rights. Despite Rousseau's precautions concerning the *is/ought* confusion, his thought was understood in the French

152 "We begin to become men properly only after having been citizens." Rousseau, *Du contract social (première version, manuscrit de Genève)*, 287 (my translation).

revolutionary context, especially by the Jacobins, as justifying rational dogmatism and legal positivism.

The French Revolution reveals a conflicting structure of rationality, which, by assigning an "objective" value to the idea of liberty, negates the fundamental philosophical presuppositions of modernity: the possibility of the subject to judge for themselves. The ambition to remodel the human world according to the requirement of pure reason results in a rational totalitarianism that marks the French conception of liberty by negating the possibility of the individual to define its content and by legitimizing the state as the instance par excellence appropriate to define even the relationship that the individual maintains with themselves. The ambition to construct *ex nihilo* and to aim for the absolute, to initiate a universe without precedent, leads to inevitable excesses, if not the failure of any such undertaking that resolves itself to a negation of subjectivity. The rationalism of the state completely absorbs the rationalism of the individual. This reflects the idea of the prudence of the Ancients, talking through the official discourse of the state as far as the opinions worthy of being heard are concerned. The French law of freedom of expression is marked by a paternalistic spirit,[153] that is by the legitimacy of the intervention of the state in defining the content of this liberty concerning the speakers and protecting the "receivers of discourse" from the danger of forming opinions judged as pernicious, "false," or potentially dangerous. It is also associated with seeing the state as having the legitimacy to outlaw modes of self-expression that are considered as eccentric and as harming the dignity of the individual, such as the dwarf-throwing case.

4.3 LOCKE, SMITH, PAINE, AND THE STATE ARBITRATOR OF THE FREE PLAY OF INTERESTS

The reluctance of jurists in the American legal system to impose limits upon freedom of expression can be understood by reference to their conception of the role of the state and of the government (*lato sensu*). It can also be understood by reference to the interplay between natural law and positive law. According to this conception, the government must exercise minimal intervention within civil society. This understanding was formed at the moment of the American Revolution as a response to the revolutionaries' political and social needs. The American revolutionaries proclaimed their independence – founding their legal order on "self-evident truths," according to which "men were doted by their creator with some inalienable rights." They aimed to create a political regime in which everybody would have the possibility to defend their own interests. The pragmatic consideration of the necessary equilibrium of interests is opposed to the ambition of the

[153] In the sense attributed to the term in Immanuel Kant, *Théorie et Pratique*, trans. Françoise Proust (Paris: GF-Flammarion, 1994), 65 ff. For a deep philosophical exploration of the concept, see Rolf Sartorius, ed., *Paternalism* (Minneapolis: University of Minnesota Press, 1987).

French revolutionaries to establish an ideological structure transcending circumstances. The thought of Locke and of the thinkers of the Scottish Enlightenment was influential in this respect.

A conception of state paternalism is missing in the United States. So is an understanding that the reason of the state must define the reason of the citizens. This is why limitations to modes of self-expression that seem eccentric are not accepted in the United States. This conception can also help understand why the US Supreme Court is reluctant to accept legal sanctions upon false statements.[154] This understanding emerged through the combination of various elements. It is consistent with some important political ideas elaborated during the founding. The Supreme Court was able to make sense of these ideas during the twentieth century when it issued its important decisions on free speech. Contemporary law on freedom of expression reflects the conception of the role of the government that Locke and the thinkers of the Scottish Enlightenment had in mind.

In France, the conception of the moralizing role of the state would be necessary to respond to the needs of a nation that wanted to reconceive itself. The optimistic discourse of Locke and of the Scottish Enlightenment thinkers was of interest to the Americans, who aimed to assert another vision for the state, to arbitrate interactions within civil society.[155] Locke and the theorists of the Scottish Enlightenment are optimists for the possibility of humanity to conceive natural law independently of the state. They consider morality as inherent in social life and the natural sociability of the individual. This conception leads to a moderate role for the state in the proper realization of society.[156] If society can be held together on the basis of "moral sentiments" for the Scottish Enlightenment, or thanks to reason, according to Locke, the state is established in order to regulate limit cases of conflicts. It does not have a moralizing role because society can assume this task best by itself. The

154 See *United States* v. *Alvarez*, 132 S. Ct. 2537 (2012).

155 See for example Thomas Jefferson, "Letter to Thomas Mann Randolph" [New York, May 30, 1790], in *Political Writings*, ed. Joyce Appleby and Terence Ball (Cambridge University Press, 1999), 261, in which Jefferson praises Smith's *Wealth of Nations*, and Montesquieu and Locke's theory of government; see also "Letter to Thomas Law" [Poplar Forest, June 13, 1814] in *Political Writings*, 288. In "Letter to John Norvell" [June 14, 1807], in *The Works of Thomas Jefferson*, vol. 10 (New York and London, G.P. Putnam's Sons, 1905), 416, Jefferson praises Hume, Locke, and Smith. See also Samuel Fleischacker, "Adam Smith's Reception among the American Founders, 1776–1790," *The William and Mary Quarterly* 59 (2002) 897–924; Craig Yirush, *Settlers, Liberty and Empire: The Roots of Early American Political Theory, 1675–1777* (Cambridge University Press, 2011), 2; Thomas G. West, *The Political Theory of the American Founding: Natural Rights, Public Policy and the Moral Conditions of Freedom* (Cambridge University Press, 2018), 21–22. For a description of Locke's theory of government as "umpirage," see Michael Oakeshott, *Morality and Politics in Modern Europe* (Yale University Press, 1993), 55.

156 Ibid. For the influence of Adam Smith in a conception of limited government in America, see also Richards, *Foundations of American Constitutionalism*, 55; Caroline Winterer, *American Enlightenments* (New Haven, CT: Yale University Press, 2016), 210. More generally, on the influence of the Scottish Enlightenment upon the American Founders, see Kloppenberg, *Toward Democracy*, 270 ff.

optimism of the Scottish Enlightenment, attributing the "natural" character of the social bond to "moral sentiments," aims to delegitimize any state intervention that would have the role of imposing some conception of the good upon civil society. Locke's description of the prepolitical state leads to the same result.

Locke's thought can constitute the prism through which the American conception of freedom of speech can be understood. He contributed substantially to the formation of the ideas of the American revolutionaries.[157] Inversely, his ideas also express the dominant understanding of the role of the government in America. In his thought there are elements that are repeated in the conception of natural law underlying positive law in the United States, as well as in the conception of the reciprocal relation between natural law and positive law. The distinctive characteristic of Locke's thought consists in the conception of natural law as universal, founded upon divine will. It is intelligible thanks to rationality, inherent in every person, allowing them to interpret what is right or wrong, their obligations and their rights. In opposition to the ancient conception, for Locke, individuals are not identified with their community. The law of nature dictates obligations that can be obeyed by beings capable of reason and liberty. Politics is subordinated to morality thanks to acts of human will that are reasonable. Political community has the development and the good of the individual as its principal end. Locke is different from Aristotle as he does not justify legislative and judiciary prudence on the basis of natural wisdom but upon convention, agreement of all equally able members of society.

In France, political theory expressed a claim for unity, seeing in the unified and absolute sovereign elements of rational order that justify the omnipotence of the monarch.[158] Locke provides a different ratio for state authority with the view of limiting its impact on liberty. He is seen as having brought the absolutist substance of sovereignty to a crisis.[159] He emphasizes individual judgment. This leads him to a conception of government as a simple function of society. His key idea is that natural law is intelligible to human beings and can hold a society together. This legitimizes a reduced role for the government. Government intervenes when individual reason is dysfunctional. Locke's thought had a particular appeal to American revolutionaries, as his ideas extolling trust in reason, in epistemological independence, in science and in self-improvement by personal labor, gave expression to the concerns of Americans during the colonial times because of the circumstances of their everyday life.[160]

157 See for instance John Adams, *Novanglus*, in *The Works of John Adams* (Boston Charles C. Little and James Brown, 1851), 15; Bernard Bailyn, *The Ideological Origins of the American Revolution*, (Cambridge, MA: Harvard University Press, 1967) 24–34, 36; Higonnet, *Sister Republics*, 202; Ralph Lerner, "The Constitution of the Thinking Revolutionary," in Richard Beeman, Stephen Botein, and Edward C. Carter II, eds., *Beyond Confederation: Origins of the Constitution and American National Identity* (Chapel Hill: University of North Carolina, 1987), 38–68, 45.

158 Simone Goyard-Fabre, *John Locke et la raison raisonnable* (Paris, Vrin, 1986), 34–35.

159 Jaume, *Liberté et la Loi*, 72.

160 Jerome Huyler, *Locke in America: The Moral Philosophy of the Founding Era* (Lawrence: University Press of Kansas, 1995), 207; Barbara Arneil, *John Locke and America: The Defence of English Colonialism* (Oxford: Clarendon Press, 1996), 24; Steve Pincus, *The Heart of the Declaration: The*

Locke seems to renew the tradition of Christian natural law, a tradition for which God is the author of divine as well as natural law.[161] The law of nature is inscribed for Locke in a teleological conception of the order of the world created by God. Despite accepting a teleology in the universe, he does not have an organic vision of society. His Calvinism, which stresses the importance of individuality in the relationship with God and the experience of the divine, provides the foundation of a modern natural rights theory.[162] For Locke, natural law is intelligible to a creature gifted with reason. Therefore, the person must make good use of their God-given faculties, in order to discover the relation between right and wrong, which are moral ideas necessary to their existence.[163] The law of nature can be known thanks to the light of nature, which consists in the intellectual faculties of human beings.[164] Reason is not the creator of this law, but its interpreter.[165] It is our fault if we do not succeed to make ourselves sure about the truth of moral principles.[166] Locke rejects authority as a source of knowledge. Thus, he thinks that the extreme difference that we find in the ideas of men arises from the different use that they make of their faculties. At times human beings submit themselves to the authority of others as a result of cowardice, when it is their duty to examine ideas by themselves.[167] This element against paternalism is particularly important for the understanding of the legal regime of free speech in the United States.

The American conception of a minimal role for the government has its origins in Locke's conception. In his thought, it is associated with the possibilities of humanity and society to conceive natural law and to regulate itself. Locke presents sociability as being natural in man, while admitting that political society has an artificial foundation, a contract. If every person can equally grasp natural law, authority is founded on individual consensus. He reconciles two elements which seem *prima*

Founders' Case for an Activist Government (New Haven, CT: Yale University Press, 2016), 30. On Locke's influence on Whig ideology, see Richard Ashcraft and M. M. Goldsmith, "Locke, Revolution Principles and the Formation of Whig Ideology," *The Historical Journal* 26, no. 4, 773–800.

161 John Locke, *Questions Concerning the Law of Nature*, Folio 84, trans. Robert Horwitz and Jenny Strauss Clay (Ithaca, NY: Cornell University Press, 2008), 205, 211. See also, John Locke, *Essay on Human Understanding*, ed. Roger Woolhouse (London: Penguin Books, 1997), bk. 2, chap. 28I, § 8, 317. James Otis follows exactly this conception in *The Rights of the British Colonies Asserted and Proved* (Boston and London: J. Almon, 1764), 15, 16. On the religious elements underlying the conception of natural law dominant in the colonies during the Founding Era, see also James Kloppenberg, "The Virtues of Liberalism: Christianity, Republicanism, and Ethics in Early American Political Discourse," *The Journal of American History* 74 (1987), 9–33, 23; S. B. Drury, "John Locke: Natural Law and Innate Ideas," in Richard Ashcraft, ed., *John Locke, Critical Assessments*, vol. 2 (London and New York: Routledge, 1991), 84–97, 87.

162 See Quentin Skinner, *The Foundations of Modern Political Thought*, vol. 2 (Cambridge University Press, 1979), 239; John Dunn, *Locke* (Oxford University Press, 1984), 2.

163 Locke, *Questions Concerning the Law of Nature*, 155–56.

164 Ibid., 153.

165 Ibid., 101.

166 Locke, *Essay on Human Understanding*, 75.

167 Ibid., 166–68.

facie contradictory: sociability, which is governed by the law of nature, and the artificial element in the constitution of the state resulting from the social contract. In the state of nature, natural law, which is intelligible to everyone thanks to reason, is enough to make human beings realize that they have obligations. The law of nature is binding and leads them to limit their liberty by themselves. It makes social life possible. It is the expression of the natural sociability of men: they can live in conformity with reason peacefully because mutual assistance and preservation are possible. Political society is artificial and it must be in conformity with the law of nature.

This conception explains well the prima facie incompatibility between the writings of Locke on the natural sociability of the human being and the necessity to establish a government that will resolve conflicts of interpretation on natural law. Human beings have the ability to conceive natural law as they have the ability to err and to be carried away from the right interpretation. Locke discusses the divergence in the interpretation of natural law that history reveals and the diversity of mores between different people. He also refers to the inability of children to interpret it.[168] Even if all humans have the potential to develop their reason, it is not activated in the same way in everyone. This means that, in the absence of government, a situation of peaceful coexistence emerges among some mature individuals capable of reason, but less so among others. All human beings are born with the potential to become rational, although they are unequally situated to become so, because of their virtues or vices, or their situation.

Locke's antipaternalistic spirit is obvious in that he thinks that human beings do not need to learn forms of syllogisms taught in the schools: the faculty to perceive the compatibility or incompatibility of different ideas is a natural faculty. The human being is gifted by God with powers that they must discover through the good use of their understanding. A human being is defined as a reasonable existence. This reasoning is the exact reverse of Rousseau's. Rousseau thinks that since the general will guarantees the reasonable use of liberty, the community has a liberating action that can force the individual to become free. For Locke, the reasonable society is one that respects inalienable negative rights and the ability of the individual to form their own reason. The idea of a natural order in the world that humans can grasp if they use their reason exists in Madison, as does the idea that although humans have the potential to use their reason, they do not always use it.[169]

This conception prepares the doctrine of the Lockean social contract in the *Second Treatise on Civil Government*. In a prepolitical state, natural law dictates the obligation to live in a social state of peace and reciprocal security. In a hypothetical prepolitical situation, peaceful coexistence would be possible thanks to the possibility to conceive the obligation to limit one's freedom. Humans have the

168 Locke, *Questions Concerning the Law of Nature*, 145.
169 See Matthews, *If Men Were Angels*, 35–40.

same faculties, despite the differences in their capacities, and they can share everything without hierarchies.[170] Locke's writings on knowledge and the formation of moral conscience and those on civil government meet in the idea that human beings do not need the mediation of the general will, the moralizing discourse of the state, to arrive at the ability to form their conscience. According to Locke, individual reason does not need the mediation of political power to enforce respect of self-imposed obligations. In this, he is opposed to Rousseau who sees the mediation of the general will as indispensable to the access of the subject to rationality. If Rousseau considers as necessary this mediation of the general will to assure the common good and the general interest, for Locke nothing is more appropriate than the law of nature to assure the common good, the general interest, and to safeguard human affairs in security. In Locke's scheme, the free human gives their assent to a civil government ordered according to reason to safeguard natural rights. This is a key idea that underlies the conception of government in the United States in opposition to France and can assist our understanding of the legal regime of freedom of speech. American constitutional thinkers followed this conception, rejecting perfectionistic ideas about the role of the government.[171] In this context, the rights to conscience and free speech were important as they preserved this distance between the state and the individual's capacity for moral independence.[172]

For Rousseau, as understood and applied by the French, the people are conceivable only through the absorption in the general will expressed by the state. For Locke, who has influenced the American conception of the role of the government, what keeps the people together and constitutes them as such is individual rationality, even in the absence of the state. Locke considers the people reasonable enough to judge the conformity of the decisions of the governors with the mission entrusted to them. The people retain the ability to withdraw this trust.[173] In the *Second Treatise on Civil Government*, Locke demonstrates concerns with applying natural law to the organization of social life. He postulates in the state of nature the possibility of the perfect liberty of the human being respecting the limits of natural law. Political society is a work of reason, necessary for the cases in which reason does not operate in the natural state.

Locke legitimizes the construction of the political order on the necessity to establish a common judge to settle the cases where a divergence in the interpretation of natural law emerges. Political society is created for Locke to compensate for the cases of insufficiency of individual reason. Political power is formed to institute an interpreter of natural law recognized by all, whose judgments will be binding in order to guarantee the common good, to safeguard individuals. Locke does not

170 Locke, *Second Treatise*, §§ 4 and 6.

171 Richards, *Foundations of American Constitutionalism*, 44.

172 Ibid.

173 Locke defends the people against accusations of ignorance, instability, and incertitude in their opinions. Locke, *Second Treatise*, chap. 19, §§ 223, 230.

conceive the political community as having a value in itself, nor as having a sufficient end in itself. Even if the safeguard of the social contract can require the sacrifice and the death of those who disobey, the preservation of society does not outweigh the protection of the individuals that make it up. According to the *First Treatise on Government*, the public good is "the good of everyone of the particular members of a community so long that it can be according to the common rules."[174] He arrives at a conception of the public good associated with peace and security for the liberties and properties of persons, which can be the object of general laws so that the supreme end of the existence of the community resides in the safeguarding of individuals. Political power is based on the consensus of every individual, who aims to have their "life, liberty and estates," which Locke calls "property" *lato sensu*, safeguarded.[175] Political power thus instituted guarantees the qualities "proper" to every human being, their rights and property. Locke uses the concept of property *lato sensu* to signify life, liberty the individual state proper to each person. The same broad understanding of "property" exists in James Madison's thought, as does the idea that the purpose of government is to protect this "property of every sort."[176]

In order to construct political power, human beings concede to the central power the executive power (which they have in the state of nature) to defend themselves against offenses. Contrary to Rousseau's conception of the moralizing reason for the state, Locke justifies political power (from the point of view of natural law) as the transfer of the natural executive power of every person but for strictly limited aims.[177] The individual concedes, through the contract instituting political power, the power to interpret natural law and to execute it for the cases where conflicts of interpretation emerge. They also concede the power to punish according to their conception of natural law. They accept that positive law will define relations with other human beings while conserving the rights and powers that the law of nature confers, which do not disappear in the political state. In Locke the interaction between natural and positive law persists, whereas in Rousseau positive law, the expression of the general will, is incarnating the "integral" that absorbs natural law and expresses the transcending public good. Locke is close to Rousseau when considering that in political society being free consists of living under the legislative power to which we have consented – by incorporating ourselves into the commonwealth and obeying the laws established by it. Nevertheless, in opposition to Rousseau, he thinks that these laws must not

174 John Locke, *First Treatise of Government*, in *Two Treatises of Government* (London: Thomas Tegg, 1823), 62.

175 Locke, *Second Treatise*, chap. 9, § 123, 324–25.

176 And it "embraces everything to which a man may attach a value and have a right." See James Madison, "Property," in Gaillard Hunt, ed., *The Writings of James Madison*, vol. 6 (Boston: G.P. Putnam's Sons, 1906), 101. See also Wilfrid E. Rumble, "James Madison on the Value of Bills of Rights," in J. Roland Pennock and John W. Chapman, eds., NOMOS XX, *Constitutionalism* (1979), 122–62.

177 Jean Roy, "La 'Prérogative' chez Locke," in Simone Goyard-Fabre, ed., *La pensée libérale de John Locke* 5 (Caen: Cahiers de Philosophie Politique et Juridique de l'Université de Caen, 1984), 149–55, 150.

entirely absorb natural law. They must respect negative liberty, the possibility of the individual to choose their conception of the good, their plans for life, and their opinions on the world. This conception presupposes extended protection for freedom of expression, to facilitate the diffusion of ideas and opinions and the formation of individual personality. If it is appropriate for a person to be obliged to liberty, they must have the possibility of having options in forming and exercising this liberty.

The American revolutionaries were able to draw the implications of Rousseau's thought that only "A society of Gods would govern themselves democratically."[178] The impossibility of realizing pure democracy makes any attempts to form this democracy likely to lead to disastrous results if left unchecked. Their experience showed them that a republican government left unchecked would be dangerous for individual liberty. In 1787, around the time of the elaboration of the Federal Constitution, Americans had realized that the abuse of the legislative power was more dangerous than that of the executive and that the importance of rights was that they would protect minorities and individuals against factions.[179] Locke's thought was thus more appealing to the extent that the majority legislative power is not, for him, an arbitrary power: Locke uses the term "sovereign" in a descriptive sense, as a reference to the individual "free and sovereign" in the state of nature.[180] The legislative power is not an ultimate power. According to the Lockean conception, the individual finds their full natural liberty when political power goes against the laws of nature or violates its mission in cases of "breach of trust."

For Locke, the majority should tend to produce laws that express the center of gravity – the conformity of political decisions with the greatest part of the interests of the members of society. This conception of the possibility of a center of gravity for all interests is qualitatively different from the role of the general will and the moralizing role assigned to it by Rousseau.[181] Locke, participating in the idea of the sovereign people, accepts the force of the majority to the extent that it expresses natural law and accepts the right of resistance to this majority when positive law is opposed to natural law. Locke defines the purpose of majority decision-making as promoting the good of the people associated with the protection of individual liberty, property *lato sensu*.[182] If

[178] For this element in Adams's thought, see for instance *Thoughts on Government* in *Works of John Adams*, vol. 4, 303. See also Douglas Adair, "Experience Must be Our Only Guide," in *Fame and the Founding Fathers*, ed. Trevor Colbourn (Virginia: Institute of Early American History and Culture, 1974), 113.

[179] James Madison, "No. 10," in Hamilton, Jay, and Madison, *The Federalist*, 42. See also Jack N. Rakove, *Original Meanings: Politics and Ideas in the Making of the Constitution* (New York: Alfred A. Knopf, 1996), 290.

[180] Edward S. Corwin, "The 'Higher Law' Background of American Constitutional Law, in Randy E. Barnett, ed., *The Rights Retained by the People: The History and Meaning of the Ninth Amendment* (Fairfax: George Mason University Press, 1989), 67–106, 72.

[181] Cf. Oakeshott, *Morality and Politics*, 57.

[182] Locke, *Second Treatise*, chap. 11, § 134, 329. See also Loughlin, *Foundations of Public Law*, 384; Oakeshott, *Morality and Politics*, 36, C. B. Macpherson, *The Political Theory of Possessive Individualism: Hobbes to Locke* (Oxford University Press, 1969), 20.

the positive laws do not fulfill their purpose, to promote the good of the people, the governors have violated the contract and the trust that the people had invested in them.[183] The people who consent to the commonwealth reserve the right to choose those to whom they delegate this power. They have the right to take back the original liberty to assume legislative power by themselves or to invest someone else with their trust.[184]

The moral philosophy of the Scottish Enlightenment also reflects the conception of liberty and the reduced moralizing role of the state in the United States in comparison to France.[185] Hutcheson's "moral sense," as an "epistemological tool,"[186] provides the factor that keeps a society together and legitimizes a weaker sovereign, who does not need to exercise a moralizing role to keep society together. Adam Smith redeveloped the concept later as "moral sentiments."[187] If human beings are kept together on the basis of their "moral sense" or their "moral sentiments," the role of the sovereign is limited to arbitrating limit cases where disputes arise. It is not legitimate for the sovereign to impose a vision of the good upon civil society. These ideas provide the prism to understand coexistence in society in the United States and the libertarian conception of freedom of speech.

A comparison with France makes it possible to note some subtle differences in the interplay between the role of society and the state in America. Although some conception of the public good also exists in America, this conception is qualitatively different.[188] Hutcheson underlines the role of political power for the promotion of

183 This is precisely the meaning of the American Declaration, which proclaims as the ends of state government the assurance of the rights of the individuals, conceived as associated intrinsically to collective security. Cecelia M. Kenyon, "The Declaration of Independence: Philosophy of Government in a Free Society," in Aspects of American Liberty, Philosophical, Historical and Political (Philadelphia: The American Philosophical Society, 1977), 114–25, 117–20. For a similar reading of Locke, see also Jeremy Waldron, *God, Locke and Equality* (Cambridge University Press, 2002), 131 ff.

184 This point in Locke's thought is followed almost word for word in Otis, *Rights of the British Colonies*, 18, 33–35. The work was extremely influential in the formation of consciousness for independence. For a similar reasoning as a justification for a revolution, see John Adams, *Novanglus*, in *Works of John Adams*, vol. 4, 16, 84.

185 Douglas Adair, "That Politics May Be Reduced to a Science: David Hume, James Madison and the Tenth Federalist," in Douglas Adair, *Fame and the Founding Fathers*, ed. Trevor Colbourn (Virginia: Institute of Early American History and Culture, 1974), 93–106. Adair notes that in America the treatises of the thinkers of the Scottish Enlightenment "dealing with history, ethics, politics, economics, psychology, and jurisprudence … had become the standard textbooks of the colleges of the late colonial period." Ibid., 95. See also Douglas Adair, "James Madison," in Douglas Adair, *Fame and the Founding Fathers*, ed. Trevor Colbourn (Virginia: Institute of Early American History and Culture, 1974), 128; Gordon S. Wood, *Empire of Liberty: A History of the Early Republic, 1789–1815* (Oxford University Press, 2009), 12; Richards, *Foundations of American Constitutionalism*, 55, Armitage, *Declaration of Independence*, 9; Kloppenberg, *Toward Democracy*, 271.

186 According to Gary Wills' expression in *Inventing America: Jefferson's Declaration of Independence* (Boston and New York: Mariner Books, 2002), 178.

187 Smith, *Theory of Moral Sentiments*.

188 See Chapter 5.

the common good. In his work A *System of Moral Philosophy*,[189] he discusses the artificial character of government. He founds political power upon individual consent. He also rejects Rousseau's conception that the sovereign should provide for the regeneration of human beings in citizens through their membership in the political body. Hutcheson assigns to the sovereign the role of arbitrating conflicts that emerge inside society in limit cases, reminiscent of Locke. He accepts Locke's social contract theory in regard to creating government, while stressing that "society is stronger and more durable than government."[190] Hutcheson thinks that in their "natural state," human beings are, thanks to their "moral faculty," under the natural bonds of benevolence and humanity. Conflicts rarely emerge when some members act in opposition to the dictates of their nature.[191] These occasional and rare violations do not prove that the natural state of humanity is conflictual. Natural law, which defines the rights and the obligations of human beings and is known thanks to the "moral faculty," indicates the self-limitation of their egoistic passions. For Hutcheson, The "moral faculty" and "instrumental reason" cooperate when assuring general agreement on the interpretation of natural law and a peaceful natural state. For Hutcheson, alluding to Hobbes, the theorists who hypothesize the natural state as a state of *belum omnium contra omnes*, and the possibility of transcending this state thanks to instrumental reason, contradict their own theory. If reason, inherent in every human being, can help them out of this universal war, the natural state is a peaceful state.[192]

The majority of human beings are not corrupt and unjust, thanks to "moral sentiments," as every human possesses a sense of what is just and unjust and has a natural indignation toward justice and injustice.[193] The role of the state would be limited to punishing a minority that cannot be dissuaded from causing harm by moral principles. The power to settle disputes and to decide upon the life and the death of the guilty is not a *quantum* of power that is more important than the one assumed by "any of our fellows"[194] in a state of "natural liberty." Hutcheson distances himself from organicism postulating that civil government must seem attractive to everybody, even when considering personal interest only.[195] He recognizes the

189 Francis Hutcheson, A *System of Moral Philosophy* [1755] (London, Continuum, 2005).

190 Daniel Walker Howe, "Why the Scottish Enlightenment Was Useful to the Framers of the American Constitution," *Comparative Studies in Society and History* 31 (1989), 572–87, 578. On the proximity between Locke and Hutcheson and the influence of both on Jefferson, see Ronald Hamowy, "Jefferson and the Scottish Enlightenment: A Critique of Garry Wills's *Inventing America: Jefferson's Declaration of Independence*," *William and Mary Quarterly* 36 (1979), 503–23. On the influence of the Scottish Enlightenment more broadly toward a peaceful conception of the state of nature in pre-independence America, see Mark Somos, *American States of Nature: The Origins of Independence*, 1761–1775 (Oxford University Press, 2019), 42 ff.

191 Hutcheson, *System of Moral Philosophy*, 281.

192 Ibid., 282.

193 Ibid., 215.

194 Ibid., 222.

195 Ibid., 223.

pedagogical mission of the law, which must aim to civilize the mores and to improve the temperament of the people "to virtue." All laws must promote the public good, which coincides with the moral good, having "a tendency toward general happiness."[196] The sovereign does not have the role to provide for the regeneration of humanity in citizenship, as in Rousseau's conception, but to enforce natural law, uniform and knowable to everybody by their "moral faculty," in the rare cases when it might be violated. Positive law legislated by the sovereign must enforce natural law. Hutcheson, postulating natural equality, refutes the Aristotelian idea of organic unity in the social body and of natural inequalities that would justify servitude. He explicitly refutes the legitimacy of political power on the basis of superior wisdom. These elements provide a *ratio* necessary for the American revolutionaries to justify their independentist movement.[197]

Likewise, for Adam Smith, society can be held together on the basis of immanent elements. However egoistic, there are some principles in human nature that motivate a person to provide for the good of others.[198] Human beings are capable of sympathy, an imaginary projection of the self in the position of another person. Coexistence is possible on the basis of these "natural" qualities. The moral development of individuals inside society makes it possible for them to adopt an impartial point of view. If society can be held together by "moral sentiments," it is not legitimate for the government to elevate its own judgment about right and wrong to a supreme standard. This would be a sign of arrogance.[199] Although Rousseau refers to human pity in order to propose the possibility of a "general will" as the foundation of a strong government that has the potential to regenerate its citizens, Smith refers to human sentiments in order to justify minimal government. Even if the sovereign must be guided by a systematic idea concerning the perfection of politics and the law, it must not insist on establishing it despite any opposition. In his capital work *The Wealth of Nations*, Smith is in favor of taxation for the maintenance of the sovereign and the Constitution.[200] He conceives the sovereign though as the necessary arbitrator of differences that can sometimes arise in society. This goes together with the idea that a government sure of itself can allow the widest possible liberty within civil society. In the same book, Adam Smith is in favor of government intervention in order to do away with monopolies and guarantee the functioning of the free market and economic growth within civil society. The sovereign should

196 Ibid., 272.

197 Caroline Robbins, "'When It Is That Colonies May Turn Independent': An Analysis of the Environment and Politics of Francis Hutcheson (1694–1746)," *William and Mary Quarterly* 11 (1954), 214–51, 243 ff.

198 Smith, *Theory of Moral Sentiments*, 9.

199 Ibid., 234. See also Louis Schneider, ed., *The Scottish Moralists on Human Nature and Society* (University of Chicago Press, 1967). Michael Frazer, *The Enlightenment of Sympathy* (Oxford University Press, 2010).

200 Samuel Fleischacker, "Adam Smith's Reception among the American Founders, 1776–1790," *William and Mary Quarterly* 59 (2002), 897–924, 905 ff.

engage in action that guarantees the free functioning of the market, such as providing infrastructure. This conception of the role of the government is qualitatively and quantitatively different from accepting that the government must intervene to impose a comprehensive vision of the good upon civil society. If it is not legitimate for the sovereign to impose his vision of the good upon society, as in Adam Smith, the sovereign does not have legitimacy to limit the content of freedom of expression on the basis of this conception of the good. The US Supreme Court's refusal to make content distinctions reflects this view.

In his early writings, Thomas Paine also insists on the possibility of the free, peaceful, and harmonious play of individual interests. His 1776 pamphlet *Common Sense*[201] was particularly influential on the actors of the Declaration of Independence. In his opinion, the state is a "necessary evil."[202] It should only have a minimal role as "the simpler anything is, the less liable it is to be disordered."[203] Society can accomplish by itself almost any task usually assigned to the state. This conception underlies the understanding of government in America. The foundation of government on human rights and on the respect of freedom within civil society allows all social members to live harmoniously, despite the fact that the variety of nations and persons accustomed to different forms of government, speaking different languages, and having various religious beliefs suggest that coexistence would be impossible.[204] Social order has its origins in the natural constitution of human beings and in the principles of society for mutual dependency and reciprocal interest. Society can accomplish by itself almost any activity assigned to the government. The starting point is the individual created for social life. The constitution of the human being, the diversity of needs and talents, the possibility for a harmonious coexistence in regard to the mutual accommodation of needs, the propensity of being in society, and the necessity to preserve the resulting advantages justifies a limited *quantum* of power. A great part of what is called government comes from imposition alone.[205] Government is necessary only in order to provide for exceptional cases, when society and civilization are not enough.[206] There are many cases where it is evident that the tasks of the government, although beneficial, can be accomplished by the common consent of society. Abolition of formal government would not lead to dissolution; it would strengthen social bonds. The part of its organization that society trusted to government would return to society, which can

201 On Paine's influence upon the American revolutionaries, see Pauline Maier, *American Scripture: Making the Declaration of Independence* (New York: Alfred A. Knopf, 1997), 28 ff.; Kloppenberg, *Toward Democracy*, 321. Paine expresses distrust toward the government in 1776, when he writes *Common Sense*, whereas he moves toward a thesis in favor of some redistribution in 1792, when he writes *Rights of Man*.

202 Thomas Paine, *Common Sense* (New York and Toronto: Everyman's Library, 1994), 253.

203 Ibid.

204 Thomas Paine, "The Rights of Man, Part II," in *Political Writings*, ed. Bruce Kuklick (Cambridge University Press, 1989), 158.

205 Ibid., 156.

206 Ibid.

by the appropriate coordination of interests serving the common interest act so as to produce common security by itself. As long as human beings are accustomed to social and civilized life, these principles can help them bring any change that they find necessary or convenient to their government. This natural tendency of humanity to society is often upset and destroyed by government, when instead of accomplishing the task entrusted to it in the origin of its Constitution, the protection of natural rights, it claims to exist for itself, becoming the cause of the wrongs that it should prevent.

Locke, Paine, and the thinkers of the Scottish Enlightenment all insist on the importance of the free play of interests within civil society. Government should intervene rarely, only when society cannot accomplish a task by itself. These ideas were very influential upon the American revolutionaries and the American Founders later on as the next section demonstrates.

4.4 THE AMERICAN FOUNDERS AND LIBERAL INDIVIDUAL REASON

Locke's thought extolling trust in reason, in epistemological independence, in science and improvement by personal industrial effort, gave expression to the concerns of colonial America due to the circumstances of their everyday life.[207] His metaphysical and epistemological ideas and their political and moral implications helped Americans form their own ideas on government. If, for Locke, human virtue consists in the full use of reason and has as its immediate corollary epistemological independence and independence of spirit, this spirit extends to the social arena, underlining the principle of liberty against authority. Inventivity toward the improvement of the human condition were thought to be important human qualities. Locke's political philosophy was part of the everyday experience of the colonies. His attitude against paternalism was inspiring for the American conception of liberty.[208] The Declaration of Independence, written by Jefferson, has a set of classical republican concerns added to a theory of resistance, which has its origins in the language of natural law.[209] These rights are frequently accompanied by allusions to the fundamental aims and to the just limits of political authority. The text of the Declaration reveals the Lockean rationalism, which inspired its author: Jefferson refers to "self-evident rational truths," which could be certified by intuitive reason and which "could verify and lend support to the moral sense, which … intimated that the principles of natural law were true."[210]

207 Huyler, *Locke in America*, 207; Arneil, *John Locke and America*, 24.

208 In Mary Ann Glendon, *Rights Talk: The Impoverishment of Political Discourse* (New York: Free Press, 1991), the author criticizes, from a communitarian point of view, the antipaternalistic reading of Locke by the American Founders that constituted the foundation of the American conception of liberty. See also Gordon Wood, *The Radicalism of The American Revolution* (New York: Alfred A. Knopf, 1992), 147; Higonnet, *Sister Republics*, 100.

209 Carl Becker, *The Declaration of Independence* (New York: Vintage Books, 1958), 8.

210 Morton White, *The Philosophy of the American Revolution* (New York: Oxford University Press, 1978), 115.

Jefferson's conception of liberty is founded upon the idea of the self as moral, associated with the ancient political rhetoric of self-government, giving it an individualistic sense that it did not have in the past.[211] There was a general agreement in the American revolutionary context on the idea that every human possesses the right to self-government. This was seen as a "natural" right exercised by individuals and societies.[212] The vision underlying the American Declaration of Independence, rejecting paternalism, consists in the idea that whatever the inequalities among human beings, of intelligence, virtue, beauty, or force, authority of one person upon another cannot be justified. The conception of natural law underlying the American Declaration stresses equality and independence in the enjoyment of inalienable rights, which are not associated nor derive from duties or obligations.[213]

Jefferson's theory of government is virtually lifted out of the conception of Locke and Smith. Following the insights of the Scottish Enlightenment, he discusses "moral sense" as an element that defines humanity.[214] This moral sense, guided by reason, can, for Jefferson, hold a society together.[215] If this is the case, then Adam Smith's and Locke's conception of the role of the government is the best possible way to organize social coexistence.[216] If civil society is to be trusted, government is not. Government must be limited as it "degenerates when trusted to the rulers of the people alone."[217] Jefferson is famous for having noted in 1787 that "were it left to me to decide whether we should have a government without newspapers, or newspapers without a government, I should not hesitate a moment to prefer the latter."[218] American republicanism seems paradoxically founded on resistance to the power of the government.

The Americans reject the conception of the classical republic not founded on the principle of natural equality, which led to the production of tumultuous republics.[219] These republics ultimately lost their republican character. If the government existed in

211 Knud Haakonssen, "From Natural Law to the Rights of Man," 51 ff.

212 Thomas Jefferson, *A Summary View of the Rights of British America* [1774], in Ford, ed., *Works of Thomas Jefferson*, vol. 2, 83; Thomas Jefferson, "Letter to Peter Carr," in *Political Writings*, ed. Joyce Appleby and Terence Ball (Cambridge University Press, 1999), 253 (discussing the "moral sense").

213 Zuckert, *Natural Rights Republic*, 24.

214 See for example Jefferson's "Letter to Thomas Law" [Poplar Forest, June 13, 1814], in *Political Writings*, 288 (insisting on the fact that moral sense defines virtue despite the differences in the understanding of utility in different places). See also Jefferson's "Letter to John Adams" [October 14, 1816]. This develops on the idea that the moral sense is as much a part of our constitution, as that of "feeling seeing or hearing": "every human mind feels pleasure in doing good to another." Ibid., 296. On this point, see also James Kloppenberg, "The Virtues of Liberalism: Christianity, Republicanism, and Ethics in Early American Political Discourse," *The Journal of American History* 74 (1987), 9–33, 22.

215 Jefferson, "Letter To Peter Carr," 252–56.

216 Thomas Jefferson, "Letter To Thomas Mann Randolph" [New York, May 30, 1790], in *Political Writings*, 260–63.

217 Thomas Jefferson, "Notes on Virginia: Query XIV," in *Political Writings*, 259.

218 Thomas "Letter to Edward Carrington" [January 16, 1787], in *The Papers of Thomas Jefferson*. ed. Julian P. Boyd et al. (Princeton University Press, 1950), 11: 48–49.

219 See John Adams, "A Defence of the Constitutions of Government of the United States of America," chaps. VII-IX [1778], in *Works of John Adams*, vol. 4, 469–578.

order to assure the rights of all, everybody (adult men) would possess a right to collective political decision-making as a guarantee of their personal security.[220] Adams defends the system of limited government of the American states in comparison to the French. He discusses, among other things, Hobbes, Mandeville, and even Rousseau's *Discourse on the Origins of Inequality* in order to draw conclusions different from those that Rousseau draws in *The Social Contract*.[221] Adams read Rousseau as providing a theory of peaceful coexistence in the state of nature thanks to pity, a prereflective sentiment. Although the French read in Rousseau the need to use state coercion in order to activate the citizens' positive emotions toward one another and to eliminate corruption, Adams emphasizes the need for a system of divided government to protect citizens from abuse inherent in power. The influence of the Scottish Enlightenment on the American Founders is clear in the attempt to design a system of government that would promote the public good, even if its agents are guided by personal interest.[222] Public good is guaranteed by the design of institutions that would take personal interest, which is seen as an inevitable human propensity, into consideration. The Constitution, through its system of "checks and balances," would lead to the desired result even in the absence of a spirit of enlightened republicanism founded on public virtue, by directing the vices, through an appropriate combination, to accomplish the task of virtues.[223]

Locke accepts limitations to the omnipotence of the majority, which is a source of inspiration for Dworkin's conception of rights as "trumps," the principal concern of the judiciary control of majority decisions in the United States. The judiciary is the *institution* that makes positive elements of natural law that the legislative did not consider, the Lockean natural rights.[224] Even if Locke does not refer explicitly to the judiciary power, his theory has implications that contribute to the doctrine of judicial review.[225] It is John Adams who explicitly makes this link when discussing the judiciary as the institution that holds the balance between the legislative and the executive, referring to Locke.[226] Locke's philosophy, and in particular, his conception of the relation between natural law and positive law, reflects the conception of liberty in the legal order of the United States. An exemplary liberty in this respect is freedom of speech.[227] Contemporary Supreme Court doctrine against content

220 Zuckert, *Natural Rights Republic*, 221.

221 John Adams, "A Defense of the Constitutions of Government of the United States of America" [1778], in *Works of John Adams*, vol. 5, 35.

222 Walker Howe, "Why the Scottish Enlightenment Was Useful," 584; Caroline Robbins, "When It Is That Colonies May Turn Independent," 248; Matthews, *If Men Were Angels*, 22–27.

223 Walker Howe, "Why the Scottish Enlightenment Was Useful," 585.

224 In John Strayer, "The Rule of Law," in *Aspects of American Liberty, Philosophical, Historical and Political* (Philadelphia, The American Philosophical Society, 1977), 16–36, 35, the author stresses the idea that the US Supreme Court is the strongest instrument known in the world to assure the guarantee of the "rule of law" in opposition to any rule of "reason of state."

225 Corwin, "The 'Higher Law' Background," 75.

226 See John Adams, *Thoughts on Government*, in *Works of John Adams*, vol. 4, 196, 207.

227 On the association between Locke's natural rights theory and freedom of speech, see Jud Campbell, "Natural Rights and the First Amendment," *Yale Law Journal* 127 (2017), 246–321.

distinctions (with the narrow exceptions of obscenity and commercial speech, among other things) expresses the same spirit.[228]

For Locke, once the people have formed political society, they maintain the supreme power to change the legislative power when they estimate that its acts exceed the power entrusted to it. Power is entrusted to the legislature for concrete aims and trust is withdrawn when these aims are not accomplished as society maintains a perpetual supreme power to save itself from any attempt or design, which would violate its liberty and "properties."[229] This conception is at the heart of the understanding of the American Framers both at the level of state constitutions as well as at the level of the Federal Constitution. Citizens transfer some rights to the government but they retain their natural rights. Some rights need to be specified in constitutions as "they are preeminent in the scale of political security."[230] Nevertheless, this does not negate that all rights are reserved unless a constitution specifies otherwise. According to the American Founders, the English parliament's Declaration of 1689 was not a good model for Americans to imitate, as its articles "were never intended to limit the authority of Parliament."[231]

The understanding that it is the mission of the legislative branch to protect the negative liberties of the citizens was widespread among the writers of the American state constitutions of 1776. So was the idea that bills of rights were expressing principles that the legislative bodies had to respect.[232] The American Founders of the Federal Government also opted for a form of government that would maintain the majority principle of republican government, which they combined with elements of mixed government. These elements would moderate the impact of majority decision-making upon liberty.[233] For Madison, the federal government could act as a "disinterested and dispassionate umpire in disputes between different passions and interests in the State" (meaning the states), and thus limit "the aggressions of interested majorities on the rights of minorities and of individuals."[234] Democracy would be moderated by aristocratic elements such as the Senate and the Supreme Court.

228 Geoffrey R. Stone, "Restrictions of Speech Because of Its Content: The Peculiar Case of Subject-Matter Restrictions," *University of Chicago Law Review* 46 (1987), 81–115; Geoffrey R. Stone, "Content Regulation and the First Amendment," *William and Mary Law Review* 25 (1983), 189–252; Frederick Schauer, "Categories and the First Amendment: A Play in Three Acts," *Vanderbilt Law Review* 34 (1981), 265–307; Frederick Schauer, "Uncoupling Free Speech," *Columbia Law Review* 92 (1992), 1321–57.

229 Locke, *Second Treatise*, § 149, 337.

230 Rakove, *Original Meanings*, 326, citing Thomas Hartley.

231 Thomas Hartley, cited in Rakove, *Original Meanings*, 326.

232 Rakove, *Original Meanings*, 308–13.

233 Douglas Adair, "Experience Must be Our Only Guide," in Douglas Adair, *Fame and the Founding Fathers*, ed. Trevor Colbourn (Virginia: Institute of Early American History and Culture, 1974) 120.

234 Letter from Madison to Washington, April 16, 1787, in William T. Hutchinson, William M. E. Rachal, Robert Rutland, et al., eds., *The Papers of James Madison* (University of Chicago Press, 1962–91), vol. 9, 383–84.

The development of civility is a private question in the "quasi-Lockean" political order[235] of the United States. Even if the Americans sought to cultivate public virtue, understood as participation in the public sphere, they also meant to guarantee negative liberty and not to ensure the formation of citizens according to a precise form of classic civic virtue. The influence of Locke, is visible again in both the Federalists and the Anti-Federalists. For Locke civic virtue was indispensable in the maintenance of the well-being of republics and legitimate communities. Nevertheless, Locke distinguishes politics from morality, any form of civic morality included, estimating that it is not proper for the legislator to decide on questions of moral virtues and vices.[236] Madison discusses the importance of good moral qualities for republicanism to function.[237] Republicanism, though, should serve the natural rights of the citizens, and the formation of virtue, necessary as it is, should be a private matter.

Madison aimed to create a large commercial republic promoting the free development of a variety of interests, in the context of a natural environment that would allow the development of acquisitive spirit and individual self-interest.[238] This element was important in the conception of democracy and the role of the state in the United States, as Madison saw it, following Locke and Adam Smith.[239] The political problem was moderating self-interest in a nation founded on this principle. The large commercial republic would render the establishment of a majority difficult.[240] Peace and liberty in the political sphere would be guaranteed if everyone would be allowed to promote their personal material well-being in a large commercial republic where disputes on moral conceptions would be privatized, instead of taking place among citizens in the public sphere.[241] American republicanism is founded on economic independence due to land possession, independence seen as begetting virtue, and this as begetting republican liberty.[242] Madison's procedural republic was criticized as "depoliticized" and as leading to an inevitable reduction of the extent of the contribution of politics to the search for what is "just" and advantageous for society to a simple reflection of interests in competition within

235 Robert Horwitz, "John Locke and the Preservation of Liberty: A Perennial Problem of Civic Education," in Horwitz, ed., *Moral Foundations*, 129–56, 156.

236 Locke, *Second Treatise*, 328–36.

237 James Madison, "No. 55," in Hamilton, Jay, and Madison, *The Federalist*.

238 Ibid., 133.

239 Locke notes that "as different degrees of industry were apt to give men possessions in different proportions, so this invention of money gave the, the opportunity to continue and enlarge them." Locke, *Second Treatise*, chap. 5, § 48, 285.

240 The American system of government was criticized on the grounds that being designed in a way as to prevent majorities to bring the changes that they wish, privileged minorities can prevent changes they do not want; in this way the American system is oriented in favor of maintaining status quo against reform. Robert A. Dahl, "On Removing Certain Impediments to Democracy in the United States," in Horwitz, ed., *Moral Foundations*, 234–56, 240 ff.

241 Walter Berns, "Religion and the Founding Principle," in Horwitz, ed., *Moral Foundations* (Charlottesville, University Press of Virginia, 1979), 178–79.

242 McDonald, *Novus Ordo Seclorum*, 262.

civil society.[243] Madison's strategy for resolving the democratic problem of economic factions was considered as depoliticizing political opinion.

Hamilton expresses a version of the "doux commerce" thesis nothing that mutual interest can cultivate a spirit of "mutual amity and concord."[244] According to this thesis, commercial exchange has itself a positive impact upon human mores.[245] The effective market economy would form the "national character" of the American republic. Internally government would be weak. Externally it would project strength by deploying a navy in order to defend its commercial interests.[246] If in the ancient world, a superior aristocratic social class, inspired by an organic conception of the relation between the state and the civil society, would dictate social norms to inferior classes, America saw itself as having not only one ruling class in order to promote the standards of moral behavior and justice. Stressing individual morality is a component of American politics in the context in which the free and morally responsible individual is the foundation of communal solidarity.[247] The Founders of the American commercial republic read in Montesquieu the idea that commercial republics are more compatible with human liberty, as they satisfy fundamental human needs of survival.[248] They also preserve a sense of exact justice, which is opposed to illegitimate appropriation and to the moral virtues that lead a person to neglect private interest for the advantage of others.[249] In their opinion a federal commercial republic substitutes external balancing of interests for an internal concern for the public good, where formal equality becomes the functional attribute of a system of relations of exchange.[250]

Tocqueville had also noted during the nineteenth century the reconciliation of the protection of political liberties with negative liberties dominant in America: participation in political decision-making was motivated by "self-interest properly understood."[251] Participation in politics ensures the protection of negative liberties.[252] For Tocqueville, the doctrine of self-interest is the best suited of all philosophical theories to the want of men in democratic times: men are made citizens but the republic does not aim for the high standards of virtue that the

243 Martin Diamond, "Ethics and Politics: The American Way," in Horwitz, ed., *Moral Foundations*, 39–72, 56.
244 Alexander Hamilton, "No. 6," in Hamilton, Jay, and Madison, *The Federalist*, 23–24.
245 On the influence of the Scottish Enlightenment on this thesis, see Richards, *Foundations of American Constitutionalism*, 64.
246 See Alexander Hamilton, "No. 11," in Hamilton, Jay, and Madison, *The Federalist*, 51–52.
247 Lipset, *American Exceptionalism*, 271.
248 Charles Louis de Secondat Baron de Montesquieu, *l'Esprit des lois*, bk. 20, "Des lois dans le rapport qu'elles ont avec le commerce considéré dans sa nature et ses distinctions," in *Oeuvres complètes de Montesquieu*, ed. D. Oster (Paris: Seuil, 1964), 650.
249 Ibid., 651.
250 Wilson Carey McWilliams, "On Equality as the Moral Foundation for Community," in Horwitz, ed., *Moral Foundations*, 183–213, 203.
251 Tocqueville, *Democracy in America*, 527.
252 Ibid., 235–36.

ancient *polis* aimed for. American institutions are also exemplary in having recognized rights (negative and political) and ensuring in return consensus and obedience to any state authority, as well as vivid interest in political affairs.[253]

The background of the defense of the Constitution was also the tradition of the Anglo–Scottish Enlightenment dominated by the opposition between modern civil society and the antique and medieval world where the state was seen as absorbing civil society. The authors of the *Federalist Papers* underline the limits of the experience and the interests of the classic citizen, erasing all the elements that seem anachronistic and irrelevant to the American situation. The creation of the American republic and of the political body took place at the price of abandoning some elements of Whig radicalism and the anterior republican tradition. The new large republic would be more the republic of commerce than virtue. This system of government would define public interests as the result of the confrontation of personal interests at the state and federal levels.[254] This new civic humanism would be associated with the idea of negative liberty. Virtue would be a personal question and to a great extent promoted by commerce, according to a thesis present in the Scottish Enlightenment as well. Pocock has characterized this conception as Machiavellian to the extent that civic morality does not always accord with personal morality.[255]

During the debates on the adoption of the Federal Constitution, the Anti-Federalists considered self-government realizable only inside relatively small republics. According to their opinion, both political and negative liberty can be protected more efficiently when the government remains within the citizens' reach.[256] Even they saw the protection of negative liberty as one of the principal aims of self-government.[257] The former colonies, liberated from a monarchy supposed tyrannical and a strong parliament, were not inclined to cede a significant part of their

253 Ibid., 242, 509–13.

254 Benjamin R. Barber, "The Compromised Republic: Public Purposelessness in America," in Horwitz, ed., *Moral Foundations*, 30, Richards, *Foundations of American Constitutionalism*, 55. For a discussion of the shift from a focus on civic virtue in the early years of the revolutionary movement to a distancing from the idea in the Framers of the Federal Constitution, see Michael Sandel, *Democracy's Discontent, America in Search of a Public Philosophy* (Cambridge, MA: Harvard University Press, 1998), 129–36.

255 See Pocock, *Machiavellian Moment*, 466–67, discussing the interplay between the Whig ideology and self-interest as a motivating interest in public affairs, as a theory that migrated from Britain to America. For the philosophical foundations of a conception of morality and politics where self-seeking and the pursuit of happiness replaces the pursuit of virtue, see also M. M. Goldsmith, "Liberty, luxury and the Pursuit of Happiness," in Antony Pagden, ed., *The Languages of Political Theory in Early-Modern Europe* (Cambridge University Press, 2009), 225.

256 See Luther Martin's intervention on June 20 in Max Farrand, ed., *The Records of The Federal Convention of 1787*, vol. 1 (New Haven, CT: Yale University Press, 1911), 340–41. See also Brutus, "To the Citizens of the State of New-York" [October 17, 1787], in *The Complete Anti-Federalist*, vol. 2, 2.9.11, 368.

257 See for Instance Brutus, "To the Citizens of the State of New-York" [New York Journal, November 1, 1787] in Storing and Murray, eds., *Complete Anti-Federalist*, vol. 2, 372 ff.

liberty to the demands of civic virtue.[258] In a climate of political tensions, the opinions of the Federalists gained ground, according to which neither the classical republican model, which would have as its ultimate aim the creation of virtuous citizens, nor its modification by the Anti-Federalists was realizable. Leaving aside the question of virtue, they attempted to develop political institutions that would guarantee the existence of the Union and its security even in the absence of political virtue. The *Federalist Papers* contain frequent references to the dangers that ancient republics posed to the property and personal security of the citizens. Madison notes the "tyranny of the passions" in the democracy of ancient Athens, which led it to "decreeing to the same citizens, the hemlock on one day, and statues on the next."[259]

The dangers for minority rights inherent in majority decision-making were a concern for the American Founders. American republicanism is an idiosyncratic combination of a concern with finding common interests that are to be defended and promoted by the role of the government, and a concern against a wide sphere of intervention of the government within civil society. Madison expresses a concern against injustice coming from one part of society against another, which brings him close to the neo-Roman conception of liberty as independence. He noted that it was important to protect within the American constitutional system one part of society against the injustice of the other part.[260] In this respect, he had in mind the protection of negative interests. This conception is very far from Rousseau's and the French revolutionaries' conception of the entire redefinition of a person's interests through the prism of the general will that the state should teach to the citizens. He did not express a wish to reform society in a way that would prevent the very emergence of difference in interests, unlike the political theory dominant in France. Contrary to the French conception of a strong state, inevitably marked on the imaginary level by its past and having as its aim to provide for the physical existence and the virtue of its citizens, in America, since the Declaration of Independence, government is seen as having a reduced role and scope of action. The French state is still considered as almost identified with civil society, which makes it legitimate for it to assure the formation of character and to enforce civility rules. The American state is considered as separate from civil society and as having less ambitious aims, guaranteeing the protection of individual life, property, and the pursuit of private happiness. Instead of having a wide moralizing role, the aims of the American government would be to promote economic growth within civil society.[261]

The American Founders were concerned with "instructing the art of self-government."[262] Many state constitutions noted the importance of personal virtue

258 Horwitz, "John Locke," 132.

259 James Madison, "No. 63," in Hamilton, Jay, and Madison, *The Federalist*, 327.

260 James Madison, "No. 51," in Hamilton, Jay, and Madison, *The Federalist*, 270.

261 Steve Pincus, *Heart of the Declaration*, 19–20. The government would be activist on the basis of a Smithian conception – doing away with obstacles to the free functioning of the market – rather than in the sense of imposing a comprehensive vision of the good upon civil society.

262 Samuel Adams, "Letter to John Adams" [October 4, 1790], in *Works of John Adams*, 414.

in order to preserve "free government" and the "blessings of liberty."[263] In this spirit, the 1776 Pennsylvania Declaration of Rights provides that "laws for the encouragement of virtue shall be made," and the same clause provides that the state will encourage religious societies.[264] Such clauses in legal texts, which enumerate a catalogue of negative liberties and other "due process rights" and refer to "natural rights," should be understood as providing for the preconditions that can hold a society together. Historians have analyzed the virtues discussed by the American Founders, these being justice, moderation, temperance, industry, and frugality.[265] Any society cannot survive as such unless it creates a "collective consciousness," as Durkheim notes. This consciousness has stabilized in the United States around the need to protect negative liberties. State governments would encourage the virtues that are necessary in order to make everyone's external liberty compatible with everyone else's. The states would encourage the existence of a peaceful civil society through public education. This is a form of minimal government intervention, which is compatible with Adam Smith's thought as necessary to the peaceful functioning of civil society.[266] Smith had noted the need for minimal government intervention in order to eliminate the negative unintended consequences of the free market and the division of labor, such as the stultification of the workers.[267] He was in favor of basic public education for everyone. In fact, Smith discusses public education together with the institutions that facilitate commerce.

Elements of communitarianism existed in the colonial settlements and some of them survived in the creation of the new independent states.[268] The understanding was widespread that these communities could coexist peacefully if the same negative liberty was recognized equally to all. A consciousness of individualism emerged in the life of the colonies during the pre-independence period and was reinforced after independence and after the creation of the federal government. The absence of uniformity and the plurality of religious communities was also a factor that contributed to individualistic elements as an element that could ensure peaceful coexistence among various religious groups. In the United States, during the years following the creation of the Federal Constitution, states would encourage the protection of personal virtue indirectly by funding religious groups to accomplish this task. Pennsylvania's Declaration of Rights expresses this mentality too. The state

263 Quotes from Virginia's Declaration of Rights, 1776, § 15. The constitutions of Vermont, New Hampshire, Massachusetts and Pennsylvania contain similar references.

264 Pennsylvania Declaration of Rights, 1776, Sect. 45, in Schwartz, *Bill of Rights*, 274.

265 Thomas G. West, *The Political Theory of the American Founding*, 270 ff.

266 Adam Smith, *An Inquiry into the Nature and Causes of the Wealth of Nations* [1795] (Indianapolis: Liberty Fund, 1981). "Some attention of government is necessary in order to prevent the almost entire corruption and degeneracy of the great body of the people." Smith, *Wealth of Nations*, bk. 5, chap. 1, 781.

267 Ibid., 782.

268 Patrice Higonnet discusses the communitarian-minded communities of Puritans in America during the seventeenth century. Higonnet, *Sister Republics*, 14.

would not have the comprehensive mission to form men into citizens. The mission of the state would not be to regenerate citizens entirely as it was understood to be in France.[269]

During the nineteenth century, the necessity to establish a viable democracy and the challenge of ensuring government stability brought about the need to establish a historical conscience in America. The Whig party replied to this popular need, and contractualist theories were weakened and ceded their place to an organicist discourse concerning the aims of the state.[270] This organicism was moderated by empiricism, as the state was seen as an experiment. The writings of the Whigs of this period on the origins of government are a fascinating synthesis of Lockean contractualism and organic developmentalism.[271] Adam Ferguson,[272] who speaks about a propensity of man to unite himself with his fellow human beings, was influential. According to his thought, the formation of society follows deliberation and profound reflection on the advantage that humankind finds in commerce and mutual support. From this union derive the happiest sentiments, if not the whole of his rational character. Even if the political frame of the Whigs was protestant piety, moral philosophy, and classic teachings, the idea of sovereignty of civil society remains dominant in a context of distrust toward the state and the government despite classical influences. The constitution of government must always reflect the constitution of society. Even if the radical Whigs of the nineteenth century accepted the moralist discourse of Scottish philosophers like Thomas Reid, who stressed that liberty implies responsibilities and duties, they similarly shared the generalized discourse of liberty of the political body and the distrust toward government.[273] Their moralist discourse ran parallel to their conception of the role of the state as planning and intervening in opposition to the discourse of their democratic contemporaries. However, the moralizing role of the state was limited for them as well, as they insisted on personal responsibility for virtue.[274]

During the nineteenth century, many states enacted legislation regulating individual behavior in conformity with these ideas by exercising extended police power. Limitations to freedom of expression were common. Some states prohibited the sale and consumption of alcohol, gambling, interracial marriage, and even

269 The comparison with France and the reference to Adam Smith helps include in a broader context and somehow relativize Thomas G. West's emphasis on virtue in his discussion of the political theory of the Founding Era, as well as his discussion on government funding of religion. See Thomas G. West, *The Political Theory of the American Founding*, 208 ff.

270 Daniel Walker Howe, *The Political Culture of the American Whigs* (University of Chicago Press, 1979), 76–81.

271 Ibid.

272 Adam Ferguson, "Of the Principles of Union among Mankind," in *An Essay on the History of Civil Society*, 8th ed.[Philadelphia, 1819], in Louis Schneider, ed., *The Scottish Moralists on Human Nature and Society* (University of Chicago Press, 1967), 77–89, 78.

273 Walker Howe, *Political Culture*, 30.

274 Ibid., 36–37.

contraception.[275] This legislation was an exception to this logic. It can also be understood in reference to the need to ensure peace and stability. These bans were short lived. It was during the twentieth century that the Supreme Court started to invalidate legislation on issues of personal morality, establishing a link with the libertarian tradition of the Founding Era.[276] Freedom of expression is par excellence a negative liberty worth protecting within the American system of government. Its rigorous protection during the twentieth century in the United States can be traced back to the political theory dominant during the Founding Era.

Contemporary case law on freedom of expression can be understood as part of this general attitude of distrust toward the state. The US Supreme Court has held that it is not the mission of the state to put forward an official version of the truth. Even demonstrably false statements are protected provided that the speaker does not aim to defraud or obtain some economic benefit. The government should not be allowed to compile a list of subjects about which false statements are punishable.[277] The decision makes a compelling case for self-regulation in the area of speech: "The remedy for speech that is false is speech that is true."[278] Justice Kennedy's opinion reflects Smith's trust toward civil society and Mill's optimism that truth wins over error: "the response to the unreasoned is the rational; to the uninformed, the enlightened; to the straight-out lie, the simple truth."[279] The decision repeats a theme existing in many other speech decisions that "the best test of truth is the power of the thought to get itself accepted in the competition of the market."

Protests that for some are verbal assaults are also protected in reference to an expansive protection of the public sphere. The protest of a religious group close to the funeral of a dead soldier arguing that soldiers die because God is punishing the American military for accepting homosexual soldiers was considered to be protected speech.[280] The First Amendment can serve as a defense in state tort suits for intentional infliction of emotional distress. Despite the coincidence of the protest with the funeral, the church engaged in speech that is of public concern as it is related to any matter of political, social, or other concern to the community. "Speech cannot be restricted simply because it is upsetting or arouses contempt." "Outrageousness" is a highly malleable standard with inherent subjectiveness.[281] Even if its contribution to public debate is negligible in this case, and even if it inflicts great pain, speech should be protected.[282] A trust toward civil society to work

[275] Gary Gerstle, Liberty and Coercion: The Paradox of American Government from the Founding to the Present (Princeton and Oxford: Princeton University Press, 2015), 79; John J. Dinan, The American State Constitutional Tradition (Lawrence: University Press of Kansas, 2006), 248.

[276] For the case of interracial marriage, see *Loving* v. *Virginia*, 388 US 1 (1967).

[277] *United States* v. *Alvarez*, 132 S. Ct. 2537, 2547 (2012).

[278] Ibid., 2550.

[279] Ibid.

[280] *Snyder* v. *Phelps*, 562 US 443 (2011).

[281] Ibid., 458.

[282] Ibid., 460–61.

out by itself the importance of speech that can easily be considered low value and degrading is reflected in the relevant decision. Political correctness, the idea that social consequences follow speech that is offensive, is a form of self-regulation consistent with the optimism of Locke, Smith, and Paine about the potential of society itself.

In 1943, the Supreme Court noted in relation to the distribution of religious leaflets that "a community may not suppress, or the state tax, the dissemination of views because they are unpopular, annoying or distasteful."[283] The Court has also held that under the First and the Fourteenth Amendment, it is not legitimate for a state to ban a film because it is considered to be "sacrilegious."[284] As a general matter the same Court holds that government has no power to restrict expression because of its message, its ideas, its subject matter, or its content. The trust toward civil society to discover truth by itself and to distinguish right from wrong is reflected in decisions that concern symbolic expression even associated with the ideology of racial inequality of the Ku Klux Klan. According to the Supreme Court, the burning of the cross, despite its association with the Ku Klux Klan, may be constitutionally protected core political speech, unless the person is engaging in intimidation.[285] "Burning a cross at a political rally, would almost certainly be protected expression."[286] Even if the burning of a cross at a political rally arouses a sense of anger or hatred among the vast majority of citizens, it is protected speech, according to the same Court.[287]

As I argued in this chapter, the thought of Locke and of the Scottish Enlightenment can constitute the prism through which the American conception of freedom of expression can be understood. These thinkers can help us to understand the conception of the role of the government in the United States upon a self-regulating civil society. The legal status of freedom of expression in the United States builds off this conception. It is marked by an antipaternalistic spirit, as content distinctions are accepted only exceptionally. Harm caused by speech is not considered significant enough to mobilize state coercion for its retribution. Political correctness, this self-regulating potential of society can assume this mission by itself.

In France, there is greater acceptance of state paternalism, a conception that builds on Rousseau's moralizing role of the state. If in Rousseau's thought, the ethical-moral sphere, the political sphere, and the social sphere are confounded with potentially dangerous implications for subjectivity, in Locke's thought the three spheres are kept separate. Every human being possesses the potential to know the moral principles so that it is a person's own fault if they do not arrive at assuring oneself about their exactitude.[288] He thinks thus that the extreme difference between

283 *Murdock* v. *Pennsylvania*, 319 US 105, 116 (1943).
284 *Joseph Burstyn, Inc.* v. *Wilson*, 343 US 495.
285 *Virginia* v. *Black*, 538 US 343, 365.
286 *R.A.V.* v. *St. Paul*, 505 US 377, 402.
287 Ibid., 366.
288 John Locke, *Essay on Human Understanding*, ed. Roger Woolhouse (London, Penguin Books, 1997), bk. 1, chap. 3, § 1, p. 75.

the ideas of humans comes from the different use that they make of their faculties. Often as a result of laziness, humans submit their spirit to the authority of others concerning elements that they should examine themselves. Locke is a defender of freedom of spirit as the capacity to think for oneself.

For Locke, every human being can have access to natural law by using the faculties that are given by God. In a hypothetical situation, where political power is absent, peaceful coexistence would be possible. Therefore, if for Hobbes the dialogue between natural law and positive law can end by the decision of the sovereign concerning the rules that will become positive, for Locke it continues infinitely so that the sovereign must respect the natural law in any attempt to enunciate a positive rule. If for Locke natural law is comprehensible thanks to the natural light, political power exercised by the government must only provide for the cases in which human beings are carried away from their ability to use their reason to discover natural law: in other words, only for the cases where the human beings allow themselves to be carried away by their passions, giving up the proper use of their reason. If for Rousseau imposing obligations upon oneself is mediated through the general will, for Locke the moral qualities allow already in the state of nature the imposition of obligations upon oneself. If for Rousseau one's self-conception as a person and the realization of individual reason presupposes the mediation of the general will, for Locke rationality can assure one's self-conception as a person capable of laws. For Rousseau, it is the general will that guarantees the reasonable use of liberty, expressing the integral of all possible opinions inside one community. The rationality that is latent in any individual can come to surface thanks to the liberating action of the general will, which can even "force" the individual to be free. For freedom of speech, this means that it is legitimate for the state to dictate to the citizens the content of their speech and to protect them from modes of self-expression that show that they are not really "free," as the cases of the burka ban and dwarf-throwing show.[289] There is also greater legitimacy for the state to enforce rules of civility and respect toward others. For Locke reasonable society is one that respects negative inalienable rights, as the individual is able to form and exercise their reason by themselves. The distrust toward the government that Locke's thought allows for leads to rejecting content distinctions for speech and to accepting a wide role for speech criticizing the government. In this respect, even inaccurate statements concerning government action are protected provided that they were not made with reckless disregard as the *New York Times Co.* v. *Sullivan* case shows.[290]

In parallel, thanks to the thought of the Scottish Enlightenment, if a society can be held together on the basis of moral sentiments, the sovereign must intervene as little as possible. This conception is reflected in the political correctness doctrine omnipresent today within the United States. Social restrictions in the United States play

[289] See Chapter 1 for an analysis of the relevant cases.
[290] *New York Times Co.* v. *Sullivan*, 376 US 254 (1964).

the role that legal restrictions play in France. It is in this sense that the essential premise of the American Founders is that government exists in order to assure the negative natural rights and not to cultivate virtue.[291] In the United States, it is less legitimate for the government to enforce rules of civility and respect. Tocqueville had discerned the fact that in the United States religion provided the moral bond necessary to substitute for the loosening of the political bond. Religion is thought to guarantee the appropriate use of liberty in a context where regulation is relatively light. The republican conception in the United States was associated with a conception of virtue as a private quality. It was the private quality of virtue that could ensure the extraordinarily moral character of the people.

***

To conclude, the significance of the revolutionary and declaratory task on each side of the Atlantic can help deepen our understanding of the meaning that liberties have in the two legal systems today. In America, the revolutionary movement sought to liberate the spontaneous forces of self-regulation in harmony with natural law. In France, it attempted to affirm a constitution in conformity with natural law against a deprived society and a corrupt human nature of the Ancien Régime.[292] Rousseau's ideology of the Fall was inspiring for the French revolutionaries. In this same line of thought, the question of "social rights" presupposes a conception of the state of nature, of the prepolitical state as a social state, whose members are bound by an organic unity that makes government action in the political state legitimate in order to realize these social rights. The state will help the citizens realize their liberty and protect them from the danger of reaching dangerous and "wrong" opinions. In this respect, precise elements in Rousseau's thought were particularly inspiring to the French revolutionaries. Rousseau's thought meets the Ancients in many respects, in particular with respect to the close association that he sees between morality and politics, civil society, and political society.

On the contrary, the American conception of freedom of expression reflects the optimism of Locke and the Scottish Enlightenment for individual reason. According to this conception, societies can be held together due to their reason or sentiments. Individuals can conceive natural law by themselves and limit their liberty. Positive law is necessary in order to compensate when individual reason (for Locke) and/or sentiments (for Adam Smith) are dysfunctional. For Locke, with the acceptance of the contract of institution of political power, the individual yields the power to interpret the natural law and to execute it in cases where conflicts of interpretation arise, thereby accepting that positive general laws will define their relations with

[291] Zuckert, *Natural Rights Republic*, 26; Gerber, Scott D., "Whatever Happened to the Declaration of Independence? A Commentary on the Republican Revisionism in the Political Thought of the American Revolution," *Polity* 26 (1993), 207–31, 230.

[292] Cf. Habermas, *Theorie und Praxis*, 105.

other human beings with whom they live. The individual retains the natural rights which do not disappear in the political state.

For Locke, every human being can have access to natural law by using the faculties that are given by God. In a hypothetical situation where political power is absent, peaceful coexistence would be possible. For Locke the same dialogue continues infinitely, so that the sovereign must respect the natural law in any attempt to enunciate a positive rule. If for Locke natural law is comprehensible thanks to the natural light, political power and the government must only provide for the cases in which human beings are carried away from the possibility to use their reason to have access to natural law. In other words, only in cases where the human beings allow themselves to be carried away by their passions, giving up the proper use of their reason. For Rousseau, imposing obligations upon oneself is mediated through the general will. For Locke, the moral qualities of humanity make it possible for a person to impose obligations upon oneself already in the state of nature. If for Rousseau one's self-conception as a person and the realization of individual reason presupposes the mediation of the general will, for Locke rationality can assure one's self-conception as a person capable of laws. For Rousseau it is the general will that guarantees the reasonable use of liberty. It expresses the integral of all possible opinions inside one community, the rationality which is latent in any individual coming to surface thanks to the liberating action of the general will, even "forcing" the individual to be free. In Locke's thought, reasonable society is the one that respects negative inalienable rights, that is the possibility of the individual to form their reason by themselves.

Locke is close to Rousseau in thinking that in political society liberty is guaranteed only by a legislative power. For Locke these laws should respect individual liberty in its negative form, the possibility of the individual to choose their vision of the good, their life plans, or their opinions on the world, in general. This last conception presupposes the recognition of extended freedom of expression in order to facilitate the diffusion of ideas and opinions necessary for the formation of individual personality. If any human being can be obliged to liberty, Locke's individual would not need state paternalism to define which opinions are worthy of being heard and appreciated. If the individual concedes some of their rights to interpret the natural law, they conserve the right to judge if an act or a command that endangers one's life is opposed to the law. Locke accepts limitations to majority decision-making. By definition he defines the mission of the majority to define the "properties" of the individual, by which he means negative liberty more broadly. Although Locke does not refer explicitly to the judiciary power, his theory has implications that contribute to the doctrine of judicial review for the protection of negative liberty.[293] In the legal system of the United States, the judiciary is the medium through which elements of

293 Corwin, "The 'Higher Law' Background," 75.

natural law that the legislature avoided to take into consideration become positive. This particularly applies to elements pertaining to the protection of natural rights.

The philosophy of Locke and his conception of the relationship between natural law and positive law is reflected in the conception of liberty in the legal and political order of the United States, especially concerning the legal status of freedom of expression and the reluctance of the Supreme Court to make content distinctions between categories of speech and accepting such distinctions for some rare cases such as obscene speech. More generally, the distrust toward the reason of the state dominant in America makes jurists less willing to accept regulation of the content of speech. It is not legitimate for the state to impose an official version of the truth as is evident from the Supreme Court cases concerning inaccurate statements.[294] Furthermore, it is not legitimate for the state to outlaw modes of self-expression that are considered by a majority to be eccentric and incomprehensible.[295] If benevolence is not to be enforced by the state then it is not legitimate for the state to act in order to overcome the distinction between "real" freedom and "formal" freedom, to participate in the political debates and to affect electoral results by imposing limits to independent expenditures usually coming from corporations.[296] It is not legitimate for the state to equalize the possibility for all individuals to exercise their freedom of speech.

294 *United States* v. *Alvarez*, 132 S. Ct. 2537 (2012).

295 *Zacchini* v. *Scripps – Howard Broadcasting Co.*, 433 US 562 (1977).

296 *Citizens United* v. *FEC*, 558 US 310 (2010).

5

Foundation of the Rights of Man on the Rights of the Citizen versus Foundation of the Rights of the Citizen on the Rights of Man

As I argue in this book, the divergence in the balancing of freedom of expression and other values between France and the United States can be understood in reference to the broader historical, social, and philosophical context in which jurists operate. The balancing of freedom of speech and other values in the two legal systems can be understood by reference to the role of the government and the understanding of liberty. This understanding affects how jurists define the content and limits of a liberty and strike a balance between liberties in conflict. Courts and jurists in the United States today refer to the political tradition formed during the Founding Era to justify a less restrictive doctrine for free speech. This chapter expands on the difference in the understanding of liberty in France and the United States since the American and the French revolutions.

The difference in the protection freedom of expression in the two legal systems relates to political ideas on the role of the government and the understanding of liberty. Judges in the United States see themselves as having legitimacy to declare invalid legislation limiting freedom of speech. It is less the case in France, where legislative limitations to the content and limits of freedom of expression are seen as legitimate. The legislative branch is seen as having legitimacy to define the content and limits of freedom of expression, in other words, to amplify and realize liberty. This conception stems from a deeper tradition on the authority of the legislative power in France. It is already obvious in the texts declaring liberties. These texts can offer very important insights on the understanding of liberty within a legal system.

The role that the French Declaration of the Rights of Man and the Citizen attributes to the law in the definition of the content and limits of liberty shows that rights depend on the act that records them.[1] The state by its laws is trusted to realize liberty as a metaphysical quality of every human being. This means accepting an extended role for the state in making liberty "positive." Paradoxically, and despite

[1] Blandine Barret-Kriegel, *Les droits de l'homme et le droit naturel* (Paris: Presses Universitaires de France, 1989), 24. In the same spirit see Claude Nicolet, *L'idée républicaine en France, 1789–1924* (Paris: Gallimard, 1982).

the metaphysical universalism in the understanding of liberty analyzed in previous chapters, the trust toward the state means that liberty exists only to the extent that it is guaranteed by the state. Liberty appears in France as having only a positive foundation. Rights were seen during the elaboration of the Declaration of the Rights of Man and of the Citizen in the summer of 1789 as rules that ensure social coexistence rather than as "natural" qualities of the individual. The American Declaration, on the contrary, presupposes that rights are "natural" qualities of the individual referring to God, creator of nature. The Americans of the Founding Era saw themselves as proclaiming "pre-existent" rights.[2] They saw their Bills of Rights as guaranteeing reserved natural rights.[3] In France rights are protected to the extent that they are compatible with the common good. In America the common good is defined in reference to the need to protect rights. These ideas are reflected in contemporary law on freedom of expression.

The differences in the political imaginary in France and in the United States affect the understanding of liberty in the two legal systems. In French republicanism a vision of organic unity between state and civil society is latent. In American republicanism, the idea of an artificial relation between political power and civil society is latent. According to the American conception, political power is an artifice in the service of civil society. In France, the fiction of the incorporation of the citizens in the *corpus mysticum* of the king, which the French Revolution inherited, leads to an inverse reasoning. It leads to the idea that civil society was progressively separated and liberated from the state. French republicanism implies the consideration of negative liberty as quasi-artificial to the extent that it is associated with the common good. The quality of being a citizen is primary. The rights of man make sense only as rights of the citizen. The state has the mission to realize the universal conception of liberty for all citizens conceived abstractly. This leads to accepting a wide sphere of government intervention in defining the content and limits of liberty and in particular of freedom of speech. The French positivistic conception associates liberty with its enactment by the state. American republicanism makes an amalgam between the necessity to protect the common good while respecting "natural" liberties. The American jusnaturalist discourse presupposes interpreting the "constitutional" rights that citizens have through the prism of "natural rights."[4] In France, the moralizing role of the government in defining the content and limits

2 James Madison, Speech to the House of Representatives, June 8, 1789, in *The Writings of James Madison*, vol. 5, 1789–1790, ed. Gaillard Hunt (New York and London: G. P. Putnam's Sons, 1904), 381.

3 See for instance Gov. Randolph in his "Speech to the Virginia Ratifying Convention" on June 15, 1788 noting that bills of rights exist in order to restore the proper rights of the government not to define the rights that the citizens have. Rights that always remain with the people are the liberty of the press and the right of conscience. It is the enumeration of rights in texts that might limit their protection. See Jonathan Elliot, ed., *Debates in Several State Conventions On The Adoption Of The Federal Constitution*, vol. 3 (US Congress, 1836), 469.

4 Zuckert, *Natural Rights Republic*, 116.

of liberty goes together with a positivist conception of the law: once the instances authorized to accomplish this role have decided, judges do not see themselves as having legitimacy to limit the action of the government through the reference to extralegal criteria. A conception of rights as "trumps" does not seem to apply in the area of expressive freedoms in France to the same extent that it applies in the United States.[5]

While ideas of republicanism and of the common good were present on both sides of the Atlantic, there are nuances in the understanding of these ideas in the two social and political contexts. French republicanism is based upon a paternalistic conception of the role of the state, which is seen as permitted to dictate to the citizens the proper exercise of reason. Rousseau's thought expresses an idealized vision of politics, which was inspiring for the French revolutionaries. An important idea dominant in the French revolutionaries was that society and the role of the state helps elevate a human being to the dignity of being human. In the United States, the dominant understanding of republicanism attempts to reconcile the natural rights philosophy with the conception of the common good. The dominant conception is that the political sphere is instrumental to the private sphere. The public sphere is only the medium to protect and preserve the private sphere, which is the sphere of happiness.

Thus, the difference in the content of the two declarations can be attributed to the difference in ideology underlying the two texts, concerning the conception of society and its aims.[6] In America, the dominant conception of natural law is the modern, which focuses on the negative rights of the individual. The bills of rights are seen as setting limits upon the government. In other words, the rights of the citizen are founded on the rights of man. In France, the dominant conception of natural law echoes that of the Ancients, according to which the natural state of humanity is social. Men and their liberty reach their perfection in society. If it is being a citizen that makes a human being, then the rights of a person are those that they are recognized as having by political society. The rights of man are founded upon the rights of the citizen. For the French Declaration, the rights of man have meaning only as rights of the citizen. The aim of the French Declaration is to determine the mission of the legislator. The *legicentrist* character of the Declaration of Rights of 1789 means that the law has the mission to form the liberty of the citizens. This *legicentrism* (centrality of the law) aims to guarantee the primacy of the realization of collective aims. On the contrary, institutional design that favors judicial review of legislation defining liberties favors the protection of negative liberty. For freedom of speech this means that in France there is greater legitimacy for the state to define the content of speech and impose limits to it. According to the American conception, it is less legitimate for the state to regulate the natural liberty of freedom of speech.

5 According to the title of Ronald Dworkin's conception in *Taking Rights Seriously*.

6 Cf. Troper, "Jefferson et l'interprétation de la Déclaration des droits de l'homme de 1789," *Revue Française d'Histoire des Idées Politiques* 9 (1999), 3–23, 17.

The idea of a right, of a liberty in the negative sense, was not entirely unknown to the Ancients. Aristotle discusses private liberty[7] and the Roman jurists discuss the concept of *dominium*. According to the legal thought of classical antiquity, in order to establish the right of each person (*jus suum cuique*), or of everything, the starting point would not be the individual but the mass of the social goods to share objectively. The right of everyone would be a *quotient*, not the "attribute" of an individual, but an objective thing ("incorporeal thing"), a delimited quantity of prerogatives.[8] Michel Villey proposes to instead use the term "zone" of power, a sector of delimited action in relation to other sectors attributed to other members of society, rather than power to accomplish one activity, like circulating or expressing one's opinion.[9] For Roman law, the law, understood as a status of every man or everything, would not only imply advantages but also responsibilities.[10] This terminology expresses very subtle nuances. Talking about negative rights in the sense of "powers" presupposes a conceptual division between two spheres of action, the state's sphere of action and the individual's.

The defensive character of liberty as personal security is clear in Locke. For Locke, the people concede to the legislative branch only a power to preserve their properties in the personal, immaterial, and material sense.[11] Citizens concede to the executive and judicial power the natural right to "pursue the execution of one's own individual judgment."[12] Locke attributes a central role to the law and this element considerably influenced the French as much as the Americans. However, he thinks that this role should be limited. The purpose of the legislative power is to protect natural liberties understood as negative liberties. The importance of the role of the law as such influenced the French. The elements in Locke's thought that point toward the necessity to limit the legislative power appealed to the American Founders of the state and federal constitutions.[13] As analyzed earlier, historians agree that the American Revolution was a revolution against the legislative activity of the British parliament. In France, the revolution placed the parliament at the center of French society and its system of government.

Rousseau's thought was very influential in this respect upon the French revolutionaries.[14] For Rousseau the law ensures life and property. It elevates the person above their physical existence. It helps persons who are alienated to find

7 Aristotle, *Politics*, 1253b, 30.

8 Villey, "Abrégé du droit naturel classique," 25–72, 68.

9 Ibid.

10 Ibid.

11 John Locke, *The Second Treatise*, in *Political Writings*, ed. David Wootton (London: Penguin, 1993), 335; cf. Lucien Jaume, *La liberté et la loi: les origines philosophiques du libéralisme* (Paris: Fayard, 2000), 152.

12 Locke, *Second Treatise*, 305.

13 See Stéphane Rials, "Ouverture: généalogie des droits de l'homme," *Droits* 2 (1985), 3–12, 12.

14 In fact, there were even suggestions to publish the Declaration preceded by the text of *The Social Contract*. See Keith Michael Baker, "The Idea of a Declaration of Rights," in Dale Van Kley, ed., *The French Idea of Freedom: The Old Regime and the Declaration of Rights of 1789* (Stanford University Press, 1994), 189.

themselves. It restitutes liberty.[15] Rousseau insists on the role of the law to guarantee the concrete reality of rights, as the rights of man are true rights only in the state where they are affirmed by the act of the legislative power as the rights of the citizen.[16] Rights are not postulated as having an existence *a priori* in view of founding political legitimacy in reason and constituting a limit to political power. They emerge only to the extent that they are enacted by the state.[17] "Where the American Declaration was looking for the rights of man in the respect of natural law, the French declarations construct the rights of the citizen in the foundation of civil society."[18] Rights are those of the citizens of a state. They become concrete thanks to the state.

The background understanding of the origins of liberty has important implications related to the legitimacy of the role of the law in defining its content and its limits. For Rousseau, by creating the ideal social contract human beings give up all their liberty, but not only do they lose nothing, on the contrary, they are freer than before. In the civil state positive law "fixes" these rights.[19] For the French constituents, liberty has an ethical meaning. It is thought of as belonging by nature to man as man, but mediated legally by the law or the Constitution and determined by the quality of the citizen. The natural and inalienable liberty of man takes form in the idea of the absorption of the individual in the general will. It comes from a voluntary and transformative association in which "everyone by uniting with everyone else obeys only themselves and remains as free as before,[20]" since nobody would agree to harm themselves. Liberty makes sense only in relation to a political association founded on the idea of popular sovereignty. Rights can only exist as rights of the citizen and they depend on a specific mode of exercise of sovereignty made legitimate by the consent of the social contract, as the Declaration of 1789 proposed to form the basis of any legitimate political body.[21] "Natural rights recognised a priori are

15 John-Jacques Rousseau, *Discours sur l'économie politique*, in *Œuvres complètes*, vol. 3 (Paris: Gallimard, 1964), 248; commentary in Philonenko, *Jean-Jacques Rousseau et la pensée de malheur*, vol. 1, *Le traité du mal*, 250.

16 Simone Goyard-Fabre, "La Déclaration des droits ou le devoir d'humanité: une philosophie de l'espérance," *Droits* 8 (1988), 41–54, 45; Yves-Charles Zarka, "La notion de droit naturel dans la Déclaration des droits de l'homme et du citoyen de 1789," in Bernard Bourgeois and Jacques d'Hondt, *La philosophie et la Révolution française* (Paris: Vrin, 1993), 59–67, 65 ff.; Manent, *Naissances de la politique moderne*, 177.

17 Zarka, "Notion de droit naturel," 66. In Patrick Wachsmann, "Déclaration ou Constitution des Droits?", in Michel Troper et Lucien Jaume, eds., 1789 *et l'invention de la Constitution* (Paris: LGDJ and Bruylant, 1994), 44–54, the author notes the paradoxical conception underlying the Declaration that it is the legal order that determines the supposed natural rights: "the natural law is fixed to the principles that are enunciated: it is finite." Ibid., 48.

18 Barret-Kriegel, *Les droits de l'homme et le droit naturel*, 27.

19 Rousseau, *Du contrat* social, bk. 2, chap. 6, 378.

20 Rousseau, *Du contrat social*, bk. 1, chap. 6, 360.

21 Barret-Kriegel, *Les droits de l'homme et le droit naturel*, 21; J. K. Wright, "National Sovereignty and the General Will: The Political Program of the Declaration of Rights," in Van Kley, ed., *The French Idea of Freedom*, 199–233.

thus cut off their theoretical, if not theological, foundation." The recognition of natural rights does not carry any normative value in relation to the laws of the state, as it is these laws that define their limits and their content.[22] The reference to natural rights does not provide the principles a priori of a refoundation of the political and legal space to regulate the exercise of state authority.[23]

The dialectical transition from the man to the citizen made plausible interpretations of the French declarations that ceded the antique model of the *polis*, the conception of the law as liberating and the association between the legalism of rights and the loyalism of the citizens.[24] "The civic obligation is neither the inverse nor the counterpart of the rights of man but the concrete figure of their existence; it implies the indivisibility between the rights and the duties of man."[25] During the French declaratory work, Rousseau's ideas that the rights of man cannot be unconditional, were omnipresent. Declaring the rights of man and of the citizen is an act of posing norms that indicates to humanity its *ought*. The Declaration founded the existence of humanity on the one of citizenship.[26] The ideal foundation of the rights of the citizen, and, through the citizen, of the rights of man, forms a contradiction that affects the very foundation of the rights of man. Recognizing the foundation of the rights upon the rights of the citizen as such, without consideration of the rights of man, makes legitimate greater government intervention in defining their content and their limits as is the case with freedom of expression.

The philosophy of the French revolutionaries defines the relations between the individual and the state and the idea of a person in a teleological perspective of humanity. According to this conception of rights as posed by the state and bound to the political obligation of the citizen, they are not a natural privilege that everyone could use and abuse. If the American Founding Era expresses an idea of human dignity founded on the necessity to protect negative liberty,[27] the conception of the rights of man of the period of the French Revolution designates a normative conception of humanity inscribed in Rousseau's ideal citizen.[28] As an idea of reason that is to be implemented by the state, they led to two antithetical currents of thought in France, and later in all of Europe: individualism and socialism.

The debates around the right to property show this tension between jusnaturalism and artificialism, latent in the conception of liberty. These conceptions indicate an attitude toward rights more generally. Locke's theory of legitimacy of property referring to self-preservation and work was useful in the revolutionary self-understanding of the Americans. As analyzed earlier, they aimed to liberate themselves from the legislative activity of the British parliament. According to this

22 Zarka, "Notion de droit naturel," 66.
23 Ibid.
24 Goyard-Fabre, "La Déclaration des droits ou le devoir d'humanité," 41–54, 48.
25 Ibid.
26 Bourgeois, *Raison Moderne*, 130.
27 Zuckert, *Natural Rights and the New Republicanism*, 318.
28 Goyard-Fabre, "La Déclaration des droits ou le devoir d'humanité," 48.

conception, the government has the role of protecting against dangers, of guaranteeing the natural form of self-preservation. For Rousseau, this reference to the idea of work is a "rationalization," a legitimizing myth on behalf of the wealthy, of their "property."[29] These ideas caused a polemic, still open, on whether he is a partisan or an adversary of modern natural law, as he insists on the conventional origins of the right to property.[30] According to his *Discourse on the Origins of Inequality*, property of material goods is not a human quality nor a natural right, but an artificial source of inequality among men. It is the result of convention and human institution. Everyone can dispose at will what they possess but not the essential gifts of nature, such as life and liberty, which everyone is allowed to enjoy.[31] Returning to a hypothetical starting point with a pedagogical aim in order to indicate another normative solution, Rousseau provides a pragmatic history of humanity:[32] "The first [person] who, having enclosed a piece of land, decided to say 'this is mine,' and found men simple enough to believe him, is the true founder of civil society."[33] Following a reasoning that is comparable to the one that Marx developed later on in the idea of "primitive accumulation," Rousseau discusses the origins of property and law in force, exploitation, and ugliness: the rich and strong usurped the supreme power, instituted for everyone, just like they usurped the land common to all.[34] The Lockean theory of legitimizing property in reference to the idea of work constitutes for Rousseau a theory of rationalization, a gratuitous justification.[35]

When, in his *Discourse on Political Economy*, Rousseau discusses property as a fundamental right, he recognizes that it obtains its legitimate existence from the social contract instituting the political body. The positivistic filter is here again. He sees in property a "fundamental" but "instrumental" right that can serve the consolidation of the quality of citizenship.[36] Government must prevent inequalities of property by preventing accumulation of property.[37] Following Rousseau's distinction between law and fact, property in the state of nature belongs to the order of fact and not of the law. It cannot be legitimized and obtain the status of "law" on the level of the *ought* if it is not recognized by the general will. In *The Social Contract*, Rousseau recognizes a status of *ought* in the right to property in the natural state as "everyone would naturally have right to everything that is

29 Rousseau, *Discours sur l'origine*, 164.

30 Barny, *Les contradictions de l'idéologie révolutionnaire des droits de l'homme*, 139. Among thinkers who note that the idea of natural rights as prepolitical does not imply limitations upon popular sovereignty, see Loughlin, *Foundations of Public Law*, 345.

31 Rousseau, *Discours sur l'origine*, 184. On the difference between the conception of the right to property in Locke and Rousseau, see the analysis in Florence Gauthier, *Triomphe et mort du droit naturel en Révolution, 1789–1795–1802* (Paris: Presses Universitaires de France, 1992), 15.

32 Philonenko, Jean-Jacques Rousseau et la pensée de malheur, vol. 1, Le traité du mal, 209 ff.

33 Jean-Jacques Rousseau, *Discours sur l'origine*, 164.

34 *Discours sur l'origine*, 187.

35 Ibid., 176–77.

36 Rousseau, *Discours sur l'économie politique*, 263.

37 Ibid., 258.

necessary to him."[38] He also notes that the general will, at the level of the "ought," can do whatever it wants to any property that belongs to the world of reality.[39]

In the preamble to the Constitution read by Sieyès in the National Assembly on the of July 21, 1789, there are elements that resonate with Rousseau's theory.[40] Sieyès notes that when the strong oppress the weak there is a de facto situation that does not create a right for the strong. On the contrary, the weak have a natural duty to react to this oppression. In fact, Sieyès notes, this act of resistance of the weak is a duty toward themselves. The social state favors and increases liberty. A human being does not sacrifice their liberty when they enter society. Society extends and guarantees the use of liberty. It removes obstacles and threats to liberty by private forces. Society which is omnipotent can guarantee liberty. Following Rousseau, Sieyès notes that liberty makes more sense in the social state than what is called the natural state.

Other radical French thinkers and political actors show even greater proximity to Rousseau's thought. Saint-Just talks about selflessness as a "natural social law" and property as a "sad situation."[41] The earth does not belong to human beings – it is human beings as "sterile dust" that belong to the earth, he notes. Robespierre considers that society's first goal is to maintain existence.[42] He thinks that the first law of society is the one that guarantees to all members the means to survive and that all other laws are subordinated to it. Property was created only in order to affirm this law. Therefore, it cannot be conceived in a way that brings it in opposition to subsistence. What is indispensable in order to preserve life belongs to society as a whole.[43] In his opinion, nothing distinguishes the holder of a monopoly from a simple murderer if their actions threaten humanity, which suffers.[44] He makes a case in favor of forcing merchants of crops to make them available to the market.[45] He is in favor of using the law to define the liberty of property in order to prevent abuse and to even force speculators and holders of monopolies "to be honest."[46] His

38 Ibid., 365. In earlier parts *of Discourse on the Origins of Inequality*, Rousseau discusses the possibility that the savage has to appropriate things in order to survive. Those parts could have been influential also upon James Otis in the United States as argued in Mark Somos, *American States of Nature: the Origins of Independence, 1761–1775* (Oxford University Press, 2019), 68. These are not the implications though that Rousseau considers later on for the role of the government in the ideal social contract toward eliminating the wrong pragmatic social contract, which led to exploitation.

39 Cf. Manent, *Naissances de la politique moderne*, 173. Rousseau to some extent read in Locke, without elaborating the idea, that "work and culture" are the "only sign of property that, in the absence of legal titles. must be respected by others." Rousseau, *Du Contrat Social*, bk. 1, chap. 9, 366.

40 "Préliminaire de la Constitution, reconnaissance et exposition raisonnée des droits de l'homme et du citoyen," read in the National Assembly by Sieyès on July 21, 1789, *Archives parlementaires*, vol. 8, 256–61.

41 Saint-Just, "Ésprit de la Révolution," 284.

42 Maximilien Robespierre, "Discours sur les subsistances et le droit à l'éxistence" [December 2, 1792], in *Discours pour le bonheur et pour la liberté*, ed. Yannick Bosc, Florence Gauthier, and Sophie Wahnich (Paris: La Fabrique, 2000), 183.

43 Ibid.

44 Ibid., 184.

45 Ibid., 186.

46 Ibid., 189.

fury in describing the abuses of the right to property is not very far from the famous Marxist critique of the same right in *The German Ideology*.[47] In this text Marx also discusses the injustice of the *ius utendi* and *abutendi* in relation to property and how it can threaten human life. In the draft declaration of rights that Robespierre introduced in April 1793, he included an article that defined property as the right to enjoy and dispose of the goods that are guaranteed to a person by the law, which are limited by the obligation to respect the rights of others.[48] He even provides for a clause establishing a duty of those who have "surplus" to give some of it to those who are deprived of what they need.[49]

Babeuf, being even more radical, calls property a "deplorable creation of our fantasies."[50] Babeuf made a compelling case in favor of the collective character of goods.[51] In his opinion, anything an individual appropriates to themselves beyond what they need to survive is "social theft." Hereditary property isolates the members of a society from one another. Thus, it is just for society to recover what that individual has unjustly obtained. Society is the primary owner of goods and should apportion them on the basis of need.

In the transcendental future that Rousseau envisions for humanity following the principles of his ideal contract, he envisions a complete renunciation of all the rights of the natural state.[52] Rousseau declares that the citizens renounce the "natural right that they must enjoy in their quality of men" and instead of true alienation, they have made an "advantageous exchange." This transformation by the social contract restores to the civil man "under another form the essential goods that he enjoyed in the state of nature." Total alienation is an artifice to guarantee man living in society against "any personal dependency and to allow him to be as free as in the state of nature."[53] The total alienation of every member with all their rights to the community is a methodological fiction, a constructive rule, necessary to demonstrate how the rights of the individual, while inseparable from their nature, must be formally conferred to them by the state. Rights are conceived only as legal to the extent that they are recognized through state enactment by an instance that incarnates reason. Furthermore, Rousseau has a doubtful conception of constitutionalism

47 See Karl Marx, "The German Ideology," in *The Marx-Engels Reader*, ed. Robert Tucker (New York: Norton, 1978), 188.

48 Maximilien Robespierre, "Discussion of April 24, 1793," in Marc Bouloiseau, Georges Lefebvre, and Albert Soboul, eds., *Œuvres de Maximilien Robespierre*, vol. 8 (Paris: Presses Universitaires de France, 1958), 461.

49 Ibid., 466.

50 Gracchus Babeuf, "Contre la Propriété. Pour la Communauté" 30 frimaire an IV (21st December 1795), in Maurice Dommanget ed., *Pages choisies de Babeuf* (Paris: Armand Colin, 1935) 250–264, 269.

51 Gracchus Babeuf, "Manifeste des plébéiens: 9 frimaire an IV," (November 3, 1795) in Maurice Dommanget ed., *Pages choisies de Babeuf* (Paris: Armand Colin, 1935), 250–64, 258.

52 Rousseau, *Du Contrat Social (première version, manuscrit de Genève)*, 294.

53 As noted in Robert Dérathé, *Jean-Jacques Rousseau et la science politique de son temps* (Paris: Presses Universitaires de France, 1950), 171.

to the extent that he subordinates any idea of fundamental law to the will of the people.[54] There is no law such as a law protecting fundamental rights that cannot be undone by popular sovereignty. In this line of thinking, freedom of speech is to exist only to the extent that it is recognized by the general will and it should have the content assigned to it by the general will.[55]

Rousseau's conception of the realization of the rights of man combines the love of self, and the sentiment of humanity.[56] In the *Discourse on the Origin of Inequality*, Rousseau affirms that pity is older than the work of reason and reflection and is a condition of universality.[57] It is an innate, spontaneous, prereflexive virtue, which is activated by imagination and not by reason.[58] Contrary to the Madisonian conception according to which the establishment of a limited constitutional government is enough for the protection of rights, the generalization of the sentiments of humanity can, for Rousseau, lead to the realization of the rights of man and guarantee a nondespotic government. Fichte was also a thinker who rejected the idea of natural rights as such, postulating that rightful relations between human beings can exist only within a commonwealth and under positive law.[59] In this respect, his thought is very close to what the French revolutionaries had in mind. In his opinion, although the appellation of a right serves to denote a moral claim in how we relate to others, it is the recognition of society that makes a right a right in the legal sense. He applauded the French Revolution for aiming to create a republic that would establish these rightful relations among human beings and would lead to a proper recognition of rights. For Fichte, it is the state through its positive laws that recognizes rights and allows for this flourishing through the creation of a common will.

Reflecting this spirit of a social origin of rights, the French Declaration classes property among the "natural and imprescriptible rights of man," to underline that it is society that can make a human being holder of property. "Man possesses a natural law right to enter in society in order to begin to be holder of property."[60] The French

54 Rousseau, *Du contrat social*, bk. 3. See Martin P. Thompson, "The History of Fundamental Law in Political Thought from the French Wars of Religion to the American Revolution," *The American Historical Review* 91 (1986), 1103–28, 1126.

55 For the dangers inherent in this conception associating the general will with state rationalism in France, see Chapter 4.

56 Terence Marshall, "Les droits de l'homme et la politique constitutionnelle: un dialogue franco-américain à l'époque révolutionnaire," in Bourgeois et d'Hondt, eds., *La philosophie et la Révolution française*, 29–48, 39.

57 Rousseau, *Discours sur l'origine*, 154.

58 Cf. Derrida, *Grammatologie*, 259.

59 J.G. Fichte, *Foundations of Natural Rights According to the Principles of the Wissenschaftslehre* [1796], trans. Michael Baur, ed. Frederick Neuhouser (Cambridge University Press, 2000), 132. See also Alain Renaut, *Le système du droit, philosophie et droit dans la pensée de Fichte* (Paris: Presses Universitaires de France 1986), in which Renaut notes the subtlety in Fichte's thought that transcends individualism, and notes that it is the legal relation with others that makes intersubjectivity possible, and thus subjectivity as well. Ibid., 351.

60 Troper, "Jefferson et l'Interprétation," *Revue Française d'Histoire des Idées Politiques* 9 (1999), 3–23, 18.

revolutionaries, during the elaboration of the text of the French Declaration in the summer of 1789, invoke ancient and modern theories of natural law. They vacillate between conceptions of artificialism as well as naturalism for liberty. The social conception of natural law wins over in the relevant debates.[61] This was the case for political actors across the ideological spectrum. In the summer of 1789, many of the participants in the National Assembly referred to the situation in America in order to distinguish it from France. They engaged with natural rights discourse, in order to dismiss it in favor of a social conception of rights. According to the dominant opinion, rights are rules that regulate social interaction. They do not make sense outside of society. According to a part of the Assembly, theories that were good for America were not relevant in France. Mounier, for instance, notes that the French are not "a new people" that" has just come out of the forest."[62] On the contrary, they are a "large society," which needs to strengthen the links that unify all its parts.[63] Rights "are not to be abandoned," "but they shouldn't be exaggerated either."[64] Lafayette notes that the purpose of a Declaration of rights was to be the guide that leads all institutions of the stage "to the source of natural and social law."[65]

The aristocrat Lally Tollendal considers that a declaration of natural rights would threaten social disorder.[66] Unlike the Americans, who are now being born as a nation, the French are, in his opinion, an "ancient, enormous people," who have had government for fourteen hundred years.[67] Natural rights should be immediately associated with positive rights. References to natural law should be immediately associated with a conception of social unity between the various parts of French society. This social unity can be made effective thanks to positive law. Only positive law can ensure political and social reform as well as social relief. Mirabeau wanted to call his draft the "Declaration of the Rights of Man in Society."[68] For Duport, another aristocrat, the revolutionary value of natural law in its social conception can come from its conception of man as a social being against some other aristocrats who

[61] Cf. Barny, *Le droit naturel à l'épreuve de l'histoire*, 31 ff. For the influence of classical models particularly on the Constitution of 1793, which means abandoning a discourse of natural rights and focusing on rights as "postpolitical" or social, see Andrew Jainchill, *Reigmagining Politics after the Terror: The Republican Origins of French Liberalism* (Ithaca, NY: Cornell University Press 2008). Marcel Gauchet also notes that this attitude was dominant throughout the various stages of the French Revolution and the constitutional instability that followed it. See Gauchet, *La Révolution des droits de l'homme*, 100–101.

[62] M. Mounier, Speech in the National Assembly, Thursday July 9, 1789, *Archives parlementaires*, vol. 8, 215.

[63] Ibid.

[64] Ibid.

[65] Speech in the National Assembly, July 10, 1789, *Archives parlementaires*, vol. 8, 221.

[66] Speech in the National Assembly, July 11, 1789, *Archives parlementaires*, vol. 8, 222. See also Keith Michael Baker, "The Idea of a Declaration of Rights," in Van Kley, ed., *The French Idea of Freedom*, 174.

[67] Speech in the National Assembly, July 11, 1789, *Archives Parlementaires*, vol. 8, 222.

[68] Barny, *Le droit naturel à l'épreuve de l'histoire*, 31 ff.

are enemies of metaphysical speculations.[69] The monarchist Champion de Cicé notes that "there is nothing that cannot bend before the public interest."[70]

Some bourgeois thinkers insist on solitary natural law in a conservative intention against those on the left who discuss the transformation of the solitary nature by the social state. Still, even the thinkers identified as "bourgeois," who use a solitary conception of natural law to propose a foundation for the right to property (Sieyès or Condorcet), are not indifferent to the right of subsistence.[71] Those thinkers insist on the negative aspect of natural liberty against the privileges of the feudal regime. Nevertheless, the idea of an opposition between the solitary state of nature – and the social state – gradually faded in the relevant debates. It vanished against the movement of the lowest social strata and the necessity to respond to the social question.[72] This necessity led to the idea that the natural state of man is not solitary but social, a reflection that implies that property is not a natural right, but an artificial right.

The idea of a positivism related to rights, of a quasi-artificial character of rights, was dominant. For Crenière, rights do not make sense outside of the social state. In the social state human beings give up their independence and exchange it with political liberty.[73] In the state of nature human beings have neither rights nor duties.[74] It is within society that human beings take on duties while acquiring equivalent rights. In other words, rights are only a creation of the social state and they are correlative to duties. They have value and utility only within society. And he means political society. Although he uses the terms "natural and imprescriptible" in association with rights, he thinks that rights take their form only through agreeing to a voluntary association that determines social relationships in the form of rights. For Crenière, rights are imprescriptible not in the sense dominant in America as natural pre-social characteristics of the individual. They are imprescriptible in the sense that abolishing those rights means dissolving the society that recognizes them and returning to the state of nature, where rights do not exist. It is the formation of the general will to which everybody contributes that defines those rights. Those who created society imposed upon themselves the duty to obey the law. They have naturally and imprescriptibly acquired the right to make their own laws and to determine the authority that executes them. For Crenière, who follows Rousseau on this point, liberty and equality and in consequence life, security, and happiness are values whose protection is founded on the general will. Crenière concludes that the

69 Ibid.

70 Speech in the National Assembly, July 27, 1789, *Archives parlementaires*, vol. 8, 281.

71 See Chapter 4.

72 Barny, *Le droit naturel à l'épreuve de l'histoire*, 33.

73 Speech in the National Assembly, August 1, 1789, *Archives parlementaires*, vol. 8, 318.

74 "Man in the state of nature is neither free nor slave … he has neither rights to exercise nor duties to fulfill. Nature gives nothing useless and if the isolated man had rights, against whom and how would he exercise them?" By exchanging natural independence, man has access to political liberty. *Archives parlementaires*, vol. 8, 318.

general will is constituted in the state and society and that any law, even that which could be called "natural," has its foundation only in it and not in some order anterior to the state.[75] Paradoxically, Crenière defines rights – whose protection is the purpose of a Constitution of a nation – as being exclusively submitted to general laws and to the general will from which law originates.

Delandine notes that, for the French people, it is not necessary to go back to the origins of the social state, but to improve the existing social state.[76] It is not the natural man that is important to consider but the civilized French man. Any declaration of rights should, in his opinion, be preceded by a declaration of the "rights of the nation," which are anterior to any other right and from which all other rights emanate.[77] This vision that the rights in any declaration concern the rights of the man in society was shared by most of the orators during the elaboration of the Declaration of 1789.[78]

Even those who discuss rights as natural, like Rabaud de Saint-Etienne, accept that it is society that favors and amplifies liberty. It is society that fulfills the goal of liberty, which is the conservation and improvement of human existence.[79] Aristotelian teleological elements in the understanding of liberty are present in his thought, to the extent that he sees liberty as something to be perfected within society. If this is so, it does not make sense to talk about "sacrifice of liberty" in the case of taxation, Rabaud de Saint-Etienne notes.[80] Legislation enacted within political society only embellishes the existence and the liberty of man. Even thinkers who discuss liberty as natural, insist on the importance of society in an existential sense. Liberty makes sense only in society that amplifies it and makes it meaningful through its laws. Similar philosophical discourse is entirely absent from the debates related to the foundations of the American constitutional texts.

Under the pressure of the peasants' struggles theories emerge tending toward the reestablishment of social equality, despite reactions from the conservatives. Egalitarian theories for agrarian reform support the generalization of the small property for the peasants. The right to property seems to be par excellence a right – social creation. It appears legitimate to control it in the name of the general interest. The right of the owner over the products of their land is limited by the right to existence of the consumers of these products. In the Abbé de Cournant's *De la propriété ou la cause du pauvre*, the reference to Rousseau legitimizes submission of the right to property to the general will, which can annihilate it provided that the measure is applicable to all without distinction.[81] Cournant considers an agrarian

75 Ibid.

76 Speech in the National Assembly, August 1, 1789, *Archives parlementaires*, vol. 8, 324.

77 Ibid., 325.

78 See for instance, Desmeuniers, Speech in the National Assembly, August 3, 1789, *Archives parlementaires*, vol. 8, 334; Le comte D'Antraigues, ibid.

79 Rabaud de Saint-Étienne, "Idées sur les bases de toute constitution," submitted to the National Assembly on August 12, 1789, *Archives parlementaires*, vol. 7, 403–4.

80 Ibid., 405.

81 Cited in Barny, *Le droit naturel à l'épreuve de l'histoire*, 130.

law that should redistribute the land of the peasants and was the result of the egalitarian correction of the bourgeois social contract.[82] Popular egalitarianism serves the *sans-culottes*' demands. The image of the state of nature provided by Rousseau serves, in this sense, the struggle against social inequality, the most general principles of slavery of enslavement of man to man. If the state of nature only knows independent individuals, the social state should only allow reciprocal dependencies without inequality.[83] For Saint-Just, a claim to "natural rights," which is against the liberty as established in the civil state by the law, is wrong.[84] For him, it is being a member of society that makes a human being truly independent. An idiosyncratic compromise took place between the consideration of the right to property as a right "imprescriptible and inalienable," and a "social right." If the right to property can be developed only on the basis of a social convention, it is a quasi-artificial and not a natural right. Although a frontal attack on the right to property did not come about, this philosophy affected the understanding of the mission of the state toward liberty.

Even the Physiocrats who wrote before the French Revolution, providing a foundation of natural rights similar to Locke's, arrive paradoxically at the need for a despotic power to guarantee the natural order of society and to realize the subjective rights of the citizens.[85] They start from the axiom that political laws must accommodate economic laws, since economic laws are established by nature, whereas the political laws are human work, subject to fallibility.[86] The Physiocrats accept Locke's legitimization of private property. They consider property as the result of inequality of talent, of forces and faculties of body and spirit.[87] They pose the "laissez-faire" principle in economics, while considering that this natural order can be maintained only by a despotic power. Monarchical absolutism will see to the formation of public reason, by civic education, necessary for the constitution of the political body. This political body presupposes the necessary unity of opinion that presumes a common interest and only one and the same will in which sovereignty resides. Thomas Paine notes that the moral maxims of the Physiocrats concerning government aim to reform and economize the administration of government as it is, not government itself.[88] Despite following Locke in some respects, the Physiocrats accept subjective rights as rights proper to the citizens; liberty can exist for them only in the political state.[89] The natural order of society is actualized for them by means of political power.

82 Ibid., 123–24.

83 Ibid., 131.

84 Saint-Just, "Ésprit de la Révolution," 303.

85 On the proximity between the physiocrats and Locke, see Cheryl B. Welch, *Liberty and Utility: The French Ideologues and the Transformation of Liberalism* (New York: Columbia Press, 1984), 9.

86 Georges Weulersse, *La Physiocratie sous les ministères de Turgot et de Necker (1774–1781)* (Paris: Presses Universitaires de France, 1950), 109 ff.

87 Ibid., 107.

88 Thomas Paine, "The Rights of Man, Part I," in *Political Writings*, ed. Bruce Kuklick (Cambridge University Press, 1989), 101.

89 Jürgen Habermas, *Theory and Praxis*, trans. John Viertel (Boston: Beacon Press, 1973), 101.

Mirabeau's conception of rights seems to be virtually lifted out of Rousseau's. In his opinion, citizenship reconciles humanity with its nature by an act of reason that actualizes the rights of man. Human regeneration can come only from the realization of the rights of the citizen.[90] Sieyès makes a triple distinction in relation to rights.[91] First, he thinks that men united in society in order to enjoy property in tranquility. A second category of rights derives from association but is not established by the law, the law having the mission of protecting them. A third category is the rights upon which there is "agreement" in society, concerning which the political body is the "master who wants or accords what it likes" in relation to their social utility, such as the right to "dispose one's goods, when one does not exist." He thinks that the right to property is natural, while considering succession rights as artificial. Succession rights should be submitted, in his opinion, to the creative or attributive will of the nation "according to its utility or its pleasure." In *What Is the Third Estate?*, Sieyès proposes an amalgam of some natural rights and physiocratic ideas, which are to be absorbed and realized by the nation.[92] In this respect, he is very close to Rousseau's conception, who, having as his starting point some concept of rights, ends up proposing a conception that absorbs those rights in the general will.

The French Declaration of 1789 affirms the rights of a politically constituted society, rights that are politically crucial for the Physiocrats: liberty, property, and security. Nevertheless, despite this nominal reference to rights that sound "natural," it seems that these rights are recognized only as rules that serve social interaction. They are inseparable from the rights of the citizen and from the rights of the nation. The nation has the mission to define these rights through its representatives. Stéphane Rials notes insightfully that if the French Declaration seems placed "under the 'civilization' of natural law," it expresses at the same time a "radical positivism."[93] It proclaims the rights of the citizen, instituted rights, which are valid because they are positively recognized. These encompass the rights of the human being, of the physical human existence. The institutionalization of the natural rights in Rousseau's thought reflects the absorption of civil society by the political society, the state. This is far from Smith's and Paine's approach.

90 Cited in Stéphane Rials, "La Déclaration de 1789: le mystère des origins," *Droits* 8 (1988), 3–21.

91 Emmanuel-Joseph Sieyès, "Lois," in *Ecrits politiques*, 87–88.

92 Sieyès "Qu'est-ce-que le Tiers état?," 162 ff. See also J. K. Wright, "National Sovereignty and the General Will," 199, 209.

93 Stéphane Rials, *La Déclaration des droits de l'homme et du citoyen* (Paris: Hachette, 1988), 353–54. This positivism is particularly visible in Article 4: "Liberty consists in being able to do anything that does not harm others: thus, the exercise of the natural rights of every man has no bounds other than those that ensure to the other members of society the enjoyment of these same rights. These bounds may be determined only by law." It is also visible in Article 5: "The law has the right to forbid only those actions that are injurious to society. Nothing that is not forbidden by Law may be hindered, and no one may be compelled to do what the Law does not ordain." These two articles, as Stéphane Rials shows, seem to exclude the references to natural law. They seem to provide a vehicle for the idea that for someone to be able to invoke harm before a judge it must be taken into consideration by the law.

The declarations of rights that followed made this conception more explicit. The Declaration of Rights of June 24, 1793 includes rights of social participation, like the one to work and to public education. The Declaration of 1795 refers in its first article to "the rights of man in society," omitting any reference to natural rights. The idea, already present in the earlier stages of the revolution, matured and was expressed in a constitutional text in 1795. Immediately after the Terror, the Thermidorian predominance more clearly expressed a conception that shows an understanding of natural law closer to antiquity. Rights are not natural and transcending time and place. Rights exist to the extent that they are recognized by a politically organized society. By analogy, in this context, freedom of speech is also a right that exists only to the extent that its content is recognized and protected by the laws of the state. This general conception of rights, makes government intervention in defining the content and limits of freedom of speech more legitimate.

Locke's conception of natural rights implies the recognition of the rights existing before the emergence of the state. The state has the end to preserve the natural order of rights. The members of society retain the right to institute government and to keep it under control.[94] This spirit is expressed by the American Declaration of Independence. In France, the new Constitution reorganized society against the Ancien Régime. The new political will, which is omnipotent, reflecting the one preceding it, guarantees the liberty recognized only as posed by the law. The Constitution guarantees the rights of human existence, everything necessary to the physical preservation, under a positive form, following an institutionalization of these rights, of the human being as a citizen. The reference to the rights of man plays "the role of a founding detour, of an operator of the rights of the citizen."[95] In this context, the reference to the natural rights in the text of 1789 cannot play the role of a prepolitical norm. Commentators note that if such an a priori foundation, theological or otherwise, seems to be taken away from rights, from the moment that an "eclipse" of the natural law has taken place, the danger exists that rights lose their immunity more easily.[96]

In France it is legitimate to limit speech on the basis of an ancient conception of natural law, the idea that the content of a liberty must be in accordance with the justice of the *cosmos*. This points toward reducing the possibility of the subject to choose for themselves the opinions that are worth listening to. The revolutionary legicentrism inaugurates a French tradition that makes the state the "institutor of the social sphere," articulating every realization of an individual right as what might be compared to the common interest, according to the idea that makes it the governing power.[97] In this context, as analyzed earlier, property is a second order liberty of variable content and protection in relation to liberties, having a positive content,

94 Habermas, *Theory and Praxis*, 104.

95 Rials, *La Déclaration*, 353.

96 Zarka, "Notion de droit naturel," 67.

97 Lucien Jaume, *Individu effacé*, 80.

such as the right to education, which consists in the formation of citizenship.[98] By analogy, for freedom of speech, this means that it is legitimate for the state to define its content and to make sure that everyone can exercise it in terms of equality. It also means that there is less tolerance toward social harm caused by freedom of expression. It is legitimate for the state to limit speech in order to protect against offense caused to others and offense caused to important social values, as the prohibition of the denial of crimes against humanity shows.

The American Declaration of Independence, the state bills of rights and the Amendments to the Federal Constitution emerged in a different intellectual atmosphere. A conception of rights as "natural" was dominant in the period that led to the Declaration of Independence. This conception was building on a tradition of constitutionalism emerging in the American colonies in the seventeenth century. The charters accorded to the colonies as a matter of privilege and grace were seen as the written source of their basic freedoms. "The colonists were quick to oppose any infringements upon their Charter rights."[99] Locke himself was the co-author of the *Fundamental Constitutions of Carolina 1669*, which contain a core of negative liberties such us property (section thirteen, fourteen), freedom of religion and worship (section one hundred and one), and trial by jury (section one hundred and eleven).[100] These charters together with the intellectual debate against the legislative activity of the British parliament led to conceiving the state declarations of rights as ensuring rights seen as prepolitical, God-given qualities.

The American Declaration of Independence presents "doctrinal and verbal" similarities with Locke's thought.[101] The end of government is the security of negative rights, qualities proper to every person. American intellectuals in the years preceding the Declaration of Independence discuss extensively the natural negative rights of the individual.[102] This discussion was part of a movement against taxation imposed by the British parliament on the colonies, which were seen as unfair. In 1764 the book by James Otis, *The Rights of the English Colonies: Asserted*

98 Louis Favoureu, "La jurisprudence du Conseil constitutionnel et le droit de propriété proclamé par la Déclaration de 1789," in *La Déclaration des droits de l'homme et du citoyen et la jurisprudence* (Paris: Presses Universitaires de France, 1989), 125–50, 138.

99 Schwartz, *Bill of Rights*, 50–51. The First Charters were the Virginia Charter of 1606, the Fundamental Orders of Connecticut of 1639, and the Maryland Act for the Liberties of the People of 1639.

100 The Concessions and Agreements of West New Jersey of 1677 also guarantees the protection of negative rights such as religious liberty (Chapter XVI), trial by jury (Chapter XVII), fair public trials (Chapters XX-XXIII), and no arrest or imprisonment without summons (Chapter XVIII). The text was an important step toward the federal Bill of Rights. Ibid., 125–26. Freedom of religion and trial by jury was protected in the Pennsylvania Frame of Government of 1682 (Section XXXV), the New York Charter of Libertyes and Priviledges of 1683, and the Pennsylvania Charter of Privileges of 1701 (Article I).

101 Zuckert, *Natural Rights and the New Republicanism*, 18.

102 For a discussion of some of these ideas see Mark Somos, *American States of Nature: The Origins of Independence, 1761–1771* (Oxford University Press, 2019)

and Proved, contributed to the idea of natural rights, inherent in the quality of man and citizen and inalienable by any government act that would make them positive, enacted rights.[103] Otis discusses the "natural absolute personal rights of individuals," by which he means the right of personal security, personal liberty, and private property.[104] Otis refutes Blackstone's opinion that those rights and privileges depend on the local charters. Jefferson also associates natural rights with the natural instinct for security. The guarantee of reciprocity is associated with the negative character, as rational calculus of the appropriate means to guarantee this security to all human beings.[105] He discusses the absolute limits established by God and by the nature of the legislative power in the form that would become the one adopted by the American Bills of Rights.[106] He writes against the authority to tax, which was the principal reason for dissension between the colonies and the British Empire.[107] Following Locke, Otis considers it appropriate to impose restrictions to the power of the parliament, those dictated by "divine and natural law."[108] Virtually repeating Locke, Otis defends negative liberties as natural rights. Some of those liberties were later included in the Declaration of Independence.

The Rights of the Colonists and a List of Infringements and Violations of Rights of 1772 (prepared in Boston by a Committee of Correspondence at the suggestion of Samuel Adams) also refers directly to Locke, developing a natural rights theory.[109] It enumerates among the rights of the colonists "the absolute Rights of Englishmen, and all freemen in or out of Civil society" as "personal security, personal liberty and private property," and "liberty in matters spiritual and temporal." Throughout his writings from his *Summary View of the Rights of British America*, written in 1774,[110] until late into the life of the new federal government, Jefferson refers to the natural rights of the individual. John Adams reasons in the same way in many of his works. In his *Dissertation on the Canon and Feudal Law*, written before the Declaration of Independence, Adams notes that rights are "antecedent to all earthly government" and "cannot be repealed or restrained by human laws," as they are "derived from the

103 Otis, *Rights of the English Colonies*, 29, 31, 42.

104 James Otis, "A Vindication of the British Colonies" [1765], in Richard Samuelson, ed., *Collected Political Writings of James Otis* (Indianapolis, IN: Liberty Fund, 2015), 189, Otis, *Rights of the British Colonies*, 29, 31, 42.

105 See for example Thomas Jefferson, *A Summary View of the Rights of British America* [1774], in Ford, ed., *Works of Thomas Jefferson*, vol. 2, 64. On the link between liberty and security in the Age of the American Revolution, see Reid, *Concept of Liberty*, 70–73.

106 Otis, *Rights of the British Colonies*.

107 Ibid., 55–57.

108 Ibid., 45.

109 See Schwartz, *The Bill of Rights*, 200–202. The same document provides limitations of the Legislative power upon "the lives and the fortunes of the people." Schwartz, *Bill of Rights*, 203. In the Infringements section it criticizes the taxation without representation imposed by the British parliament and refers to trial by jury as a fundamental right of which the colonies are deprived. The same liberties are stressed in the Declaration and Resolves of the First Continental Congress of 1774.

110 Thomas Jefferson, *Summary View of the Rights of British America*, in Ford, ed., *Works of Thomas Jefferson*, vol. 2, 68.

great Legislator of the Universe."[111] For Adams, it is absurd to suppose that men by entering society "renounce their essential natural rights, or the means of preserving those rights."[112] He notes that the end of the institution of government is "to furnish the individuals who compose it with the power of enjoying . . . their natural rights."[113]

From the right to use material things to ensure self-preservation, the right to life, derives the right to appropriate material things.[114] The reference to natural rights is omnipresent in the works of Jefferson and Madison. Locke's conception of natural rights was interesting to them, as well as the idea that the passage from the pre-political state to the political meant conceding one's individual "natural," "executive" power to the state. If rights are less protected in the absence of government, the only end and the only reason for the existence of the government is the guarantee of these rights. Modern natural rights theories underly the American texts declaring rights. They express the idea of a prepolitical state anterior to the state and to any positive law. This conception aims to emphasize the artificial character of government, constructed by human beings in order to serve specific goals, the guarantee of "natural" rights.[115]

In opposition to Rousseau's conception of liberty, which underlies the French Declaration and associates liberty to enactment by the state, in Thomas Paine's works *Common Sense* and *The Rights of Man*, he situates the foundations of rights on the human being, independently from the quality of being a citizen of a state, and independently from any constitution or charter.[116] The works eloquently express the understanding of rights in America in the Founding Era. Following a contractualist reasoning, legal rights have their origins in the natural rights and not the other way around, since human beings did not enter society in order to deteriorate their situation, that is in view of having less rights, but in order to have these rights better guaranteed.[117] For Paine, natural rights are rights that belong to the human being on the basis of their very existence. They consist of intellectual rights, rights of the spirit, and individual rights that concern action and do not violate the rights of others. Civil rights are rights that belong to the human being on the basis of their quality as a member of society. Following Locke, Paine considers that every civil right has its foundation in a pre-existing natural right for the protection of which individual

111 John Adams, *Dissertation on the Canon and Feudal Law* [1765], in *Works of John Adams*, vol. 3, 449.

112 Samuel Adams, "The Rights of the Colonists: Report of the Committee of Correspondence to the Boston Town Meeting," Nov. 20, 1772, *Old South Leaflets* 173, https://memory.loc.gov/service/gdc/scd0001/2009/20090211001ri//20090211001ri.pdf.

113 See John Adams, *The Report of a Constitution or Form of Government for the Commonwealth of Massachusetts, Preamble* [1779], in *Works of John Adams*, vol. 4, 219. The reference to "natural rights" exists also in Article 1 of the *Declaration of the Rights of the Inhabitants of the Commonwealth of Massachusetts* written by John Adams., Ibid., 220.

114 Zuckert, *Natural Rights and the New Republicanism*, 18.

115 Zuckert, *Natural Rights Republic*, 81 ff.

116 Tomas Paine, *Common Sense* [1776] (New York: Alfred Knopf, 1994); Thomas Paine, "The Rights of Man, Part I" [1791], in *Political Writings*; "The Rights of Man part II" [1792], in *Political Writings*.

117 Paine, "The Rights of Man, Part I," in *Political Writings*, 78.

power is not enough.[118] Once in political society, persons retain the natural rights for which their power of protection is sufficient. They accept conversion into civil rights for those rights for which their power of protection is defective. If every civil right comes from the conversion of a natural right, civil power comes from the aggregation of natural rights for which the individual power of defense is missing. Civil power, produced by the aggregation of natural rights, cannot be employed to invade the natural rights retained by the individual, for which the power of protection is perfect in the individual as the right itself. Freedom of expression is a natural right always retained.[119]

Paine understands rights in the negative sense. He stresses that every right is correlative to an obligation of respect, of abstention, so that any declaration of rights is by reciprocity a declaration of duties of abstention.[120] This understanding of "duties" is a thinner version of what the French meant by the same term. The French placed more emphasis on the duties of positive state action to guarantee human existence. Paine is in favor of some positive action of the government in providing the necessary preconditions for the exercise of liberty including progressive taxation and poor relief. He accepts a positive role of the state to guarantee equality of negative liberty and security.[121] For him, property is a civil right.

The understanding of natural law evolved in America in the period before independence and throughout the creation of the federal state.[122] Before independence, a period of political revolt, the Americans aimed to justify their claims to some rights and thus a negative theory of rights against the government was the most appropriate. Once independence was won, and the political needs had changed, the theory of republican government became dominant while references to negative natural rights persisted.

Republican elements, along with a conception of the common good, also existed within the American Founders. There are nevertheless qualitative differences between France and America of the time in the understanding of the common good and of how natural rights relate to it. According to the American conception, natural rights are not to be entirely converted into positive rights. Although social coexistence and serving the common good requires political coercion, some scope for natural liberty is to be preserved. This difference can be understood by reference to the ideological background and the different social and political needs to which the two revolutionary movements were responding.[123] The American conception of the public good expressed by the majority associates it with an empirical majority,

118 Ibid., 79.

119 Ibid., 117.

120 Ibid.

121 Thomas Paine, *Rights of Man*, II (New York, Toronto: Everyman's Library 1994), 225. See also Francis Canavan, S. J., "Thomas Paine," in Strauss and Cropsey, eds., *History of Political Philosophy*, 685–86.

122 B. F. Wright, Jr., "American Interpretations of Natural Law," *The American Political Science Review* 20, no. 3 (1926) 524–47, 528–29.

123 See Chapter 2.

expression of the interests of society, itself plural and divided, and not with a public good expressed by the state.[124] As discussed in Chapter 2, in France, the common interest is not the result of the confrontation of various private interests, as it is in the United States for Madison.[125] It is instead something qualitatively different. It is the one "by which citizens resemble one another."[126] It is something with which all citizens identify. Sieyès follows Rousseau in considering the common interest as the result of the harmonization of individual interests.[127] For Madison, private and local interests are to be represented and it is their confrontation that leads to the discovery of the common good.

This conception of the relation between government and liberty was the result of the influence of many generations of British political thinkers. *Cato's Letters* by John Trenchard and Thomas Gordon was very influential in America.[128] These texts are famous for their synthesis of Lockean political philosophy and the anterior political science of the Whigs. *Cato's Letters* contains the terms that were repeated later by the Declaration of Independence almost word for word. The political science of liberty shows the way to ensure a free government and how this can assure the liberty and security of rights.[129] Following Locke, *Cato's Letters* discusses the original state as one of equal liberty. It expresses a demystifying vision of politics. Political society and government are an artifact constructed by human beings who were originally free and equal.[130] Elements of Aristotelian organicism are absent. The "public" is conceived as "the collective body of abstract human beings" and the "public spirit" as the protection of "liberty, plenty, ease and security."[131] "The affairs of all should be minded preferably to the Affairs of One."[132] The starting point is the individual and the public good is measured by reference to their liberty, which stands in opposition to the French conception, where the very relationship that a person maintains with themselves is mediated by the state. Natural rights are the foundation of government. As divine gifts, they cannot be alienated by submission to absolutist or arbitrary power.[133] Liberty and property are the power that every person has over their actions

124 Cf. Jaume, *Individu effacé*, 76.

125 James Madison, "No. 57," in Madison, Hamilton, and Jay, *The Federalist*, 297–98; Madison, "No. 10," in Madison, Hamilton, and Jay, *The Federalist*, 42.

126 Emmanuel Joseph Sieyès, "What is the Third Estate?," in *Political Writings*, trans. Michael Sonenscher (Indianapolis/Cambridge: Hackett, 2003), 154.

127 Ibid., 40.

128 Thomas Gordon and John Trenchard, *Cato's Letters, or Essays on Liberty, Civil and Religious, and other Important Subjects* (New York: Da Capo Press, 1971), 1720–21.

129 Gordon and Trenchard, *Cato's Letters*. See for example, "No. 25" (April 15, 1721), in ibid., vol. 1, 184 ff.; "No. 35" (July 1, 1721), vol. 2, 13. See. Zuckert, *Natural Rights and the New Republicanism*, 312.

130 In Gordon and Trenchard, "No. 33" (June 17, 1721), in *Cato's Letters*, vol. 1, 259, the author exposes how distrustful power is, because human beings are governed by their insatiable passions. See also Zuckert, *Natural Rights Republic*, 301 ff.

131 Gordon and Trenchard, "No. 35" (July 1, 1721), in *Cato's Letters*, vol. 2, 13–14.

132 "As the preservation of property is the source of national happiness; whoever violates property, or lessens or endangers it, common sense says, that he is an enemy to his country." Ibid., 17.

133 Gordon and Trenchard, "No. 59" (December 30, 1721), in *Cato's Letters*, vol. 2, 216.

and their "right to enjoy the fruit of his Labour, Art and Industry."[134] The asocial character of desires that require mutual recognition requires a government with the power to impose rules and to enforce them in view of guaranteeing these rights. The idea underlying *Cato's Letters* is that happiness concerns liberty understood as negative liberty rather than citizenship.[135] The natural state of the human being is outside political life. The latter emerges not for personal fulfillment but out of necessity.

The logic expressed in *Cato's Letters* is the opposite to that of the French Declaration, which aimed to guide the state toward realizing the rights of the citizens. The public sphere is instrumental to the private. The public is only the medium used to protect and preserve the private sphere of happiness.[136] The understanding of the general interest expressed in *Cato's Letters* is different from Rousseau's conception of the same interest. If the only purpose for which humans enter political society is the preservation of their natural rights, the aim of government must be to guarantee to everyone their own goods.[137] Prudent indulgence of self-interest and not of self-sacrifice makes peaceful coexistence and patriotism possible, the devotion to the city being a "personal-collective interest."[138] In Tocquevillian terms it would be "self-interest properly understood."[139] Tocqueville has further noted that interest in political affairs originates in America out of a concern that political decisions will have an impact upon negative liberty. If human nature is dominated by the desire to acquire, engendering insecurity consumed by anxiety, the political remedy is not a citizenship of virtue, but of laws and institutions. Concentration of power can be a source of public danger and tools must be developed to assure the minimization of its impact upon liberty to what is strictly necessary.[140]

As Michael Zuckert has shown, *Cato's Letters* synthesizes Locke's political philosophy and the political science of the Whigs.[141] It expresses doubts on the desirability of submitting a person's interests to others.[142] Gordon and Trenchard conceive politics according to the spirit of the new science, as mechanistic: checks upon magistrates are indispensable to freedom.[143] The political science of *Cato's Letters* attempts to combine two elements that are partly contradictory: that the government

134 Gordon and Trenchard, "No. 62" (January 20, 1722), in *Cato's Letters*, vol. 2, 245; Gordon and Trenchard, "No. 59," in ibid., vol. 2, 228.

135 Gordon and Trenchard, "No. 62" (January 20, 1722), in *Cato's Letters*, vol. 2, 245.

136 "True and impartial liberty is therefore the right of every man to pursue the natural, reasonable, and religious dictate of his own mind; to think what he will and act as he thinks, provided he acts not to the prejudice of another." Ibid., 248.

137 Ibid., 246, 248; Gordon and Trenchard, "No. 90" (August 18, 1722), in *Cato's Letters*, vol. 3, 200.

138 Ibid., 199–200.

139 Tocqueville *Democracy in America*, 527.

140 Gordon and Trenchard, "No. 75" (May 5, 1722), in *Cato's Letters*, vol. 3, 75.

141 Zuckert, *Natural Rights and the New Republicanism*, 164–66.

142 Zuckert, *Natural Rights and the New Republicanism*, 315 ff.

143 Gordon and Trenchard, "No. 97" (October 6, 1722), in *Cato's Letters*, vol. 4, 81.

is founded on a pact of trust in view of serving the interests of the governed, which are better served by making the interests of the governors identical to those of the governed. Public interest – honoring the trust of this government – is in the interest of all perfectly rational beings.[144] The appeals to the public spirit are seen as necessary supplements to the system of personal interest upon which *Cato's Letters* is founded.[145] Virtue is associated with self-interest by the reference to the desire to win the appreciation of others. The Americans invented an idiosyncratic combination of a "natural rights republic."[146] Michael Zuckert has suggested that it is possible to conceptualize a political science that is dominant in the American revolutionaries and Founders as separate from their political philosophy. The elements of classical republicanism belong to the political science of the Founders, whereas their liberalism is a reflection of their political philosophy. This fusion contributed to a syncretism of traditional republican elements with the necessity to protect negative liberty, solidifying a new type of Whiggism that became dominant in America toward 1776.[147] American republicanism is based on an idiosyncratic combination of civic spirit and a conception of natural rights.

In *The Machiavellian Moment*,[148] J. G. A. Pocock shows the links between American republicanism and "civic humanism," a term which associates self-government to the humanist tradition of the Renaissance and not to Aristotelian naturalism. As Pocock notes, the humanism of the Renaissance produced an important modification to classical republicanism, and the American foundation can be understood as expressing a Machiavellian moment rather than an Aristotelian one.[149] Pocock's contribution consists in underlining that citizenship and political participation were important for American republicanism as well, but the subordination of the part to the whole was not.[150] In the civic humanist ethos, the individual was seen as combining self-interest with the role of being a citizen in the republic.[151] In the world of values, the idea of the civic man was very important, while this idea had to be reconciled with the historic actuality of the economic man.[152] In the emerging commercial society, humanity is not to be understood merely as associated with political virtue, as *zoon politikon*. The recurrence of this conception, which was dominant in antiquity and in France in the Revolutionary Era is due to its own political and social circumstances. In America, Florentine

144 Gordon and Trenchard, "No. 63" (January 27, 1722), in *Cato's Letters*, vol. 2, 259.

145 Gordon and Trenchard, "No. 89" (August 11, 1722), in *Cato's Letters*, vol. 3, 193 (developing how everybody's private interest benefits from seeing the public flourish: only when the public is secure can private property and the means of acquiring property flourish).

146 Zuckert, *Natural Rights and the New Republicanism*, 299.

147 Zuckert, *Natural Rights and the New Republicanism*, 299.

148 J. G. A. Pocock, *The Machiavellian Moment: Florentine Political Thought and the Atlantic Republican Tradition* (Princeton University Press, 1975), 462 ff.

149 Ibid., 466–67.

150 Ibid., 464.

151 Ibid., 466.

152 Ibid., 466.

thought was appealing to the extent that it reached a better equilibrium between political participation and self-interest. Pocock notes that the values dominant in American culture were "a civic and patriot ideal in which the personality was founded in property, perfected in citizenship but perpetually threatened by corruption; government figuring paradoxically as the principal source of corruption."[153] This is the exact opposite conception to the one dominant in France. In the American context of distrust toward the possibility of the state exercising a moralizing role, virtue was to be a personal matter.

Cato stresses that the role of political liberty is to encourage commerce, which assures abundance.[154] In Locke's thought the right to property consists in the necessity to appropriate the things of the external world, to associate with the internality of the self the things which belong to the external world.[155] It is justified by the survival and the quality of the human being as a *homo faber*. Persons – in search of security – invest their work in the external world. Locke provides a moral foundation for property. The correlative duty to abstain from violating property is founded on the moral idea of work and of the time spent obtaining a good from the external world. This moral justification associating it to work in respect to self-preservation can generate an exclusive and transcendent natural right. The combination of inequality in talents, of devotion to the work of force means justifying inequality in the possession of wealth.[156] Madison follows this exact conception of property, accepting that "the protection … of the diversity of the faculties of human beings, in which have their origins the rights to property, is the first aim of government."[157] In the same spirit, Madison discusses explicitly freedom of speech as one of the "natural rights retained."[158] Madison distinguishes between natural rights, such as the right to free speech, and government-created rights, such as trial by jury. Jefferson's understanding of liberty that underlies the American Declaration is in line with Locke's.

Contrary to the French Declaration, which establishes the recognition of the rights of man on the rights of the citizen, the American texts establish the rights of the citizen on the "private" man, meaning the self-sufficient man. Jefferson and others read in Locke the language of inalienable rights,[159] which was used in the

153 Ibid., 507.

154 Gordon and Trenchard, "No. 64" (February 3, 1722), in *Cato's Letters*, vol. 2, 267; Gordon and Trenchard, "No. 68" (March 3, 1722), in *Cato's Letters*, vol. 2, 321.

155 Locke, *Second Treatise*, § 27, 274.

156 Polin, *Politique morale de John Locke*, 271 ff.

157 Madison, "No. 10," in Madison, Hamilton, and Jay, *The Federalist* (Indianapolis, IN: Liberty Fund, 2001), 43. See also Matthews, *If Men Were Angels*, 118.

158 James Madison, Speech, House of Representatives, 8 June 1789, *in The Writings of James Madison*, vol. 5, 1789–1790, ed. Gaillard Hunt (New York and London: G. P. Putnam's Sons, 1904), 381. On freedom of speech understood as a natural right during the Founding Era, see Thomas G. West, "Free Speech in the American Founding and in Modern Liberalism," *Social Philosophy & Policy* 21, no. 2 (2004), 310–84.

159 Zuckert, *Natural Rights and the New Republicanism*, 245. More generally on the negative aspect of rights dominant in America during the Founding Era, see Richard Primus, *The American Language of Rights* (Cambridge University Press, 1999), 83.

Declaration of Independence, the Declaration of Massachusetts of 1780, and the constitutions of Vermont, Pennsylvania, and Virginia.[160] The Declaration of Rights that Jefferson, as an Ambassador of the United States in France, proposed to Rabaut Saint-Etienne in 1789 contained a list of negative procedural liberties, which was close to the dominant conception of liberty of the American revolutionaries.[161] The republicanism of natural rights as conceptualized by the American Framers insists on the centrality of political economy and of economic growth. This logic of natural rights republicanism is far from the republican vision of antiquity.

Writing shortly after the French Revolution, Richard Price notes that it is possible to promote one's "private interest" together with promoting "the interest of our country."[162] In his opinion, during the Glorious Revolution, the British became the "instructors of the world" in ensuring security of property and enlarging the bounds of free enquiry.[163] The mission of civil government is to protect negative liberties.[164] He approves of the American Revolution for contributing to this way of thinking too.

The rights proclaimed in the Declaration of Independence – life, liberty, and property – are complementary. The state must protect their negative aspect through positive actions. They are equally associated with moral sense, natural compassion, and benevolence.[165] The mutual and intersubjective character of security leads to moderating egoistic passions. Associated with security, the right to life enjoys primary protection in the American Declaration.[166] Contrary to the conception of the French Declaration, for which the right to life is an essentially positive right to which the right to property is subordinated, Jefferson's conception remains focused on the negative aspect of this right. A positive right to life, meaning a right entailing positive obligations for the state to assure its realization, would not succeed in the American context as it could lead to unlimited control of a person's life. The "slippery slope" argument is present here: a positive right to meet one's needs would institute a vague legal responsibility threatening to put the personal work and its fruit to the service of others.[167] Benevolence deriving from "moral sense" or "sympathy" is a moral virtue that the state does not have the legitimacy to enforce. This would create insecurity and undermine the motivation to work.[168]

The necessity to protect the negative aspect of self-government was one of the major political claims of the Founding Era. Civic ideology and the need to liberate oneself

160 According to the Virginia Constitution: "all men ... have certain inherent rights, of which, when they enter into a state of society, they cannot by any compact, deprive or divest their posterity."

161 Thomas Jefferson, "Letter to Rabaut de St. Etienne, Paris, June 3, 1789," in *Political Writings*, ed. Joyce Appleby and Terence Ball (Cambridge University Press, 1999), 349–51.

162 Richard Price, *A Discourse on the Love of Country*, 2nd ed. (London: T. Cadell, 1789), 47–48.

163 Ibid., 32.

164 Ibid., 20–21.

165 Thomas Jefferson, "Letter to John Adams, October 14, 1816," in *Political Writings*, 296.

166 Ibid., 104.

167 Zuckert, *Natural Rights Republic*, 81.

168 Ibid. See Thomas Jefferson, "Letter to DuPont de Nemours, April 24, 1816," in *Political Writings*, 292.

from the oppressive legislative activity of a parliament whose acts were applicable to the colonies without representation were omnipresent. Despite disagreement on the concept of rights dominant among the Founders, the principled commitment in favor of liberty reflects an idea in opposition to that which underlies the French Declaration. According to the vision expressed by the American Declaration, the pursuit of happiness is a personal question and not a social one. American republicanism is founded on an amalgam between classical republicanism and civic humanism, with the protection of "natural" rights. According to this interpretation, the spirit of the American Declaration is that the object of politics is the protection of natural and prepolitical rights. It does not attribute human self-accomplishment to political participation but to the search for individual happiness. Likewise, the idea that political life would require, as a duty or sign of virtue, the submission of personal interests to the common good, is absent from the American Declaration. This seems to derive from the coordination of the satisfaction of fundamental individual interests called "rights," and from the conditions necessary for the guarantee of these rights. The authors of *The Federalist* noted that a "new political science" was necessary to harmonize elements that seemed up to then incompatible: the promotion of the common good by a republican government and the protection of negative liberty.

Jefferson's conception of this political orientation contributed to the emergence of "natural rights republicanism." According to this conception, government, derived from his philosophy of natural rights, is an instrument to assure property in the broad Lockean sense.[169] The system of government is founded on the idea that human beings possess inalienable rights over themselves, their person, and their property.[170] Jefferson thinks that the real foundation of republican power is not in the idea of "public happiness" in opposition to private happiness, nor in the classical idea, but in the equal rights of citizens.[171] Jefferson criticizes ancient republicanism as having no structure of government for the protection of personal liberty.[172] Public institutions must be handled in conformity with their aim as guaranteeing rights and their nature as "acquisitions." Government must be edified and conducted in a way that proceeds from a real and active consensus, from the will of the governed. Jefferson's republicanism is associated with the assimilation of the public sphere with the theory of private property, that is with the consideration of the state through the prism of the Lockean theory of property and rights to property.[173] Jefferson's defense

169 Thomas Jefferson, *A Summary View of the Rights of British America* [1774], in Ford, ed. *Works of Thomas Jefferson*, vol. 2, 64. See also " Letter to John Norvell" in *Works of Thomas Jefferson*, vol. 10 (New York and London: J. P Putnam's Sons, 1905), 416.

170 Thomas Jefferson, "Letter to P. S. DuPont de Nemours," in *Political Writings*, 292.

171 On personal happiness as covered by an individual right in the thought of the American Founders see also Cecelia M. Kenyon, "Constitutionalism in Revolutionary America," in J. Roland Pennock and John W. Chapman, eds., *Constitutionalism: NOMOS XX* (1979), 84–120, 87.

172 Thomas Jefferson, "Letter to Isaac H. Tiffany, August 26, 1826," in *Political Writings*, 217–18.

173 Cf. Zuckert, *Natural Rights Republic*, 234. On this broad understanding of property see also Reid, *Concept of Liberty*, 72.

of the right to democratic self-government combines deontological and consequentialist elements. This right expresses a fundamental right in itself, while being instrumental to other rights. This theory of the Jeffersonian republic leads to a harmonious combination between stability and security in association with the requirement of principle that governments must be reduced to instruments of protecting natural rights.[174]

The thinkers who discussed natural rights in the Founding Era saw that they were incompatible with slavery. In his influential book *The Rights of the English Colonies*, James Otis denounced slavery in 1763, underlying that all men are "of nature free born" and that slavery "threatens to reduce both Europe and America to the ignorance and barbarity of the darkest ages."[175] The Declaration served as a catalyst for northern states to abolish slavery. The contradiction between the natural rights philosophy of the American Revolution and slavery led to a wave of abolitionism and the firm proclamation of equality during the following century in the United States.[176] Universal suffrage in America was not only a requirement of the equality principle but corresponded to the industrial and commercial needs of a social state profoundly different from the one in France.[177] Jefferson himself made a compelling case against slavery in the first version of the Declaration of Independence, denouncing it as "a cruel war against human nature itself violating its most sacred Rights of Life and Liberty."[178] Even earlier he had written that the colonies desired to abolish slavery, which was "unhappily introduced" there.[179] James Madison also characterized slavery as a sign of "barbarism," an "unnatural traffic," expressing the wish that the federal government would discourage it.[180]

A conception of natural rights existed in the declarations enacted in the American states before the creation of the federal government. It was also dominant during the debate between Federalists and Anti-Federalists on the opportunity of enacting a bill

174 Zuckert, *Natural Rights Republic*, 234–5

175 Otis, *Rights of the English Colonies*, 43–44.

176 Pensylvannia abolished slavery in 1780. Vermont had abolished slavery in 1777, but it was its own country until 1791. In 1790 Benjamin Franklin helped submit a petition to Congress abolishing slavery for all states. See Allen, *Our Declaration*, 241–42. On the contradiction between the content of the Declaration and slavery, see Michael Klarman, *The Framers' Coup*, 259; Jedediah Purdy, *A Tolerable Anarchy: Rebels, Reactionaries and the Making of American Freedom* (Vintage: New York, 2010), 17. Nevertheless, slavery had legal consequences. Slave states could count three fifths of the slave population in their population number for the apportionment of seats in the House of Representatives and in the "electoral college" that elected the president, see US Constitution, Article I, Section 5(3), which was changed by Section 2 of the Fourteenth Amendment. See Madison, Hamilton, and Jay, *The Federalist*, 526–7. Slavery was abolished by the Thirteenth Amendment (1865) in the United States. See Amar, *Bill of Rights*, 163.

177 Émile Boutmy, *Etudes de droit constitutionnel: France, Angleterre, Etats-Unis* (Paris: Plon, 1888), 219.

178 Thomas Jefferson, "Declaration of Independence, First Draft," in *Writings of Thomas Jefferson*, vol. 2, 210.

179 Thomas Jefferson, "A Summary View of the Rights of British America," in *Writings of Thomas Jefferson*, vol. 2, 79.

180 James Madison, "No. 42," in Madison, Hamilton, and Jay, *The Federalist*, 217.

of rights during the elaboration of the Federal Constitution.[181] Alexander Hamilton, considering it impossible to list all natural rights, saw any attempt to make natural liberty positive "unnecessary" and "dangerous."[182] It could create the impression of protecting only the enumerated rights to the exclusion of unenumerated ones.[183] The people have not "surrendered" any of their rights by creating the Constitution.[184] According to this view, only an enumeration of the powers delegated to the federal government would be necessary.[185] The Ninth Amendment was the compromise that assured the ratification of the Federal Constitution.[186] This conception has significant implications for judicial interpretation in deciding the constitutionality of a law that limits the content of a liberty. French judges are inclined to adopt the interpretation that saves the validity of the law. In the area of expressive freedoms, American judges are more willing to favor interpretations giving primacy to liberty. A conception of liberty as "natural" underlies these interpretations.

For the French, formal general laws are mediums of exercise of sovereignty by a general will and essential elements of democracy. The French do not conceive the sphere of society as separated from that of the state, considering that the sphere of commodities and of exchange must be realized and affirmed in the context of a Constitution that encompasses society.[187] *Cato's Letters* implies that the government is nothing more than an object in the service of the aims and interests of the governed and concludes that freedom of expression should be strictly protected, particularly the freedom to criticize the government.

This conception of negative natural rights is reflected today in the current First Amendment doctrine.[188] It is not legitimate for the state to regulate the content of speech. The right to freedom of expression is protected in the United States as a negative right and not a positive one in the sense that it would be required by the state either to provide rights of access to the media[189] or to guarantee the material

181 Thomas Jefferson insisted on the necessity to elaborate a bill of rights in "Letter To James Madison, Paris, December 20, 1787," in *Political Writings*, 349–51.

182 Alexander Hamilton, "No. 84," in Madison, Hamilton, and Jay, *The Federalist*, 445. See also, Cornelia Geer LeBoutillier, *American Democracy and Natural Law* (New York: Columbia University Press, 1950), 110 ff.

183 Alexander Hamilton, "No. 84," 446.

184 Ibid., 445.

185 Randy E. Barnett, "James Madison's Ninth Amendment," in Randy E. Barnett, ed., *The Rights Retained by the People: The History and Meaning of the Ninth Amendment* (Fairfax, VA: George Mason University Press, 1989), 1–49.

186 Ibid. See also Edward S. Corwin, "The 'Higher Law' Background of American Constitutional Law," in Randy E. Barnett, ed., *Rights Retained*, 67–106, 70.

187 Habermas, *Theorie und Praxis*, 104.

188 For an analysis of these cases, see Chapter 1.

189 As discussed in Chapter 4, the Supreme Court has rejected a right to respond for offensive publications that would limit editorial freedom in *Miami Herald Publishing Co.* v. *Tornillo*, 418 US 241 (1974). This argument is valid with the reservation that at the times when the scarcity of audiovisual frequencies made necessary some government intervention, the Supreme Court accepted government intervention in the

conditions that facilitate its exercise. Along the same line of thinking, the government should not intervene in political debate by limiting independent expenditures by corporations.[190] The idea that some social forces have excessive economic power and thus their speech can affect and even distort the public debate is not important enough to mobilize state coercion in favor of equalizing effective speech rights. The state will merely guarantee the protection of its negative aspect by rejecting content distinctions. In this conception of the negative aspect of freedom of expression, the state will not protect individuals from themselves when they engage in modes of self-expression that are considered eccentric by others, for instance when the wearing of conspicuous signs of religious affiliation is at stake.[191]

Natural rights discourse was omnipresent in the area of freedom of religion. The Americans had already realized in the Founding Era that equal freedom of religion for all religious sects would ensure peaceful coexistence among religious groups. Civic identity in the United States is constructed around the idea of equal negative liberty, which emerged to a great extent out of the need to ensure peaceful coexistence among religious communities. The first, mostly protestant colonial communities were not always tolerant of newcomers.[192] Massachusetts and Virginia had legislation against religious minorities, while New York and New Jersey had a policy of de facto religious toleration.[193] Only some colonies were established explicitly as safe spaces for religious dissenters: Maryland, Rhode Island, Pennsylvania, and Carolina. By the beginning of the eighteenth century, Americans realized that peaceful coexistence would be possible if they recognized equal negative liberty for all religious groups. Jefferson authored the Bill for Establishing Religious Freedom, which was largely inspired by Locke's *Letters on Religious Toleration*.[194] The Bill discusses freedom of religion as a natural right and notes that all attempts by civil government to influence religion "beget habits of hypocrisy and meanness."[195] It notes that civil rights should not depend on religious opinions and thus obliging public employees to give up their freedom of religion is a violation of the same natural right. The Bill is against government support of

allocation of the possibility to broadcast. Similarly under the "fairness doctrine," established by the Federal Communications Commission, requiring that public issues be presented by broadcasters and that each side of those issues be given fair coverage was accepted as valid by the Supreme Court, in *Red Lion Broadcasting Co., Inc.* v. *FCC*, 395 US 367 (1969).

190 *Citizens United* v. *FEC*, 558 US 310 (2010).

191 *Zacchini* v. *Scripps – Howard Broadcasting Co.*, 433 US 562 (1977). For an analysis of the relevant cases, see Chapter 1.

192 Thomas Curry, *The First Freedoms: Church and State in America to the Passage of the First Amendment* (Oxford: University Press, 1986), 21.

193 See, Michael W. McConnell, "The Origins and Historical Understanding of Free Exercise of Religion," *Harvard Law Review* 103 (1990), 1409, 1422; Philip Hamburger, "Constitutional Right of Religious Exemption: An Historical Perspective," *George Washington Law Review* 60 (1992), 915, 946

194 Thomas Jefferson, "A Bill for Establishing Religious Freedom" (introduced to the Assembly of Virginia in June 13, 1779 and passed by the Assembly of Virginia in 1786), in *Writings of Thomas Jefferson*, vol. 2, 438–41.

195 Ibid., 439.

religion, noting that obliging a person to contribute for the propagation of religious opinions they do not believe in is tyrannical. The Bill influenced the religion clauses of the First Amendment regarding the separation of church and state. At the time of the Bill of Rights, some states maintained multiple establishments of religion, but mostly Anglican. An establishment had a different meaning in America compared to Europe. It meant mostly financial government support, not necessarily associated with preferential treatment for any one religious group.[196] The First Amendment was agnostic in relation to establishments at the time it was enacted, allowing these issues to be regulated by the states.

Madison also discusses religion as an inalienable natural right that is not abridged when man enters society.[197] On the contrary, the preservation of a free government requires, in his opinion, not only a separation of powers but also that none of them infringes upon the rights of the people.[198] The rulers who limit this right exceed the commission by the people that legitimizes their authority.[199] Madison is also famous for noting that the multiplicity of religious sects was itself a guarantee for religious liberty, because no majority would emerge out of this variety that could "oppress and persecute the rest."[200] Following the incorporation of the Bill of Rights, the First Amendment's prohibition of legislation limiting free exercise of religion became even more compelling and enforceable against the states.

For the French, liberty is meaningful only as liberty of the citizen on the basis of which negative liberties are recognized. According to the American conception, the declaratory and constitutional texts recognize only a part of the liberties of human beings. In case of doubts on whether a liberty exists, it is the presumption in favor of the "retained" liberty that is dominant and it is with this aim that the Ninth Amendment of the Federal Constitution was adopted.[201] The discourse of "retained rights" indicates that natural rights cannot be enumerated, because any enumeration would risk causing an inverse presumption that only the enumerated rights are

196 Leonard Levy, *Origins of the Bill of Rights* (New Haven, CT: Yale University Press, 1999), 92; Curry, *First Freedoms*, 213.

197 James Madison, *Memorial and Remonstrance against Religious Assessments*, [1785], addressing the General Assembly of the Commonwealth of Virginia on a Bill "Establishing a provision for Teachers of the Christian Religion," in *The Writings of James Madison*, vol. 2 (New York: G. P. Putnam's Sons, 1901), 184.

198 Ibid., 185.

199 Ibid., 185.

200 Jonathan Elliot, ed., *Debates On The Adoption Of The Federal Constitution*, Jonathan Elliot (Ayer Co. 1987), 330.

201 Calvin R. Massey, *The Ninth Amendment and the Constitution's Unenumerated Rights Philadelphia* (Philadelphia: Temple University Press, 1995); Daniel A. Farber, *Retained by the People: The "Silent" Ninth Amendment and the Constitutional Rights Americans Don't Know they Have* (New York: Basic Books, 2007); Eugene M. Van Loan III, "Natural Rights and the Ninth Amendment," in Randy E. Barnett, ed., The Rights Retained by the People: The History and Meaning of the Ninth Amendment (Fairfax, VA: George Mason University Press, 1989), 149–177, 163. Norman Redlich, "Are there 'Certain Rights retained by the People?,'" in Barnett, ed., *Rights Retained by the People*, 127–147, 138.

protected. "Natural" rights are thought to exist in the world of the contents of thought, independently from whether they are made positive (in the sense of enacted) by the state. Constitutional protection is not necessary, and it has the simple status of "declaring" their inviolability. The clause of the Ninth Amendment indicates that the written constitutional texts are not the only instruments that codify "higher law," because there are also obligatory unwritten principles.[202] Akhil Reed Amar has emphasized a federalist reading of the clause, in which the clause initially served to protect the self-government of the states against the federal government.[203] From a comparative perspective, it is possible to add that, considerations of federalism aside, the concern with protecting negative liberty was also dominant, and to a greater extent in relation to France. If, as Amar notes, "the Ninth [Amendment] warns readers not to infer from the mere enumeration of a right in the Bill of Rights that implicit federal power in fact exists in a given domain,"[204] this is a concern to limit the powers of the federal state in order to protect the negative aspect of self-government of the states as well as negative liberties. Beyond debates concerning the interpretation of a constitutional text, independently of whether originalism is accepted, the dominant presumption that guides judges when they must decide on the protection of the negative aspect of freedom of speech or any other liberty, is in favor of the protection of liberty.[205] The Supreme Court has developed sophisticated criteria on the basis of which it evaluates limitations to individual liberties. For Laurence Tribe and Michael Dorf, the Ninth Amendment today constitutes a rule of interpretation; it is in reality the same rule of interpretation explicitly enunciated in the Constitution, which aims at strengthening a presumption in favor of liberty.[206]

In America, the reference to natural rights constitutes the prism through which jurists interpret the Constitution on both levels, state and federal. In the political imaginary of the French, the reference to the regenerating role of the general will constitutes the point that gives legitimacy to the state. In the United States, the reference to the respect of natural rights constitutes the legitimizing fiction of state action.[207] According to American republicanism, private liberty is protected exactly

202 Thomas C. Grey, "Do we Have an Unwritten Constitution?," *Stanford Law Review* 27 (1974–75), 703–18, 716. On the same topic, see Paul Brest, "The Fundamental Rights Controversy: The Essential Contradictions of Normative Constitutional Scholarship," *Yale Law Journal* 90 (1980–81), 1063–109; Jack N. Rakove, *Original Meanings: Politics and Ideas in the Making of the Constitution* (New York: Alfred A. Knopf, 1996), 328–29.

203 Amar, *Bill of Rights*, 120, 123.

204 Ibid., 124.

205 Randy Barnett discusses the opinions of Robert Bork, Antonin Scalia, Ronald Dworkin, and Bruce Ackerman to argue that in the majority of cases they pronounce themselves in favor of interpretations that refer to the "original meaning of the text." Randy E. Barnett, *Restoring the Lost Constitution: The Presumption of Liberty* (Princeton University Press, 2004), 92 ff.

206 Laurence Tribe and Michael C. Dorf, *On Reading the Constitution* (Cambridge, MA: Harvard University Press, 1991), 14.

207 Barnett, *Restoring the Lost Constitution*, 32 ff.

because it promotes this republicanism, which makes the distinction between the private and the public indispensable. For French republicanism, liberty is consubstantial with the public good. This version of republicanism recognizes the practical effectiveness of the rights of the citizen by conceiving them in a "legal horizon of coercion."[208]

The analysis in this chapter on the understanding of liberty in France and the United States corresponds to my earlier point that the difference in the understanding of the concept of liberty and of the role of the government pertains to a difference in the understanding of natural law and the interplay between natural law and positive law. According to the conception of ancient-classic natural law, human beings are naturally sociable. The conception of a moral sphere of individuality as such has not emerged yet. Modern natural law expresses an interplay between individuality and sociability. If this conception of modern natural law is in conformity with the idea of a separation between the three spheres – the political sphere, the social sphere, and the moral/ethical sphere – it seems that the French Declaration was elaborated in the context of circumstances where a conception of natural law closer to the ancient one was dominant. The conception of natural law underlying the French Declaration and the French conception of liberty is close to the one of the Ancients in relation to the natural character of society. Rights are rules that ensure social coexistence. This conception is parallel to a rationalist conception of the role of the state, which is supposed to incarnate wisdom and thus assign meaning to liberty. The idea of the general will is at the heart of the device of the state and the emancipation of society must go through the realization of the principles of pure practical reason by the submission of the particular (the interest, the mores, and society) under the universal (reason, the law, and the state). This conception is close to the essentialism of the Ancients. It is very close to the Aristotelian idea that the legislator is prudent, wise, and well informed and that "the law is intelligence without passion."[209] According to this conception, the legislator works on the basis of natural justice by concluding the search for what is naturally just. At the same time, the legislator determines by his own will what is just.[210] Of course, classical natural law could not have revolutionary implications, while modern natural law does. By a paradoxical detour, however, the French conception of natural law finds the ancient conception passing by Rousseau's individualism with revolutionary implications.

If rights exist to the extent that society and the state recognizes them, as is the case in France, this means that they exist only to the extent that they are made "positive," that is they are recognized by positive law. If liberty exists only to the extent that its content and limits are defined by society then this allows for an overdetermination of

208 Rials, *La Déclaration*, 395.

209 Aristotle, *Politique*. See also Aristotle, *Ethique à Nicomaque*; Villey, *Formation*, 93, Pierre Aubenque, "La loi chez Aristote," *Archives de Philosophie du Droit*, 25 (1980), 147–57, 156.

210 Villey, *Formation*, 94–95.

the content of freedom of expression. This conception is strengthened by a general understanding of a moralizing role for the state and of distrust toward individual reason. For freedom of speech, this means greater legitimacy for the state to define the content and its limits when it is in conflict with other rights and collective considerations. In this case, it is legitimate for the state to impose an official version of the truth in order to protect the sensibilities of some social members as is evident in the cases related to the denial of crimes against humanity.[211] It is also legitimate to outlaw eccentric modes of self-expression,[212] as it is legitimate to intervene in order to make sure that citizens have a real and equal possibility to exercise their freedom of expression, as can be seen in the strict regulation of independent expenditures for political campaigns.[213]

211 CC, Decision 2015–512 QPC, Jan. 8, 2016, JO, Jan. 10, 2016, 20.

212 CE Ass., Oct. 27, 1995, 136727, available at: www.legifrance.gouv.fr/affichJuriAdmin.do?idTexte=CETATEXT000007877723.

213 For an analysis of these cases, see Chapter 1.

6

Conclusion

Should the state overdetermine or underdetermine the content of liberty? Is hyperprotection of freedom of speech better than hypersensibility toward competing values? The protection of a liberty and the definition of its content varies in time and space in relation to which activity is valued the most in a culture.[1] Distrust toward the government makes Americans particularly sensible to any limitation of freedom of expression, even when the protection of other rights is at stake. In France, a spirit of prudence and moderation is obvious in jurists' ex ante understanding of the limits of freedom of speech when it is in conflict with other values. The trust toward the government to limit freedom of expression when it violates other rights extends to the point of trusting it to limit this freedom even in cases of self-expression that violate the dignity of the person expressing themselves, as the dwarf-throwing case and the burka ban show. The negative presumption of the Americans toward the government is in opposition to the trust of the French in its positive character. In France, the government *lato sensu* is considered as the legitimate regulator of interpersonal respect. In America, this role is to a great extent undertaken by society itself in the form of political correctness.

The difference in the protection of freedom of speech in France in relation to America depends on a difference in the conception of the role of the government in the structure of contemporary democratic states. The process of understanding the meaning and application of legal norms is the work of the subjectivity and the creative activity of the interpreter. Every interpretive approach toward a text involves a fusion of horizons – of the historical context of the text's authors and the actualizing reading of any jurist.[2] Any jurist interprets a legal text in a way that makes sense for the moment in time they live in. This adaptation depends on some important ideas formed at founding moments that define traditions. A retrospective inquiry into the ideological and political foundations of the French and American democracies, just like the study of the respective revolutionary circumstances that were the

[1] Giovanni Sartori, *Théorie de la démocratie* (Paris: Armand Colin, 1973), 224.

[2] Gadamer, *Vérité et méthode*, 312 ff.

historical foundations of the two democracies, helps to illuminate the difference in how freedom of speech is balanced when in conflict with other values.

American republicanism associates constitutionalism with direct limitations on the power of the government by declarations of rights. The American version of the separation of powers means that institutions are conceived according to the system of checks and balances. This system is permeated with the ideology of "limited government" against a civil society seen as able to regulate itself. The press, despite being an element of civil society, is considered as part of the system of checks and balances. The "abuses" of freedom of the press are rarely considered worthy of repression.[3] The exceptional legal status of freedom of speech, recognized by American courts, can be understood in reference to the structure of the government *lato sensu*. It is not legitimate for the state to intervene within civil society to readjust an equilibrium which already exists there, a situation in which freedom of speech has already affected other rights and liberties. This distrust toward the government was formed out of the political and social needs of the Declaration of Independence. The extraordinary immunity of the American press against defamation and violation of privacy actions can be partially explained by considering the press as having a quasi-institutional role, as control on the power of government.

The "common character"[4] of the French people was formed in relation to different political problems. The distrust toward the holders of power at the moment of the French Revolution was the reverse of the belief in their positive character once those who had usurped it were removed.[5] The transfer of sovereignty from the king to the people was a sufficient guarantee. The reference to sovereignty in the French imaginary of power, dating from the success of the royal power to unify the French territory against the feudal power, can be explained as an attempt to affirm the pre-eminence of the state upon society, and to transcend cultural and political particularisms. The political and administrative centralization established by the monarchy before the revolution had the same aim. As Arendt notes, Sieyès's theory of representation uses the notion of unity of the nation, substituting it for the monarchic will. In his writings, representation must, in the name of the primacy of the general interest upon any particularity, make society speak with one voice and not express the geographic, cultural, social, or economic differences.[6] In this framework, representation is conceived by Sieyès as a consequence of the division of social labor, liberating citizens from the tasks accomplished by their representatives, allowing them to enjoy individual rights and to look after their own affairs external to public life. Citizens, judges in principle of everything, in reality choose those who will be in

3 Peter B. Edelman, "Free Press v. Privacy: Haunted by the Ghost of Justice Black," *Texas L.R.* 68 (1989–90), 1195–234.

4 According to Montesquieu's phrase, in *Œuvres complètes*, 173.

5 Gauchet, *Révolution des droits de l'homme*, 38.

6 According to this theory of representation, every deputy must be free in his decisions, but himself a representative of the entire nation. Jaume, *Discours jacobin*, 285.

a position to make political decisions in their place.[7] In the French representative system, the Assembly, once chosen, is identified with the nation.

The comparison of the broader ideological origins of the protection of free speech can be instructive toward reflecting on the just limits of speech. Understanding the social and political context that led to the emergence of a legal rule can inspire a reflection on whether there are still reasons to maintain a rule or whether the rule needs to change. Some scholars have expressed skepticism over efforts to elaborate universal standards for regulating speech.[8] For some others, understanding the ideologies behind the emergence of a legal rule and the historical trajectory of the emergence of this legal rule does not mean accepting historical determinism.[9] It is possible to reflect *in abstracto* about just criteria for limiting speech. Habermas notes that cultural values and norms are candidates to be considered in a philosophical reflection as to the justifiability of rules: we should engage in a normative reflection on whether these norms are just. The two historical traditions analyzed in this book can inspire a philosophical reflection that takes into consideration the importance of exercising state power to define the limits of free expression in order to protect others from harm and to eliminate social power dynamics.

As Habermas notes, the law extends between facts and norms.[10] A part of the legal rules that we have is conditioned by our situation in a lifeworld and the coercion that this situation entails. This coercion can be consolidated social power as well as consolidated understandings of justice. Nevertheless, the law is also by definition a normative phenomenon. As such it always evolves as our standards of normativity evolve. Habermas also offers a theory test of the validity and justice of norms, the ideal speech situation. Habermas thinks that it is possible to transcend the diversity of backgrounds of the various interlocutors and claims of relativity of values, thanks to the rationality that is inherent in all communicative processes. Communicative processes all around the world are oriented toward reaching understanding. Therefore, all participants who engage in them in all languages make some normative presuppositions. Habermas builds off Karl-Otto Apel's formulation that every person who engages in argument presupposes a real communication community, which they have become a member of through a process of socialization, and an ideal communication community, which would be capable of adequately understanding the meaning of their arguments and judging their truth in a definitive manner.[11] Everywhere

7 Benjamin Constant is known as having formulated the need for representation in terms of division of labor, identifying the liberty of the moderns in the security of private enjoyments in " De la liberté des Anciens comparée à celle des Modernes" in Marcel Gauchet ed., *Écrits politiques* (Paris: Gallimard, 1997).

8 Robert Post, in Robert Post and Peter Molnar, "Interview with Robert Post," in Michael Herz and Peter Molnar, eds., *The Content and Context of Hate Speech: Rethinking Regulation and Responses* (Cambridge University Press, 2012), 30.

9 Cf. Eric Heinze, *Hate Speech and Democratic Citizenship* (Oxford University Press, 2016), 183.

10 Habermas, *Between Facts and Norms*.

11 Ibid., 322.

concepts such as "truth, rationality, justification and consensus, even if interpreted differently and applied according to different criteria, play the same grammatical role."[12] Participants in argumentation make validity claims that transcend their context. This rationality inherent in our everyday communicative processes makes it possible to envision an ideal speech situation where only the force of the best argument is valid.

Despite the criticisms that have been addressed to him on the very possibility of an ideal speech situation, the importance of the dialectic in his theory is what also conditions any normative comparative approach to institutions. It can provide the starting point for a normative evaluation of the relevant solutions. As William Ewald notes, comparative law is "an essentially philosophical enterprise"[13] aiming to uncover the reasons and justifications that underlie legal rules and seeking answers to legal questions. This study, by analyzing the intellectual foundations of the protection of free speech in France and in the United States, aims to incite a reflection on whether principles and rules elaborated in the past to meet concrete sociopolitical needs are still relevant to address contemporary concerns in the understanding of the limits of rights. How can the variety in the protection of freedom of speech be instructive in view of reaching criteria of balancing between the expressive freedoms and other values when they are in conflict?

A deontological defense of freedom of expression would justify the protection of one's liberty if it passes the universalizability test, according to which the liberty of the agent must be able to accord itself with the liberty of everyone else according to a universal law.[14] If speech causes harm, it is not universalizable. The question thus becomes one of evaluating when harm exists. A consequentialist theory would argue that it is important to weigh consequences. Dworkin offers a theory that combines elements from deontology and consequentialism. According to Dworkin, there are three grounds for limiting a right:[15] firstly, in marginal cases when the values protected by the right are not really at stake; secondly, when the right defined to include the marginal case would abridge some other competing right; thirdly, when the right defined to include a marginal case implies a cost to society of a degree that would be enough to justify an assault on dignity or equality by limiting the right. For freedom of expression it is important thus to evaluate the cost of tolerating a violation of another right or the social cost of protecting expression overall.

Popular sovereignty is associated with the exchange of arguments. Since there is disagreement on questions of politics, democracy establishes that it is the popular will that must be prevalent upon any other method of reaching collective decisions.

12 Ibid., 311.

13 William Ewald, "Comparative Jurisprudence (I): What Was it Like to Try a Rat?," *University of Pennsylvania Law Review* 143 (1995), 1898–2251, 1947.

14 Emmanuel Kant, *Métaphysique des moeurs: deuxième partie: doctrine de la vertu*, trans. Alexis Philonenko, 5th ed. (Paris: Vrin, 1996), 52.

15 Dworkin, *Taking Rights Seriously*, 200.

It presupposes the possibility to decide on what is right and what is wrong in politics on the basis of majority decision-making. Does this mean that the majority becomes the measure of knowledge? Should societies follow majority decision-making to avoid the risk of an infinite regression? Is democratic argumentation enough to protect negative liberties, by definition conceived as beyond majoritarian control? Alternatively, the acceptance of the possibility that the majority can err confirms the idea that the "falsity" of an idea cannot be a criterion to exclude it from public debate, to refuse people the right of access to information and opinions that can have an effect on their decisions. Whatever might be the force of the majority and its eventual errors, the consideration of the liberty to criticize it helps the majority to see its errors and to recognize its fallibility. Enlightenment thought that stresses the need to use one's own understanding and Tocqueville's fears against the uniformity of thought that social majorities lead to are relevant here.

An ex ante understanding in favor of state action can legitimize its action to limit freedom of speech. The conception dominant in France has the potential to lead to excesses of determination of the content of freedom of expression and a regulation of the marketplace of ideas that ends up harming the development of free personality. A negative presumption of the role of the state and the consideration that freedom of expression, as an exceptional human activity exposing defects of government, make state intervention to limit this freedom illegitimate, even when the protection of other values is at stake. In the United States, distrust toward the state and the necessity for transparency for public officials leads to an underestimation of the normative claim to privacy and a reticence to protect other values when freedom of expression is in conflict with them, even for vulnerable persons like minor delinquents or victims of sexual violence.[16] As *Citizens United* shows, this is the case when freedom of expression means disproportionately affecting the political debate.[17]

The American approach allows self-realization, by permitting access to a quantity of information that a person needs to deepen their reflection in order to form and realize their ends in life. The concern with guaranteeing the flow of information necessary to form individuality has the power to negate individuality. The American approach, by negating the protection of privacy in its informational aspects indispensable to self-realization, seems to refuse the possibility of a self-realization. In this way, the individual is provided with the elements they need to develop their authentic self, while at the same time the spatial sphere, inside which this development can take place, is negated. The French legal order, while protecting other values when they are in conflict with freedom of speech, does not sufficiently protect its aspect as people's freedom to make decisions for themselves, to the extent that the positive presumption in favor of the role of the state ends up depriving individuals of

[16] *Cox Broad. Corp.* v. *Cohn*, 420 US 469 (1975); *Florida Star* v. *B.F.J.*, 491 US 524 (1989); *Globe Newspaper* v. *Superior Court*, 457 US 596, 607–8 (1982); *Smith* v. *Daily Mail Publ'g Co.*, 443 US 97, 108–9 (1979).

[17] *Citizens United* v. *FEC*. 558 US 310 (2010).

the information that would be necessary to define their subjectivity and individuality. It also leads to limiting the possibilities for self-expression that derive from considerations of autonomy. This is obvious in the dwarf-throwing case as well as in the headscarf ban cases.

The crucial question consists in knowing who incarnates and who best expresses "reason": individuals or the state? The response in France favors the state, as is inevitable given the residue of divine sovereignty of the antecedent political formation. The democratic state in France, having succeeded the *dignitas* of the king, and the parliament, which expresses the general will of the nation, will ensure that the citizens attain their *dignitas*. By providing what is necessary to guarantee a life that is worthy of being human for everyone, this may lead to excessive regulation that negates the *dignitas* of the citizen in the sense of internal liberty and autonomy. In the legal and political context of the United States, a less ambitious conception of the state is dominant. The distrust toward the role of the state is not converted into trust. *Novus ordo seclorum* is associated with a conception of the state as arbitrator of the free play of individual reason in the social sphere. The political realism of Americans corresponds to a different normative conception of democracy.

Guaranteeing to everyone the possibility of using their reason and conceiving in this respect a positive role of the state has the potential to lead to defining this very reason, which is evident from the situation in France. The reason of the law defines the reason of liberty. The idealist vision of the law and the state as reconstructing reality leads to the negation of the possibility for individual reason. National sovereignty can only produce good laws, which do not threaten individual reason but contribute to its realization. This definition of individual reason runs the risk of leading to its total absorption: the individual will be forced to use their reason in a way dictated by the state against their wish to give a different content to it, even when their acts do not harm others.

The political and legal order of the United States and the dominant procedural conception of democracy are characterized by the multiplication of instances that express the reason of the state in relation to filtering and controlling the final result and its impact upon individual reason. The distrust toward the "reason" of the law goes together with checks and balances on various levels. The optimism of the Enlightenment leads the French to hope that human reality will respond to the rational legal ordering of the law, which is in conformity with the interest of everyone and of all. The same optimism leads Americans to hope that this will be the result of individual reason. In America, priority is given to the possibility to develop individual reason, which will lead to the best results for everyone.

The moralizing role of the state includes the danger of the "slippery slope." In states where it is legitimate to regenerate humanity and to guarantee to everyone the material possibilities of the exercise of reason there is the risk of overdetermining the reason of the individual in a way that negates individuality. It can lead to state paternalism in relation to the ideas that must be allowed to circulate. Insisting on the continuity between the internal dialogue and the external dialogue from its proximity to the theoretical scheme of Rousseau, France ends up negating subjectivity. If it is being a citizen that helps someone elevate themselves to human dignity, the distinction between the personal and the political becomes almost impossible, with negative consequences for subjectivity. The distinction between internal liberty and external liberty seems to be almost negated to the extent that every action has the potential to present social interest. France distrusts the use of individual reason: this reason needs to be guided and formed by the state, to some extent reminiscent of the Hegelian rational state, which always constitutes the best possible instantiation of reason in history.

Is distrust toward individual reason associated with the distrust of the postmoderns – in relation to the very possibility to think "rationally" – or to the paternalism of the premoderns to compensate this insufficiency of individual reason? The distrust toward individual reason was reaffirmed by the atrocities of the Second World War, and the need to avoid any repetition of this movement in Europe led to this paradoxical union between postmodern and premodern elements: distrust toward individual reason, and trust in state reason to form individual reason. The reaffirmation of the reason of the state as the purifying entity after the Second World War expresses a deeper tradition of trust present in Europe.

The prohibitions of holocaust denial stem from the same paternalistic conception of the state, which has the mission in France and other European countries to protect its citizens against the danger of arriving at erroneous understandings of historical facts. It is part of the same moralizing role toward its citizens that is recognized in the government. If it is legitimate for the state to intervene and define the content of freedom of speech, then it is legitimate for it to protect an official version of the truth through the criminalization of speech denying it. However, this ban can be interpreted as expressing feelings of guilt within European collective consciousness arising from the atrocities that happened in its midst.[18] There are very significant dangers in the use of the punitive mechanism of the state in this way. It is motivated by paternalistic and irrational considerations within collective consciousness, such as this feeling of guilt. Furthermore, outlawing the denial of the holocaust can be discriminatory unless France and other European countries outlaw the denial of other genocides that have taken place. This can lead to the danger of a "slippery slope" where speech of crucial importance to democratic political debate is outlawed. Existing legislation has led to legal adventures before courts for historians expressing interpretations of historical facts that are not in conformity with dominant understandings of the same facts.[19] The bans can lead to versions of official national truths that are in tension with the idea of liberal democracy. In

[18] For this approach, see Ioanna Tourkochoriti, "Challenging Historical Facts And National Truths: An Analysis Of Cases From France And Greece," in Uladzislau Belavusau and Aleksandra Glyszczynska-Grabias, eds., *Law And Memory: Towards Legal Governance of History* (Cambridge University Press, 2017), 151–74.

[19] Ibid.

the area of holocaust denial, the causal link between speech and harm is very weak. It is difficult to see harm in a comment that a person makes about the external world in the absence of an individualized offense or incitement to hatred.

The distrust toward government intervention that is dominant in the American legal system led to a Supreme Court decision that even protected untruthful speech.[20] According to the Supreme Court, the threat of criminal prosecution can inhibit speakers from making true statements, thereby "chilling" speech, which would be characteristic of a totalitarian Orwellian government. For the Court:

> Permitting the government to decree this speech to be a criminal offense, whether shouted from the rooftops or made in a barely audible whisper, would endorse government authority to compile a list of subjects about which false statements are punishable. That governmental power has no clear limiting principle. Our constitutional tradition stands against the idea that we need Oceania's Ministry of Truth."[21]

In this case, the justification offered by the Supreme Court is compelling. Maintaining laws that criminalize the denial or trivialization of crimes against humanity, can have pernicious unintended consequences upon important constitutional freedoms such as academic freedom and the freedom of association.[22] These laws are usually the result of collective disapproval of some of the worst atrocities committed throughout history. As a matter of principle though, giving legal form to the collective consciousness in this way in association with a conception of state paternalism can lead to a situation where it is difficult to halt the irrational elements within collective consciousness. The paradox here is obvious in that state rationality, defined by irrational elements, uses the punitive function of the state to impose itself upon individual rationality.

The paternalistic vision of the state that is dominant in France leads to accepting limitations to self-expression, such as in the burka ban and dwarf-throwing cases. In these cases, a reference to a conception of human dignity as imposing obligations toward the self that are enforceable through state coercion is dominant. In France, it is legitimate to limit speech when it violates another person's dignity as it is legitimate to limit self-expression when a person violates their dignity. In France, "dignity" is protected according to the Roman conception of the term, and the individual can be forced to be "dignified" in the same way that they can be forced to be "free," when their opinions prevent them from realizing their "liberty" and their "dignity," as the dwarf-throwing case shows. Dignity is not understood as the expression par excellence of the possibility to assert one's plans for life and make one's most important

[20] *United States* v. *Alvarez*, 132 S. Ct. 2537 (2012).

[21] Ibid., 2547, quoting George Orwell, *Nineteen Eighty-Four* [1949] (Centennial ed., 2003). Even the dissenting opinion in this case agrees that false statements about historical events cannot be banned as it is impossible to know "how certain must it be that a statement is false before the ban may be upheld" and "who should make that calculation." Ibid., 2564 (Alito, J., dissenting).

[22] See Ioanna Tourkochoriti, "Challenging Historical Facts," 153–64.

life decisions. There is a performative contradiction in any attempt to "force someone to be free," as the burka ban and dwarf-throwing cases show. Referring to the concept of human dignity to limit a person's freedom is a performative contradiction, an enunciation whose force, in a context of communication, contradicts its content.[23] This means using one conception of dignity against another: dignity as social status against dignity as liberty. The ban on dwarf-throwing ostensibly promotes dignity and liberates the individual, but in reality it negates it to the extent that it negates the liberty of the individual to undertake this activity as an opportunity to make money that does not harm others. Allowing the person to define the meaning that life has for them, even if that means being a human cannonball, is based on a conception of dignity as autonomy and inviolability. The problem with dignity as social status here is that this social status is defined by an external point of view and not by the point of view of the person in question. Sanctions should not be imposed upon behaviors that come across as eccentric. If the state considers some spectacles as being of inferior value compared to others, then it has the ability to dissuade its citizens by making spectacles of a higher value available to them. In this case the state addresses their reason. There is something deeply problematic with using the mechanism of state constraint to promote these goals. The Lockean principle of reliance on individual reason that underlies the American conception of liberty must be given preference in this case.

Similarly, in the case of the burka ban, the French government proposes that the ban liberates women to the extent that it allows them to dress as they wish. Wearing a burka voluntarily, according to this conception, means that the women in question are suffering from false consciousness. The ban allows them to find "authenticity" of will. It liberates women from the domination of religion according to the precepts of the French Enlightenment. The question emerges whether France has gone too far. And whether this kind of prohibition is the best possible way to promote gender equality. We need to consider if it is legitimate for the state to protect women from themselves and to intervene in the relationship that a woman has with herself as expressed in her dress choices. The French conception of *laicité* was imposed from the top to bottom as opposed to the conception of secularism in America that emerged from the bottom to top.[24]

One of the reasons put forward by the French government to justify the burka ban was the refusal of fraternity of the very possibility of social coexistence associated with the will to hide oneself, and thus incivility.[25] The inability to tolerate this behavior has its origins in the values of the French republic. The mission of the

[23] See Jürgen Habermas, *Morale et Communication*, trans. Christian Bouchindhomme (Paris, Cerf 1989), 101.

[24] Ioanna Tourkochoriti, "The Burka Ban: Divergent Approaches to Freedom of Religion in France and in the U.S.A.," *William and Mary Bill of Rights Journal* 20 (2012) 791–852.

[25] Assemblée Nationale, "Rapport d'information fait en application de l'Article 45 du Règlement n°2262 (2010)," citing the hearing of Élisabeth Badinter (Sept. 9, 2009), 118.

government is supposedly to liberate individuals from poverty but also from their "immaturity." One can argue against this by noting that a major idea of the Enlightenment is to allow the individual to make mistakes and learn from them. There is a performative contradiction in liberating women from the domination of one authority, the authority of religion, while establishing domination by the authority of the state. A basic element of the philosophical discourse of modernity lies in allowing individuals to define for themselves the degree of their allegiance to community.[26] Eccentric behavior that seems incomprehensible from the point of view of a majority is to be accepted in the name of protecting freedom. The state adopts an internal point of view and projects an interpretation of the meaning of wearing a religious symbol upon the persons who are wearing it themselves. The ban is consistent with a conception according to which it is citizenship that dignifies human beings, by defining how human beings should treat themselves and what opinions about religion they should be exposed to. This conception is consistent with the idea that civil society coincides with political society. If it is belonging to a community that, thanks to language, contributes to moralization and the development of the discursive, reasonable faculties of man, the nexus between the importance of this membership to the community and the overdetermination on behalf of the community of the spheres that should belong to the judgment of the subject becomes obvious. It is dictated by accepting the possibility for the state to overdetermine liberty and to limit the very possibility of reflexivity for the subject. If it is society that makes the reflexivity of the subject possible, the individual should preserve the possibility of critical appreciation of the norms of society. The subject should retain the possibility to withdraw from the community and to reflect critically for themselves on their very membership to a community.

The French government defended its position as intervening in order to annihilate social power, the power exercised upon women by their families. It is extremely difficult to adopt an internal point of view and be aware of the reasons why women decide to wear a burka. The state should not engage in an interpretation of the content of a liberty. Frequently wearing a burka is self-imposed. The burka can be a choice liberating women from the social constraints of fashion, which they see as part of a materialistic way of life. Freedom contains the possibility of some voluntary servitude.[27] If it is social pressure that the French state aims to eliminate then penalties for the members of the families who force women to cover their faces can be justified, but not upon women themselves. Similarly, regulation of covering one's face in schools can be justified if it is proven that it seriously impedes the educational process. However, outlawing the hijab, which does not cover the face, is unlikely to have a similar effect.

26 For analysis from this perspective, see Tourkochoriti, "Burka Ban," 847.

27 Étienne Balibar, "Dissonances dans la laïcité," in Charlotte Nordmann, ed., *Le foulard islamique en questions* (Paris: ed. Amsterdam, 2004), 15, 24.

The French state is seen as having legitimacy to make sure that the citizens can enjoy "real" liberty and not merely "formal" liberty, an idea omnipresent in the debates around the moment of the revolution. Nevertheless, in this case it is not legitimate for the state, instead of the citizen, to interpret what "real" freedom is, as it inevitably distorts the internal perspective of the individual. Unlike the cases of socioeconomic inequality where it is legitimate for the state to intervene and engage in redistribution, in the cases of religious freedom any attempt to make sense of a religious doctrine from an external perspective runs the risk of leading to misunderstandings detrimental to individual liberty. In France, it is legitimate to protect the citizens from poverty as it is legitimate to protect the citizens from their own immaturity. Government intervention in the economic sphere does not need to go together with government intervention in the sphere of ideas and self-expression, to the extent that there is no harm to others. In France, it is legitimate to limit freedom of speech in order to protect the rights of others, in the same way that it is legitimate for the state to have a paternalistic role in the protection of the individual from their personal immaturity. It is possible though to have one without having the other. It is possible to accept that it is legitimate for the state to intervene to limit freedom of expression when there is harm to others, while it is not legitimate for the state to intervene in cases of self-expression, such as the dwarf-throwing and the burka ban.

In the case of the burka ban, the French state should have offered the possibility to reflect upon the practice of wearing a burka. It is persuasion and not coercion that respects those whose beliefs and religious self-expression seem incomprehensible to others. Our *demoi* must today be engaged in reflexive acts of self-constitution due to the inevitable movement of populations.[28] As Habermas notes, the public sphere is composed of the fluid networks of our everyday communicative practices on issues of public concern.[29] These everyday interactions are the best medium that societies of reception have to express to women and members of their family their ideas about wearing the burka. If there are elements of gender inequality and gender oppression in a woman's decision to cover herself by wearing a headscarf or a burka, then it is by engaging in a conversation with them and their families that these elements can be dissipated. Dialogue and not prohibition is what respects the women's self-expression and dignity in this case. It is dialogue that shows respect toward them and the unconditional value of their humanity.

The American solution, which finds inspiration in distrust toward political power and the "fear" of "slippery slopes" – of seeing the state involved in the domains that affect other aspects of autonomy, such as the possibility of the subject to think and act for themselves – leads to the impasse of underprotecting important values like privacy. The American legal and political order allows the individual to reflect and judge by themselves, thereby recognizing a sphere of interiority and of the

[28] Seyla Benhabib, *Another Cosmopolitanism* (Cambridge University Press, 2006), 35–36.

[29] Habermas, *Between Facts and Norms*, 365–66.

fundamental personal decisions beyond the control of politics. The moral sphere seems to be clearly distinguished from the political sphere, and internal liberty separated from external liberty. The use of individual reason will help the citizens arrive at the best possible conclusion in determining questions of morality and politics. The dominant optimism in the capacities of reason and the distrust toward state coercion give rise to the hope that the personal use of reason will lead to the best possible results for the liberty and the dignity of the individual and of society. In cases of self-expression, such as headscarf bans and bans of other clothing, when no harm to others exists then the American solution for protecting this aspect of liberty is compelling.

However, the costs of this general liberty seem at times too heavy and particularly for the persons upon whom they are imposed in cases of violations of other rights, such as the right to privacy. The negative presumption against the state risks causing considerable harm to those who are socially vulnerable. The fundamental principle that regulates the very possibility of coexistence, the one of universalizability of the recognition of a liberty or a right, is not taken into consideration in relation to some uses of freedom of expression, which risks causing severe harm to the persons affected. Would social democracy, with its potential risk to overdetermine the content of liberty and its undesirable consequences for the sphere of subjectivity, be preferable, or is libertarian democracy and its negative potentialities for the rights and the sensibilities of others the better option? Delinquent minors and victims of sexual violence are the inverse slippery slopes, those of a legal and political system that displays an exaggerated trust toward the self-regulating possibilities of individual reason. The state is not always a "generating source of disorder," as Paine thought, and the protection of vulnerability is an aim, which legitimizes state action.

Does the good of the *polis* require the sacrifice of other values? The emergence of privacy as a value is also an important element of modernity. Can the objectivation of a person's privacy be relevant to democratic debate?[30] Privacy understood as the necessity for the individual to keep a sphere of activities protected against social or state intervention is important and legitimate. The right to privacy is founded on the notion of autonomy and the dignity of the human person. The core of the same right is founded on the respect that human beings owe each other to keep a distance from one another, on the basis of their only quality of being human, transcending geographical limits and cultural differences. The periphery of its protection, however, finds its foundation in the conventions and the way of life of every society.[31] The definition of the concept of "privacy" always necessitated a latent normative choice both in time and in space, concerning its meaning amidst the indefinite scope of the possible understandings of the term. Even if there is consensus upon

30 Cr. Guy Haarscher, "Paradoxes de la liberté d'expression," in Guy Haarscher, ed., *Les médias entre droit et pouvoir* (Editions de l'Université de Bruxelles, 1995), 112.

31 Frederick Schauer, "Free Speech and the Social Construction of Privacy," *Social Research* 68 (2001), 221–31.

a solid foundation of a core right to privacy, differences persist in social rules concerning the facets and the particular manifestations that will be protected by the law. In this sense, privacy and "human dignity," concepts used interchangeably, are both protean.[32]

Privacy is necessary for the exercise of activities in public life. Protecting the "dignity" of someone in the sense attributed by the Romans to this term – in the sense of public *persona* – allows the person to arrive at self-realization, to deepen their reflection and to make decisions that are authentically theirs. Privacy is essential to the process of construction of personal identity and for the search of self. The protection of this same value serves psychological aims; it is associated with the psychic and intellectual needs of man. The "maturity" of a person is appreciated in relation to their possibility to develop a public *persona*, which could correspond harmoniously with the world of others. The possibility to obey social morality presupposes the development of individuality that can take place in the intimacy of the private sphere. The crucial question becomes finding the equilibrium between the public and the private personality, the possibility to interact peacefully in public without being exposed in ways that would be emotionally traumatic or would inhibit the free operation of sentiments, thought, and imagination.

Privacy is an important liberty that derives from autonomy. It denotes the need to protect a condition of being apart from others, which favors the development of mental activities. Emotional vulnerability is a foundation for the protection of privacy. Isolation from others favors psychological ends like peace and mental health. It allows the individual to define their existence against the pressure to conform to social expectations.[33] The impossibility to control one's appearance before others can have negative effects upon the conception of the self. The impossibility to define and control our public person can result in a loss of self. Privacy is considered a condition in arriving at autonomy, as the extent of the social and legal space left to the individual, so that they can develop the emotional, cognitive, spiritual, and moral powers of an autonomous agent. It constitutes the sphere par excellence inside which the relation that every individual maintains with themselves is developed. The right to privacy is equivalent to the protection of this core of existence of the person, which is crucial to our understanding of us as persons

[32] For the difficulties in defining privacy, see W. A. Parent, "A New Definition of Privacy for the Law," *Law and Philosophy* 2 (1983), 305–38; Hyman Gross, "The Concept of Privacy," *New York University Law Review* 42 (1967), 34–54; Judith Wagner DeCew, "The scope of Privacy in Law and Ethics," *Law and Philosophy* 5 (1986), 145–73; Raymond Wacks, "The Poverty of 'Privacy,'" *The Law Quarterly Review* 96 (1980) 73–89; Jack Hirshleifer, "Privacy: Its Origin, Function and Future," *Journal of Legal Studies* (1980), 649; H. J. McCloskey, "The Political Ideal of Privacy," *Philosophical Quarterly* (1971), 303; Richard Epstein, "A Taste for Privacy? Evolution and the Emergence of a Naturalistic Ethic," *Journal of Legal Studies* (1980), 665.

[33] Sidney Jourard "Some Psychological Aspects of Privacy," *Law & Contemporary Problems* 31 (1966), 307–18, 308.

capable of having a conception of the good and of devoting ourselves to activities that are dictated by this conception.[34]

Treating a human being like an end and never as a means is equivalent to recognizing in them the possibility to assert their own ends and to allow them the space to pursue these ends by themselves. The right to privacy is indispensable to understanding the person as capable of having their own conception of the good and to devote themselves to activities, dictated by this conception. Privacy is articulated in concentric spheres of intimacy protecting many types of human relations. The relationship that every person maintains with themselves in order to progressively add the various levels of social relations and many objectives of association would be included in the core. Deciding which kind of information on someone will be circulated derives from personal autonomy, from one's decision to choose, for a territory, the protection of privacy for information that a person or a group would not want to make known to others. The legal knowledge and the capacity of the person to control who will have access to information concerning them is associated with their aptitude to develop various types of interpersonal relations concerning the quantity and the type of information that they decide to make known, and is associated with the idea of the variety of the social contexts of communication. Having control over cognitive appropriation, in which part of one's physical existence is experienced by someone else, is necessary for self-realization. Obtaining information on someone without their consent means refusing them due respect, as this makes them perceive themselves as an object of control, violating their understanding of themselves as a moral agent. The impossibility to control how one appears before others can have negative effects on the conception of the self; the impossibility to define and control our persona can lead a person to a loss of an identity. Hard cases include speech on politicians' privacy, since in the United States it is accepted that a part of the electoral body can consider these elements to have a value for political debate. In this respect, the narrow conception of "newsworthiness," which is dominant in French law, seems to be preferable to the extensive protection of freedom of speech. Even for public figures, French law requires strict relevance with the needs of information for aspects related to private life.

In thinking about hate speech, both models, the French and the American should be appreciated critically. The reluctance to limit hate speech in the American legal system overlooks the performative dimensions of speech. European legal systems provide for enhancements of responsibility in the area of defamation and insults when these take place on the basis of membership of a "racial" group. In this case, the social consequences of hate speech are not negligible in the cases of an individualized attack against a person. The American conception is based on

[34] Michael. A. Weinstein, "The Uses of Privacy in the Good Life," NOMOS XIII 99; Sissela Bok, *Secrets: On the ethics of Concealment and Revelation* (New York: Vintage, 1998), 15 ff.

a distinction between speech and acts and considers the harm caused to others by hate speech as not being significant enough to mobilize state coercion. American law contains penalty enhancements for hate crimes where acts are involved. It is doubtful whether this distinction holds. In a context of oppression and marginalization, speech is equivalent to action on the basis of the performative aspects of discourse, which J. L. Austin has made us aware of.[35] Austin notes that speech is equivalent to action in certain contexts of communication. Depending on the time, space, and circumstances in which they take place, some statements commit actions either by being said – an illocutionary effect – or by the fact of being said – the perlocutionary effects of hate speech. For Austin, in a pragmatic context of enunciation, a speech act can have such an illocutionary force as to produce effects in the Popperian world of the contents of thought,[36] considered through a phenomenological prism. In a context of marginalization and discrimination, hate speech perpetuates this marginalization. The crucial characteristic that makes these enunciations speech acts is the sensibility and vulnerability of the addressees. Hate speech causes serious harm, which implies the use of words to preserve division, inequality, and subordination between social groups, relativizing the distinction between speech and act. Hate speech operates as an act to the extent that it reproduces the oppression experienced by the victims and leads even to internalizing racist mental forms.[37]

Hate speech negates the effective exercise of the principle of equal citizenship. The primary good that Rawls calls "the social basis of self-respect"[38] is refused to the addressees of hate speech because their status in the community, their opportunities, their self-worth, and enjoyment of life are limited, as social status and self-respect are defined dialectically in reference to their recognition by others.[39] When historically oppressed individuals speak, they are not heard. Feminist scholars have made this argument in the case of women[40] and it is also relevant in the area of racist speech.[41] Social power dynamics is a factor that needs to be considered here. The law can and

35 John Austin, *How to Do Things with Words* (Cambridge, MA: Harvard University Press, 1975).

36 Karl Popper, "Epistemology without a Knowing Subject," in *Objective Knowledge* (Oxford University Press, 1972), 106 ff.

37 Pierre-Andre Taguieff, *La force du préjugé: essai sur le racisme et ses doubles* (Paris: Gallimard, 1990), 56.

38 Rawls, *Political Liberalism*, 366.

39 Philosophers and sociologists have stressed the need for intersubjective recognition for the formation of one's personality. See Georg Friedrich Hegel, *Phenomenology of Spirit*, §187, 113–14; Erving Goffman, *The Presentation of Self in Everyday Life* (London: Penguin 1990), 28.

40 Catharine MacKinnon, *Only Words* (Cambridge, MA: Harvard University Press, 1996); Rae Langton, "Speech Acts and Unspeakable Acts," *Philosophy & Public Affairs* 22 (1993), 293–330; Rae Langton, "Whose Right? Ronald Dworkin, Women and Pornographers," *Philosophy & Public Affairs* 19 (1990), 311–59. In the same spirit, cf. Pierre Bourdieu, *Ce que parler veut dire: l'économie des échanges linguistiques* (Paris: Fayard, 1982).

41 See Ioanna Tourkochoriti, "Should Hate Speech Be Protected? Group Defamation, Party Bans, Holocaust Denial and the Divide between (France) Europe and the United States," *Columbia Human Rights Law Review* 45 (2014) 552–622.

should be used in a way that eliminates social power dynamics.[42] Hate speech introduces constraints, as Habermas would say, upon the participations of some people in discussions that take place in the communicative network of the public sphere.[43] In this case, the focus should be on the social aspect of exercising the right to free speech. This means that instead of referring to a "natural rights" theory in order to justify extended protection, an approach that focuses on the social value of speech for citizenship, such as the one dominant in France, can provide a basis for limiting speech to avoid harm to others.

Critical race theory scholars note the psychological harm that hate speech causes upon "racialized" individuals.[44] They also note the social and economic inequalities that prevent historically oppressed social groups from exercising their freedom of expression. Their freedom of speech is merely formal and not real. A First Amendment understanding of government abstention toward hateful insulting speech seems to perpetuate real social inequalities within American society.

When speech causes harm to others, the equality rationale that Dworkin discusses is not plausible.[45] As Schauer notes, the principles of equality and dignity are not always helpful in all cases of speech.[46] When a speaker uses hate speech to target an individualized person, they exclude themselves from the protection of equality due to the harm they inflict upon others. The harm here consists of the projection of a stereotype upon a person that negates their autonomy. Individualized racist defamatory speech projects a stereotypical identity upon a person and does not allow them to show to others their identity. Racial stereotypes can be associated with negative personality traits that are projected upon a person in a way that deprives them of the possibility to show others their own identity. By not allowing a person to project their identity as they understand it there is an offense to human dignity in the sense of self-determination. The offender does not recognize in the person they offend the possibility to form their own personality and to show it to others. The French tradition of protectionism of vulnerability toward those who have historically experienced discrimination seems preferable in very narrowly limited circumstances. Government intervention in this area is legitimate to protect social groups that have historically experienced discrimination. Expression of general viewpoints are hard to capture within this conception. Some caution is required here. A general ban against broad expressions of hate in the absence of an individualized target and in the absence

42 For a similar conception in the area of feminist discourse, see Catharine MacKinnon, *Towards A Feminist Theory of the State* (Cambridge, MA: Harvard University Press, 1991).

43 Habermas, *Between Facts and Norms*, 323.

44 Charles R. Lawrence III, "The Id the Ego and Equal Protection: Reckoning with Unconscious Racism," *Stanford Law Review* 39 (1987), 317; Mari J. Matsuda, et al., eds., *Words that Wound: Critical Race Theory, Assaultive Speech and the First Amendment* (Boulder, CO: Westview Press, 1993); Richard Delgado and Jean Stefancic, Must We Defend Nazis? Hate Speech, Pornography and the New First Amendment (New York University Press, 1997).

45 See Chapter 1.

46 Schauer, *Free Speech*, 63.

of incitement to harmful action would extend to too much speech as Heinze persuasively argues.[47] Only when individualized offense takes place, where the speaker offends a person and accentuates this offense by reference to racial background, is it legitimate for the state to intervene. Therefore, limitations on hate speech in the form of aggravating circumstances for offenses already existing in a criminal code such as defamation and insult can be justified. The United States maintains narrowly defined time, context, and manner restrictions. Hate speech that is not part of public discourse, addressed by one employee to another in the context of government employment, will receive minimal forms of constitutional protection.[48] In France, engaging in hate speech that refers to an individual's race independent of context, and which is directed toward an individualized target, is not protected. In this narrow case restrictions can be justified by reference to state protectionism.

For Heinze, consequentialist rationales cannot override a deontological foundation for free speech in longstanding, stable, and prosperous democracies. Heinze advocates in favor of government action to eliminate discrimination in education, employment, and the delivery of goods and services, as practiced in his conception of longstanding democracies. State institutions, far from being value neutral, should maintain, through antidiscrimination regimes, enforceable policies of civic and social pluralism. Democracies should also be able to deal with policing acts of violence or discrimination against vulnerable groups or persons without the state having to impose viewpoint-selective penalties within public discourse, in order to be considered stable. And prosperous democracies are those that are sufficiently wealthy to assure adequate measures against violence and discrimination. This argument inevitably has a context-dependent component built into it. A very narrow restriction upon individualized attacks against individuals can be considered part of these enforceable policies of civic pluralism.

Furthermore, the libertarian spirit of protection of freedom of expression dominant in the United States may lead to erring on the side of overprotecting the speech of powerful social actors and to neglecting the distinction between real freedom and formal freedom. Expecting that the state may protect public debate from distortion by corporations that use their corporate funds for independent campaign expenditures, and thus protecting citizens from brainwashing by placing ultimate limits on independent expenditures, is also a compelling consideration. The US Supreme Court concluded in *Citizens United* that neither equality, nor distortion, nor eliminating corruption can count as constitutionally compelling interests capable of justifying legislation prohibiting corporations from spending in political campaigns. While the concern for self-government was capital during the Founding Era in America, a conception of the free marketplace of ideas as a sphere of absolute freedom overlooks the dynamics of power within civil society. The distinction

47 Heinze, *Hate Speech and Democratic Citizenship*, 139.
48 Post and Molnar, "Interview with Robert Post," 12.

between formal liberty and real liberty is pertinent in this case as well. The average citizen does not have the real liberty to engage in independent expenditures. Thus, *Citizens United* failed to understand the relationship between ordinary commercial corporations and First Amendment rights.[49] The Court did not ask the question of whether allowing the speech of corporate independent expenditures in favor of political candidates promotes or undermines informed public decision-making. The Court instead referred to criteria such as rules against speaker discrimination and a "chilling effect," which are of doubtful relevance to the speech of commercial corporations.[50] The Court expressed the logic that undue pressures on the body politic will be cleansed by the competitive character of the electoral process.[51] The decision shows trust toward the market, which contains a large number and a wide range of speakers of diverse interests overlooking the domination of aggregations of concentrated wealth.[52] The idea that government intervention to redistribute speaking power may be justified on grounds of market failure is missing.[53]

The decision reflects a vision of free speech on the basis of which it is unacceptable for government to intervene for paternalistic or redistributive reasons.[54] This vision overlooks equality considerations. Political equality is advanced by governmental regulation limiting corporate influence, which decreases the diversification of electoral debate.[55] The social power of corporations in this case is extremely important and it is legitimate for the state to intervene to moderate the influence upon political debates. The power dynamics consolidated within societies make the exercise of freedom of speech more meaningful for corporations and less meaningful for individuals. The Court entirely neglected the distinction between formal freedom and real freedom. The theoretical possibility for everyone to exercise freedom of speech does not correspond with a real possibility to exercise this freedom. In this respect the French conception has the considerable advantage of engaging in a "redistribution" of speech rights, of limiting excessive influence of conglomerates of interests upon the public debate. *Citizens United* is not the only instance in which the Supreme Court has shown hostility toward campaign finance restrictions.[56] Following the decision,

[49] See Robert Post, *Citizens Divided: Campaign Finance Reform and the Constitution* (Cambridge, MA: Harvard University Press, 2014); Kathleen M. Sullivan "Two Concepts of Freedom of Speech," *Harvard Law Review* 124 (2010), 143; Samuel Issacharoff, "On Political Corruption," *Harvard Law Review* 124 (2010), 118; Lucian Bebchuk and Robert Jackson, Jr., "Corporate Political Speech: Who decides?," *Harvard Law Review* 124 (2010), 83.

[50] See Ibid.

[51] Samuel Issacharoff, "On Political Corruption," 133–34.

[52] *Citizens United*, 130 S. Ct., 904–8.

[53] Ibid., 906–7.

[54] Sullivan "Two Concepts of Freedom of Speech," 145.

[55] Ibid., 154–55.

[56] This has led scholars toward suggesting alternative ways to mitigate the influence of funding in politics such as enacting legislative recusal rules that elected officials can use in legislation serving the interests of corporations that have engaged in independent expenditures for them. See Eugene Mazo, "Regulating Campaign Finance through Legislative Recusal Rules," in Timothy K. Kuhner and

political money has altered the possibility for accountability for political candidates. They may be made electable thanks to the support of independent expenditures. The principle that every citizen has an equal vote is distorted.[57]

Protecting the public political debate from distortions and corruption is a legitimate mission for the government, as it is in this political debate that the citizens are able to develop the public use of their reason as advocated by Kant. It is through keeping oneself informed about current political debates that citizens can transcend their private identities and see themselves as citizens of the state. Allowing for independent expenditures is a medium that undermines their possibility to elaborate their public reason and keeps them trapped in their private reason. It prevents the very possibility of the emergence of a discursive democracy. Government action that would allow the emergence of deliberative democracy and would help citizens realize their liberty of freedom of expression in terms of equality is extremely valuable in this respect. If, as Robert Post notes, public opinion is elusive and in constant flow, then making sure that there is no undue influence distorting public opinion is very important. Discursive democracy is a value in itself and it presupposes "a structure of government that connects official decision-making to public opinion."[58] In this respect elections are the mechanism par excellence that express public opinion. Electoral integrity might be an ideal that is difficult to realize. Nevertheless, it is legitimate for the government to engage in all measures that it can in order to promote this goal. It is a mission of a democratic government to establish institutions that make democracy effective to the extent that democracy is the political regime that respects human dignity.

In other words, regulating political campaign spending facilitates deliberation in the various networks of the political public sphere that is decentered in contemporary societies, as Habermas notes. Government intervention that equalizes the terrain and allows as many opinions as possible to be expressed facilitates the deliberation that takes place and allows the citizens to reflect while protected from undue influence. A hands-off approach in the area of campaign funding, with a natural rights philosophy in the background like the one dominant in the United States, can accentuate social power imbalances. The French insight that political society should try to eliminate this imbalance as much as possible holds sway in this case. Government intervention in this area inspired by the philosophy of rights dominant in France is legitimate.

In the context of globalization, this study has aimed to offer pointers toward ways of thinking in order to evaluate the regulation of freedom of expression in France and the United States. This interpretation of how legal traditions emerged aims to help us think critically about the legitimate limits to freedom of expression. It aims to provide criteria for the adjustment of the dialectic relationship between government and liberty in the area of freedom of expression.

Eugene D. Mazo, eds., *Democracy by the People: Reforming Campaign Finance in America* (Cambridge University Press, 2018).

57 Sullivan "Two Concepts of Freedom of Speech," 169.

58 See Post, *Citizens Divided*, 59.

Bibliography

Ackerman, Bruce. *We the People*, vol. 1, *Foundations*. Cambridge, MA: Harvard University Press, 1991.

Ackerman, Bruce. *We the People*, vol. 2, *Transformations*. Cambridge, MA: Harvard University Press, 1998.

Adair, Douglas. "Experience Must Be Our Only Guide." In Douglas Adair and Trevor Colbourn, eds. *Fame and the Founding Fathers*. Virginia: Institute of Early American History and Culture, 1974.

Adair, Douglas. "'That Politics May Be Reduced to a Science': David Hume, James Madison and the Tenth Federalist." In Douglas Adair and Trevor Colbourn, eds. *Fame and the Founding Fathers*, 93–106. Virginia: Institute of Early American History and Culture, 1974.

Adams, John. "A Defence of the Constitutions of Government of the United States of America." In *The Works of John Adams*, vol. 4, 469–588, vol. 5, 3–478. Boston: Charles C. Little and James Brown, 1851.

Adams, John. *Declaration of the Rights of the Inhabitants of the Commonwealth of Massachusetts*. In *The Works of John Adams*, vol. 4, 213–18. Boston: Charles C. Little and James Brown, 1851.

Adams, John. *Novanglus*. In *The Works of John Adams*, vol. 4, 15–177. Boston:Charles C. Little and James Brown, 1851.

Adams, John. *The Report of a Constitution or Form of Government for the Commonwealth of Massachusetts, Preamble*. In *The Works of John Adams*, vol. 4, 219–67. Boston: Charles C. Little and James Brown, 1851.

Adams, John. *Thoughts on Government*. In *The Works of John Adams*, vol. 4, 189–207. Boston: Charles C. Little and James Brown, 1851.

Adams, Samuel. "The Rights of the Colonists: Report of the Committee of Correspondence to the Boston Town Meeting." In *Old South Leaflets*, No. 173 (Boston: Directors of the Old South Work, 1906).

Allen, Danielle. *Our Declaration: A Reading of the Declaration of Independence in Defense of Equality*. New York: Norton 2014.

Amar, Akhil Reed. *America's Unwritten Constitution: The Precedents and Principles We Live By*. New York: Basic Books, 2012.

Amar, Akhil Reed. *The Bill of Rights: Creation and Reconstruction*. New Haven, CT: Yale University Press, 1998.

Amar, Akhil Reed. "The Creation, Reconstruction and Interpretation of the Bill of Rights." In Barry Alan Shain, ed. *The Nature of Rights at the American Founding and Beyond*, 163–80. Charlottesville and London: University of Virginia Press, 2007.

Alféri, Pierre. *Guillaume d'Ockham: le singulier*. Paris: Minuit, 1989.
American Philosophical Society. *Aspects of American Liberty, Philosophical, Historical and Political*. Philadelphia: The American Philosophical Society ed., 1977.
Anderson, Alexis J. "The Formative Period of First Amendment Theory." *The American Journal of Legal History* 24 (1980), 56–75.
Anderson, David. "The Origins of the Press Clause." *University of California Los Angeles Law Review* 30 (1983), 455–541.
Arendt, Hannah. *On Revolution*. London: Penguin Books, 1990 [1963].
Aristotle. *The Nicomachean Ethics*. Revised Oxford translation, vol. 2. Edited by Jonathan Barnes. Princeton University Press, 1995.
Aristotle. *Politics*. Revised Oxford translation, vol. 2. Edited by Jonathan Barnes. Princeton University Press, 1995.
Armitage, David. *The Declaration of Independence: A Global History*. Cambridge, MA: Harvard University Press, 2007.
Arneil, Barbara. *John Locke and America: The Defence of English Colonialism*. Oxford: Clarendon Press, 1996.
Aron, Raymond. *Essai sur les libertés*. Paris: Hachette, 1998 [1967].
Ashcraft, Richard and M. M. Goldsmith. "Locke, Revolution Principles and the Formation of Whig Ideology." *The Historical Journal* 26, no. 4 (1983), 773–800.
Assemblée Nationale, *Archives parlementaires de 1787 à 1860*, vol. 8.
Assemblée Nationale, *Rapport d'information fait en application de l'article 145 du réglement*, no. 2262 (2010).
Aubenque, Pierre. "La loi chez Aristote." *Archives de Philosophie du Droit* 25 (1980), 147–57.
Aubenque, Pierre. *Le problème de l'être chez Aristote: essai sur la problématique aristotélicienne*. Paris: Presses Universitaires de France, 1962.
Aulard, François Alphonse. *Le culte de la raison et le culte de l'être suprême (1793–1794): essai historique*. Paris: F. Alcan, 1892.
Aulard, François Alphonse. "Les philosophes et la Révolution." In Auguste Dide, ed. *La Révolution française: revue historique*, 193–203. Paris: Siège de la Société de l'Histoire de la Révolution Française, 1892.
Aumètre, Jacques. "La Révolution: réalisation et révélation de la raison." In Josiane Boulad-Ayoub and Jacques Aumètre, eds. *Les Lumières et la Déclaration des droits de l'homme: rupture ou continuité?*, 11–29. Québec: Presses de l'Université de Québec, 1990.
Austin, John. *How to Do Things with Words?* Cambridge, MA: Harvard University Press, 1975.
Azouvi, François. *Descartes et la France: histoire d'une passion nationale*. Paris: Fayard, 2002.
Azouvi, François and Jean-Marie Beyssade. "Descartes." In Philippe Raynaud et Stéphane Rials, eds. *Dictionnaire de philosophie politique*, 155–59. Paris: Presses Universitaires de France, 2003.
Babeuf, Gracchus. *Oeuvres de Babeuf*, vol. 1, *Babeuf avant la révolution*. Edited by V. Daline, A. Saitta, and A. Soboul. Paris: Bibliothèque Nationale, 1977.
Babeuf, Gracchus. *Pages choisies de Babeuf*. Edited by Maurice Dommanget. Paris: Armand Colin, 1935.
Casali de Babot, Judith and Guillermo Salvatierra. "Mably: utopie ou réalisme dans la pensée pré-révolutionnaire?" In Peter Friedemann, Florence Gauthier, Jean-Luc Malvache, and Fernanda Mazzani Pepe, eds. *Colloque Mably: la politique comme science morale*, vol. 1, 85–99. Bary: Palomar Casa Editrice, 1995.
Bailyn, Bernard. *The Ideological Origins of The American Revolution*. Cambridge, MA: Harvard University Press, 1967.

Baker, C. Edwin. "Scope of the First Amendment Freedom of Speech." *University of California Law Review* 25 (1978), 964–1040.

Baker, Keith Michael. "The Idea of a Declaration of Rights." In Dale Van Kley, ed. *The French Idea of Freedom: The Old Regime and the Declaration of Rights of 1789*,154–98. Stanford University Press, 1994,

Balibar, Étienne. "Dissonances dans la laïcité." In Charlotte Nordmann, ed. *Le foulard islamique en questions*, 5–27. Paris: ed. Amsterdam, 2004.

Balkin, Jack. *Living Originalism*. Cambridge, MA: Harvard University Press, 2011.

Barber, Benjamin R. "The Compromised Republic: Public Purposelessness in America." In Robert H. Horwitz, ed. *The Moral Foundations of the American Republic*, 19–38. Charlottesville: University Press of Virginia, 1979.

Barker, Ernest. "Edmund Burke et la Révolution française." In E. Barker et al., eds. *La Révolution de 1789 et la pensée moderne*, 1–32. Paris: Presses Universitaires de France, 1940.

Barnett, Randy E. "James Madison's Ninth Amendment." In Randy E. Barnett, ed. *The Rights Retained by the People: The History and Meaning of the Ninth Amendment*, 1–49. Fairfax, VA: George Mason University Press, 1989.

Barnett, Randy E. *Restoring the Lost Constitution: The Presumption of Liberty*. Princeton University Press, 2004.

Barny, Roger. *Les contradictions de l'idéologie révolutionnaire des droits de l'homme, droit naturel et histoire*. Paris: Les Belles Lettres, 1993.

Barny, Roger. *Le droit naturel à l'épreuve de l'histoire: Jean Jacques Rousseau dans la Révolution (débats politiques et sociaux)*. Paris: Les Belles Lettres, 1995.

Barny, Roger. *Prélude idéologique à la Révolution française: le rousseauisme avant 1789*. Paris: Les Belles Lettres, 1985.

Barny, Roger. *Le triomphe du droit naturel: La constitution de la doctrine révolutionnaire des droits de l'homme (1787–1789)*. Paris: Les Belles Lettres, 1997.

Barret-Kriegel, Blandine. *Les droits de l'homme et le droit naturel*. Paris: Presses Universitaires de France, 1989.

Barret-Kriegel, Blandine. *L'État et les esclaves*. Paris, Payot, 1989 [1979].

Beard, Charles. *The Economic Interpretation of the Constitution*. New York, MacMillan, 1913.

Bebchuk, Lucian and Robert Jackson, Jr. "Corporate Political Speech: Who Decides?" *Harvard Law Review* 124 (2010), 83–117.

Becker, Carl. *The Declaration of Independence*. New York: Vintage Books, 1958.

Benhabib, Seyla. *Another Cosmopolitanism*. Cambridge University Press, 2006.

Bentham, Jeremy. "Anarchical Fallacies: Being an Examination of the Declaration of Rights Issued during the French Revolution." In Jeremy Waldron, ed. *Nonsense Upon Stilts: Bentham, Burke and Marx on the Rights of Man*, 46–76. London and New York: Methuen, 1987

Berghausen, Mark E. and Skylar Albertson. "The Rise and Fall of the Separation of Powers." *Northwestern University Law Review* 106 (2012), 527–50.

Berlin, Isaiah. , "John Stuart Mill and the Ends of Life." In *Four Essays on Liberty*. Oxford University Press, 2002.

Berlin, Isaiah. "Two Concepts of Freedom." In *Four Essays on Liberty*. Oxford University Press, 1969.

Berns, Walter. "Religion and the Founding Principle." In Robert H. Horwitz, ed. *The Moral Foundations of the American Republic*, 178–79. Charlottesville: University Press of Virginia, 1979.

Bilder, Mary Sarah. *The Transatlantic Constitution: Colonial Legal Culture and the Empire*. Cambridge, MA: Harvard University Press, 2004.

Black, Jr., Charles L. "Foreword: State Action, Equal Protection, and California's Proposition. *Harvard Law Review* 69 (1967), 69–262.

Bland, Richard. *An Inquiry into the Rights of the British Colonies, Intended as an Answer to the Regulations Lately Made concerning the Colonies, and the Taxes Imposed upon Them Considered*. Williamsburg: Alexander Purdie & Co., 1766.

Bloch, Ernst. *Droit naturel et dignité humaine*. Translated by Denis Authier and Jean Lacoste. Paris: Payot, 2002.

Böckenforde, Ernst-Wolfgang. "La naissance de l'État: processus de sécularisation." In *Le droit, l'État, et la constitution démocratique*. Translated by Olivier Jouanjan, Willy Zimmer, and Olivier Beaud. Paris: Bruyland LGDJ, 2000.

Bodéüs, Richard. *Le philosophe et la cité: recherches sur les rapports entre morale et politique dans la pensée d'Aristote*. Paris: Les Belles Lettres, 1982.

Bodin, Jean. *Les six livres de la république*. Paris: Jacques du Puys, Librairie Juré, 1576.

Bok, Sissela. *Secrets: On the Ethics of Concealment and Revelation*. New York: Vintage, 1998.

Bollinger, Lee C. *Images of a Free Press*. Chicago: University of Chicago Press, 1991.

Boudon, Julien. *Les Jacobins: une traduction des principes de Jean-Jacques Rousseau*. Paris: LGDJ, 2006.

Bourdieu, Pierre. *Ce que parler veut dire: l'économie des échanges linguistiques*. Paris: Fayard, 1982.

Bouretz, Pierre. "Egalité et liberté." *Droits* 8 (1988), 71–82.

Bouretz, Pierre. *La république et l'universel*. Paris: Gallimard, 2000.

Bourgeois, Bernard. "Hegel." In Philippe Raynaud and Stéphane Rials, eds. *Dictionnaire de philosophie politique*, 267–74. Paris: Presses Universitaires de France, 2003.

Bourgeois, Bernard. *Philosophie et droits de l'homme, de Kant à Marx*. Paris: Presses Universitaires de France, 1990.

Bourgeois, Bernard. *La raison moderne et le droit politique*. Paris, Vrin, 2000.

Boutmy, Émile. "La Déclaration des droits de l'homme et du citoyen et M. Jellinek." *Annales des Sciences Politiques* 17 (1902), 415–43.

Boutmy, Émile. *Etudes de droit constitutionnel: France, Angleterre, Etats-Unis*. Paris: Plon, 1888.

Bowen, John R. *Why the French Don't Like Headscarves*. Princeton University Press, 2006.

Brennan Jr., William. "The Constitution of the United States: Contemporary Ratification." *University of California Davis Law Review* 19 (1985), 2–15.

Brest, Paul. "The Fundamental Rights Controversy: The Essential Contradictions of Normative Constitutional Scholarship." *Yale Law* Journal 90 (1908–1981), 1063–109.

Burke, Edmund. *On Conciliation with America*. In *The Writings and Speeches of Edmund Burke*, vol. 3. Edited by Paul Langford. Oxford University Press, 1996.

Burke, Edmund. *Reflections on the Revolution of France*. In *The Writings and Speeches of Edmund Burke*, vol. 8. Edited by L. G. Mitchell. Oxford University Press, 1989.

Burke, Edmund. *Second Speech on Conciliation, 16 November 1775*. In *The Writings and Speeches of Edmund Burke*, vol. 3. Edited by Paul Langford. Oxford University Press, 1996.

Campbell, Jud. "Natural Rights and the First Amendment." *Yale Law Journal* 127 (2017), 246–321.

Cassirer, Ernst. *The Question of Jean-Jacques Rousseau*. Translated by Peter Gay. Bloomington: Indiana University Press, 1963.

Castoriadis, Cornelius. *L'institution imaginaire de la société*. Paris: Seuil, 1975.

Canavan, S. J., Francis. "Thomas Paine." In Leo Strauss and Joseph Cropsey, eds. *History of Political Philosophy*, 3rd ed., 685–86. University of Chicago Press, 1987.

Cayla, Olivier. "La notion de signification en droit: contribution à une theorie du droit naturel de la communication." Unpublished doctoral dissertation, University Paris II, 1992.

Cayla, Olivier. "Rousseau Jean-Jacques, Du contrat social." In Olivier Cayla and Jean-Louis Halpérin, eds. *Dictionnaire des grandes oeuvres juridiques*, 495–505. Paris: Dalloz, 2008.

Censer, Jack R. and Lynn Hunt. *Liberty, Equality, Fraternity: Exploring the French Revolution*. Pennsylvania State University Press, 2001.

Chafee, Jr., Zechariah. "Freedom of Speech in Wartime." *Harvard Law Review* 32 (1919), 932–73.

Chafee, Jr., Zechariah. *Free Speech in the United States*. Cambridge, MA: Harvard University Press, 1941.

Chafee, Jr., Zachariah. *How Human Rights Got into the Constitution*. Boston University Press, 1952.

Cobban, Alfred. *The Social Interpretation of the French Revolution*. Cambridge University Press, 1964.

Cohen, Joshua. "Freedom of Expression." *Philosophy and Public Affairs* 22 (1993), 207–63.

Coisne, Martine and Collin, Jean. "Le droit de réponse dans la communication audiovisuelle." In Dupeux Jean-Yves and Lacabarats Alain, eds. *Liberté de la presse et droits de la personne*, 17–30. Paris: Dalloz, 1997.

Commager, Henry Steele. *The Empire of Reason*. New York: Anchor Press and Doubleday, 1977.

Condorcet, Marie-Jean-Antoine-Nicolas de Caritat, Marquis de. *Esquisse d'un tableau historique des progrès de l'ésprit humain*. Edited by Monique and François Hincker. Paris: Editions Sociales, 1966.

Constant, Benjamin. "De la liberté des Anciens comparée à celle des Modernes" [1819]. In *Écrits politiques*. Edited by Marcel Gauchet. Paris: Gallimard, 1997.

Constant, Benjamin. *Manuscrit des principes*. In *De la liberté chez les modernes*. Edited by Marcel Gauchet. Paris: Pluriel, 1980.

Corwin, Edward S. "The 'Higher Law' Background of American Constitutional Law." In Randy E. Barnett, ed. *The Rights Retained by the People: The History and Meaning of the Ninth Amendment*, 67–106. Fairfax, VA: George Mason University Press, 1989.

Courtney Cecil P. "Burke et les Lumières." In *La Révolution française entre Lumières et Romantisme*, 53–64. Cahiers de philosophie politique et juridique, no. 16. Centre de Publications de l'Université de Caen, 1989.

Cowie, Jefferson. *The Great Exception: The New Deal and The Limits of American Politics* Princeton University Press, 2016.

Curry, Thomas. *The First Freedoms: Church and State in America to the Passage of the First Amendment*. Oxford University Press, 1986.

Dahl, Robert A. "On Removing Certain Impediments to Democracy in the United States." In Robert H. Horwitz, ed. *The Moral Foundations of the American Republic.*, 234–56. University Press of Virginia, 1979.

DeCew, Judith Wagner. "The Scope of Privacy in Law and Ethics." *Law and Philosophy* 5 (1986), 145–73.

Delgado, Richard and Jean Stefancic. *Must We Defend Nazis? Hate Speech, Pornography and the New First Amendment*. New York University Press, 1997.

Dellannoi, Gil. *Éloge de la prudence*. Paris: Berg International Editeurs, 1993.

Delannoy, Benjamin. *Burke et Kant: interprètes de la Révolution française*. Paris: L'Harmattan, 2004.

Dérathé, Robert. *Jean-Jacques Rousseau et la pensée politique de son temps*. Paris: Presses Universitaires de France, 1950.

Derrida, Jacques. "*Declarations of Independence.*" In *Negotiations: Interventions and Interviews 1971–2001*, 46–54. Stanford University Press, 2002.

Derrida, Jacques. *De la grammatologie*. Paris: Minuit, 1967.

Derrida, Jacques. *Otobiographies: l'enseignement de Nietzsche et la politique du nom propre*. Paris: Galilée, 1984.

Descartes, René. *Discours de la méthode*. In *Oeuvres et lettres*. Collection Bibliothèque de la Pléiade. Paris: Gallimard, 1937.

Dewey, John. *Characters and Events: Popular Essays in Social and Political Philosophy*, vol. 2. Edited by Joseph Ratner. New York: Henry Holt and Company, 1929.

Dewey, John. "Liberalism and Civil Liberties." *The Social Frontier* (February 1936), 137–38.

Dewey, John. *Liberalism and Social Action*. New York: G.P. Putnam's Sons, 1935.

Dewey, John. "Philosophy and Democracy." In *Political Writings*, 38–47. Edited by D. Morris and Ian Shapiro. New York: Hackett, 1993.

Dewey, John. "Philosophies of Freedom." In *On Experience, Nature and Freedom*, 271–72. Edited by Richard J. Bernstein. Indianapolis/New York: Bobbs-Merrill, 1960.

Diamond, Martin. "Ethics and Politics: The American Way." In Robert H. Horwitz, ed. *The Moral Foundations of the American Republic*, 39–72. Charlottesville: University Press of Virginia, 1979.

Dinan, John J. *The American State Constitutional Tradition*. Lawrence: University Press of Kansas, 2006.

Drury, S. B. "John Locke: Natural Law and Innate Ideas." In Richard Ashcraft, ed. *John Locke, Critical Assessments*, vol. 2, 84–97. London and New York: Routledge 1991.

Duguit, Léon. *Traité de droit constitutionnel*, vols. 1 and 2. Paris: Ed. de Boccard, 1921.

Dumont, Louis. *Essais sur l'individualisme*. Paris: Seuil, 1985.

Dunn, John. *Locke*. Oxford University Press, 1984.

Durkheim, Émile. *The Division of Labor in Society*. Translated by Lewis A. Coser. New York: The Free Press, 1984.

Durkheim, Émile. *The Elementary Forms of Religious Life*. Translated by Karen E. Fields. New York: The Free Press 1995.

Durkheim, Émile. *Les formes élémentaires de la vie religieuse: le système totémique en Australie*. Paris: F. Alcan, 1912.

Duverger, Maurice. *Les constitutions de la France*. Paris: Presses Universitaires de France, 1944.

Dworkin, Ronald. *Taking Rights Seriously*. Cambridge, MA: Harvard University Press, 1977.

Edelman, Peter B. "Free Press v. Privacy: Haunted by the Ghost of Justice Black." *Texas Law Review* 68 (1989–90), 1195–234.

Edling, Max. *A Revolution in Favor of Government: Origins of the U.S. Constitution and the Making of the American State*. Oxford University Press, 2003.

Elliot, Jonathan, ed. *Debates in Several State Conventions On The Adoption Of The Federal Constitution*, 5 vols. US Congress, 1836.

Emerson, Thomas. *The System of Freedom of Expression*. New York: Random House, 1970.

Emerson, Thomas. "The Affirmative Side of the First Amendment." *Georgia Law Review* 15 (1981), 795–849.

Epstein, Richard. "A Taste for Privacy? Evolution and the Emergence of a Naturalistic Ethic." *Journal of Legal Studies* 9 (1980), 665–81.

Eskridge, William and John Ferejohn. *A Republic of Statutes: The New American Constitution*. New Haven, CT: Yale University Press, 2010.

Ewald, William. "Comparative Jurisprudence (I): What Was it Like to Try a Rat?" *University of Pennsylvania Law Review* 143 (1995), 1898–2251.

Fallon, Jr., Richard. *The Nature of Constitutional Rights: The Invention and Logic of Strict Judicial Scrutiny*. Cambridge University Press, 2019.

Farber, Daniel A. *Retained by the People: The Silent Ninth Amendment and the Constitutional Rights Americans Don't Know they Have*. New York: Basic Books, 2007.

Farrand, Max, ed. *The Records of The Federal Convention of 1787*. 3 vols. New Haven, CT: Yale University Press, 1911.

Favoureu, Louis. "La Déclaration de 1789 et le juge: une problématique américaine?" *La Revue Tocqueville* 14 (1993), 147–55

Favoureu, Louis. "La jurisprudence du Conseil constitutionnel et le droit de propriété proclamé par la Déclaration de 1789." In *La Déclaration des droits de l'homme et du citoyen et la jurisprudence*. 125–50. Paris: Presses Universitaires de France, 1989.

Favoureu, Louis and Loïc Philip. *Les grandes décisions du Conseil constitutionnel*. 10th ed. Paris: Dalloz, 1999.

Faye, Emmanuel. *Philosophie et perfection de l'homme: de la Renaissance à Descartes*. Paris: Vrin, 1998.

Felcher, Peter L. and Edward L. Rubin. "Privacy, Publicity, and the Portrayal of Real People by the Media." *Yale Law Journal* 88 (1979), 1577–622.

Ferguson, Adam. "Of the Principles of Union among Mankind." In Louis Schneider, ed. *The Scottish Moralists on Human Nature and Society*, 77–89. Chicago: The University of Chicago Press, 1967.

Ferry, Jean-Marc. "La rationalisation habermassienne de la prudence." In Philippe Raynaud et Stéphane Rials, eds. *Une prudence moderne*. Paris: Presses Universitaires de France, 1992.

Ferry, Luc. "Actualité de la querelle de l'Aufklärung et du romantisme." In *La Révolution française entre Lumières et romantisme*, 195–209. Cahiers de Philosophie Politique et Juridique, no. 16. Centre de Publications de l'Université de Caen, 1989.

Ferry, Luc. *Le droit: la nouvelle querelle des Anciens et des Modernes*. Paris: Presses Universitaires de France, 2007.

Ferry, Luc. "Kant." In François Furet et Mona Ozouf, eds. *Dictionnaire critique de la Révolution française: interprètes et historiens*, 157–64. Paris: Flammarion, 2007.

Ferry, Luc and Alain Renaut. *Philosophie politique 3: des droits de l'homme à l'idée républicaine*. Paris: Presses Universitaires de France, 1992.

Ferry, Luc and Alain Renaut. *Système et critique: essais sur la critique de la raison dans la philosophie contemporaine*. Bruxelles: Ousia, 1984.

Fichte, Johann Gottlieb. *Considérations destinées à rectifier les jugements du public sur la Révolution française*, Translated by Jules Barni. Paris: F. Chamerot, 1859.

Fichte, Johann Gottlieb. *Foundations of Natural Rights According to the Principles of the Wissenschaftslehre* Translated by Michael Baur. Edited by Frederick Neuhouser. Cambridge University Press, 2000.

Finnis, John. *Natural Law and Natural Rights*. Oxford University Press, 1980.

Finnis, John. "Natural Law: The Classical Tradition." In Jules L. Coleman, Kenneth Einar Himma, and Scott J. Shapiro, eds. *The Oxford Handbook of Jurisprudence and Philosophy of Law*, 1–60. Oxford University Press, 2004.

Fleischacker, Samuel. "Adam Smith's Reception among the American Founders, 1776–1790." *The William and Mary Quarterly* 59 (2002), 897–924.

Forbath, William E. "Constitutional Welfare Rights: A History, Critique, and Reconstruction." *Fordham Law Review* 69 (2001), 1821–91.

Forbath, William E. "The New Deal Constitution in Exile." *Duke Law Journal* 51 (2001), 165–222.

Franz, Paul. "Unconstitutional and Outlawed Political Parties: A German-American Comparison." *Boston College International and Comparative Law Review* 5 (1982), 51–89.

Fraser, Steve. "The Labor Question." In Steve Fraser and Gary Gerstle, eds. *The Rise and Fall of the New Deal Order, 1930–1980*, 55–84. Princeton University Press,1990.

Frazer, Michael. *The Enlightenment of Sympathy*. Oxford University Press 2010.

Fried, Charles. *Modern Liberty and the Limits of Government*. New York: Norton and Company, 2007.

Friedman, Michel. *Les droits de réponse*. Paris: Editions du Centre de formation et de perfectionnement des journalistes, 1994.

Friedrich, Carl J. and Robert G. McCloskey. *From the Declaration of Independence to the Constitution: The Roots of American Constitutionalism*. New York: The Liberal Arts Press, 1954.

Fuller, Timothy. "Jeremy Bentham and James Mill." In Leo Strauss and Joseph Cropsey, ed. *History of Political Philosophy*. 3rd ed., 710–31. University of Chicago Press, 1987.

Fuller, Timothy. "Thomas Hobbes and Emergent Modernity." In Edward McLean, ed. *An Uncertain Legacy: Essays on the Pursuit of Liberty*, 73–90. Wilmington, DE: Intercollegiate Studies Institute 1997.

Furet, François. "Ancien Régime." In François Furet and Mona Ozouf, eds. *Dictionnaire critique de la Révolution française: idées*, 39–40. Paris: Flammarion, 1992.

Furet, François. "Babeuf." In François Furet and Mona Ouzouf, eds. *Dictionnaire critique de la Révolution française: acteurs*, 25–35. Paris: Flammarion, 1992.

Furet, François. "L'idée de république et l'histoire de France au XIXe siècle." In François Furet and Mona Ozouf, eds. *Le siècle de l'avènement républicain*, 289–312. Paris: Gallimard, 1993.

Furet, François. "Jacobinisme." In François Furet and Mona Ouzouf, eds. *Dictionnaire critique de la Révolution française: idées*, 241. Paris: Flammarion, 1992.

Furet, François. *Penser la Révolution française*. 2nd ed. Paris: Gallimard, 1978.

Furet, François. *Marx et la Révolution française*. Paris: Flammarion, 1986.

Furet, François and Ozouf, Mona, eds. *Dictionnaire critique de la Révolution française: acteurs*. 2nd ed. Paris: Flammarion, 2007.

Furet, François and Mona Ouzouf, eds. *Dictionnaire critique de la Révolution française: interprètes et historiens*. Paris: Flammarion, 2007.

Gadamer, Hans-Georg. "Hegel's Philosophy and Its Aftereffects until Today." In *Reason in the Age of Science*,21–37. Translated by Frederick G. Lawrence. Cambridge, MA: MIT University Press, 1986.

Gadamer, Hans-Georg. *Vérité et méthode*. Translated by Pierre Fruchon, Jean Grondin, and Gilbert Merlio. Paris: Seuil, 1976.

Gardner, James A. *Interpreting State Constitutions: A Jurisprudence of Function in a Federal System*. University of Chicago Press, 2005.

Gauchet, Marcel. *L'avènement de la démocratie*, vol. 1, *La révolution moderne*. Paris: Gallimard, 2007.

Gauchet, Marcel. *Le désenchantement du monde: une histoire politique de la religion*. Paris: Gallimard, 1985.

Gauchet, Marcel. *La religion dans la démocratie*. Paris: Gallimard, 1998.

Gauchet, Marcel. *La révolution des droits de l'homme*. Paris: Gallimard, 1989.

Gauchet, Marcel. *La révolution des pouvoirs: la souveraineté, le peuple et la représentation 1789–1799* Paris: Gallimard, 1995.

Gauthier, Florence. *Triomphe et mort du droit naturel en Révolution, 1789–1795–1802*. Paris: Presses Universitaires de France, 1992.

Geer LeBoutillier, Cornelia. *American Democracy and Natural Law*. New York: Columbia University Press, 1950.

Gengembre, Gerard. "Burke." In François Furet and Mona Ouzouf, eds. *Dictionnaire critique de la Révolution française: interprètes et historiens*, 51–61. Paris: Flammarion, 2007.

Gengembre, Gérard. "La Contre-révolution et le refus de la Constitution." In Michel Troper and Lucien Jaume, eds. *1789 et L'Invention de la Constitution*, 55–74. Paris: LGDJ and Bruylant, 1994.

Gerber, Scott D. "Whatever Happened to the Declaration of Independence? A Commentary on the Republican Revisionism in the Political Thought of the American Revolution." *Polity* 26 (1993), 207–31.

Gerstle, Gary. *Liberty and Coercion: The Paradox of American Government from the Founding to the Present*. Princeton University Press, 2015.

Gewirtz, Paul. "Privacy and Speech." *Supreme Court Review* (2001), 139–200

Gierke, Otto Friedrich von. *Natural Law and the Theory of Society 1500 to 1800*. Translated by Ernest Barker. Cambridge University Press, 1934.

Glendon, Mary Ann. *Rights Talk: The Impoverishment of Political Discourse*. New York: Free Press, 1991.

Glennon Robert and Novak, John E. "A Functional analysis of the Fourteenth Amendment 'State Action' Requirement." *Supreme Court Review* (1976), 221–61.

Goffman, Erving. *The Presentation of Self in Everyday Life*. London: Penguin 1990.

Goldsmith, M. M. "Liberty, Luxury and the Pursuit of Happiness." In Pagden, Antony, ed. *The Languages of Political Theory in Early-Modern Europe*, 225–52. Cambridge University Press, 2009.

Goldschmidt, Victor. *Anthropologie et politique: les principes du système de Rousseau*. Paris: Vrin, 1974.

Gordon, Thomas and Trenchard, John. *Cato's Letters, or Essays on Liberty, Civil and Religious, and other Important Subjects*. 4 vols. New York: Da Capo Press, 1971.

Gouhier, Henri. *Les méditations métaphysiques de Jean-Jacques Rousseau*. Paris: Vrin, 1984.

Goyard-Fabre, Simone. "La Déclaration des droits ou le devoir d'humanité: une philosophie de l'espérance." *Droits* 8 (1988), 41–54.

Goyard-Fabre, Simone. *John Locke et la raison raisonnable*. Paris: Vrin, 1986.

Goyard-Fabre, Simone. "Les Lumières ont-elles préparé la Révolution?" *La Révolution française entre Lumières et romantisme*, 23–43. Cahiers de philosophie politique et luridique, no. 16. Centre de Publications de l'Université de Caen, 1989.

Goyard-Fabre, Simone. *Politique et philosophie dans l'oeuvre de Jean-Jacques Rousseau*. Paris: Presses Universitaires de France, 2001.

Graber, Mark. *Transforming Free Speech: The Ambiguous Legacy of Civil Libertarianism*. Oakland: University of California Press, 1991.

Greenawalt, Kent. *Fighting Words, Individuals, Communties and Liberties of Speech*. Princeton University Press, 1995.

Greenawalt, Kent. "Free Speech Justifications." *Columbia Law Review* 89 (1989), 125–29.

Grey, Thomas. "Constitution as Scripture." *Stanford Law Review* 37 (1984), 1–25.

Grey, Thomas. "Do We Have an Unwritten Constitution?" *Stanford Law Review* 27 (1974–75), 703–18.

Gross, Hyman. "The Concept of Privacy." *New York University Law Review* 42 (1967), 34–54

Guenée, Bernard. *States and Rulers in Later Medieval Europe*. Translated by Juliet Vale. Oxford: Blackwell, 1985.

Gusdorf, Georges. *Naissance de la conscience romantique au siècle des Lumières*. Paris: Payot, 1976.

Gusdorf, Georges. *Les révolutions de France et d'Amérique: la violence et la sagesse*. Paris: Librairie Académique Perrin, 1988.
Gusdorf, Georges. *Les sciences humaines et la pensée occidentale*, vol. 8, *La conscience révolutionnaire des idéologues*. Paris: Payot, 1978.
Haakonssen, Knud. *The Science of a Legislator: The Natural Jurisprudence of David Hume and Adam Smith*. Cambridge University Press, 1981.
Haarscher, Guy. "Droits de l'homme." In Philippe Raynaud and Stéphane Rials, eds. *Dictionnaire de philosophie politique*, 190–97. Paris: Presses Universitaires de France, 2003.
Haarscher, Guy. "Paradoxes de la liberté d'expression." In Guy Haarscher, ed. *Les médias entre droit et pouvoir*, 103–14. Brussels: Editions de l'Université de Bruxelles, 1995.
Haarscher, Guy. *Philosophie des droits de l'homme*. 4th ed. Brussels: Editions de l'Université de Bruxelles, 1993.
Habermas, Jürgen. *Between Facts and Norms*. Translated by William Rehg. Cambridge, MA: The MIT Press, 1996.
Habermas, Jürgen. *De l'éthique de la discussion*. Translated by Mark Hunyadi. Paris: Flammarion, 1991.
Habermas, Jürgen. *Morale et communication*. Translated by Christian Bouchindhomme. Paris: Cerf, 1989.
Habermas, Jürgen, *Theory and Practice*. Translated by John Viertel. Boston: Beacon Press, 1973.
Habermas, Jürgen. *Theory of Communicative Action*. Translated by Thomas McCarthy. Boston: Beacon Press, 1995.
Hamburger, Philip. "Constitutional Right of Religious Exemption: An Historical Perspective." *George Washington Law Review* 60 (1992), 914–48.
Hamilton, Alexander, John Jay, and James Madison. *The Federalist*. Edited by George W. Carey and James McClellan. Indianapolis, IN: Liberty Fund, 2001.
Hamowy, Ronald. "Jefferson and the Scottish Enlightenment: A Critique of Garry Wills's *Inventing America: Jefferson's Declaration of Independence*." *William and Mary Quarterly* 36 (1979), 503–23.
Hampson, Norman. *Will and Circumstance: Montesquieu, Rousseau and the French Revolution*. London: Duckworth, 1983.
Hart, H. L. A. "Are There Any Natural Rights?" *Philosophical Review* 64 (1955), 175–91.
Hartz, Louis. *The Liberal Tradition in America*. New York: Harcourt, Brace and World, 1955.
Hassner, Pierre. "Georg W. F. Hegel." In Leo Strauss and Joseph Cropsey, eds. *History of Political Philosophy*. 3rd ed., 732–60. University of Chicago Press, 1987.
Hauriou, Maurice. *Précis de droit constitutionnel*. Paris: Sirey 1929.
Hayek, Friedrich *The Constitution of Liberty*. University of Chicago Press, 1960.
Hayek, Friedrich. *The Road to Serfdom*. University of Chicago Press, 1944.
Hayek, Friedrich. "Social or Distributive Justice." In Chiaki Nishiyame, Kurt R. Leube, eds. *The Essence of Hayek*, 62–99. Stanford: Hoover Institution Press, 1984.
Hegel, G. W. F. *Elements of Philosophy of Right*. Translated by H. B. Nisbet. Cambridge University Press, 1991.
Hegel, G. W. F. *Introduction to the Philosophy of History*. Translated by Leo Rauch. Indianapolis and Cambridge: Hackett, 1988.
Hegel, G. W. F. *Phenomenology of Spirit*. Translated by A. V. Miller. Oxford University Press, 1977.
Hegel, G. W. F. *The Philosophy of History*. Translated by J. Sibree. New York: Dover, 1956.
Heidegger, Martin. *Being and Time*. Translated by John Macquarrie and Edward Robinson. New York: Harper and Row, 1962.

Henkin, Louis. "Human Dignity and Constitutional Rights." In Michael Meyer and William Parent, eds. *The Constitution of Rights: Human Dignity and American Values*, 210–28. Ithaca, NY: Cornell University Press, 1992.

Henkin, Louis. "Rights: American and Human." *Columbia Law Review* 79 (1979), 405–25.

Heinze, Eric. *Hate Speech and Democratic Citizenship*. Oxford University Press, 2016.

Hennette Vauchez, Stéphanie. *Disposer de soi*. Paris: L'Harmattan, 2004.

Higonnet, Patrice. *Sister Republics: The Origins of French and American Republicanism*. Cambridge, MA: Harvard University Press, 1988.

Hinsley, F. H. *Sovereignty*. London: C. A. Watts and Co. Ltd., 1966.

Hirshleifer, Jack. "Privacy: Its Origin, Function and Future." *Journal of Legal Studies* 9 (1980), 649–64.

Hobbes, Thomas. *The Elements of Law: Human Nature and De Corpore Politico*. Edited by J. C. A. Gaskin. Oxford University Press, 1994.

Hobbes, Thomas. *Leviathan*. Edited by Richard Tuck. Cambridge University Press, 1991.

Hofstader, Richard. "The Founding Fathers: An Age of Realism." In Robert H. Horwitz, ed. *The Moral Foundations of the American Republic*, 73–85 Charlottesville: University Press of Virginia, 1979.

Holmes, Oliver Wendell. "The Path of the Law." *Harvard Law Review* 10 (1897), 457–78.

D'Hondt, Jacques. *De Hegel à Marx*. Paris: Presses Universitaires de France, 1972.

D'Hondt, Jacques. "Hegel et Napoléon." In Jacques d'Hondt, ed. *Hegel et les Français*,. New York: Georg Olms Verlag Hildesheim, 1998.

D'Hondt, Jacques. "Le Parcours hégélien de la Révolution française." In Jacques d'Hondt. *Hegel et les Français*, 139–54. New York: Georg Olms Verlag Hildesheim, 1998.

Horwitz, Morton J. *The Transformation of American Law, 1870–1960*. Oxford University Press, 1992.

Horwitz, Robert. "John Locke and the Preservation of Liberty: A Perennial Problem of Civic Education." In Robert H. Horwitz, ed. *The Moral Foundations of the American Republic*, 129–56. Charlottesville: University Press of Virginia, 1979.

Howe, Daniel Walker. *The Political Culture of the American Whigs*. University of Chicago Press, 1979.

Hume, David. "Of the Liberty of the Press." In *Political Essays*, 1–3. Edited by Knud Haakonssen. Cambridge University Press, 1994.

Hume, David. "That Politics May Be Reduced to a Science." In *Political Essays*, 4–15. Edited by Knud Haakonssen. Cambridge University Press, 1994.

Hutcheson, Francis. *A System of Moral Philosophy*. London: Continuum, 2005.

Hutson, James H. "The Emergence of the Modern Concept of a Right in America: The Contribution of Michel Villey." In Barry Alan Shain, ed. *The Nature of Rights at the American Founding and Beyond*, 25–42. Charlottesville and London: University of Virginia Press, 2013.

Huyler, Jerome. *Locke in America: The Moral Philosophy of The Founding Era*. Lawrence: University Press of Kansas, 1995.

Hyppolite, Jean. "La signification de la Révolution française dans la "phénoménologie" de Hegel." In E. Barker, et al., eds. *La Révolution de 1789 et la pensée moderne*, 193–224. Paris: Presses Universitaires de France, 1940.

Jainchill, Andrew. *Reigmagining Politics after the Terror: The Republican Origins of French Liberalism*. Ithaca, NY: Cornell University Press, 2008.

Jaume, Lucien. "Préface aux droits de l'homme." In Lucien Jaume, ed. *Les déclarations des droits de l'homme (Du débat 1789–1793 au préambule de 1946)*, 27–65. Paris: Flammarion, 1989.

Jaume, Lucien. *Le discours jacobin et la démocratie*. Paris: Fayard, 1989.
Jaume, Lucien. *L'individu effacé ou le paradoxe du libéralisme français*. Paris: Fayard, 1997.
Jaume, Lucien. *La liberté et la loi: les origines philosophiques du libéralisme*. Paris: Fayard, 2000.
Jaurès, Jean. *Histoire socialiste de la Révolution française*. Paris: Jules Rouff, 1900.
Ingber, Stanley. "The Marketplace of Ideas: A Legitimizing Myth." *Duke Law Journal* (1984), 1–91.
Issacharoff, Samuel. "On Political Corruption." *Harvard Law Review* 124 (2010), 118–42.
Jefferson, Thomas. *The Papers of Thomas Jefferson*. Edited by Julian P. Boyd, et al. Princeton University Press, 1950.
Jefferson, Thomas. *Political Writings*. Edited by Joyce Appleby and Terence Ball. Cambridge University Press, 1999.
Jefferson, Thomas. *The Works of Thomas Jefferson*. 12 vols. Edited by Paul Leicester Ford. New York and London: G. P. Putnam's Sons, 1904–5.
Jellinek Georg, *La Déclaration des droits de l'homme et du citoyen: contribution à l'histoire du droit constitutionnel moderne*. Translated by Georges Fardis. Paris: Albert Fontemoing, 1902.
Jennings, Jeremy. *Revolution and the Republic: A History of Political Thought in France since the Eighteenth Century*. Oxford University Press, 2011.
Jones, H. S. *The French State in Question: Public Law and Political Argument in the Third Republic*. Cambridge University Press, 1993.
Jouvenel, Bertrand de. *De la souveraineté: à la recherche du bien politique*. Paris: Génin, Librairie de Médicis, 1955.
Jourard, Sidney. "Some Psychological Aspects of Privacy." *Law and Contemporary Problems* 31 (1966), 307–18.
Judt, Tony. "Rights in France." *La Revue Tocqueville* 1 (1993), 67–108.
Kahn, Robert. *Holocaust Denial and the Law: A Comparative Study*. New York: Palgrave, 2004.
Kairys, David, ed. *The Politics of the Law*. New York: Basic Books, 1998.
Kalven, Harry. *The Negro and the First Amendment*. University of Chicago Press, 1966.
Kalven, Harry. "The New York Times Case: A Note on the Central Meaning of the First Amendment." *Supreme Court Review* (1964), 191–221.
Kammen, Michael. *A Machine That Would Go of Itself: The Constitution in American Culture*. New York: Knopf, 1987.
Kant, Immanuel. "An Answer to the Question: 'What is Enlightenment?'" In *Political Writings*, 54–60. Translated by H. B. Nisbet. Edited by H. Reiss. Cambridge University Press, 1970.
Kant, Immanuel. "On the Common Saying: 'This May be True in Theory, but it does not Apply in Practice.'" In *Political Writings*, 61–92. Translated by H. B. Nisbet. Edited by H. Reiss. Cambridge University Press, 1970.
Kant, Emmanuel. *Le conflit des facultés en trois sections*. Translated by J. Gibelin. Paris: Vrin, 1935.
Kant, Immanuel. *Fondements de la métaphysique des moeurs*. Translated by J. Barni. Paris: Librairie philosophique de Lagrange, 1848.
Kant, Emmanuel. *Métaphysique des moeurs: deuxième partie: Doctrine de la vertu*. Translated by Alexis Philonenko. Paris: Vrin, 1996.
Kant, Emmanuel. *Projet de paix perpétuelle*. Translated by Jean Darbellay. Paris: Presses Universitaires de France, 1958.
Kant, Immanuel. *On Perpetual Peace*. Translated by H. B. Nisbet. Cambridge University Press 1970.

Kant, Emmanuel, *Théorie et pratique*. Translated by Françoise Proust. Paris: GF-Flammarion, 1994.

Kantorowicz, Ernst H. *The King's Two Bodies: A Study in Mediaeval Political Theology*. Princeton University Press, 1997.

Katz, Stanley N. "The American Constitution: A Revolutionary Interpretation." In Richard Beeman, Stephen Botein, and Edward C. Carter II, eds. *Beyond Confederation: Origins of the Constitution and American National Identity*, 23–37. Chapel Hill and London: University of North Carolina Press, 1987.

Katznelson, Ira. *Fear Itself: The New Deal and the Making of Our Time*. New York: Norton, 2014.

Kelsen, Hans. *General Theory of Law and State*. Translated by Anders Wedberg. Cambridge, MA: Harvard University Press, 1949.

Kelsen, Hans. "Justice et droit naturel." In *Le droit naturel: annales de philosophie politique III*. Paris: Pressses Univeritaires de France, 1959.

Kelsen, Hans. *Reine Rechtslehre*. Translated by Charles Eisenmann. Paris: LGDJ, 1999.

Kennedy, Duncan. *The Rise and Fall of Classical Legal Thought*. Washington, DC: Beard Books, 2006.

Kenyon, Cecelia M. "Constitutionalism in Revolutionary America." In J. Roland Pennock and John W. Chapman, eds. *Constitutionalism, NOMOS* xx (1979), 84–120

Kenyon, Cecelia M. "The *Declaration* of Independence: Philosophy of Government in a Free Society." In *Aspects of American Liberty: Philosophical, Historical and Political*, 114–25. Philadelphia: The American Philosophical Society 1977.

Keohane, Nannerl O. *Philosophy and the State in France: The Renaissance to the Enlightenment*. Princeton University Press, 1980.

Kessler, Jeremy. "The Early Years of First Amendment Lochnerism." *Columbia Law Review* 116 (2016), 1915–2004.

Klarman, Michael. *The Framers' Coup: The Making of the United States Constitution*. Oxford University Press, 2016.

Kloppenberg, James. *Toward Democracy: The Struggle for Self-Rule in European and American Thought*. Oxford University Press, 2016.

Kloppenberg, James. *Uncertain Victory: Social Democracy and Progressivism in European and American Thought 1870–1920*. New York: Oxford University Press 1986.

Kloppenberg, James. "The Virtues of Liberalism: Christianity, Republicanism, and Ethics in Early American Political Discourse." *The Journal of American History* 74 (1987), 9–33.

Kondylis, Panayotis. *Περί Αξιοπρέπειας*. Translation of the text "Würde" in Historisches Lexicon zur politisch-sozialen Sprache in Deutschland Geschichliche Grundbegriffe. Athens: Ίνδικτος,2000.

Krotoszynski, Ron. *Privacy Revisited: A Global Perspective on the Right to be Left Alone*. New York: Oxford University Press 2016.

Kuhn, T. S. *The Structure of Scientific Revolutions*. University of Chicago Press, 1970.

Lacorne, Denis. "Le débat des droits de l'homme en France et aux Etats-Unis." *La Revue Tocqueville* 14 (1993), 5–31.

Langton, Rae. "Speech Acts and Unspeakable acts." *Philosophy and Public Affairs* 22 (1993), 293–330.

Langton, Rae. "Whose Right? Ronald Dworkin, Women and Pornographers." *Philosophy & Public Affairs* 19 (1990), 311–59.

Larrère, Catherine. "Rousseau." In Philippe Raynaud et Stéphane Rials, eds. *Dictionnaire de philosophie politique*, 687–95. Paris: Presses Universitaires de France, 2003.

Laurence, Jonathan and Justin Vaisse. *Integrating Islam: Political and Religious Challenges in Contemporary France*. Washington, DC: Brookings Institution Press, 2006.

Lawrence III, Charles R. "The Id, the Ego and Equal Protection: Reckoning with Unconscious Racism." *Stanford Law Review* 39 (1987), 317–88.

Lebovic, Sam. *Free Speech and Unfree News: The Paradox of Press Freedom in America*. Cambridge, MA: Harvard University Press, 2016.

Lecomte, Catherine. "Des dignités à la dignité." In *Fondations et naissances des droits de l'homme*, vol. 1, *L'odyssée des droits de l'homme*. 159–66. Paris: L'Harmattan, 2003.

Lefort, Claude. *L'Invention démocratique*. Paris: Fayard, 1981.

Legros, Robert. "Hegel entre Lumières et romantisme." In *La Révolution française entre Lumières et romantisme*. Cahiers de philosophie politique et juridique, no. 16, 143–57. Centre de Publications de l'Université de Caen, 1989.

Leibniz Gottfried, Wilhelm. *La monadologie*. Paris: C. Delagrave, 1881.

Lerner, Ralph. "The Constitution of the Thinking Revolutionary." In Richard Beeman, Stephen Botein, and Edward C. Carter II, eds. *Beyond Confederation: Origins of the Constitution and American National Identity*, 38–68. Chapel Hill: University of North Carolina, 1987.

Lessay, Franc. "Burke et la nationalisation de la raison." *La Révolution française entre Lumières et Romantisme*. Cahiers de philosophie politique et juridique, no. 16. 65–82. Centre de Publications de l'Université de Caen, 1989.

Levinson, Sanford. *Constitutional Faith*. Princeton University Press, 1988.

Levy, Jean-Paul. "Pratique du droit de réponse dans la presse écrite et la communication audiovisuelle." In Jean-Yves Dupeux and Alain Lacabarats, eds. *Liberté de la presse et droits de la personne*, 31–35. Paris: Dalloz, 1997.

Levy, Leonard. *Emergence of a Free Press*. New York: Oxford University Press, 1985.

Levy, Leonard. *Origins of the Bill of Rights*. New Haven, CT: Yale University Press, 1999.

Lewis, Antony. *Make No Law: The Sullivan Case and the First Amendment*. New York: Vintage, 1991.

Lincoln, Anthony Handley. *Some Political and Social Ideas of English Dissent, 1763–1800*. Cambridge, 1938.

Lipset, Seymour Martin. *American Exceptionalism: A Double-Edged Sword*. New York: W. W. Norton and Company, 1996.

Lock, Geoffrey. "The 1689 Bill of Rights." *Political Studies* 37 (1989), 540–61.

Locke, John. *Essay on Human Understanding*. Edited by Roger Woolhouse. London: Penguin Books, 1997.

Locke, John. *First Treatise of Government*. In *Two Treatises of Government*. London: Thomas Tegg, 1823.

Locke, John. *Letter concerning Toleration*. Indianapolis: Liberty Fund, 2010.

Locke, John. *Questions Concerning the Law of Nature*. Translated by Robert Horwitz and Jenny Strauss Clay. Edited by Diskin Clay. Ithaca, NY: Cornell University Press, 2008.

Locke, John. *The Second Treatise of Government*. Edited by David Wootton. London: Penguin Books, 1993.

Loughlin, Martin. *The British Constitution: A Very Short Introduction*. Oxford University Press, 2013.

Loughlin, Martin. "The Constitutional Imagination." *The Modern Law Review* 78 (2015), 1–25.

Loughlin, Martin. *Foundations of Public Law*. Oxford University Press, 2010.

Loughlin, Martin. *The Idea of Public Law*. Oxford University Press, 2003.

Luchaire, François. *Le juge constitutionnel en France et aux Etats-Unis: étude compare*. Paris: Economica, 2002.
Mably, Gabriel Bonnot de. *Des droits et des devoirs du citoyen*. Paris: Librairie Marcel Didier, 1972.
Machiavelli, Nicolo. *Discourses*. In *The Historical, Political and Diplomatic Writings*. Boston: James R. Osgood and Company, 1881.
MacKinnon, Catharine. *Only Words*. Cambridge, MA: Harvard University Press, 1996.
MacKinnon, Catharine. *Towards A Feminist Theory of the State*. Cambridge, MA: Harvard University Press, 1991.
Macpherson, C. B. *The Political Theory of Possessive Individualism: Hobbes to Locke*. Oxford University Press, 1969.
Madison, James. "Amendments to the Constitution" (speech of June 8, 1789). In *A Century of Lawmaking for a New Nation: U.S. Congressional Documents and Debates, 1774 – 1875*, Annals of Congress, House of Representatives, 1st Congress, 1st Session.
Madison, James. *The Writings of James Madison*. 9 vols. Edited by Gaillard Hunt. New York and London: G. P. Putnam's Sons, 1900–10.
Madison, James. *The Papers of James Madison*. Edited by R. Rutland and W. Rachal. Charlottesville: University of Virginia Press, 1975.
Maier, Pauline. *American Scripture: Making the Declaration of Independence*. New York: Alfred A. Knopf, 1997.
Maier, Pauline. *Ratification: The People Debate the Constitution, 1787–1788*. New York: Simon & Schuster, 2010.
Maistre, Joseph-Marie De. *Considerations on France*. Translated by Richard A. Lebrun. Montreal and London: McGill-Queen's University Press, 1974.
Malberg, Raymond Carré de. *Théorie générale du droit et de l'Etat*, vol. 1. Paris: Sirey, 1920.
Manent, Pierre. *Cours familier de philosophie politique*. Paris: Gallimard, 2001.
Manent, Pierre. *Naissances de la politique moderne: Machiavel-Hobbes-Rousseau*. Paris: Payot, 1977.
Mansfield, Harvey. "Les formes de la liberté: le constitutionnalisme dans la pensée politique classique et moderne." In Terence Marshall, ed. *Théorie et pratique du gouvernement constitutionnel: la France et les Etats-Unis*, 23–33. La Garenne Colombes: Editions de l'Espace Européen, 1992.
Marcaggi, Vincent. *Les origines de la Déclaration des droits de l'homme de 1789*. Paris: Fontemoing, 1912.
Maron, Eugène. *Histoire littéraire de la convention nationale*. Paris: Poulet Malassis et de Broise, 1860.
Marshall, Terence. "Les droits de l'homme et la politique constitutionnelle: un dialogue franco-américain à l'époque révolutionnaire." In Bernard Bourgeois et Jacques D'Hondt, eds. *La philosophie et la Révolution française*, 29–48. Paris: Vrin, 1993.
Marx, Karl. *Capital*, vol. 1. Translated by Ben Fowkes. New York: Vintage, 1977.
Marx, Karl. "The Jewish Question." In *The Marx-Engels Reader*, 26–52. Edited by Robert Tucker. New York: Norton, 1978.
Marx, Karl. "The German Ideology." In *The Marx-Engels Reader*, 146–200. Edited by Robert Tucker. New York: Norton, 1978.
Mason, George. "Opposition to a Unitary Executive." In Max Farrand, ed. *The Records of The Federal Convention of 1787*, vol. 1. New Haven, CT: Yale University Press, 1911.
Massey, Calvin R. *The Ninth Amendment and the Constitution's Unenumerated Rights Philadelphia*. Philadelphia: Temple University Press, 1995.

Matsuda, Mari J. , et al., eds. *Words that Wound: Critical Race Theory, Assaultive Speech and the First Amendment*. London and New York: Routledge, 1993.
Matthews, Richard K. *If Men Were Angels: James Madison and the Heartless Empire of Reason*. Lawrence: University Press of Kansas, 1995.
Mayaud, Yves. "L'abus de droit en matière de droit de réponse." In Jean-Yves Dupeux and Alain Lacabarats, eds. *Liberté de la presse et droits de la personne*, 5–16. Paris: Dalloz, 1997.
Mazo, Eugene. "Regulating Campaign Finance through Legislative Recusal Rules." In Timothy K. Kuhner and Eugene D. Mazo, eds. *Democracy by the People: Reforming Campaign Finance in America*. Cambridge University Press, 2018.
Mazauric, Claude. *Babeuf et la conspiration pour l'égalité*. Paris: Editions Sociales, 1962.
Mazzanti Pepe, Fernanda. "Mably pour une démocratie à la mesure de l'homme." In Peter Friedemann, Florence Gauthier, Jean-Luc Malvache, and Fernanda Mazzani Pepe, eds. *Colloque Mably: la politique comme science morale*, vol. 1, 65–83. Bary: Palomar Casa Editrice, 1995.
McCloskey, H. J. "The Political Ideal of Privacy." *Philosophical Quarterly* 21 (1971), 303–14.
McConnell, Michael W. "The Origins and Historical Understanding of Free Exercise of Religion." *Harvard Law Review* 103 (1990), 1409–507.
McDonald, Forrest. *Novus Ordo Seclorum: The Intellectual Origins of the Constitution*. Lawrence: University Press of Kansas, 1985.
McWilliams, Wilson Carey. "On Equality as the Moral Foundation for Community." In Robert H. Horwitz, ed. *The Moral Foundations of the American Republic*, 183–213. Charlottesville: University Press of Virginia, 1979.
Meckstroth, Christopher. *The Struggle for Democracy: Paradoxes of Progress and the Politics of Change*. Oxford University Press, 2015.
Meiklejohn, Alexander. "The First Amendment is an Absolute." *Supreme Court Review* (1961), 245–66.
Meiklejohn, Alexander. "Free Speech and Its Relation to Self-Government." In *Political Freedom: The Constitutional Powers of the People*. Westport, CT: Greenwood Press Publishers, 1979.
Meyer, Michael and William Parent, eds. *The Constitution of Rights: Human Dignity and American Values*. Ithaca, NY: Cornell University Press, 1992.
Michel, Alain. "La dignité humaine chez Cicéron." In Pierre Magnard, ed. *La dignité de l'homme*,17–24. Actes du Colloque tenu à la Sorbonne (Paris-IV). Paris: Honoré Champion, 1995.
Michelman, Frank. "Possession v. Distribution in the Constitutional Idea of Property." *Iowa Law Review* 72 (1987), 1319–50.
Mill, John Stuart. "On Liberty." In *On Liberty and Other Essays*. Edited by John Gray. Oxford University Press, 1998.
Milton, John. *Areopagitica*. Cambridge University Press, 1918.
Minow, Martha, "Equality and the Bill of Rights." In Michael Meyer and William Parent, eds. *The Constitution of Rights: Human Dignity and American Values*, 118–28. Ithaca, NY: Cornell University Press, 1992.
Montesquieu, Charles Louis de Secondat Baron de. *Oeuvres complètes de Montesquieu*. Edited by D. Oster. Paris: Seuil, 1964.
Morelly, Étienne-Gabriel. *Code de la nature*. Paris: Paul Masgana, 1841.
Mornet, Daniel. *Les origines intellectuelles de la Révolution française 1715–1787*. Paris: Armand Colin 1954.
Moyn, Samuel. *Not Enough: Human Rights in an Unequal World*. Cambridge, MA: Harvard University Press, 2019.

Murrin, John M. "A Roof without Walls: The Dilemma of American National Identity." In Richard Beeman, Stephen Botein, and Edward C. Carter II, eds. *Beyond Confederation: Origins of the Constitution and American National Identity*. Chapel Hill and London: University of North Carolina Press, 1987.

Nelson, Eric. *The Royalist Revolution: Monarchy and the American Founding*. Cambridge, MA: Harvard University Press, 2014.

Nicolet, Claude. *L'idée républicaine en France, 1789–1924*. Paris: Gallimard, 1982.

Nietzsche, Friedrich. *Zur Genealogie der Moral*. Translated by Eric Blondel, Ole Hansen Love, Théo Levdenbach, and Pierre Pénisson. Paris: GF Flammarion, 2000.

Oakeshott, Michael. *Morality and Politics in Modern Europe*. New Haven, CT: Yale University Press, 1993.

Ossipow, William and Gerber, Dominik. "The Reception of Vattel's Law of Nations in the American Colonies: From James Otis and John Adams to the Declaration of Independence." *American Journal of Legal History* 57 (2017), 521–55.

Otis, James. "A Vindication of the British Colonies." In Richard Samuelson, ed. *Collected Political Writings of James Otis*, 183–208. Indianapolis: Liberty Fund, 2015.

Otis, James. "Essay on the Writs of Assistance Case" (*Boston Gazette*, January 4, 1762). In *Collected Political Writings of James Otis*, 15–18. Indianapolis, Liberty Fund, 2015.

Otis, James. *The Rights of the British Colonies: Asserted and Proved*. Boston and London: J. Almon, 1764.

Ozouf, Mona. *L'homme régénéré*. Paris: Gallimard, 1989.

Paine, Thomas. "The Rights of Man, Part I." In *Political Writings*. Edited by Bruce Kuklick. Cambridge University Press, 1989.

Paine, Thomas. "The Rights of Man, Part II." In *Political Writings*. Edited by Bruce Kuklick. Cambridge University Press, 1989.

Paine, Thomas. *Common Sense*. New York: Alfred Knopf, 1994.

Palmer, Robert R. *The Age of the Democratic Revolution: A Political History of Europe and America, 1760–1800*. Princeton University Press, 1959.

Palmer Robert R. "The European Enlightenment in Its American Setting." In *Aspects of American Liberty: Philosophical, Historical and Political*, 47–55. Philadelphia: The American Philosophical Society, 1977.

Pangle, Thomas L. *The Spirit of Modern Republicanism: The Moral Vision of the American Founders and the Philosophy of Locke*. University of Chicago Press, 1988.

Parent, William. "Constitutional Values and Human Dignity." In Michael Meyer and William Parent, eds. *The Constitution of Rights: Human Dignity and American Values*, 47–72. Ithaca, NY: Cornell University Press, 1992.

Parent, William. "A New Definition of Privacy for the Law." *Law and Philosophy* 2 (1983), 305–38.

Patel, Kiran Klaus. *The New Deal: A Global History*. Princeton University Press, 2015.

Pech, Lauren. *La liberté d'expression et sa limitation: les enseignements de l'expérience américaine au regard d'expériences européennes (Allemagne, France et Convention européenne des droits de l'homme)*. Presses Universitaires de la Faculté de Droit de Clermont Ferrand, LGDJ, 2003.

Pellegrin, Pierre. "Aristote." In Philippe Raynaud et Stéphane Rials, eds. *Dictionnaire de Philosophie Politique*, 28–36. Paris: Presses Universitaires de France, 2003.

Peller, Gary. "The Metaphysics of American Law." *California Law Review* 73 (1985), 1152–290.

Pettit, Philip. *Republicanism: A Theory of Freedom and Government*. Oxford University Press, 1999.

Philonenko, Alexis. *Jean-Jacques Rousseau et la pensée du malheur*, 3 vols. Paris: Vrin, 1984.

Philonenko, Alexis. *Théorie et praxis dans la pensée morale et politique de Kant et de Fichte en 1793*. Paris: Vrin, 1968.
Pico della Mirandola, Giovanni. *De la dignité de l'homme*. Translated by Yves Hersant. Paris : Editions de l'Eclat, 1993.
Pincus, Steve. *1688: The First Modern Revolution*. New Haven, CT: Yale University Press, 2009.
Pincus, Steve. *The Heart of the Declaration: The Founders' Case for an Activist Government*. New Haven, CT: Yale University Press, 2016.
Pocock, J. G. A. *The Machiavellian Moment: Florentine Political Thought and the Atlantic Republican Tradition*. Princeton University Press, 1975.
Pocock, J. G. A. "1776: The Revolution Against Parliament." In J. G. A. Pocock, ed. *Three British Revolutions: 1641, 1689, 1776*. Princeton University Press, 1980.
Polanyi, Karl. *The Great Transformation*. Boston: Beacon Press, 2001.
Polin, Raymond. *La politique de la solitude: essai sur la philosophie politique de Jean-Jacques Rousseau*. Paris: Sirey, 1971.
Polin, Raymond. *La politique morale de John Locke*. Paris: Presses Universitaires de France, 1960.
Popper, Karl. "Epistemology without a Knowing Subject." In *Objective Knowledge*,. Clarendon Press: Oxford University Press, 1972.
Post, Robert. *Citizens Divided: Campaign Finance Reform and the Constitution*. Cambridge, MA: Harvard University Press, 2014.
Post, Robert and Peter Molnar. "Interview with Robert Post." In Michael Herz and Peter Molnar, eds. *The Content and Context of Hate Speech: Rethinking Regulation and Responses*, 11–36. Cambridge University Press, 2012.
Post, Robert and Amanda Shanor. "Adam Smith's First Amendment." *Harvard Law Review Forum* 128 (2015), 165–82.
Pound, Roscoe. "Mechanical Jurisprudence." *Columbia Law Review* 8 (1908). 605–23
Pound, Roscoe. "Liberty of Contract." *Yale Law Journal* 18 (1909), 454–87
Powe, Lucas A. *The Warren Court and American Politics*. Cambridge, MA: Harvard University Press, 2001.
Price, Richard. *A Discourse on the Love of Country* 2nd ed. London: T. Cadell, 1789.
Primus, Richard. *The American Language of Rights*. Cambridge University Press, 1999.
Primus, Richard. "An Introduction to the Nature of American Rights." In Barry Alan Shain, ed. *The Nature of Rights at the American Founding and Beyond*, 15–24. Charlottesville and London: University of Virginia Press, 2007.
Proudhon, Pierre Joseph. *De la justice dans la Révolution et dans l'Eglise*, vol. 1. Paris: Libraire de Garnier Frères, 1858.
Purdy, Jedediah. *A Tolerable Anarchy: Rebels, Reactionaries and the Making of American Freedom*. New York: Vintage, 2010.
Rabban, David. *Free Speech in Its Forgotten Years*. Cambridge University Press, 1997.
Rabban, David. "The Ahistorical Historian: Leonard Levy and Freedom of Expression in Early American History." *Stanford Law Review* 37 (1985), 795–856.
Rakove, Jack N. *Original Meanings: Politics and Ideas in the Making of the Constitution*. New York: Alfred A. Knopf, 1996.
Raynaud, Phillippe. "Anciens et Modernes." In Philippe Raynaud and Stéphane Rials, eds. *Dictionnaire de philosophie politique*. Paris: Presses Universitaires de France, 2003.
Raynaud, Philippe. "Locke et les limites de la raison libérale." In Philippe Raynaud and Stéphane Rials, eds. *Une prudence moderne?*, 21–33. Paris: Presses Universitaires de France, 1992.

Raynaud, Philippe. "Lumières et Anti-lumières: de la Révolution française au romantisme politique." In *La Révolution française entre Lumières et romantisme*. Cahiers de philosophie politique et juridique, no. 16. 179–92. Centre de Publications de l'Université de Caen, 1989.

Raynaud, Philippe. "Révolution américaine." In Philippe Raynaud et Stéphane Rials, eds. *Dictionnaire de philosophie politique*, 669–76. Paris: Presses Universitaires de France, 2003.

Raynaud, Philippe. "Révolution française." In Philippe Raynaud and Stéphane Rials, eds. *Dictionnaire de philosophie politique*, 669–76. Paris: Presses Universitaires de France, 2003.

Raynaud, Philippe. *Trois révolutions de la liberté: Angleterre, Amérique, France*. Paris: Presses Universitaires de France, 2009.

Rawls, John. *A Theory of Justice*. Cambridge, MA: Harvard University Press, 1971.

Rawls, John. *Political Liberalism*. Columbia University Press, 1993.

Redlich, Norman. "Are there 'Certain Rights retained by the People?'" In Randy E. Barnett, ed. *The Rights Retained by the People: The History and Meaning of the Ninth Amendment*, 127–47. Fairfax, VA: George Mason University Press, 1989.

Reid, John Phillip. "The Authority of Rights at the American Founding." In Barry Alan Shain, ed. *The Nature of Rights at the American Founding and Beyond*, 258–79. Charlottesville and London: University of Virginia Press, 2007.

Reid, John Philip. *The Concept of Liberty in the Age of the American Founding*. Chicago and London: University of Chicago Press, 1988.

Reid, John Phillip. *Constitutional History of the American Revolution: The Authority of Rights*. Madison: University of Wisconsin Press, 1986.

Renaut, Alain. *Le système du droit: philosophie et droit dans la pensée de Fichte*. Paris: Presses Universitaires de France, 1986.

Rials, Stéphane. "La Déclaration de 1789: le mystère des origins." *Droits* 8 (1988), 3–21.

Rials, Stéphane. *La Déclaration des droits de l'homme et du citoyen*. Paris: Hachette, 1988.

Rials, Stéphane. "Ouverture: généalogie des droits de l'homme." *Droits* 2 (1985), 3–12.

Richards, David A. J. "Constitutional Liberty, Dignity, and Reasonable Justification." In Michael Meyer and William Parent, eds. *The Constitution of Rights, Human Dignity and American Values*, 73–101. Ithaca, NY: Cornell University Press, 1992.

Richards, David A. J. *Foundations of American Constitutionalism*. New York: Oxford University Press, 1989.

Richards, David A. J. "Free Speech as Toleration." In W. J. Waluchow, ed. *Free Expression, Essays in Law and Philosophy*. Oxford: Clarendon Press, 1994.

Ricoeur, Paul. "The Erosion of Tolerance and the Resistance of the Intolerable." In Paul Ricoeur, ed. *Tolerance Between Intolerance and the Intolerable*, 189–201. Providence, RI: Bergahn Books, 1996.

Ritter, Joachim. *Hegel et la Révolution française*. Translated by Xavier Tilliette. Paris: Beauchesne, 1970.

Rivero, Jean. "Intervention in the Debate on 'Les Libertés.'" In Louis Favoureux, ed. *La continuité constitutionnelle en France, de 1789 à 1989*. Paris: Presses Universitaires d'Aix-Marseille, 1990.

Robbins, Caroline. *The Eighteenth Century Commonwealthman: Studies in the Transmission, Development and Circumstance of English Liberal Thought from the Restoration of Charles III till the War with the Thirteen Colonies*. New York: Atheneum, 1969.

Robbins, Caroline. "'When It Is That Colonies May Turn Independent': An Analysis of the Environment and Politics of Francis Hutcheson (1694–1746)." *William and Mary Quarterly* 11 (1954), 214–51.

Robespierre, Maximilien. *Discours sur la liberté de la presse, prononcé à la Société des amis de la constitution le 11 Mai 1791*. Paris: Imprimerie Nationale, 1791.

Robespierre, Maximilien. "Discours sur la liberté de la presse." In *Oeuvres de Maximilien Robespierre*, vol. 8. Edited by Marc Bouloiseau, Georges Lefebvre, and Albert Soboul. Paris: Centre Nationale des Recherches Scientifiques, 2007.

Robespierre, Maximilien. "Discours sur les subsistances et le droit à l'existence." In *Discours pour le bonheur et pour la liberté*. Edited by Yannick Bosc, Florence Gauthier, and Sophie Wahnich. Paris: La Fabrique, 2000.

Robespierre, Maximilien. *Oeuvres de Maximilien Robespierre*. 10 vols. Edited by Marc Bouloiseau, Georges Lefebvre, and Albert Soboul. Paris: Presses Universitaires de France, 1958.

Rosanvallon, Pierre. *La démocratie inachevée: histoire de la souveraineté du peuple en France*. Paris: Gallimard, 2000.

Rosanvallon, Pierre. *Le modèle politique français: la société civile contre le jacobinisme, de 1789 à nos jours*. Paris: Seuil 2004.

Rosenberg, Norman L. "Another World." *Reviews in American History* 16 (1988), 554–59.

Rousseau, Jean-Jacques. *Discours sur l'économie politique*. In *Oeuvres complètes*, vol. 3. Paris: Gallimard, 1964.

Rousseau, Jean-Jacques. *Discours sur l'origine et les fondements de l'inégalité parmi les hommes*. In *Oeuvres complètes*, vol. 3. Paris: Gallimard, 1964.

Rousseau, Jean-Jacques. *Discours sur les sciences et les arts*. In *Oeuvres complètes*, vol. 3. Paris: Gallimard, 1964.

Rousseau, Jean-Jacques. *Du contrat social (première version, manuscrit de Genève)*. In *Oeuvres complètes*, vol. 3, 281–346. Paris: Gallimard, 1964.

Rousseau, Jean-Jacques. *Du contrat social*. In *Oeuvres complètes*, vol. 3. Paris: Gallimard, 1964.

Rousseau, Jean-Jacques. *Emile*. In *Oeuvres complètes*, vol. 4. Paris: Gallimard, 1969.

Rousseau, Jean-Jacques. *Lettres écrites de la montagne*. In *Oeuvres complètes*, vol. 3. Paris: Gallimard, 1964.

Rousseau, Jean-Jacques. *Oeuvres complètes*. 5 vols. Paris: Gallimard, 1959–95.

Rousseau, Jean-Jacques. "On the Social Contract." *The Basic Political Writings*. Translated by Donald A. Cress. Edited by Peter Gay. Indianapolis, Hackett, 1987.

Roy, Jean. "La 'prérogative' chez Locke." In Simone Goyard-Fabre, ed. *La Pensée Libérale de John Locke*, 149–55. Cahiers de philosophie politique et juridique, no. 5. Centre de Publications de l'Université de Caen. 1984.

Rumble, Wilfrid E. "James Madison on the Value of Bills of Rights." In J. Roland Pennock and John W. Chapman, eds. *Constitutionalism: NOMOS xx* (1979), 122–62.

Sadoun, Marc, ed. *La démocratie en France 1: idéologies*. Paris: Gallimard, 2000.

Saint-Just, Louis Antoine de. "Ésprit de la Révolution et de la Constitution de France." In *Oeuvres complètes*, vol. 1. Paris: Charpentier et Fasquelle, 1908.

Saint-Just, Louis Antoine de. "Fragments sur les institutions républicaines." In *Oeuvres complètes*, vol. 2. Paris: Charpentier et Fasquelle, 1908.

Sandel, Michael. *Democracy's Discontent: America in Search of a Public Philosophy* Cambridge, MA: Harvard University Press, 1998.

Sartorius, Rolf, ed. *Paternalism*. Minneapolis: University of Minnesota Press, 1987.

Sartori, Giovanni. *Théorie de la démocratie*. Paris: Armand Colin, 1973.

Scanlon, Thomas. "A Theory of Freedom of Expression." *Philosophy and Public Affairs* 1, no. 2 (1972) 204–226.

Schauer, Frederick. "Categories and the First Amendment: A Play in Three Acts." *Vanderbilt Law Review* 34 (1981), 265–307.

Schauer, Frederick. "Free Speech and The Social Construction of Privacy." *Social Research* 68 (2001), 221–31

Schauer, Frederick. *Free Speech: A Philosophical Inquiry*. Cambridge University Press, 1982.

Schauer, Frederick. "Uncoupling Free Speech." *Columbia Law Review* 92 (1992), 1321–57.

Schauer, Frederick. "The Exceptional First Amendment." In Michael Ignatieff, ed. *American Exceptionalism and Human Rights*, 29–56. Princeton University Press, 2005.

Schivelbusch, Wolfgang. *Three New Deals: Reflections on Roosevelt's America, Mussolini's Italy, and Hitler's Germany, 1933–1939*. New York: Metropolitan Books, 2006.

Schmitt, Carl. *The Concept of the Political*. Translated by George Schwab. University of Chicago Press, 1996.

Schmitt, Carl. *Political Theology*. Translated by George Schwab. Cambridge, MA: The MIT Press, 1985.

Schneider, Louis, ed. *The Scottish Moralists on Human Nature and Society*. University of Chicago Press, 1967.

Schwartz, Bernard, ed. *The Bill of Rights: A Documentary History*. New York: Chelsea House Publishers, 1971.

Schwartz, Paul M. "The EU-US Privacy Collision: A Turn to Institutions and Procedures." *Harvard Law Review* 126 (2013), 1966–2009.

Schwartz, Paul M. and Solove, Daniel J. "Reconciling Personal Information in the United States and European Union." *California Law Review* 102 (2014), 877–916.

Schwoerer, Lois G. "The Bill of Rights: Epitome of the Revolution of 1688–89." In Pocock J. G. A., ed. *Three British Revolutions: 1641, 1688, 1776*, 225–43. Princeton University Press, 1980.

Scott, Austin. "Holmes v. Walton: The New Jersey Precedent." *American Historical Review* 4 (1899), 456–60.

Seidman, Louis Michael and Mark V Tushnet. "The State Action Paradox." In *Remnants of Belief, Contemporary Constitutional Issues*, 49–71. Oxford University Press, 1996.

Sellers, M. N. *American Republicanism: Roman Ideology in the United States Constitution*. London: MacMillan, 1994.

Sellers, M. N. *The Sacred Fire of Liberty: Republicanism, Liberalism and the Law*. London: MacMillan, 1998.

Shain, Barry. *The Myth of American Individualism: The Protestant Origins of American Political Thought*. Princeton University Press, 1994.

Shain, Barry A. "Rights Natural and Civil in the *Declaration* of Independence." In Barry Alan Shain, ed. *The Nature of Rights at the American Founding and Beyond*, 116–62. Charlottesville and London: University of Virginia Press, 2007.

Shiffrin, Seana. *Speech Matters: On Lying, Morality, and the Law*. Princeton University Press, 2014.

Shklar, Judith. "Liberté positive: liberté négative en Amérique." In *Les usages de la liberté*, 107–35. Neuchâtel: Ed. De la Baconnière, 1990.

Shklar, Judith. *Men and Citizens: A Study of Rousseau's Political Theory*. Cambridge University Press, 1969.

Sieyès, Joseph Emmanuel. *Ecrits politiques*. Edited by Roberto Zapperi. Paris: Editions des archives Contemporaines, 1985.

Sieyès, Joseph Emmanuel. *Political Writings*. Edited by Michael Sonenscher. Indianapolis, Cambridge: Hackett, 2003.

Silier, Yildiz. *Freedom: Political, Metaphysical, Negative and Positive*. Aldershot: Ashgate, 2005.

Skinner, Quentin. *The Foundations of Modern Political Thought*, vol. 2. Cambridge University Press, 1979.

Skinner, Quentin. *Liberty before Liberalism*. Cambridge University Press, 1998.

Smith, Adam. *The Theory of Moral Sentiments*. Indianapolis: Liberty Fund, 1982.
Smith, Adam. *The Wealth of Nations*, vol. 1. Indianapolis: Liberty Fund, 1981.
Smith, Joseph Henry. *Appeals to the Privy Council from the American Plantations*. New York: Columbia University Press, 1950.
Smith, Rogers M. *Liberalism and American Constitutional Law*. Cambridge, MA: Harvard University Press, 1985.
Soboul, Albert. "Babeuf et le Babouvisme." In *Oeuvres de Babeuf*, vol. 1, *Babeuf avant la Révolution*, 7–22. Edited by V. Daline, A. Saitta, A. Soboul. Paris: Bibliothèque Nationale, 1977.
Solomon, Stephen D. *Revolutionary Dissent: How the Founding Generation Created the Freedom of Speech*. New York: St. Martin's Press, 2016.
Somos, Mark. *American States of Nature: The Origins of Independence, 1761–1775*. Oxford University Press, 2019.
Spinoza, Benedict. *Tractatus Theologicophilosophicus*. Translated by Jonathan Israel and Michael Silverthorne. Cambridge University Press, 2007.
Spitz, Jean-Fabien. "Jean-Jacques Rousseau et les droits de l'individu." In Cazzaniga, Gian Mario–Zarka, Yves Charles, eds. *L'individu dans la pensée moderne XVIe–XVIIIe siècles*, 659–74 Pisa: Edizioni, 1995.
Staël, Madame de. *Considérations sur les principaux évenements de la Révolution Ffançaise*. Paris: Delaunay Libraire, 1818.
Stern, Alfred. "Hegel et les idées de 1789." In E. Barker et al. *La Révolution de 1789 et la pensée moderne*. Paris: Presses Universitaires de France, 1940.
Stone, Geoffrey "Content Regulation and the First Amendment." *William and Mary Law Review* 25 (1983), 189–252.
Stone, Geoffrey. *Perilous Times: Free Speech in Wartime, From the Sedition Act of 1798 to the War on Terrorism*. New York: Norton, 2005.
Stone, Geoffrey "Restrictions of Speech Because of its Content: The Peculiar Case of Subject-Matter Restrictions." *University of Chicago Law Review* 46 (1987), 81–115.
Storing, Herbert and Dry Murray, eds. *The Complete Anti-Federalist*. 7 vols. Chicago: University Press, 1981.
Strauss, David A. "Persuasion, Autonomy, and Freedom of Expression." *Columbia Law Review* 91 (1991), 334–71.
Strauss, Leo. *Natural Right and History*. University of Chicago Press, 1950.
Strayer, John. "The Rule of Law." In *Aspects of American Liberty, Philosophical, Historical and Political*, 16–36. Philadelphia: The American Philosophical Society, 1977.
Sullivan, Kathleen M. "Two Concepts of Freedom of Speech." *Harvard Law Review* 124 (2010), 143–77.
Sunstein, Cass R. "Free Speech Now." In G. Stone, R. Epstein, and C. Sunstein, eds. *The Bill of Rights in the Modern State*, 255–316. University of Chicago Press, 1992.
Sunstein, Cass R. *The Second Bill of Rights: FDR's Unfinished Revolution and Why we Need it More than Ever*. New York: Basic Books, 2004.
Taguieff, Pierre-Andre. *La force du préjugé: essai sur le racisme et ses doubles*. Paris: Gallimard, 1990.
Talmon, J. L. *The Origins of Totalitarian Democracy*. London: Penguin 1952.
Tarr, G. Alan. *Understanding State Constitutions*. Princeton University Press, 1998.
Taylor, Charles. *Sources of the Self: The Making of the Modern Identity*. Cambridge, MA: Harvard University Press, 1989.
Tierney, Brian. *The Idea of Natural Rights: Studies on Natural Rights, Natural Law, and Church Law 1150–1625*. Michigan: Eerdmans, 1997.

Tocqueville, Alexis de. *L'Ancien Régime et la Révolution*. Paris: Gallimard, 1967.

Tocqueville, Alexis de. *Democracy in America*. Translated by George Lawrence. Edited by J. P. Mayer. New York: Doubleday, 1969.

Tocqueville, Alexis de. *De la démocratie en Amérique*, vol. 2. Paris: Gallimard, 1961.

Tocqueville, Alexis de. "Discours prononcé à l'Assemblée constituante dans la discussion du projet de Constitution (12 September 1848), sur la question du droit au travail." In *Oeuvres complètes d'Alexis de Tocqueville*, vol. 9, 536–52. Paris: Michel Lévy Frères, 1866.

Thompson, Martin P. "The History of Fundamental Law in Political Thought from the French Wars of Religion to the American Revolution." *The American Historical Review* 91 (1986), 1103–28.

Tosel, André, ed. *De la prudence des Anciens comparée à celle des Modernes: sémantique d'un concept, déplacement des problématiques*. Paris: Les Belles Lettres, 1995.

Tosel, André. *Kant révolutionnaire: droit et politique*. Paris: Presses Universitaires de France, 1988.

Tourkochoriti, Ioanna. "Challenging Historical Facts and National Truths: An Analysis of Cases from France and Greece." In Uladzislau Belavusau and Aleksandra Glyszczynska Grabias, eds. *Law And Memory: Towards Legal Governance of History*. Cambridge University Press, 2017. 151–74.

Tourkochoriti, Ioanna. "The Burka Ban: Divergent Approaches to Freedom of Religion in France and in the U.S.A." *William and Mary Bill of Rights Journal* 20 (2012), 791–852.

Tourkochoriti, Ioanna. "Should Hate Speech be Protected: Group Defamation, Party Bans, Holocaust Denial and the Divide between Europe and the US." *Columbia Human Rights Law Review* 45 (2014), 552–622.

Tourkochoriti, Ioanna. "The Snowden Revelations: The Transatlantic Trade and Investment Partnership and the Divide Between US –EU in Data Privacy Protection." *University of Arkansas Law Review* 36 (2014), 161–76.

Tourkochoriti, Ioanna. Speech, Privacy and Dignity in France and the USA. *Loyola Los Angeles International and Comparative Law Review* 40 (2016), 101–82.

Treanor, William Michael. "Judicial Review Before Marbury." *Stanford Law Review* 58 (2005), 455–562.

Tribe, Laurence and Michael C Dorf. *On Reading the Constitution*. Cambridge, MA: Harvard University Press, 1991.

Tribe, Laurence. *The Invisible Constitution*. Oxford University Press, 2008.

Trigeaud, Jean-Marc. "Droit." n Philippe Raynaud and Stéphane Rials, eds. *Dictionnaire de philosophie politique*. Paris: Presses Universitaires de France, 2003.

Trognon, Alain. "La Déclaration en tant qu'acte de discours." In François Borella, ed. *Les valeurs de la Révolution devant la science actuelle*, 79–96. Paris: Presses Universitaires de Nancy, 1990.

Troper, Michel. "La Déclaration des droits de l'homme et du citoyen en 1789." In *La Déclaration des droits de l'homme et du citoyen et la jurisprudence*. Paris: Presses Universitaired de France, 1989.

Troper, Michel. " Jefferson et l'interprétation de la Déclaration des droits de l'homme de 1789." *Revue Française d'Histoire des Idées Politiques* 9 (1999), 3–23.

Troper, Michel. *Terminer la Révolution: La Constitution de 1795*. Paris: Fayard, 2006.

Tuck, Richard. *Natural Rights Theories*. Cambridge University Press, 1979.

Tushnet, Mark. *The Constitution of the United States of America: A Contextual Analysis*. Oxford: Hart, 2015.

Tushnet, Mark. "The Issue of State Action/Horizontal Effect in Comparative Constitutional Law." In *International Journal of Constitutional Law* 1 (2003), 79–98.

Tushnet, Mark. "United States of America." In Markus Thiel, ed. *The Militant Democracy Principle in Modern Democracies*, 357–78. London: Routledge 2009.

Van Loan, III, Eugene M. "Natural Rights and the Ninth Amendment." In Randy E. Barnett, ed. *The Rights Retained by the People: The History and Meaning of the Ninth Amendment*, 149–77. Fairfax, VA: George Mason University Press, 1989.

Vattel, Emer de. *The Law of Nations or Principles of the Law of Nature, Applied to the Conduct and Affairs of Nations and Sovereigns*. English translation of French text. London: J. Newbery et al., 1760.

Vedel, Georges. "L'incorporation de la Déclaration de droits de l'homme dans la Constitution française." *La Revue Tocqueville* 14 (1993), 157–63.

Villey, Michel. "Abrégé du Droit Naturel Classique." *Archives de Philosophie du Droit* 5 (1960), 25–72.

Villey, Michel. *Le droit et les droits de l'homme*. Paris: Presses Universitaires de France, 1983.

Villey, Michel. *La Formation de la Pensée Juridique Moderne*. Paris: Presses Universitaires de France, 2003.

Voltaire. *Toleration and Other Essays*. Translated by Joseph McCabe. New York and London: G.P. Putnam's Sons, 1912.

Wachsmann, Patrick. "Déclaration ou constitution des droits?" In Michel Troper and Lucien Jaume, eds. *1789 et l'invention de la Constitution*, 44–54. Paris: LGDJ and Bruylant, 1994.

Wacks, Raymond. "The poverty of 'Privacy.'" *The Law Quarterly Review* 96 (1980), 73–89.

Waldron, Jeremy. "Free Speech and the Menace of Hysteria." *The New York Review of Books* 55 (May 29, 1998).

Waldron, Jeremy. "Karl Marx's 'On the Jewish Question.'" In Jeremy Waldron, ed. *Nonsense Upon Stilts: Bentham, Burke and Marx on the Rights of Man*, 119–36. London and New York: Methuen, 1987.

Waldron, Jeremy. *The Harm in Hate Speech*. Cambridge, MA: Harvard University Press, 2012.

Waldron, Jeremy. *God, Locke and Equality*. Cambridge University Press, 2002.

Walton, Charles. *Policing Opinion in the French Revolution: The Culture of Calumny and the Problem of Free Speech*. Oxford University Press, 2011.

Walker Howe, Daniel. "Why the Scottish Enlightenment Was Useful to the Framers of the American Constitution." *Comparative Studies in Society and History* 31 (1989), 572–87.

Weinrib, Laura. *The Taming of Free Speech*. Cambridge, MA: Harvard University Press, 2016.

Weinstein, Michael. A. "The Uses of Privacy in the Good Life." In J. Roland Pennock and John W. Chapman, eds. *NOMOS XIII*. New York: Atherton Press, 1971.

Welch, Cheryl B. *Liberty and Utility: The French Ideologues and the Transformation of Liberalism*. New York: Columbia Press, 1984.

West, Thomas G. "Free Speech in the American Founding and in Modern Liberalism." *Social Philosophy & Policy* 21, no. 2 (2004), 310–84.

West, Thomas G. *The Political Theory of the American Founding: Natural Rights, Public Policy and the Moral Conditions of Freedom*. Cambridge University Press, 2018.

Westbrook, Robert. *John Dewey and American Democracy*. Ithaca, NY: Cornell University Press, 1991.

Weulersse, Georges. *La physiocratie à l'aube de la Révolution: 1781–1792*. Paris: EHESS 1985.

Weulersse, Georges. *La physiocratie sous les ministères de Turgot et de Necker (1774–1781)*. Paris: Presses Universitaires de France, 1950.

White, G. Edward. "The First Amendment Comes of Age: The Emergence of Free Speech in Twentieth-Century America." *Michigan Law Review* 95 (1996), 299–392.

White, Morton. *The Philosophy of the American Revolution*. New York: Oxford University Press, 1978.

Whitman, James Q. "Consumerism versus Producerism: A Study in Comparative Law." *Yale Law Journal* 117 (2007–8), 340–406.

Whitman, James Q. "Enforcing Civility and Respect: Three Societies." *Yale Law Journal* 109 (2000), 1279–398.

Whitman, James Q. "Human Dignity' in Europe and the United States: The Social Foundations." In Georg Nolte, ed. *European and US Constitutionalism*, 108–24. Strasbourg: Council of Europe Publishing, 2005.

Whitman, James Q. "The Two Western Cultures of Privacy: Liberty versus Dignity." *Yale Law Journal* 113 (2004), 1151–221.

Williams, Robert F. *The Law of American State Constitutions*. Oxford University Press, 2009.

Wills, Gary. *Inventing America: Jefferson's Declaration of Independence*. (New York: Mariner Books, 2002.

Winterer, Caroline. *American Enlightenment: Happiness in the Age of Reason*. New Haven, CT: Yale University Press, 2016.

Wood, Gordon. *The Creation of the American Republic*, 1776–1787. University of North Carolina Press, 1998.

Wood, Gordon. "The Democratization of Mind in the American Revolution." In Robert H. Horwitz, ed. *The Moral Foundations of the American Republic*, 102–28. Charlottesville: University Press of Virginia, 1979.

Wood, Gordon S. *Empire of Liberty: A History of the Early Republic, 1789–1815*. Oxford University Press, 2009.

Wood, Gordon. "The History of Rights in Early America." In Barry Alan Shain, ed. *The Nature of Rights at the American Founding and Beyond*, 233–57. Charlottesville and London: University of Virginia Press, 2007.

Wood, Gordon. *The Radicalism of the American Revolution*. New York: Vintage, 1993.

Worms, Frédéric. "Introduction." In Frédéric Worms, ed. *Droits de l'homme et philosophie: une anthologie, (1789–1914)*, 13–63. Paris: Agora, 1993.

Wright, B. F. "American Interpretations of Natural Law." *The American Political Science Review* 3 (1926), 524–47.

Wright, J. K. "National Sovereignty and the General Will, The Political Program of the Declaration of Rights." In Dale Van Kley, ed. *The French Idea of Freedom: The Old Regime and the Declaration of Rights of* 1789, 199–233. Stanford: Stanford University Press, 1994.

Yirush, Graig. *Settlers, Liberty and Empire: The Roots of Early American Political Theory*, 1675–1775. Cambridge University Press, 2011.

Zackin, Emily. *Looking for Rights in All the Wrong Places: Why State Constitutions Contain America's Positive Rights*. Princeton University Press, 2013.

Zarka, Yves-Charles. "La notion de droit naturel dans la Déclaration des droits de l'homme et du citoyen de 1789." In Bernard Bourgeois and Jacques d'Hondt, eds. *La philosophie et la Révolution française*, 59–67. Paris: Vrin, 1993.

Zuckert, Michael P. *Natural Rights and the New Republicanism*. Princeton University Press, 1994.

Zuckert, Michael P. *The Natural Rights Republic: Studies in the Foundation of the American Political Tradition*. University of Notre Dame Press, 1996.

Index

CPSIA information can be obtained
at www.ICGtesting.com
Printed in the USA
LVHW021547100422
715809LV00006B/404

9 781316 517635